Postmodern Adventure

THE POSTMODERN ADVENTURE

||||||||||||||||||||||||||||||||||||||||||||||||||||||||||||||||||||||||||||||||||||||||||||||||||||

Science, Technology, and Cultural Studies at the Third Millennium

Steven Best
Douglas Kellner

London

First published 2001 in the UK by Routledge
11 New Fetter Lane, London EC4P 4EE

Simultaneously published in the USA and Canada
by The Guilford Press

© 2001 The Guilford Press
A Division of Guilford Publications, Inc.
72 Spring Street, New York, NY 10012
www.guilford.com

Routledge is an imprint of the Taylor & Francis Group

Printed in the United States of America

This book is printed on acid-free paper.

British Library Cataloguing in Publication Data

A catalogue record for this book is available from the British Library

ISBN 0-415-23962-1 (hbk)
    0-415-23963-X (pbk)

CONTENTS

INTRODUCTION
Between the Modern and the Postmodern

> May you live in interesting times.
> —ANCIENT CHINESE CURSE

> The road is always better than the inn.
> —MIGUEL DE CERVANTES

> Seek, Seeker.
> The future is made of seeking
> —JOSÉ ORTEGA Y GASSET

The past several decades have exhibited vertiginous change, surprising novelties, and upheaval in an era marked by technological revolution and the global restructuring of capitalism. This "great transformation," comparable in scope to the shifts produced by the Industrial Revolution, is moving the world into a postindustrial, infotainment, and biotech mode of global capitalism, organized around new information, communications, and genetic technologies.[1] This epochal process includes the growth of far-reaching transnational corporations, intensified competition on a planetary scale, and the relocation of industry and manufacturing to the developing world. Globalization has produced a world economic system and trade laws that protect transnational corporations at the expense of human life, biodiversity, and the environment. It is accompanied by computerization of all facets of production and expanding automation, generating heightened exploitation of labor, corporate downsizing, and greater levels of unemployment, inequality, and insecurity.

As we enter the Third Millennium, we are thus witnessing the advent of a digitized and networked global economy and society, fraught with promise and danger. The scientific–technological–economic revolutions of the era and spread of the global economy are providing new financial opportunities, openings for political amelioration, and a wealth of ingenious products and technologies that might improve the human condition. Yet these developments may lead to explosive conflict, crisis, even catastrophe. Hence, the turbulent trans-mutations of the current condition are highly contradictory and ambiguous, with both hopeful and threatening features being played out on political, eco-nomic, social, and cultural fronts.

This novel situation and its myriad mutations are often subsumed under the label "postmodern," although few discussions link the condition to both wide-ranging scientific and technological revolutions *and* the global restruc-turing of capitalism.[2] For us, the "postmodern" highlights what is singular and original in the contemporary era. It calls attention to discontinuities and rup-tures, and signals that an extensive range of novelties are appearing that require fresh analyses, theories, and practices. But for the discourse of the postmodern to have theoretical and political weight, it must be articulated with the pro-found alterations of the day and given concrete substance and force. We will, accordingly, attempt to show that the transition to a postmodern society is bound up with fundamental changes that are transforming pivotal phenomena from warfare to education to politics, while reshaping the modes of work, communication, entertainment, everyday life, social relations, identities, and even bodily existence and life-forms.

Within politics today, one observes a broad expanse of events, ranging from local struggles over power and identity to new types of global conflicts and movements. The emergent movements against capitalist globalization challenge powerful sociopolitical forces such as transnational corporations, the World Bank, the International Monetary Fund (IMF), the World Trade Orga-nization (WTO), and formations like the European Union (EU) and the North American Free Trade Agreement (NAFTA). The global economy and polity thus display new structures and alliances which in many cases surpass the power of the nation-state that became a key institution of the modern po-litical order. Nonetheless, the nation-state arguably continues to be a much stronger governmental force than some theories of globalization indicate (see Chapter 5). Moreover, violence and political fragmentation in the former So-viet Union and Yugoslavia, as well as in Asia, Africa, the Middle East, and nu-merous other regions, have created a new world disorder fuelled by intense ethnic and territorial rivalries.

In the United States, the "New Deal" of the 1930s and the "Great Soci-ety" of the 1960s have devolved into a dysfunctional welfare state, which in the 1990s produced a disciplinary workfare camp and prison–industrial complex, while millions continued to fall through tears in the "social safety net." Around the globe, neoliberalism has replaced social democracy. With the col-lapse of the Soviet Union, a predatory global capitalism and its hyper-commodified McCulture are now hegemonic, confronted with no alternative historical bloc. Yet novel kinds of spectacle, technopolitics, and multimedia are creating nascent oppositional public spheres and altering the locus and net-works of communication and contestation. For decades, politics has been played out significantly in broadcast media. Now, with the Internet, cyberculture, and digital technologies, new public spheres and domains of political information, debate, and struggle are arising (see Chapter 5).

On the level of society and everyday life, individuals are bombarded by a spectrum of technologies that are reconstructing every aspect of experience. The entertainment and information industries have created innovative realms of interaction, where TV zappers surf proliferating numbers of cable channels and computer users cruise an ever-burgeoning Internet. Within cyberspace, everything from UFO cults and video voyeurism of live sex and child pornography to myriad modes of politics, alternative forms of art, and interactive information networks are on display. These emergent cultural technologies, and a rapidly materializing virtual reality (VR), are producing highly original domains that alter existing notions of space, time, reality, embodiment, and identity. VR technologies can simulate any world or experience through sound, advanced graphics, and intensely immersive and interactive environments; they are already being used to transform architecture, medicine, art, entertainment, and even the activity of war (see Chapters 2–5).

Societal evolution is especially striking in the United States, the epicenter of global capital, and where we ourselves live and write. Recent years have exhibited a burst of new technologies and an erratic economy, with accelerated periods of boom and bust, displaying an ever-changing cast of winners and losers. The past decade of highly uneven economic development has seen escalating urban violence, a wave of teen murders, the proliferation of guns, intensifying hate crimes, a high level of drug and alcohol addiction, steadily increasing divorce rates, declining wages for many, unprecedented levels of consumer debt, and growing divisions between the haves and the have nots. In this grave new high-tech world, existence is becoming stranger and increasingly dangerous. The specter of apocalyptic war threatens, as more nation-states develop nuclear bombs, and rogue terrorist groups purchase weapons of mass destruction on the international market. In the global Western imaginary, Saddam Hussein, Osama bin Laden, and other "terrorists" have declared a jihad on U.S. citizens and endanger global stability with biological, chemical, and nuclear weapons of mass destruction. In response, the U.S. government launched erratic bombing excursions on these demonized "foreign others," and conspired with NATO to undertake a full-scale air war against Serbia, while resurrecting a "star wars" missile defense system.[3]

Cyberterrorism threatens the global economy, and the Y2K problem pointed to the potential collapse of the vaunted networked society. The bullish "new economy" seems headed for a sluggish recession as celebrated dot-com companies rapidly fold. At the same time, a dangerously unqualified figurehead, George W. Bush, assumes the presidency of the United States after stealing the election, with the aid of the U.S. Supreme Court, in an unprecedented crisis of legitimacy (see Kellner forthcoming). Furthermore, overdevelopment, overpopulation, rampant consumerism, ozone thinning, global warming, and rain forest destruction forecast massive species extinction and multiple ecological crises.

After an unprecedented decade of (admittedly uneven) development in the global economy and accompanying orgy of financial capital, during the early months of 2001 the economy went into crisis and stock prices dramatically declined. Market failures and financial malaise were accompanied by crises of the energy system, where deregulation and greedy energy providers produced a situation that led to frequent energy shutdowns in California. At the same time, globally transmitted viruses in the animal kingdom were producing epidemics of foot-and-mouth disease and mad cow disease, resulting in a highly controversial and, to many, barbaric wholesale slaughter of animals in Europe. Moreover, renewed dangers of global war emerged menacingly, as the Cold Warriors who took over the White House in 2001 proposed new weapons systems and accelerated political tensions to justify their military expenditures, provoking conflicts with North Korea, Russia, and, most dramatically, China in the opening months of their reign. These unsettling features of the contemporary era portend more dark and devastating dimensions to the postmodern adventure than its theorists have so far been able to countenance. In addition, the nascent "Biotech Century" is already undertaking "the most radical experiment humankind has ever carried out on the natural world" (Rifkin 1998: x). Gene therapy and biotechnology promise to cure numerous diseases, but also presage immense dangers arising from potential corporate monopoly control of the gene pool of plants, animals, and human beings. There are accordingly serious worries about the genetic engineering of the food supply and the creation of transgenic species, along with genetic pollution, eugenics, and genetic discrimination. As bioengineering technologies redesign life, the idea of "species" as something unique and inviolable is becoming obsolete and the notion of a "natural world" ever more problematic. Human identity itself is put in question with advances in cloning and the implosion of biology and technology (see Chapters 3, 4, Epilogue).

As dramatic socioeconomic, scientific, and technological developments occurred over the past decades, a paradigm shift has been underway in the realms of theory, the arts, science, and culture at large (see Best and Kellner 1997). By the 1980s, there were intense polemics over the importance of the postmodern turn, with some celebrating the evolving forms of theory and culture as an advance over moribund modern ones, and with others bitterly attacking them as irrationalist and regressive (Best and Kellner 1991). Many, especially in the older generation of theorists, went on with "business as usual," ignoring the massive alterations taking place and the controversies over their significance.

The postmodern turn thus arose in part as an attempt to describe the intense shifts and crises in many realms of life. The turbulent transformations of the present age have proliferated a bewildering variety of contending theories to explain and make sense of them. Responding to this situation, our studies explore what kinds of theory and culture can best account for the striking changes and impassioned conflicts of the current era, and what modes of politics are needed to realize contemporary potentialities for justice, peace, self-fulfillment, solidarity, and an ecological, sustainable society. Throughout this text, we raise the question of which theoretical and political perspectives can guide us into a better future and which are dead ends. Where are we going and what, if any, are our choices? Which turns lead to a viable and better future? Which paths lead to disaster and regression? And who are "we" and what are we becoming?

The many conflicting answers to these questions have generated controversies among advocates of modern and postmodern discourses. The polemics have circulated through academic and avant-garde cultural circles to media culture and everyday life, becoming a defining, albeit highly disputed, arena of the contemporary era. Theory today, like culture and politics, is a contested terrain with contrasting modern and postmodern theories claiming that they provide the most reliable account of the intricacies of the present. Leaving behind familiar guideposts and conventional wisdom thrusts us into a novel and uncharted territory. Consequently, the raging debates, controversies, and passions of the day have led many theorists, including ourselves, to interrogate the contemporary moment in order to produce fresh theoretical and political insights, to promote an incisive grasp of the prevailing situation, and to facilitate progressive social transformation.

Our two previous books documented the origin and proliferation of postmodern shifts from the 1960s into the 1990s and the rise of new paradigms in a wide range of fields. *Postmodern Theory* (1991) analyzed the genesis and trajectory of the discourse of the postmodern in philosophy and social theory and called for a multiperspectival approach that employed the best elements of modern and postmodern positions and politics. *The Postmodern Turn* (1997) analyzed mutations from the modern to the postmodern in society, culture, the arts, science, and politics, showing key commonalities across these areas. We attempted to demonstrate that the postmodern turn, far from being a fad or momentary fashion, is becoming deeper and wider in its range of influence. Aware of the extravagant and problematic positions taken by many advocates of the postmodern, we have always distanced ourselves from extreme versions of postmodern theory that postulate a complete break with modernity and a rupture between the modern and the postmodern. Accordingly, we will argue in this book for a reconstruction of theory and politics that combines the most useful modern and postmodern perspectives.

CRISES OF MAPPING AND THE DIALECTICS OF THE PRESENT

> Investigations of various topics and levels of abstraction that are collected here are united in the intention of developing a theory of the present society.
> —MAX HORKHEIMER

> What's going on just now? What's happening to us? What is this world, this period, this precise moment in which we are living?
> —MICHEL FOUCAULT

In the realm of theory, the postmodern turn consists of a movement away from the mechanistic and positivistic conception of modern science, along with a repudiation of Enlightenment optimism, faith in reason, and emphasis on transcultural values and human nature. Postmodernists typically reject foundationalism and transcendental subjectivities within theory, the modernist emphases on innovation and originality in art, and a universalist and totalizing modern politics. With the belief that modern theories and politics have become reductive, illusory, and arrogant, diverse postmodern theorists, artists, and activists emphasize the countervalues of multiplicity and difference, antirealism, aesthetic irony and appropriation, ecological perspectives, and a proliferation of diverse forms of struggle.

We share many of these positions, but advocate the reconstruction and improvement of the best elements of modern theory, culture, society, and politics, rather than their abandonment, as in some extreme versions of postmodern theory. At the same time, we reject both completely affirmative or negative stances toward assorted postmodern theories and attempt to extract and develop what we consider to be valuable postmodern positions, while criticizing problematic ones. Rather than pursuing the modern logic of the "either/or" (i.e., either the modern or the postmodern), throughout our studies we pursue a postmodern logic of "both/and," drawing on each tradition and situating the present era between the modern and the postmodern (see below).

Consequently, our "dialectics of the present" deploys a multiplicity of theories to attempt to capture the complexity and conflicts of the contemporary era. We use the notion of the "Third Millennium" to help dramatize the novelties, challenges, and possibilities of the contemporary situation. The discourse of the new millennium signals changing times, a new age, and is thus parallel to the postmodern, which signifies ruptures in history and movement into a different constellation. Both discourses reveal a penchant for periodization in the contemporary epoch, for reflecting on breaks with the past and on novelties of the present, and for considering what is coming in the rapidly approaching future. Of course, millennial discourse is based on a premodern Christian dating system and eschatology, while the postmodern is a construct of recent philosophical, social, and cultural theory.[4] Nonetheless, we find the concept of the Third Millennium useful as a marker that indicates we are moving into new constellations and should engage their defining features, challenges, and conflicts.

The Postmodern Adventure attempts to show that as we enter the Third Millennium we are in the midst of a tempestuous period of transition and metamorphosis, propelled principally by transmutations in science, technology, and capitalism. Our project is to combine critical social theory, science and technology studies, and cultural studies in a multiperspectivist and transdisciplinary framework that illuminates the dynamics of the present moment. We accordingly seek to grasp continuities and discontinuities with the earlier modern era, while mapping the changes, threats, and promises now before us.

Confronting the turbulence, excitement, and unpredictability of the day immerses us in what we are calling "the postmodern adventure."

The concept of the postmodern adventure is deployed in our studies to
describe engagement with the striking metamorphoses and the contentious
controversies over how to characterize the vicissitudes of the current era.[5]
Whereas Alfred North Whitehead (1967) charts the trajectories of Western
culture through various "adventures of ideas," we argue that fundamental
changes stem first and foremost from material transformations in the domains
of science, technology, and economics. The postmodern adventure involves
leaving behind the assumptions and procedures of modern theory and embracing a dynamic and ongoing encounter with emergent theories, sciences,
technologies, cultural forms, communications media, experiences, politics, and
identities. It involves the traversal and exploration of emerging social and cultural spaces, alive with fresh possibilities for thought, action, and personal and
social change. The adventure is also fraught with distractions and dangers, and
it contests accepted types of thought and behavior. Postmodern adventures call
for altering definitions of natural, social, and human reality, and require innovative modes of representation, mapping, and practice.

The concepts of the postmodern adventure and the Third Millennium
are thus linked. In our interpretive construct, the postmodern adventure is
coming to fruition in the contemporary epoch and is hurtling us into an unknown future. Yet, as our studies will show, the postmodern adventure has
roots in the past and continuities with modernity. As we argue, the postmodern adventure took off during World War II with the production of novel
forms of science, technology, and bureaucratic control systems that created the
nuclear bomb and other apocalyptic weapons, as well as revolutionary computer and information systems, powerful cybernetic control networks, and
new forms of society and culture (Chapter 1). The postmodern adventure is
only fully becoming apparent in our story now, however, at the commence
ment of the Third Millennium, an era rife with claims of a new postmodernity,
economy, and culture—declarations that we will historicize and interrogate, as
we criticize the hype and ideologies that exaggerate and celebrate the transformations that we engage.

The postmodern adventure thus requires innovative mappings to represent evolving social conditions, economic shifts, sciences, technologies, experiences, and identities. In his classic essay "Postmodernism, or The Cultural
Logic of Late Capitalism" (1984, rev. 1991), Fredric Jameson vividly describes
the disorientation of contemporary life, which includes the loss of spatial coordinates, the confusing "hyperspace" of postmodern architecture and culture,
the decline of historical consciousness, the waning of affect, and a consequent
emotional numbness and detachment. Jameson also describes the cooptation of
resistance and the abolition of critical distance, requiring new modes of representation and politics.

We agree with Jameson that during the postmodern adventure, the boundaries of the modern world are breaking down, requiring theoretical and practical guides that will help us understand and navigate the tempests and turmoil of the day. Accordingly, we will be engaged in a form of *meta-cartography*, reflecting on the various processes of mapping and the contributions and limitations of the classical theories of modernity and the fledgling charting of the postmodern.[6] We interrogate the blindness and insights, limitations and visions, of opposing modern and postmodern modes of representation as we try to make sense of the epochal changes drawing the entire world into a maelstrom of flux. We reflect on diverse types of representations, including theory and science, art and media culture, quantitative and qualitative, descriptive and normative, ethical and political, and utopian and dystopian modes. We argue that multiple chartings are relevant, indeed necessary, because domains of social reality and specific social contexts *are* distinct; thus it is a pragmatic question to ask which modes of representation should be used in a particular constellation.

Different people use distinctive maps to make sense of the world, deploying various ideas, models, and theories to organize their experience, to orient themselves in their environment, and to hopefully replace multiplicity and disorder with structure and order. Mappings also help construct personal identities, pointing to ways of being in the world, existential options, and sense-making activities—as when social groups emulate "heroes of production" or "heroes of consumption" (Lowenthal 1961), or individuals follow the fashions and style of celebrities. Indeed, the postmodern adventure involves the dissolution of older traditional and modern identities and the construction of alternative ones. Whereas traditional identity maintained stable roles and social functions, postmodern identity allowed varied and richer subjectivities to proliferate. The ability to switch identities intensified problems of alienation and authenticity, as individuals felt that they were being severed from their true selves while, at the same time, passionately seeking their genuine or higher nature. In turn, the postmodernization of identity has engendered both the embrace of new technological transformations of the body and identity, as well as disparate searches for the authentic and the real. Hence, ersatz identities multiply, resulting in the growth of oppositional identity subcultures and politics. An always proliferating image and media culture, supplemented by the psychological games of the Internet where one can experiment with self-construction in ludic performative modes, generates a further expansion of identity (see Turkle 1995; Chapter 4).

An affirmative and productive version of the postmodern turn appropriates the best features from modern theory, recognizes the challenge and cogency of much postmodern critique, and undertakes new reconstructive projects (see Best and Kellner 1997). From our perspective, the postmodern adventure is a navigation through the commotion and complexity of the present, a search for order in the seeming disorder, as it maps both the disorganization of the previous forms of culture and society and their reorganization into new modes and structures. This aspect of the postmodern adventure pertains to discovery and exploration of powerful technological realms such as those of genetic engineering, cloning, multimedia, cyberspace, VR, and technopolitics. These developments demand analysis of the ways that new technologies pose grave dangers and/or can be used to remake society, culture, and human beings in progressive forms. The postmodern adventure also comprises interrogating the discourses of emergent theories and sciences, engaging novel modes of culture and society, and constructing disparate identities, politics, and theories. There are, of course, hazards and dangers in this project, as there were in the modern adventure. No doubt, there will be successes and failures, triumphs and disasters, important discoveries and misadventures as well.

While there are clearly striking continuities with the modern era (Robins and Webster 1999), the changes wrought by scientific–technological revolution and the spread of a new global economy affect all aspects of politics, culture, and everyday life. One encounters startling metamorphoses that some are theorizing as the advent of a new postmodernity, qualitatively distinct from the modern era. These developments are highly ambiguous. On the positive side, there are exciting possibilities for new experiences in cyberspace, medical advances, and increased opportunities for labor and leisure. One also finds dynamic political openings and movements such as the protests against the Seattle World Trade Organization (WTO) meetings in December 1999 and anti-International Monetary Fund (IMF) and World Bank demonstrations in Washington, Prague, and Sydney in 2000, which signal evolving coalitions and activism against capitalist globalization.

But there are worrisome dangers that plague the scientific, technological, economic, and other shifts and mutations of our time. In some ways, the postmodern adventure may confront us with the dystopias that have haunted the modern mind, from Mary Shelley's *Frankenstein*, which anticipated genetic engineering and marketable body parts, to the futuristic visions of H. G. Wells whose *Island of Dr. Moreau* and *Food of the Gods* predicted that biological mutations and technologically created species would be fraught with unforeseen results. Orwell's *1984* foresaw the panoptic society of the present, with surveillance techniques becoming ever more sophisticated and privacy increasingly diminished. Similarly, Huxley's *Brave New World* prefigured the current situation, as eugenics looms on the horizon, cloning has arrived, and sundry brands of soma (e.g., Prozac, Ecstasy, and methamphetamine) and pleasure machines and multisensory spectacles are readily available in a high-tech, consumerist, pharmacopian society of the spectacle (see Chapters 3–5).

The "dialectics of the present" thus involves living through a highly chaotic and conflictual situation. Resisting both attempts to deny any fundamental ruptures or novelties of the existing sociohistorical situation, as well as hyperbolic claims for a postmodern rupture, we suggest that it is best to envisage the prevailing condition in a zone between the modern and the postmodern. Here one finds continuities and discontinuities with the past, striking changes and enduring structures, peppered with perpetual conflicts between the old and the new. Our studies imply that the contemporary moment is a contradictory amalgam of progressive and regressive, positive and negative, and thus highly ambivalent phenomena, all difficult to chart and evaluate.[7]

The postmodern adventure has already produced unprecedented phenomena, some benign and fascinating, others frightening and deadly, as new forms of war (Chapter 2), science, (Chapter 3), technology (Chapter 4), and society, culture, and politics spring forth (Chapter 5). Collectively, these evolving possibilities and dangers constitute a panorama of phenomena that require fresh social, philosophical, ethical, and legal conceptions. The rigid boundaries constructed by modernity are beginning to unravel like a DNA double helix during reproduction. Borders that once were thought to be impermeable and impassable, as solid as "matter" itself (which at the quantum level is a vast emptiness), are now dissolving and melting, as happened for the premodern world in the Marxian vision. Seen as contingent, arbitrary, and repressive, the old perimeters are in the process of being deconstructed and reconstructed. Many are as obsolete as Checkpoint Charlie and the Berlin Wall. The conceptual divisions under contestation include those between humans and animals, society and nature, biology and technology, nation-states, and diverse racial, ethnic, sexual, and gender identities in an era of multiplying hybridization. Even the distinctions between life and nonlife, the living and the fabricated, are being rethought in the light of the findings of evolutionary biology, cosmology, and computer simulation technologies (Chapter 3).

As we show throughout our studies, society, culture and identity are all undergoing a tremendous rethinking. They currently are in a state of crisis and confusion, largely through the impact of new information, communication, and genetic technologies, and scientific theories and cosmologies. We are in a condition analogous to the remapping of the cosmos in the era of Copernicus, Brache, Kepler, and Galileo. Because of intense social and technological developments not only are numerous human beings reshaping their ethnic, gender, and political identities, but humanity as a *species* is starting to seriously rethink its status in response to ecology and environmental ethics, evolutionary theory, animal cognition, and "smart machines." With supercomputers like IBM's Deep Blue outwitting chess masters, and genetic engineering and cloning technologies transcending species boundaries and portending the fabrication of individuals in a new age of designer bodies and babies, the very fate and future of the human being itself is at stake (Chapter 4, Epilogue).

The postmodern adventure, if nothing else, is indeed risky, and we do not mean just for a few entrepreneurs or finance capitalists; rather, the future of humanity and other complex life-forms is being mortgaged to a rampaging capitalism and profit-driven science and technological development. Nuclear waste and weapons proliferation, biowarfare, the growth of the global arms market, terrorism, DNA splicing, xenotransplantation (inserting animal blood and organs into humans), loss of cultural and biodiversity, the greenhouse effect, global capitalist reorganization, and other phenomena are leading the human race into dangerous ground and a possible endgame of social and ecological devolution. The postmodern voyage beyond the observable into the very stuff of life, past the limits of the human into new configurations of humans and technology, provides new powers and capacities for the human species. Technoscience not only enables humans to better manipulate the natural world, but also to produce new natures and beings, albeit with highly volatile results.

As contemporary societies continue to transgress ethical and ecological limits, begetting proliferating problems and intensifying crises, many have come to recognize the need to impose limits on the excesses of capitalist modernity and its sciences and technologies, while constructing more humane and ecological values, institutions, and practices to sustain life on earth. Without such insight, the mutating dynamics of capitalist overdevelopment might bring the adventure of evolution to a tragic close, at least here on this planet. The evolution of the universe itself is the greatest adventure story of all, a 12- to 15-billion-year odyssey, involving the maturation of organic matter from inorganic matter, life from nonlife, and its subsequent earthly unfolding over 4.6 billion years, advancing from carbon and hydrogen atoms to DNA and the first proteins, to plants, animals, and human beings. Evolution has generated boundless diversity and ever new and more complex forms of life.

Hence, critical reflection on the pathologies and illusions of the modern adventure and their continuation in the present is an important part of the postmodern adventure. A shift in mind-set consequently should be informed by an enhanced awareness of limits, contingency, and unpredictability, along with nonhierarchical thinking. A new gestalt of this type would also require repudiation of the modern will to power over society and nature, of arrogant Western-centric humanism, of a disenchanting or cynical worldview, and of the fantasy of control and belief in technofixes for critical social and ecological problems. Where the modern adventure was predicated on the values of domination, endless growth, mastery of nature, and a cornucopian world of limitless resources, a key aspect of the postmodern adventure is the systematic dismantling of this modern ideology while keeping the best aspects of modernity—humanism, individuality, enlightened reason, democracy, rights, and solidarities—to be tempered by reverence for nature, respect for all life, sustainability, and ecological balance.

TOWARD A TRANSDISCIPLINARY CULTURAL STUDIES

> There is *only* a perspective seeing, *only* a perspective "knowing," and the *more* affects we allow to speak about one thing, the more complete will our "concept" of this thing, our "objectivity," be.
> —Friedrich Nietzsche

It is our view that we are now between the modern and the postmodern, in an interim period between epochs, where we are undergoing spectacular changes in all realms of life. We therefore resist both attempts to deny fundamental changes in the existing sociohistorical situation and hyberbolic claims that we are experiencing a postmodern rupture; we stress instead both continuties and discontinuities. The Renaissance was a long period, between the premodern and the modern, that lacks easily datable beginnings and endings; today, a similar period of protracted transformation is underway. This time the interim is between the modern era and a new era, the characteristics of which we do not fully know. The term "postmodern" serves to call attention to novelties and discontinuities of the current interim period. It also happens that, at the end of the Third Millennium, the postmodern adventure both undermines and advances millennial thinking. This mode of thought is rooted in Christianity and continued through the Enlightenment, Marxism, and other utopian movements. From the dawn of Christianity through Enlightenment projects of social construction to the scientific and technological revolutions of today, Western culture has constructed a story of the gradual movement of humanity toward a state of progress and perfection (see Becker 1964; Rifkin 1998; Noble 1998).

Many of our contemporaries continue this salvationist and linear historical narrative, believing that science, technology, and capitalism will solve all human problems and create a new world of wealth, democracy, and well-being (see critical discussions of this discourse in Chapters 4 and 5). The postmodern assault against grand historical narratives has been used to undercut the metanarrative of historical progress, such as claims that we are at the "end of history" in a triumphant state of capitalism and democracy (Fukuyama 1992). Some argue that globalization will create a world of affluence and democracy (Friedman 1999), that new technologies and cyberculture will fashion utopian cultural and social spaces, and that embryonic sciences like biotechnology will do everything from curing our diseases and feeding the world's starving children, to prolonging human life and producing a state approaching immortality. In the imagination of many bioengineers, the genetic sciences allow the realization of the vision of Enlightenment visionary Marquis de Condorcet, who proudly proclaimed: "No bounds have been fixed to the improvement of the human facilities—the perfectability of man is absolute" (cited in Rifkin 1998: 170).

Thus, far from breaking with religious values and narratives, science and technology in many ways have extended them. For their advocates are claiming that genetics and eugenics will perfect us and bring us grace without the need for divine intervention. On the other hand, the juggernaut of capital, technology, and science undercuts religious cosmologies and provides a highly secular and materialist ethos, focusing people on surviving and succeeding in a rapidly shifting present. As we enter the Third Millennium, the postmodern adventure is extremely ambiguous and contradictory. There are postmodern

trends that celebrate a return to tradition, and there has been an upsurge of religious faith and millennial thinking.[8] But there are also expanding secular
forms of postmodern identity politics, possessive individualism, and a willing-
ness to embrace the destruction of the past and tradition for the glories of the
present moment (see Best and Kellner 1997).

Contemporary developments exhibit so many twists and turns, and are so
highly complex, that they elude simple historical sketches, reductive theoretical explications, and facile generalizations. What is required, we would suggest,
is a multidimensional optic on the trajectory of the postmodern adventure that
combines historical narrative, critical social theory, and cultural mappings.
Representing the contours of the postmodern adventure in the Third Millennium accordingly involves an enterprise that crosses theoretical borders into a
new transdisciplinary and multiperspectivist space.

The social maps called classical social theories are to some extent torn,
tattered, and fragmented, and in many cases outdated and even obsolete. Fresh
theories need to be constructed constantly, using both the resources of past
theories and salient sketches of the contemporary era to make sense of our
current historical condition. Maps and theories provide orientation, overviews,
and contexts. They show how parts relate to each other and to a larger whole.
If something new appears on the horizon, a good map will chart and
contextualize it, including sketches of future configurations of potential promises and perils. But while numerous older theories and authorities decay and
are discredited, others continue to provide important guideposts for thought
and action today.

Given our emphasis on mapping, it should be clear that we do not accept
the self-refuting postmodern attacks on theory that are sometimes advanced
by writers like Lyotard, Foucault, and Rorty. Nor do we embrace postmodern
rejections of a "hermeneutics of suspicion" that strive to overcome social illusions, mythologies, and fetishized appearances by locating underlying forces
and causes of domination and destruction.[9] Without theory, interpretation,
and critical charts, we are as lost and hapless as Columbus on his first voyage.
Theory and interpretation are necessary to the extent that the world is not
completely and immediately transparent to consciousness. Because our social
and cultural situation is hard to grasp, especially in a hypercapitalist culture of
spectacles, simulacra, and disinformation, we need to comprehend how our
lives are being shaped and controlled. Postmodern claims that "theory" necessarily commits the sin of illicitly totalizing irreducibly heterogeneous phenomena are themselves reductive and homogenizing. Ludic postmodern calls for
formalistic analysis oriented toward surfaces and the aesthetic pleasures of the
text disarm cultural studies and political hermeneutics that read culture in
terms of social and ideological conflicts and contradictions. To refuse interpre-
tative depth is to vitiate critique and transformative practice by reducing analysis to description of surface and form detached from radical theory and politics (see Best and Kellner 1987). The extreme postmodern argument for the

abolition of critique and transformative politics thus becomes a self-fulfilling prophecy as some pomos suspend substantive sociopolitical critique and substitute nihilistic verbal posturing for political activism.

We believe that theory can provide social maps and inform historical narratives that supply spatial and temporal contextualizations for the present age. These critical theories should study society holistically, moving from specific phenomena and modes of human experience to an ever expanding analysis. Such inquiry may extend from the individual self and its network of everyday social relations, to its more encompassing regional environment, national setting, and finally to the international arena of global capitalism. Within this dialectical framework, social maps shift from one domain to another, articulating complex connections between economics, politics, the state, science and technology, media culture, everyday life, and their contending discourses and practices. We still find that the most powerful methodology for social analysis is a historically informed, dialectical method that sees human reality as evolving and conflict-ridden. This outlook grasps societies, and history in general, as coherent wholes, with specific spheres of economics, politics, science, technology, culture, and so on. They have their own history, autonomy, and conflicts, but interact with each other in a holistic social context.

In more contemporary language, we shall investigate how key phenomena like science and technology "coevolve" in response to mutations in the economy, culture, and polity, all of which develop together and mutually shape and co-construct one another (see Chapters 2–5). We advocate a sociohistorical approach that theorizes the interaction and coevolutionary development of science, technology, capitalism, society, and human individuals as part of reciprocally interacting social processes. Our perspective emphasizes the mutual unfolding of all realms of life, such that nature is integrated into social, technological, and human development. The concept of coevolution avoids the determinism, reductionism, and monoperspectival outlooks found in many scientific and sociological perspectives. We link it to a critical social theory that avoids conflating separate forms of social development and idealizing society as one only of cooperation and harmony, thereby missing how social relations today are shaped principally by competition, conflict, struggle, and domination.

We also stress the co-construction of people, society, science, and technology, arguing that while people create the artifacts of their culture and everyday life, they are in turn shaped by major forces such as capitalism, science, and technology. The concept of co-construction serves to emphasize that science and technology are not neutral, that specific societal interests and biases enter into their production and development. The notion underscores the constructedness of our science, technology, and culture; they are fabricated in specific ways in particular contexts. But it also signals that these fields can be reconstructed to meet human needs. Societal forces and potential instruments of human liberation and domination such as science, technology, and culture can be redesigned to serve public interests and to promote the creation of a more democratic, just, humane, and ecological world—freed from the imperatives of the state, the military, and a predatory corporate capitalism.

Thus, we propose dynamic coevolutionary, co-constructivist, and reconstructive perspectives for theorizing the dynamics of the Third Millennium. Operating in the tradition of critical theory, we believe that the role of theory is to provide weapons for social critique and change, to illuminate the sources of human unhappiness, and to contribute to the goals of human emancipation and a democratic, socially just, and truly ecological society. Critical theory involves the construction of concepts to illuminate the present and historical narratives to identify how the constellations of the contemporary have been shaped by the past and are open to alternative futures.

As argued in the historicist tradition that began in the 19th century (e.g., in the work of Hegel, Marx, Weber, Dilthey, etc.), all values, worldviews, traditions, social institutions, and individuals themselves should be understood historically as they evolve through time. In the form of Foucault's genealogies, historical narratives chart the temporal trajectories of significant experiences and events, of political movements, or the forces constituting subjectivities. Against the postmodern tendency to randomize history as a disconnected series of events, we believe historical narratives should grasp continuities, as well as discontinuities. Such sociohistorical analysis should engage both negative and positive developments, criticizing forms of oppression, domination, and exploitation, while valorizing positive possibilities for moral and technical evolution.

Together, social maps and historical narratives study the points of intersection between individuals and their cultures, between power and knowledge. To the fullest degree possible, they seek to lift the veils of ideology and expose supposed givens as contingent and the present as a social construct, while providing visions of alternative futures. Theories and narratives, then, are meant to overcome quietism and fatalism, to sharpen political vision, and to encourage translation of concepts into practice in order to advance personal freedom, social justice, and ecological preservation and reclamation. Theories and narratives should not be confused with the territories and times they analyze; they are approximations of a densely constituted human world that requires theories and imagination to conceive and depict it. Nor should social mappings be seen as final or complete, because they must be constantly rethought and revised in light of new information and rapidly changing situations. Mappings and narratives can thus only be provisional, reports from diverse explorations that require further investigation, testing, and revision. Hence, we are offering *a* mapping, not *the* mapping, of our contemporary world, one that will require sustained revision and updating.

On the whole, border crossing, transgressing boundaries between fields carefully delineated and segregated under the regime of the modern, is a productive aspect of the postmodern turn in both theory and the arts. Theoretical crossings of disciplinary borders that subvert the modern academic division of labor have given rise to a wide array of studies that have provoked new insight and produced valuable results. Earlier attempts at modern and postmodern transdisciplinary work tended to be carried out in the realms of cultural and social theory. Yet we would argue that revolutions in science and technology require broadening our theoretical perspectives. Previously, calls for transdisciplinary work concerned integration of the perspectives and the methods of the social and cultural sciences, often without regard for significant components of the natural sciences or the new philosophies of science and technology. We affirm, however, inclusion of both the natural and the social sciences to overcome the gap between the "two cultures" (C. P. Snow 1964), along with analysis of the impact of technological revolutions, in order to provide more integrated and comprehensive frameworks for theory and critique today.

Formerly, major philosophers from Diderot to Dewey, and many in the humanities and social sciences, stayed in touch with cutting-edge developments in science, looked to scientific method as the source of knowledge, and critically engaged the latest works of scientific theory. Indeed, the major social theorists of the 18th and 19th centuries saw science and technology as the driving motors of change and progress that would lift humanity from the dungeons of premodernity. They regarded science and technology as major civilizing forces that would bring a rational society in their wake. Karl Marx championed science and technology as liberating forces and went so far as to equate human emancipation with advancement of the "productive forces" of society. Likewise, John Dewey directly linked science and democracy, claiming that the scientific method of experimentation was the best pedagogy for education and the form of a democratic society and culture.

However, with a variety of critiques of modern science developing in the 20th century, ranging from phenomenological and feminist assaults on scientific objectivity to critical theory attacks on positivism and the scientific method, many leading theorists and schools of thought distanced themselves from science, ignored its developments, and did not engage its results. This was and is a crucial mistake. Our argument is that science should once again become part of a transdisciplinary effort and should be returned to its status as a valuable theoretical resource. While we wish to avoid the uncritical modern embrace of science and technology, such as was advanced by classical liberalism, Marxism, and pragmatism, we also eschew totalizing critiques that reduce science and technology to one-dimensional reason and a force of social domination. Like it or not, science and technology have been major constitutent forces of modernity, and similarly are key catalysts of change for postmodernity. As such, they need to be engaged in light of their considerable importance and carefully theorized so that their positive potential can be realized through theoretical critique and political struggle.

Accordingly, we will develop critical theories of science and technology that appreciate their emancipatory aspects, but also challenge their limitations, dangers, and possible destructive effects. Such approaches strive to overcome one-sided affirmations or rejections, produce dialectical perspectives that distinguish between positive and negative features and consequences, and thus grasp contradictions and ambiguities in these highly complex and significant phenomena. Critical theories of science and technology are also transdisciplinary and historical. Transdisciplinary interpretation is necessary because science and technology have shaped our society and identities to such a profound degree that they are part and parcel of our culture, the stuff of everyday life, and are interfacing with our very bodies and subjectivities in unpredictable ways. A critical theory, for example, that synthesizes philosophy, sociology, and anthropology, but ignores the impact of science and technology on culture, is clearly limited in its ability to grasp the fundamental dynamics of the current conjuncture. Thus, a postmodern transdisciplinary theory should include reflections on science, technology, and ecology in a multiperspectivist project that integrates critical social theory, cultural studies, science and technology studies, race theory, postcolonial analysis, feminism, and environmental concerns. Such an enterprise draws on the most useful resources of both modern and postmodern theory, as well as on theoretical and fictional mappings.

Our project of reconstruction incorporates a variety of transdisciplinary enterprises, including cultural studies and the new advances of "science and technology studies" (STS). Taking its lead from Kuhn's (1970) analysis of paradigm shifts in science, STS addresses the social construction of science, questions modern philosophy and self-understandings of science, and develops alternative "social epistemologies" of science" (see Haraway 1991, 1997; Fuller 1991, 1995, and forthcoming; and Harding 1993 and 1998). In addition, a wide spectrum of related works are emerging. They range from specific studies of key episodes in modern science and analysis of current scientific research and development, to investigations of alternative forms of scientific activity and knowledge and inquiries into how disparate social groups use science and technology to promote democracy and social justice (see Harding 1999; Kleinman forthcoming).

Some versions of STS, however, tend to be scholastic and conservative. They historicize science and technology, but fail to explicitly politicize them in the context of the coevolution of science, technology, capital, the state, and the military, and thus, more generally, within social relations of power and resistance. Moreover, while sociologically oriented analysts may see science as culture—a product of a changing community of scientists, cultural assumptions, and social practices—not all STS theorists analyze science and technology from the optic of its impact on politics, identities, and everyday life, or engage how media culture represents science and technology.

In the 1980s and 1990s, numerous theorists rooted in cultural studies moved beyond their usual terrain of film, television, and other "cultural" artifacts to address science and technology. Whereas these cultural studies theorists therefore could be considered as doing STS, the converse is not necessarily true. The past decades have exhibited furious battles over the nature and effects of science and technology. Working from positions that include critical theory, feminism, multiculturalism, radical green theory, and postmodern theory, philosophical and political challenges to regnant modern paradigms led to the eruption of heated "science wars" between neopositivists and so-called social constructionists (see Ross 1996; Best and Kellner 1997; Chapter 3). Guided by the sound assumption that science and technology are too important to be left to scientists and technocrats themselves, theorists such as Sandra Harding (1986, 1993, and 1998), Donna Haraway (1989, 1991, 1997), Andrew Ross (1991, 1994, 1998), Katherine Hayles (1984, 1990, 1999), Stanley Aronowitz (1988, 1993, 1995), and others have undertaken historical, philosophical, cultural, and political approaches to these fields. In case studies and specific readings, cultural studies theorists have analyzed the ideologies and effects of science and technology on the social and natural worlds. Typically, they call for democratic, ethical, and ecological uses of science and technology (see Taylor et al. 1997). According to Peter Taylor (1997: 204), the potency of a cultural studies orientation to STS is to historically situate acontextual universal claims to Truth and Progress; to destabilize natural and self-evident facades; to disrupt oppressive linkages of knowledge with power; to advance counterdiscourses rooted in sites including domestic life, schools, workplaces, and popular culture; to work across disciplinary boundaries; and to promote intellectual and sociopolitical transformation.

Like Haraway, Aronowitz, Taylor, and others, we seek to absorb STS into the field of cultural studies, as we also work to overcome the limitations of many cultural studies approaches to science and technology themselves. We wish to avoid overly abstract, academic, and pretentious postmodern jargon, as we engage science and technology from a multidisciplinary perspective. This involves combining theoretical analyses of science, technology, and capitalism, enriched by consideration of cultural artifacts ranging from literature and science fiction to the texts of media culture, and grounded in a critical theory informed by ecological concerns. Moreover, we engage the complex interactions among science, technology, and capital in the broad context of the global restructuring of capitalism currently in process and in its constitutive scientific and technological revolutions.

Furthermore, we attempt to expand the project of cultural studies to take account of such phenomena as modernist and postmodernist literature, war and its representations, technology, science, environmental issues, politics, and critical theory itself. We engage and build on British and North American cultural studies, but believe that this tradition has been vitiated in recent years by a cultural populism that is too uncritical of media and consumer culture. This tradition is excessively dismissive of so-called elitist high culture, neglects the complex and important ways in which economics mediates cultural artifacts, and abandons the perspectives of critical social theory and radical politics too readily (Kellner 1995a).

Consequently, while it was an important move to intensely focus on media culture, it has been a mistake to turn away from literary texts and so-called high culture for sometimes exclusive focus on the "popular" in contemporary cultural studies. We also believe that both modernist and postmodernist theory have potentially emancipatory effects that have been sacrificed by a postmodern turn in cultural studies that contemptuously swings away from high art and theory, which it dismisses as "elite." We engage the politics and effects of a wide range of cultural artifacts and reject rigid and often dubious distinctions between high and low culture, interrogating examples ascribed to both categories. Our notion of a critical cultural studies combines formal analysis of style, texture, and surface with interpretation of content, ideology, and normative values.[10] Our concept of "text" encompasses theory and literature, including the writings of Thomas Pynchon, Michael Herr, Mary Shelley, H. G. Wells, Philip K. Dick, and cyberpunk; popular media like film and television; as well as a global transnational image culture, the Internet, and events like the Gulf War. Our maps deploy the resources of both "theory" and "fiction," since each provides key illuminations of social experience from different vantage points that supplement and complement each other. At stake is the development of modes of social theory and cultural criticism adequate for capturing salient aspects of our contemporary predicament, and connecting them with projects of radical democratic social transformation.

NOTES

1. In a classic work, Karl Polanyi (1957) described the "great transformation" from preindustrial to industrial society. We argue that a similarly momentous metamorphosis is taking place today. A vast literature explains the shift in terms such as postindustrialism, post-Fordism, or postmodernity, developments that we interpret as new constellations in global technocapitalism (see Chapter 5). While such theorists as Offe (1985) and Lash and Urry (1987) describe the restructuring process as "disorganized capitalism," we see this as a complex development involving disorganization and reorganization, constituting a new mode of economy and society. We are using "the postmodern adventure" to designate dramatic changes not only in the economy and society, but also in science, technology, politics, culture, nature, and human identity and existence. The focus of our studies is our own experience and situation in the United States. Yet in a globalized world, technologies, commodities, cultures, ideas, and experiences rapidly circulate throughout the world, so that, for those living outside the United States, we recall what Marx said to all in regard to his analysis of capitalism in England: "De te fabula narratur!" ("The tale is told of you").

2. As we will demonstrate throughout this book, many discourses of the postmodern make shifts in technology largely responsible for the rupture with modernity, as does that of Baudrillard (1983a, 1993) who neglects the significance of the restructuring of the economy. While Jameson (1984, 1991), Harvey (1989), and others relate postmodern culture to transformations in capitalism, they do not adequately engage the roles of scientific and technological revolution. Other theorists, such as Lyotard (1984), interpret the "postmodern

condition" largely through mutations of discourse and culture. Throughout this book, we argue that if notions of postmodernity, or a postmodern condition, are to have any force, they require sociohistorical grounding in analysis of the conjuncture of scientific and technological revolution and the resulting cultural, social, and political transformations, all in the context of the global restructuring of capitalism.

3. The recently installed Bush administration is proceeding full-speed ahead to resurrect Reagan's "Star Wars" missile defense system. Bush's Defense Secretary, Cold Warrior Donald Rumsfeld, has long been an ardent opponent of arms control and proponent of a space-based National Missile Defense system (NMD); see Michael Klare's article in *The Nation* (January 16, 2001), accessible at http://www.alternet.org/print.html?StoryID=10341.

4. Stephen Jay Gould (1997) has offered a cogent summary of the history of the discourse of the millennium and his thoughts on the significance of the concept. For Gould, the millennium, a form of dating system, is part of an apocalyptic Judeo-Christian tradition that postulates the end of history, the coming of a new reign of God, and a rupture with secular history. Gould also reminds us that the millennium discourse is bound up with how we parcel time and experience, and peculiar modes of organization of calendar time. From this perspective, the millennium is a function of the dominant mode of calendarization, of the decision to begin history with the birth of Christ, and is thus a peculiarly Christian dating system (Gould also reminds us of the controversies over exactly when the millennium began and when the new millennium commences). Notions of the Third Millennium are becoming increasingly popular: a survey of books with the concept in the title at Amazon.com reveals hundreds of texts touting the concept. We are also following Donna Haraway's *Modest_Witness* (1997), which presents the state of technoscience, society, and culture at the end of the Second Millennium. A few years down the road from her, we present our studies at the beginning of the Third Millennium as an updating of critical social theory and cultural studies that is looking forward at the same time we attempt to understand our recent past.

5. For an excellent interrogation of adventure in modernity and the notion of the modern adventure, see Nerlich (1987).

6. In *Violent Cartographies* (1997) Michael J. Shapiro argues that maps are functions of power in which borders and terrain are artificially constructed and legitimated in ideological discourses and narratives. Part of the postmodern adventure involves undoing the violent cartographies of modernity (nation-state, national borders, scientific and academic disciplines, hierarchical forms of culture, prescribed identities, etc.) in the contemporary era, and constructing alternative mappings and border crossings.

7. We do not want to imply, however, that change and complexity render theory and mapping impossible. While we continuously stress contradictions, ambiguities, and transformations, and draw on paradigms of probability, contingency, and multiplicity developed by chaos and complexity theory, we reject the assault on theory contained in some versions of extreme postmodern discourse. In general, we attempt to navigate the tricky and treacherous shoals between overtheorizing and renouncing theory in favor of flux, change, and complexity by developing analyses that are contextual, provisional, and hermeneutical.

8. We are amused by the number of books we've found in Amazon.com's data base and in other sources that link concepts of the postmodern and of the Third Millennium to religion. On the upsurge of Christian fundamentalism and its articulation with political conservatism see Diamond (1995) and Berlet and Lyons (2000); on the proliferation of depoliticizing new forms of religion and spirituality, see Boggs (2000).

9. Ironically, at the very time in which the epochal transformations that are the topic

of our studies were becoming evident, a mode of postmodern theory, promoted by followers of Lyotard and a misunderstood Foucault, argued for the suspension of "grand narratives," "totalizing theory," and the global and macrotheories of classical theory in favor of local narratives, microtheory and politics, and more modest theoretical perspectives (see
Lyotard 1984 and the critique in Best and Kellner 1991). Against this version of postmodern theory, we are arguing for a reconstructed type of the global and critical perspectives of
classical social theory that we believe are necessary to analyze contemporary social and theoretical developments. Yet we are also in favor of combining the global and the local, micro-
and macrotheory and politics, and mediating modern and postmodern perspectives (see
Best and Kellner, 1991, Ch. 8, and Cvetkovitch and Kellner, 1996, "Introduction").

    10. See our earlier critique of a postmodern cultural criticism that primarily focuses
on style, form, and surface, to the neglect of content, ideology, and hermeneutical interpretation of meaning, in Best and Kellner (1987) and the later critique in Kellner (1995a).

1

||||||||

THOMAS PYNCHON AND
THE ADVENT OF POSTMODERNITY

May God keep us
From Single vision and Newton's sleep.
        —WILLIAM BLAKE

Yet how superb, across the tumult braided. The painted rainbow's changeful
life is bending. Now clearly drawn, dissolving now and faded. And evermore
the showers of dew descending! Of human striving there's no symbol fuller:
Consider, and 'tis easy comprehending—Life is not light, but refracted color.
        —JOHANN VON GOETHE

Life's single lesson: that there is more accident to it than a man can ever
admit to in a lifetime and stay sane.
        —THOMAS PYNCHON

The alleged end of modernity and the rise of postmodernity has been much
debated, but sustained analysis and grounding of claims for a postmodern
divide in society and history are rarely advanced. Rather than opening with
abstract theoretical formulations confronting this transition, we begin by engaging Thomas Pynchon's novel *Gravity's Rainbow* (hereafter GR) which vividly illuminates a phase between the modern and the postmodern. Portraying
the origins of post-World War II society and what he calls the "Rocket State,"
Pynchon delineates in GR the beginnings of the Cold War and the concomit-
ant rise of a system of global capitalism. In our reading, Pynchon's novel
depicts the evolution of an intensified scientific and technological culture out
of the industrial and military trials of World War II, which helped generate the
postmodern adventure.

    In addition, Pynchon's texts exhibit the postmodern turn in the arts, sci-
ence, and theory, as he cultivates a mode of postmodern writing, epistemology,
and vision. The post-World War II proliferation of forms of science, technology, political and military bureaucracy, and the globalization of corporate capi-

talism requires modes of writing adequate to represent the complex array of forces that have been constructing emergent postmodern constellations. We argue that Pynchon's *GR* provides a historical vision and context which helps to clarify what is new and original about the postmodern adventure. Our reading of Pynchon also leads us to interrogate the difference between aesthetic and theoretical maps and to articulate the specificity and efficacy of each. Hence, we open by confronting the issues of Pynchon's style of writing and the postmodern turn in literature, as both underscore the need for innovative theoretical and literary mappings to capture the novelties and complexities of the contemporary era.

LITERARY MODERNISM/POSTMODERNISM

> History—at best a conspiracy, not always among gentlemen, to defraud.
> —THOMAS PYNCHON

> Everything is connected.
> —THOMAS PYNCHON

Since the 1950s, Pynchon has been a major literary figure whose works mark the passage from modern to postmodern literature and culture. Given the heterogeneity that characterizes the postmodern, it should be no surprise that the postmodern turn in literature has moved in opposing directions.[1] While some postmodern writers take a preoccupation with linguistic experimentalism into a reified realm above sociopolitical considerations, others, such as Pynchon, William S. Burroughs, Don DeLillo, and Kathy Acker, merge their aesthetic and formal innovations with social and political concerns and engage the topics of domination and emancipation within a technocratic/bureaucratic/cybernetic/media world. Of course, contestation of conventional modes of perception can assume a political character, as they did in some forms of dada and surrealism, but socially critical postmodernists employ the formalist inventions of postmodern fiction for political ends, thereby breaking out of the self-referential funhouse of language.

For some aesthetic-oriented postmodern writers, the critique of realist texts entails a solipsistic withdrawal from the social world and any efforts to directly depict or engage it. For others, rejection of realism is only part and parcel of a larger political operation that demands some new form of "representing" the social world. Thus, it makes sense to distinguish between a ludic postmodernism (Ebert 1994), or a "postmodernism of reaction" (Foster 1983), that indulges in aesthetic play for its own sake while distancing itself from a politically troubled world, or even lending tacit or explicit support to the status quo, and a "postmodernism of resistance." The latter acknowledges its reflexive appropriation of traditional literary forms, but also seeks to engage political issues and to change culture and society.

Pynchon's work exemplifies a postmodernism of resistance and the abandonment of a linear narrative in favor of a fragmented, multiperspectivist form that examines the evolution of modern Western society from scientific, technological, economic, political, cultural, journalistic, historical, and mythological standpoints. The rich, multiperspectival character of Pynchon's GR thereby naturally lends itself to a plethora of opposing interpretations, such as a Marxian or Weberian political and historical allegory, or psychoanalytic, comic, religious, or formalist readings.

We pursue a political allegorical interpretation of GR that links central Pynchonian themes to the concerns of postmodern theory.[2] Our own multiperspectivist framework, however, requires us to present our reading as one against many, as our own set of optics that seeks to illuminate significant moments in the postmodern adventure, but does not preclude and in fact encourages alternative readings.[3] GR demands a multiperspectivist account because it exhibits such a wealth of standpoints organized in an "encyclopedic narrative" that, like *Ulysses*, *Moby Dick*, or *Faust*, attempts "to render the full range of knowledge and beliefs of a national culture, while identifying the ideological perspectives from which that culture shapes and interprets its knowledge" (Mendelson 1976: 162). Pynchon's "encyclopedia," we would argue, not only accommodates a wealth of forms of knowledge and discourse, but an abundance of literary techniques and strategies, combining modern and postmodern forms. Moreover, by juxtaposing scientific, philosophical, religious, and literary discourses, Pynchon subverts the authority of each perspective. This procedure puts in question one-sided ways of seeing and knowing, while interrogating the limitations and value of competing conceptual schemes (such as science or religion, rationalism vs. irrationalism, theory or literature, and so on), suggesting the relativity and limitations of particular perspectives.

In writing his works of fiction, Pynchon not only references a dizzying array of sociohistorical and cultural phenomena, he employs myriad narrative styles, borrowing from such forms as the picaresque quest novel, expressionism, surrealism, pornography, and political allegory. One of the many important codes and genres he deploys is that of the "historical novel" insofar as his works focus on actual historical events that Pynchon has researched meticulously.[4] Yet he privileges neither history nor fiction, showing that a novel can help comprehend specific eras and situations, but that fiction benefits from historical research and insight and other forms of knowledge in order to better portray the complexities of the epoch under question.

Pynchon frequently satirizes the specific discourses that he deploys, sabotaging their pretension to Truth. Northrop Frye proposes placing Pynchon's work in the category of "Menippean satire" which, like *Gargantua and Pantagruel*, *Gulliver's Travels*, *Candide*, and other texts, ironize the pedantry of a specific culture while simultaneously demonstrating vast learning, questioning dominant views of the culture, and subtly undermining its own cultural position (1976: 308–312). This characterization accurately describes Pynchon's highly self-reflexive work, which both displays the monumentality and erudition of high modernism and mocks its conceits and questions its concepts of truth, certainty, and system.

In his literary work, Pynchon challenges the "old" modern way of seeing and knowing and anticipates "new" postmodern cultural forms. His writing points to the limitations of modern modes of perception and representation, and demonstrates the need to deploy multiple perspectives to better grasp history and social life. Consequently, he adopts a fragmented, multiperspectivist approach that jumps from science to media culture, from mythology to history, from comic opera to political economy. In the Pynchonian vision, modern structures and institutions invariably give way to chaos that produce both emergent forms of order and/or dissolution, entropy, and ultimately death.[5] For Pynchon, the world is often stranger than it seems, and our forms of reason, structure, and reality are always haunted by their opposites. A master of the surreal, Pynchon liberally spices his narratives with the fabulous, the miraculous, and the improbable. He is also a relentless critic of the modern scientific belief that reason can completely understand and control the world. Pynchon's literary mappings point to the limitations and illusions of conventional modern forms and paradigms of representation. His own writing, by contrast, yields alternative narrative structures that are more faithful to the complexity of experience, the turbulence of history, and the mysteries of life.

We shall see that Pynchon's texts abound with correlations between phenomena and imply an alternative order of connections, as well as forms of causality and law, that undermine modern conceptual schemes and paradigms. His work advances a radical critique of modern mechanistic models of causality and rationality, undercutting the positivist belief that scientific experiment and laws will incrementally supply knowledge of the ultimate structures of reality and enable the scientist to control the most minute aspects of life. For Pynchon, disorder, chaos, violence, paradox, and enigma are constantly subverting such rationalist schemes and dreams. Sometimes Pynchon unfolds linkages and forms of creative order not perceived by mechanistic paradigms and theories, while other times he portrays disintegration in a universe saturated with random events, radical disorder, *and* possibilities for increased happiness and freedom or for destruction and barbarism.

Pynchon's multilayered writing characteristically proceeds from depictions of the stuff of everyday experience and ordinary life, to depicting the natural, sociohistorical, political, economic, and cultural powers that envelop everyday life. In his writings, he exhibits the impact of the force of circumstances and the slaughterhouse of history on the human body and social relations, while reflecting on the ultimate historical, philosophical, and scientific mysteries of life. Written during the period of the Vietnam War, the antiwar movement and the counterculture, and dramatic social contestation in the 1960s and early 1970s,

GR is part of an oppositional sensibility that confronts governing institutions and especially attacks the military, the state, and the system of corporate capitalism and imperialism that has produced endless wars and misery.

Certainly, Pynchon's novel is much more than just a '60s attack on the Establishment, for it furnishes a literary articulation of the forces of history that have produced the modern world and are in the process of creating new forms of domination and destruction. This brings us, inevitably, to the themes of conspiracy and paranoia in Pynchon's work. His writing is not "paranoid" in either a clinical or a metaphorical sense, nor is he a conspiracy monger—although there are all sorts of conspiracies in his fictive worlds. We therefore reject the conspiracy motif as an ultimate explanation or key to Pynchon's world, arguing instead that there are many optics that can be deployed to read his work. Yet we see the paranoia and conspiracy thematics as a means to thwart hegemonic orderings and mappings, to suggest that something more might be going on and that malevolent forces may be at work. On this view, appearances are deceptive and our commonsensical everyday understandings of the world are flawed. In GR, paranoia is presented as the psychological state in which one believes everything is interrelated and part of some nefarious plot. It is distinguished from "antiparanoia" where one loses all sense of connection with the world and sees everything as self-constituted and fragmented. Antiparanoia is that psychic condition "where nothing is connected to anything, a condition not many of us can bear for long" (GR 506). A "creative paranoia" makes connections that were not hitherto apparent and thus is formally similar to dialectics which, as Fredric Jameson reminds us, is the art of making connections.[6]

Indeed, Pynchon's literary mappings challenge hegemonic social schemes of ideology and interpretation, demonstrating the limitations of scientific cognition, logic, and bourgeois normality. His writings intimate that particular events unsettle standard schemes of explanation and point to dimensions of contingency, disorder, and randomness that disrupt the modern project of understanding, dominating, and reshaping the world. In the midst of a frightening and incomprehensible social reality, people often construct rigid forms of order and identity to fight off meaninglessness, chaos, and that ultimate dissipation, death itself. Pynchon's depiction of seemingly perverse sadomasochism, fetishisms, peculiar rituals, and offbeat and weird forms of behavior portray a cornucopia of ways that people cope with chaos and contingency, and produce forms of order and meaning, however seemingly bizarre.

While Pynchon could be pointed to as an example of a postmodernism of resistance, we will argue that his work stands between the modern and the postmodern, drawing on both traditions. On the whole, postmodernist literature frequently concerns itself with banal aspects of everyday life and is playful, ironic, modest, and eschews the monumentality and lust for originality in modernism. Pynchon, by contrast, is much more of a modernist auteur with dedicated followers who hold that GR is the post-World War II novel and that his ouevre as a whole is the most significant of our time. There is a cult of Pynchon, with its Pynchon Notes, conferences, ever burgeoning publications, websites and Internet discussion lists—all revolving around an enigmatic writer who isolates himself from the public world. Moreover, *GR* is truly modernist in its aspirations and achievements; it is strikingly original; and its author does have a distinctive style, vision, and set of themes. He takes on the most vital issues of our time, confronting the Bomb and the Rocket State, media culture, suburbia, and the trajectory of U.S. society since World War II, as well as the global origins and vicissitudes of modernity. Pynchon's penetrating and dazzling writing also engages the textures of everyday life and experience, offering distinctive attempts to depict post-World War II society and culture. Hence, whereas some forms of postmodernism go for little truths rather than big ones, shun signification (and resist interpretation), Pynchon's texts are veritable meaning machines that invite multiple readings, demand interpretation, and make big statements about portentous events and phenomena.

Yet there is enough postmodernism in Pynchon's style and texts to justify using this term to describe certain aspects of his work. Accordingly, we argue that he articulates a postmodern vision of fundamental transitions in history and society, and provides postmodern modes of vision and thought. Pynchon employs standard postmodern representational strategies such as self-reflexive narrative, effacement of the high/low art distinction, the dismantling of subjectivity and reader's expectations, and an antideterminist worldview, while affirming political resistance and doing so in a distinctly postmodern manner that abandons traditional schemes of modern politics. His authorial stance is extremely complex, more fragmented and conflicted than the narrative style of Pound, Eliot, Hemingway, Kafka, or Joyce. Pynchon mixes more genres and voices, undermines more radically the authority of his characters and discourses, is more bitingly ironic, and draws more heavily on forms and techniques of media culture than his modernist predecessors. Crucially, as we show in our reading, Pynchon scrambles literary codes, mixing styles, genres, and discourses in a highly implosive text that disseminates portrayals of chaos, entropy, indeterminacy, and contingency, thus taking on principal themes of postmodern science and social theory (see Best and Kellner 1997; Chapter 3).

GRAVITY'S RAINBOW: MAPPING HISTORY

> Radioactive poisoning of the atmosphere and hence annihilation of any life on earth has been brought within the range of technical possibilities. . . . In the end, there beckons more and more clearly general annihilation.
> —ALBERT EINSTEIN

> Man's . . . entire modern history has been characterized by a series of breakdowns and blurrings of boundaries. And since World War Two that process has become so intense and so extreme that we may take the year 1945 as the beginning of a new historical epoch.
> —ROBERT JAY LIFTON

Situating *GR* during the final year of World War II and the first year of the postwar scramble for power, spheres of influence, and military technology, Pynchon describes the rise of a nascent form of global capitalism based on a military–industrial complex, new technologies, a proliferation of consumer goods and services, information and entertainment, bureaucracy, and expanding systems of power and social control. Thus, *GR* yields a parable of the birth of the postmodern adventure in the matrix of a simultaneously decomposing and evolving modern society, reaching its apotheosis in world war and the atomic bomb.

One of Pynchon's major themes throughout his writing has been how science, technology, the military, and reason produce a form of rationalized social organization, driven by the search for power and money, resulting in domination and death. In *GR*, history is presented as a culture of death, haunted by paranoia, conspiracy, aggression, violence, and destruction. The novel opens in London in 1944, when Germany is bombarding the city with V-2 rockets:

> A screaming comes across the sky. It has happened before, but there is nothing to compare it to now.
>
> It is too late. The Evacuation still proceeds, but it's all theatre. There are no lights inside the cars. No light anywhere. Above him lift girders old as an iron queen, and glass somewhere far above that would let the light of day through. But it's night. He's afraid of the way the glass will fall—soon—it will be a spectacle: the fall of a crystal palace. But coming down in total blackout, without one glint of light, only great invisible crashing. (*GR* 3)

This passage evokes a dark apocalypse of Western civilization. The reader is confronted with total warfare and then led into a bomb shelter, forced to experience the fear of death and confinement in the bowels of an underground sanctuary. The text, however, soon insinuates that the narration is a dream, as Pirate Prentice, one of the novel's 400-plus characters, slowly comes to wakefulness and gets out of bed. Pynchon is constantly undercutting the reader's expectations, blurring the lines between stream-of-consciousness reveries, realistic description, surrealism, and material from a wealth of sources. The novel jumps from omniscient narrator; to dream, fantasy, and hallucinations; to technical reports and data; to excerpts from songs and movies in order to create a rich literary tapestry. Undercutting classical discourses of truth and linear narrative, Pynchon demands an active reader willing to work to detect what literary strategy is being deployed, which narrative voice and mode is operative, whether or not to trust the discourse in question, and in general to produce her or his own interpretations.

Yet *GR* is neither a ludic text that avoids signification altogether in favor of textual play, nor is it a schizophrenic fragmentation of signifiers that produce no larger patterns of meaning. Rather, it is a "paranoid" text that contains a wealth of correlations, allusions, plots, and subplots that force its readers to keep track of and organize the complexity, and in so doing facilitates insight into the institutions, technologies, and forces creating the postwar world. For instance, the title of the novel is highly resonant and works on multiple levels. The rainbow is a rich literary symbol linked to gravity, technology, and other key themes of the book. A rainbow appears to be a solid reality, an object in the sky, but it is mere delightful appearance, an illusion created through inter-action between the observer, weather atmospherics, and sunlight. As such, it is a signifier of beauty, of calm after the storm, of the bounties of terrestrial exis-tence. Yet in the context of the war narrative, the title also conjures up rockets arching across the sky and exploding in a brilliant light, evoking the aestheticization of war.[7]

GR is thus, among other things, a meditation on beauty, death, and fini-tude. The title describes as well the parabola of a rocket's ascent and descent, of technological prowess, and, given Pynchon's broad concerns, metaphorizes the rise and fall of modern civilization. The latter theme is signaled by the refer-ence to the "crystal palace" in the opening passage cited above, an architectural symbol of 19th-century technological progress that had literally disappeared by World War II.[8] The parabola also describes the structure of Pynchon's narra-tive, which opens with a rocket weaving through space in London and ends with a missile hitting a movie theater in Los Angeles—a textual excursion that moves from the center of the previous capital of imperialism, to the emblem of the emerging system of global and consumer technocapitalism. The rocket—which in GR is the holy grail that all countries are searching for in the after-math of World War II—functions in Pynchon as a symbol of technological power, destructiveness, and apocalypse. Yet it also serves as a figure for life itself: both rockets and life burn bright, follow a certain trajectory, and then dissipate. The weapon is thus entropic and counterentropic at once: it operates in a thermodynamic system that ultimately disperses its energy upon explosion, both destroying and creating different configurations of life. The rocket is also a mark of indeterminacy because each launch must deal with the contingen-cies involved in its specific deployment. As an engineering problem, rocket technology must address any conditions that will deflect a rocket from its goal and thus must try to reduce indeterminacy. This was clearly the case in World War II with early German rocket technology and has continued to haunt mili-tary missile guidance to this day.

Pynchon subverts modern science via the image of the rocket playing havoc with the laws of physics as it bursts the speed of sound such that one hears the weapon approaching after it has already exploded, thus reversing cus-tomary cause-and-effect relations—a point that the narrative emphasizes con-stantly. Moreover, it is precisely the rocket technology that makes possible tran-scendence of earthly forces of gravity as formulated by Newton. Consequently, the frequently evoked images of rockets and space travel in GR allude to a condition beyond the laws of modern physics that had governed terrestrial bodies, as new rocket technologies break free of the planet's gravity for the darkness of space and novel technological adventures.

Hence, whereas the earth's gravity holds down, limits, and constrains, its transcendence opens humanity to a frightening new space without the limitations and boundaries of the previous era. The term "gravity's rainbow" thus evinces the end of a modernity constrained by earth's gravity and projects the human species into a new universe, beyond previous scientific models. Henceforth, Newton's laws are in question and the modern deterministic and mechanistic paradigm is challenged, thrusting humanity into an era of uncertainty and indeterminacy. The "rainbow" can therefore also signify the passage from classical modernity into postmodernity, whose defining features and laws are not yet apparent, but whose novelty, difference, and promise are augured by the rainbow's variegated and sparkling colors.

On the postmodern view, all we can have is probable knowledge, as indeterminacy and randomness prevail and a new vision of complexity and contingency is required—precisely what postmodern science supplies and Pynchon articulates in his novels. For the postmodern vision, life is more random, disconnected, and chaotic than previous modern schemes, paradigms, and models would have it (see Chapter 3). The universe is not a great chain of being, a machine, a clock, or a continuum of evolutionary natural selection. Rather, it is a frequently discontinuous process of indeterminacy, complexity, self-organization, and contingency—a postmodern perspective delineated throughout Pynchon's works.

The plot of GR centers on how the military culture that arose in World War II became obsessed with rocket technology and intelligence as resources of political power and established the framework for the postwar global systems. GR is partitioned into four parts. Section 1 introduces the central characters, all of whom are engaged in various sorts of research concerning German rocket technology in England. Section 2 moves to the French Mediterranean coast near the end of World War II, with the characters now intensifying their search for the secrets of the German rocket. Section 3 is located in "the Zone" in Europe near the end of the war as various nations and groups attempt to consolidate power and control through the rocket technology and intelligence that will be the key to postwar supremacy, envisaged as a Space Age. Section 4 represents a "Counterforce" opposing the new systems of domination and administration that are surfacing in the postwar military state with its culture of death.

The central story line focuses on Tyrone Slothrop, an American who works for British intelligence during the war and afterward becomes involved in the struggles between Allied and Soviet forces for control of German military technology. In Pynchon's quest narrative, Slothrop searches for the secrets of German rocket technology and becomes ensnared in copious adventures, some quite fabulous and surreal. He thus personifies a postmodern knight errant in search of the mysteries of postwar power and technology, as well as his own identity and fate. But Pynchon deploys hundreds of leading characters and subcharacters, while multiplying both plots and subplots to provide a dazzling array of perspectives on the advent of the technowarfare state out of the corpse of fascism and the entrails of German and Allied military and scientific establishments. Thus, the novel transcends mere fiction, taking literature into a new realm, just as the rocket was a vehicle to the Space Age, a global networked society, and a new economy.

Pynchon dramatizes the romance of science and invention, with its trials, errors, discoveries, failures, successes, ambitions, and dreams. He himself worked for Boeing Aircraft in Seattle and seems familiar with the science and technology of rockets. He is also aware of the more organizational side of engineering, the ways that corporate and state science, research, and technology are part of a bureaucratic apparatus. Dissection of the structure and effects of bureaucracy is a central theme of GR, with Pynchon providing a critique of its institutions, practices, and personnel far more vivid than the work of sociological theorists.

In addition to the rocket, plastics and the technoscience that produced it are also pivotal as figures of the technological sublime in GR. A highly malleable, manmade substance, plastic intimates the ways that scientists can reshape and remake nature in order to produce new materials subject to human control. A key subplot involves the history of a chemically produced artificial substance, Imipolex G, invented by Jamf, a behaviorist who conducted experiments on a young Slothrop. Plastic has come to be a symbol of the artificial technological societies of the present. In Pynchon's imaginary, it has a sinister aura as part of a state and corporate conspiracy, connected with military and capitalist machinations. It is an integral part of rocket technology and is related to fascist ideology: ". . . Plasticity's virtuous triad of Strength, Stability and Whiteness (*Kraft, Standfestigkeit, Weisse*: how often these were taken for Nazi graffiti . . .)" (GR 250).

The godlike ability to make new forms of matter, to rearrange the very stuff of nature, is related to cybernetics and the belief that human beings themselves can be subject to control and reordering through the reshaping of their relations, and maybe even the constitution of their very psychophysical being, as in the experiments the behaviorist Jamf undertakes on Slothrop. The project of refashioning individuals and society is connected in GR with behaviorism, which is depicted as a scientific enterprise concerned with the remaking as well as the understanding of human beings. It is also linked with Walter Rathenau's dream of creating a highly rationalized and organized state and society. Called forth in a seance, Rathenau advises: "You must ask two questions. First, what is the real nature of synthesis? And then: what is the real nature of control?" (167). Nature, no longer inviolate and self-contained, is now subject to reconstruction, to breaking down and resynthesizing its basic components, a project that would continue with cracking the code of the DNA, mapping the human genome, genetic engineering, cloning, and nanotechnology. Likewise, human beings, themselves part of nature as well as society, are subject to the same processes of reconstruction, through a merger of technology and the human that is becoming a salient aspect of the postmodern adventure in the Third Millennium (see Chapters 2–4).

Pynchon portrays science as penetrating deeper into life, learning its secrets and exploiting that knowledge to control nature and humans. In the Rathenau seance, the spirit of the dead German industrialist counsels that one must look beneath industrial and technological processes and understand "the technology of these matters. [Science must delve e]ven into the hearts of certain molecules—it is they after all which dictate temperatures, pressures, rates of flow, costs, profits, the shapes of towers . . ." (167). Yet the evocation of death and finitude in the Rathenau sequence intimates that there are also inexorable limits to life; indeed, Pynchon's postmodern vision links contingency with finitude, in reference to societies and human beings. *GR* presents a dying universe, a traditional world thrown into disorder and chaos by World War II, followed by a system of reconstituted order emerging out of its rubble and ruin. From chaos, decomposition, and death, new forms of procreative life may evolve. But the nascent corporate and state technoculture is depicted by Pynchon as itself a culture of death, a closed system that is bound, according to the second law of thermodynamics, to decay and disintegrate, eventually to give rise to a new system—or to take the planet down with it, an obvious possibility in an age of nuclear weapons, biotechnology, and nanotechnology.

Beyond the references to actual people and events to indict the guilty, *GR* is a metafictional text that eschews mimetic pretensions, foregrounds the act of narration (e.g., through diverse appeals to the reader and a plethora of distancing devices), and deploys a narrator who seems to be omniscient in the traditional sense, but who turns out to be paranoid and unreliable. Pynchon combines cinematic techniques, utilizing close-ups, pans, jump-cuts, parallel editing, cross-fades, and other filmic devices, to create a kinetic and multifaceted literary narrative. He often employs indeterminate streams of consciousness that cut from one voice to another in midsentence, punctuated with a wealth of surrealist fantasies, hallucinations, and historical description to map the complexities of the postwar world. The theme of mapping itself is reflected in the novel through mathematical scientist Roger Mexico's diagram of German bomb strikes in London and Slothrop's chart of his own sexual conquests (not coincidentally, it turns out there is an exact correlation between the two maps, though the novel never fully explains *how* this occurs, implying the possibility of random patterns of experience that defy rational scientific schemes, as well as nefarious government plots and experiments).

The metafictional stance of *GR* is particularly interesting for its sustained historical interpretation through the mediation of cinematic codes and its citations of popular songs and verse, thus instantiating a postmodern collapse of high and low culture. In particular, the bits of songs quoted throughout the text demonstrate the ways that popular music mobilizes sentiment and affect, portraying how media culture plays an important role in the organization of experience and meaning. The songs and verses for which Pynchon is infamous punctuate the dramatic action, commenting, often ironically, on the character's experiences, while sometimes providing utopian longing in the midst of suffering and deprivation, alluding to cultural community that transcends individual loneliness.

GR is also perhaps the first novel that concretely engages the emergent "hyperreal" realm of experience in the contemporary period. As demonstrated by theorists such as Boorstin, Debord, Eco, and Baudrillard, the saturation of images, media, simulacra, and pseudoevents in today's media and consumer culture has threatened to erode the distinction between image and reality, sign and referent, simulacrum and original, in a new "hyperreal" world of simulacra (Baudrillard 1983a, 1983b, and 1993; also see Chapter 2). As a postmodern text that collapses the opposition between high and low culture, GR challenges mimetic codes and modernist elitism by thoroughly incorporating media culture into the sensibility and perceptual apparatus of the narrator and many of its characters, and thus into the text itself. Indeed, Pynchon's "characters" are themselves sometimes simulations of literary or cinematic figures, replicating their gestures, thoughts, and codes. Other personae, such as Slothrop, dissolve and mutate, hinting at the instability of character and personality in the evolving postwar world.

As a paradoxical, ambiguous, and self-deconstructive text, GR therefore at once seeks to engage the metatextual field of "real history" while problematizing its own attempts at representation through metafictional devices. It tries to show how "objective reality" has been vitiated in a postwar society of media, advertising, propaganda, and publicity, and to reawaken a sense of history to help grasp and illuminate the seemingly hallucinated past and present. Hence, despite the linguistically and historically mediated nature of its narrative structures, GR does not succumb to a solipsistic, nihilistic, or purely playful deconstructionist stance. Rather than falling into the density of its own discursive machine, GR seeks to critically engage contemporary history and to pursue a political dissection of dominant social powers, institutions, technologies, psychologies, and practices.

THE ROCKET STATE: TECHNOCAPITALISM, PATRIARCHY, AND IMPERIALISM

> Oh, a State begins to take form in the stateless German night, a State that spans oceans and surface politics, sovereign as the International or the Church of Rome, and the Rocket is its soul.
> —GR (565)

Weaving together Slothrop's picaresque adventures and the frequently bizarre interactions among the central characters provides the literary structure to map the emergence of what Pynchon calls "the Rocket State" and the new social system structured around advanced forms of military technology and organization. In Pynchon's vision, the rocket is a central component not only of the system of warfare that materialized in World War II, but of future advanced modes of missile technology and of communication based on satellite transmission, as well as space travel. He describes the effort to develop rocket technology in Germany, the first nation to exploit this potential, by assembling a team of scientists and engineers to manufacture what became the V-1 and V-2 missiles used by Hitler against England (coincidentally or not, *V.* was the title of Pynchon's first published novel [1962]).

Members of the German rocket research group continued their work after the war—mostly in the United States, but a smaller number also ended up in the Soviet Union. The offspring of their work include intercontinental ballistic missiles armed with nuclear warheads, global communications satellites and networks, spacecraft, space travel, and *Star Wars*-like fantasies. In their book on the German team that built the first rockets, Ordway and Sharpe (1979) recount how Albert Speer (and ultimately Hitler) deemed it more useful to the German war effort to spend millions of marks on the Peenemuende rocket test facility than to supply money for tanks and artillery. Wernher von Braun and other key scientists were brought to the United States after the war and helped to produce the rocket technology that became a crucial feature of Cold War competition between the United States and the Soviet Union, as well as the vehicles of the Space Age and a new global culture beamed through satellite transmission (see McDougall 1985).

GR depicts the growth of the *multi*national component of the new system of global capitalism. American, British, German, Dutch, African, Asian, South American, and other nations and corporations weave in and out of the plot and pursue their varied and usually conflicting goals within the shifting matrixes of power and control that characterize the passage from the wartime state of World War II to the national security state of the postwar period. Many of the characters are hybrids, such as the Schwarzcommando troops deployed by the Germans to help launch the V-2 rocket who blend African with European identities. In the alliances between I. G. Farben and other industrial corporations, such as Standard Oil in the United States and ICI in Great Britain, Pynchon points to a world where corporations are as powerful as nation-states.

Hence, Pynchon's historical vision depicts the *trans*national features of the emerging system of global capitalism with intricate details of alliances and deals between American, British, German, and other corporations for new technologies and new products like plastics and the rocket. He alludes to how Standard Oil, General Electric, and other U.S. corporations cooperated with German corporations before, during, and after the war, thus prefiguring the system of alliances between transnational corporations, nation-states, and the global political institutions of the current capitalist economic system.

Throughout the novel, we see the buying and selling practices of various capitalist nations during the war, and thus the co-construction of business, the state, and the military. Dramatizing one of the most cynical moments in the history of U.S. capitalism, Pynchon describes how U.S. corporations traded with the Nazis to help sustain their genocidal practices, profiting from and contributing to massive destruction. *GR* allows us to experience these operations by giving fictive flesh to its operatives and showing how its machinations harmed ordinary human beings.

Pynchon also charts primary forms of male domination, the connections between militarism and patriarchy, and the extension of male power throughout the interstices of everyday life. Rarely missing an opportunity for correlating rocket technology with libidinal dynamics, Pynchon depicts an explosive sexuality that erupts throughout his narrative. *GR* presents sexuality as a domain of power and control; its sublimation and expression find a prime target and outlet in the erection of military technologies, pornography, and sadomasochism. The most repressed (Major Pointsman) and the most demonic of Pynchon's characters (Major Blicero) engage in extreme sexuality to regain a sense that they are alive, drained as they are of feelings or vital energies by the system of bureaucracy and death in which they function.

Throughout the novel, Pynchon makes connections between militarism and sexual domination and violence. From this perspective, the frequent pornographic interludes can be seen as depictions of the forms of sexuality produced by militarism, which fuse Eros and Thanatos, Life and Death. Likewise, the objectifications of the body in pornography can be seen as an extension of dehumanization in the modes of technological rationality. Since men are the dominant group, and since most of the sexual fantasies and pornography exhibited are explicitly coded as male fantasies, the extreme fetishization of the body and sexuality in these passages can be read from a feminist register as a critique of patriarchy and its sexual distortions. For example, in one passage Pynchon describes a U.S. officer, Major Marvy, who represents the male tendency to brutalize and oppress others, mixing sex and death in a perverted will to domination:

> Well, that's all reet. He isn't fucking her eyes, is he? He'd rather not have to look at her face anyhow, all he wants is the brown skin, the shut mouth, that sweet and nigger submissiveness. She'll do anything he orders, yeah he can hold her head under the water till she drowns, he can bend her hand back, yeah, break her fingers like that cunt in Frankfurt the other week. Pistol-whip, bite till blood comes . . . visions go swarming, violent, less erotic than you think—more occupied with thrust, impact, penetration, and such other military values. (*GR* 606)

The victim here is a woman of color; throughout his novel Pynchon critically engages the synergistic tendencies toward colonialist imperialism, racism, the will to domination, and the eradication of otherness and difference in militarist and totalitarian systems.[9] Pynchon consistently deploys color symbolism that has racial, political, and other connotations. The names of one of his leading characters, *Weisman* (literally "white man"), and that of *Blicero* ("bleached man") signify that it is white men who are the vehicles of colonialization. The ultracolonialist character, Weisman, is engaged in the slaughter of the Herero tribe in Africa in both *V.* and *GR*. Pynchon also focuses on the deployment of African slave labor to produce the V-2 rocket, and a group of Hereros plan mass suicide as a protest against their uprootedness and exploitation.

Constantly calling attention to the shadow side of modernity, Pynchon depicts with great sympathy a product of the colonialist conquest of Africa, Enzian, who has a white father and an African mother and who Blicero takes back to Germany as his personal servant and lover. Enzian looms as a charismatic counterforce, embodying a different relation to nature and a holistic philosophy that rejects the system of binary metaphysics upon which Western reason is founded. In fact, *GR* depicts the modes of thought out of which the Western domination of nature and colonial subjugation of the world arise, while also sketching the contours, structures, psychology, and effects of a technological culture of death and destruction produced by the imperialist powers.

The novel thus allegorically depicts the rise of an emergent neoimperialist capitalist system organized around science and powerful technologies. The new ruling elites portrayed range from military men who want to appropriate their warfare potential, to capitalists who desire to exploit their economic potential, to scientists who seek to pursue their research and augment their power. They also include bureaucrats who utilize technology as tokens of power within systems of social control, media moguls who produce fantasies for mass consumption, and shadowy figures who use intelligence and technology as modes of domination and power. Throughout the novel, Pynchon delineates the contours of a system—variously called "the Firm," "They," or "It"—which he opposes to ordinary human beings, nature, and values such as love, empathy, cooperation, individuality, struggle, and resistance.

Bureaucracy, Determinism, and Domination

> "We're all going to fail," Sir Marcus primping his curls, "but the Operation won't." . . . Each of us has his place, and the tenants come and go, but the places remain. . . .
>
> —GR (616)

> "The Man has a branch office in each of our brains, his corporate emblem is a white albatross, each local rep has a cover known as the Ego, and their mission in this world is Bad Shit."
>
> —GR (712–713)

Pynchon's complex symbolism sets the "one" of freedom, singularity, and the body against the "zero" of systems of domination and control, thus portraying forces of life struggling against entropy and destruction. In Pynchon's vision, just as closed mechanical systems gradually lose energy and dissipate, so too do societies run down, tend toward disorder, and ultimately collapse. War, of course, also increases entropy, unleashing systems of military destruction that ultimately produce ruin and disorder. Slothrop, too, disintegrates and disappears in the course of *GR*, and one could read Pynchon's 1997 novel, *Mason & Dixon*, as an elegiac mediation on the entropy in the lives of the two main characters.

Yet chaos and entropy also provide the space for action and intervention, for chance and indeterminacy, for resistance and struggle, and for new forms of order and self-organization. Thus, there is both an optimistic and a pessimistic strain in Pynchon's work operating simultaneously: as with some forms of chaos and complexity theory, new forms of order originate out of disorder, but as with classical entropy theory, dynamic systems wind down and collapse. Chaos and disorder thus foster such positive potentials as the breaking up and dissolution of oppressive forms of thought, society, and conformist behavior, but also the danger of calamitous dissolution into nothingness.

In Pynchon's "dialectics of entropy," any system or structure that represses life forces will sooner or later dissipate, leading to decomposition—or to new forms of creative order. Pynchon seems to suggest that closed systems necessarily lead to stasis and death, while open systems can evolve into new forms of procreative life. It is the fate of the human being to be a relatively closed system with a limited ability to maintain evolving life—hence the drama of finitude, of the fragility of the body and human existence, which is a primary obsession of Pynchon's writings.

Whereas determinists deny the possibility of accident and chance, Pynchon describes it as "the entropies of loveable but scatterbrained Mother Nature" (*GR* 324). Yet seeming disorder and chaos may conceal underlying patterns of order. The correlation between Slothrop's erections and the impact and explosion of German rockets that is a main narrative thread of the novel intimates structures and connections not perceivable by conventional scientific logic and modes of explanation. The constant allusions to conspiracies in Pynchon's works imply, among other things, that there are social connections and forces at work that elude our grasp. Thus, Pynchon is not so much rejecting causality and linear cause–effect schemata per se, as indicating that these forms are often reductive and sometimes miss key causal forces and connections.

World War II stands, for Pynchon, as the transitional stage to a late modernization that depersonalizes individuals, sets objects and bureaucracy over freedom, turns people into things, and breeds fear and paranoia. Pynchon cites Max Weber's concept of the routinization of charisma and frequently uses Weber's notion of instrumental rationality to describe the nature and mind-set of the social system whose origins, structures, practices, and effects he depicts.[10] For Pynchon, societies are crystallizations of power and charisma—of

leaders or technologies—that must be tamed and sublimated into social normality. In Pynchon's vision, technological and charismatic powers are also
channeled into war, which is presented as an excuse to develop technology and
to produce new forms of control that would generate a postwar social reorganization. Indeed, World War II fostered immense scientific and technological
growth, as well as corporate organization on a huge new scale. At that time,
dominant corporations solidified their hold on the economy, and giant government bureaucracies mushroomed along with new modes of control and
domination.[11] Out of the relatively benign Office of Strategic Services (OSS)
the malevolent CIA materialized; the FBI became ever more sinister; television
stupified subjects with media spectacles; and industrial technology generated
novel forms of mass production and consumption that produced a new type of
consumer society. Moreover, out of World War II arose a new global struggle
between capitalism and communism, the beginnings of which are apparent in
Pynchon's narrative.

While the ostensible time frame of GR is the years 1944–1945, its historical "countermemory" (Foucault) stretches from the early to the potentially last
days of European and American colonization of the planet, from the grotesque
extermination of the dodo bird by Dutch settlers and the American war on
the Indians, to the genocidal war machines of the Nazis and the portent of
postwar domination and disaster. Just as T. W. Adorno emphasized the continuity of disaster from the slingshot to the atom bomb, Pynchon traces the continuous catastrophic advance of modern civilization from colonialism to the
Space Age.

Whereas nearly all cultures kill, European civilization surpassed all previous ones in its "obsession" with and "addiction" to death. As Captain Blicero
exclaims: "In Africa, Asia, Amerindia, Oceania, Europe came and established
its order of Analysis and Death. What it could not use, it killed or altered" (GR
722). In Pynchon's political vision, the impulse for empire produced the construction of systems of domination that lead into fascism. The military–industrial complex is thus the latest and most technologically lethal phase of a European death culture, producing a megamachine of death that does away with
pomp and ceremony to perfect the forms of killing in a rationalized and routinized administration. Within the Western "culture of death," all forms of
life—natural, animal, and human—are "being broken and reassembled every
day, to preserve an elite few" (GR 230). War becomes an extension of business
in which death is the main commodity in an "economy of pain" (GR 348), indicating the coevolution of the military and industrial systems.

Pynchon depicts an entropic structure of "control that is out of control"
(GR 277), a system addicted to money and power and technology that breaks
with the previous laws of nature to produce a new technological universe. The
novelistic equivalent of a George Grosz painting, GR savagely criticizes and
satirizes global capitalism. Rendering an enigmatic "They," a Kafkaesque "System" run by a million bureaucrats in a thousand departments and networks to

drive the necropolitical machine, Pynchon depicts a vast, intricate, and systemic structure involving corporations, scientists, universities, the military, and a host of acronymic intelligence agencies that are "all in it together" (GR 466) as components of a huge system of domination.

In this global organization of power/knowledge where the "normal" subjective response is paranoia, Pynchon draws a clear connection between the theory and practice of natural and cultural annihilation. He implicates positivistic models of cause and effect and "analysis" in general. Analytic modes of understanding are represented as the epistemology proper to a will to power that seeks to vanquish everything that is other to the norm of civilized/white/male power and resistent to scientific apprehension. The implications of the positivistic mind-set are forcefully dramatized in the figure of Pointsman, a Pavlovian-inspired behaviorist whose mania is to reduce the human world to precise laws of calculation and prediction and whose motto is "we must never lose control" (GR 109).

Against the Pavlovian-behaviorist Pointsman, Pynchon offers the mathematician Roger Mexico and a variety of parapsychologists, mystics, and paranormals who represent other ways of seeing. For Pointsman, all behavior has a physiological basis and can be predicted, controlled, and determined. Mexico, by contrast, represents a probabilistic and nonbehaviorist model of science that accepts indeterminacy and openness. As Pynchon puts it:

> If ever the Antipointsman existed, Roger Mexico is the man. Not so much, the doctor admits, for the psychical research. The young statistician is devoted to number and to method, not table-rapping or wishful thinking. But in the domain of zero to one, not-something to something, Pointsman can only possess the zero and the one. He cannot, like Mexico, survive anyplace in between. Like his master I. P. Pavlov before him, he imagines the cortex of the brain as a mosaic of tiny on/off elements. . . . But to Mexico belongs the domain *between* zero and one—the middle Pointsman has excluded from his persuasion—the probabilities. (GR 55)

GR thus pits numerous modes of knowing against each other—Pointsman's behaviorism, Mexico's indeterminacy, various forms of parascience, and the Hereros' mode of nature mysticism—as well as posing science against the discourses of history, literature, philosophy, and so on. The various scientists at "The White Visitation" all have their own theories to explain the mysterious correlation between Slothrop's erections and the German rocket explosions: some explain it as psychokinesis, others as paranormal, whereas Pointsman searches for the single casual mechanism. Roger Mexico thinks it's a statistical oddity: "But he feels the foundations of that discipline trembling a bit now, deeper than oddity ought to drive. Odd, odd, odd" (GR 85).

The name "Mexico" connotes the borderland between the United States, with its highly evolved science and technology and southern cultures, whose people are more integrally rooted in nature and tradition. Yet, in a sense, Roger Mexico prefigures an emerging postmodern science, built on the positions of Boltzmann, Poincaré, and quantum mechanics, that is based on statistical regularities and probabilities, and not on certainties or mechanistic causal links. *GR* relentlessly satirizes Pointsman's desperate Pavlovian endeavor to provide a stimulus–response nexus to explain the correlation between Slothrop's sexual exploits and the falling of the rockets. It thus calls into question the central tenets of modern science as articulated by Pointsman's expression of Pavlov's hope "for a long chain of better and better approximations. His faith ultimately lay in a pure physiological basis for the life of the psyche. No effect without cause, and a clear train of linkages" (89).

Mexico answers that "there's a feeling about that cause-and-effect may have been taken as far as it will go. That for science to carry on at all, it must look for a less narrow, a less   sterile set of assumptions. The next great breakthrough may come when we have the courage to junk cause-and-effect entirely, and strike off at some other angle" (89). That "other angle" leads to a postmodern science that suspends the modern paradigm for less determinist models. The "X-Stimulus," the Beyond the Zero, that would explain the correlation between Slothrop's "scores" and the rocket explosions is exactly that which eludes scientific understanding, which is not subject to casual mechanism and determinism. Thus, *GR* signals that randomness is a fundamental part of existence, and that underlying connections may not be perceivable or even accessible to the diligent investigator.[12]

From a conspiratorial perspective, the correlation between Slothrop's erections and German bombing insinuate an alternative order of connections, a possible mode of causality and law that would prove extremely useful to the modern project of controlling and mastering a complex and dangerous social reality. Pynchon presents science and technology as the demiurges of a new civilization that will intensify the instrumental rationality of the modern industrial world to a higher level. The novel frequently invokes SF-inspired anticipations of a future Rocket City and State that is growing out of the technological culture of death that Pynchon describes. Inside a secret German rocket production site, hidden in a mountain, Slothrop sees a vision of the Rocket City of the future with its elegant space suits, its high-tech helmets, and its futuristic architecture and design illumined by translucent lighting (*GR* 295ff.).

Pynchon also portrays a new Rocket State springing out of the industrial corporate mode of organization and the future Rocket cartel. His vision of this expansive "System" anticipates the organization of all the competitive capitalist nations into an interlocking global structure of multinational corporations under the hegemony of the United States, leading to even more technologically sophisticated societies of the future. This involves a passage from the "Oven State" of overt force and military extermination to the postwar "Rocket State" where domination is exercised via consent achieved through intensive propaganda and mass media, and where technological development threatens to vanquish spontaneity and freedom.

GR thus equates the production of rocket technology with the emergence of an entire system of social organization and control. The opening and closing presentations of the rocket furnish a metaphorical rendering of the contours of the system, with the initial evocation dramatizing the military terror from permanent warfare and the final image of the young German soldier Gottfried sacrificed in a rocket launching symbolizing the fusion of humans and technology and the ritual surrender of the human for the greater good of technological deification. In the ending parable, the demonic Captain Blicero sacrifices his handsome lover Gottfried ("God's Peace" in the English translation of his name) to the god of rocket technology. The ooooo-Rocket in which Gottfried is inserted is described as a "womb" and a "coffin" to which he is entombed (GR 750).

The passage suggests the birth of the new Space Age out of the ruins of World War II and the entrapment of humanity in a constraining political and technological apparatus that it is condemned to serve. Consequently, in our reading, GR depicts the birth of postmodernity out of the institutions and spirit of modernity by exhibiting the technological fetishism and system of analysis and death that was begetting new modes of technoscience and global technocapitalism. The charisma of rocket technology was stabilized in new structures of control and domination, but was eventually shared by the two competing postwar superpowers, the United States and the Soviet Union. It thus generated as well the Cold War, whose beginnings Pynchon symbolically portrays in the contending quests for rocket technology in what he calls "the Zone" that sprung out of the ruins of postwar Europe.

In the Zone

> But here in the Zone categories have been blurred badly.
> —GR (303)

In the latter half of GR (281ff.), the Zone emerges as the space between the collapse of European fascism and the coming system of global technocapitalism. In the postwar turmoil, the Zone stands as a site of possibility and resistance, as well as the locus of chaos and disorder. The novel's ostensible subject matter is the last year of World War II and the transformative phase to a postwar society—a short era of disorder and openness before the systems that became hegemonic during the Cold War could congeal. Pynchon thus highlights the historical moment when prewar power structures proved dysfunctional and a new multinational political and economic constellation was created, grounded in military technologies and competition between the superpowers. Although in Pynchon's vision, World War II marked the defeat of

German national socialism, new forms of fascist control of everyday life proliferated in the modes of social organization that survived World War II. Domination was thus streamlined through the erection of Soviet Stalinist and U.S.
national security state institutions, media and information technologies, and, in
the West, the consumer society.

In Pynchon's imaginary, the territory of multinational technocapitalism is
dominated by a host of secret powers whose complexity can paralyze efforts to
map and control the processes and dynamics of the present. As the narrator
asks after giving a catalogue of various intelligence and military agencies,
"Who can find his way about this lush maze of initials?" (GR 76). A multinational arena, the Zone is divided into various sectors governed by British, German, French, Soviet, and U.S. troops. It is emblematic of the chaotic social terrain and irreducible multiplicity that Michel Foucault terms "heterotopia."[13]
The Zone is strewn with the detritus of the old system and is the symbol both
of the demise of an earlier capitalism and of the beginnings of the novel postwar rocket/media state to come.

As a transitional site, the Zone is a place where chaos reigns, which lacks
the routinization of power that would soon occur again in the postwar world.
As Tanner (1982) notes, "the Zone" is distinguishable from "the System."
Where everything in the System is fixed and categorized, the Zone exhibits
anomie, chaos, and an erasure of boundaries. The Zone is the symbolic space
of "the new Uncertainty" anticipating as well the germination of a new postmodern scene of implosion and "endless simulation" (GR 570). It is a
decentered topos of multiple codes that is populated by lost and displaced persons. The Zone is thus a twilight regime between the old and the new, where
everything and everyone is adrift, and behavior is not regulated in terms of
fixed social structures and practices.

The Zone therefore points to a liminal expanse, a betweenness, where
boundaries are blurred and new borders, structures, and contours are being negotiated. The Zone is a sphere of openness, of indeterminancy, in which people have options, can make choices, and may create their own domains, cultural forms, and life. It is a sphere where corporate and state powers do not yet
rule, where bureaucracy and instrumental rationality do not yet dominate, and
where freedom and meaning, to use Weber's classical couplet, still are possible.
Pynchon's Zone is conflicted between normalizing powers that strive to create
new systems of control and domination, and "Counterforces" that resist instrumental control and reason, pursuing their own goals. The Zone is thus torn
between the old and the new, the dominant and the resistant. The denizens of
the Zone accordingly have to choose their sides and invent appropriate codes
of behavior and survival. Moreover, precisely the chaos and complexity of the
Zone render room to maneuver. Through the portrayal of the various characters pursuing their own aims within these circumstances, Pynchon evokes a
sense of possibility for action, even within perplexing and oppressive situations.

For us, the Zone is a resonant representation of that arena between the modern and the postmodern, between the old socioeconomic structure institutionalized in state capitalism and the new system of global technocapitalism. It is a figure of an interregnum where boundaries are more open, fluid, and subject to negotiation and contestation. The Zone thus points to the emergent conditions of postwar life, marked by a constant shifting of boundaries, creation of more fluid identities, and eruption of new sciences, technologies, opportunities, dangers, and experiences for which the term "postmodern" is now commonly used. It is therefore an apt metaphor for what we see as the current interstices between the modern and the postmodern in the Third Millennium, as individuals negotiate novel experiences, spaces, and forms, trying to produce concepts and practices adequate to the emergent social organization with all its tensions and novelties.

In retrospect, we can see that the origins of the postmodern adventure emerge from the conflicts of World War II and its aftermath. The year 1945 marks the shift from hot war to cold war, from imperial domination and conflict to a neoimperialist global order rooted in an expanding form of technocapitalism. Thus, in Pynchon's vision, transnational capitalism shifted from a power based on force to one rooted in hegemony, from a society of death camps to the engineered utopia of "Happyville," and from the nightmare of Orwell's *1984* (1948) to the somascape of Huxley's *Brave New World* (1931). This process, we suggest, helped create our current condition of a global network of multinational banks, corporations, communications systems, and biotechnologies.

Pynchon emphasizes that this conjuncture should be understood in terms of evolution of new forms of control and domination, an abandonment of overt violent mechanisms for more efficient covert ones. As the narrator tells us, "The Germans-and-Japs story was only one, rather surrealistic version of the real War. The real War is always there. The dying tapers off now and then, but the War is still killing lots and lots of people. Only right now it is killing them in more subtle ways. Often in ways that are too complicated, even for us, at this level, to trace" (*GR* 645). Thus, while his wartime lover, Jessica, embraces the "new world," Roger Mexico sees it only as more of the same; the postwar "peace" is only another propaganda ploy, a "rationalized power-ritual" (*GR* 177). In the paranoid vision of *GR*, the "They" structure embraces possibilities "far far beyond Nazi Germany" (*GR* 25). The excesses of Nazi power are only a vulgar symptom of what would emerge as more efficient systems of domination, achieving their goals through far more subtle, routinized means of social control and hegemony.

The historical shift to new configurations of society and culture are also symbolically negotiated in Slothrop's circumnavigations through the increasingly complex and chaotic postwar world. In the words of one of his contacts, Slothrop represents "the wave of the future," and emergence of a fragmented subjectivity that would become ever more common in the postwar world. In his adoption of layer upon layer of disguises, assumed personas, and simulated identities (soldier, war correspondent, Rocketman, Pigman, transvestite, and eventually Everyman/No-man), Slothrop anticipates the invention of the postmodern self, the resourceful *bricoleur* who invents himself over and over by constructing identities mediated through rapidly changing consumer and media culture, technologies, fads, and social roles.

In his shifting from identity to identity, Slothrop provides a preview of novel modes of transnational identities that are hybrid, flexible, mobile, and infinitely malleable. He starts out as an American working with British intelligence, then poses as an English correspondent as he wanders through the Zone, in search of the secret to the V-2 rocket which he had studied with the Allied secret services. Trying to break free from the old order and those hunting him down, and straying into the no-man's-land of the Zone, Slothrop is disconnected from social relations and enters into an existential void where, unable to adapt to a changing social world and lacking any adequate mapping strategies, he disintegrates. Having gone AWOL and left the French Riviera to seek the secret rocket technology that the various superpowers are all after, Slothrop is buffeted about in adventure after adventure, now totally reactive to the forces of history. Himself a product of behaviorism whose father had sold him to a Harvard laboratory as a child, Slothrop is a victim of causal forces that elude his mastery and the force of circumstances that knock him one way and then another like a pinball. Anticipating a later fluid and hybrid postmodern subjectivity, Slothrop must seek new identities and orient himself and survive in a hostile and confusing environment.

In this space, Slothrop leaves behind his national identity and enters into the new multinational world devoid of any "real sense of nationality." Sent to recover some hashish buried outside the Allied housing compound in Neubabelsburg during the Potsdam Conference, Slothrop is captured and drugged outside the compound by Soviet agents and awakens in the studio of a German film company. He is thus transported from the old imperial world to the new constellation that retains aspects of fascist power structures within an expanding system of global capitalism, scientific reason, media culture, and political bureaucracy. For the rest of the narrative, he finds it increasingly difficult to navigate the boundaries of this bewildering zone and eventually disappears.

Read allegorically, Slothrop's gradual psychological disintegration is symptomatic of the fate of the postmodern self whose personal power is understood as arbitrary choice and whose identity is chipped away through the bombardment of signifiers within electronic and digital culture. As the narrative proceeds, Slothrop seems to disintegrate into conflicting selves and eventually disappears from the narrative altogether: "Some believe that fragments of Slothrop have grown into consistent personae of their own. If so, there's no telling which of the Zone's present-day population are offshoots of his original scattering" (GR 742).

Through this symbolic presentation of the critical historical passage to the novel forms of hegemony in the postwar world and its impact on personal identity and everyday life, Pynchon is able to dramatize a complex series of events that helped shape the postmodern adventure. He points to emergent forms of power, domination, and identity that require new cognitive mappings. In the words of the narrator, "We have to look for power sources here, and distribution networks we were never taught, routes of power our teachers never imagined, or were encouraged to avoid . . . we have to find meters whose scales are unknown in the world, draw our own schematics, getting feedback, making connections, reducing the error, trying to learn the real function . . . zeroing in on what incalculable plot?" (*GR* 521). Thus, new maps and vision are required that are more sophisticated in method than modern mappings and are better able to delineate connections, conflicts, and transformations. In addition, alternative forms of practice and politics are needed to respond to the challenges of the novel forms of power and domination.

Changing the System?

> For every kind of vampire, there is a kind of cross.
> —*GR* (628)

A cognitive mapping that explored various lines of force and domination would do little but reinforce submission to power if it did not thematize these lines in terms of possibilities of resistance and transformation. As Foucault (1977) has emphasized, there is no power without resistance, and as Bruce Sterling (1988: vii) has indicated, there is no dominant culture without a counterculture. Thus, adequate presentation of domination should simultaneously analyze these forces for their contingency and points of vulnerability, while seeking forces of resistance and alternatives to the existing system. How, then, does Pynchon's mapping of scientific–technological–political systems of domination and destruction present possible means of resistance?

In section 4 of *GR*, Pynchon presents examples of what he calls "the Counterforce" in which various outsiders, rebels, outcasts, marginals, and those who don't fit into the system of instrumental rationality resist its structures of domination and struggle for freedom, dignity, or at least their own pleasures. *GR* was initially going to be titled *Mindless Pleasures* and indeed Pynchon catalogues the passions and practices of outsiders and bohemian subcultures throughout his texts. *GR* includes scores of characters who revolt against authority, are highly eccentric, and stand outside the system of organized authority.

The concluding section on "The Counterforce" gets underway with a distraught Roger Mexico seeking Slothrop in the Zone; a flashback portrays him confronting Pointsman at a bureaucratic meeting: "Roger has unbuttoned his fly, taken his cock out, and is now busy pissing on the shiny table, the papers, in the ashtrays and pretty soon on these poker-faced men themselves, who, although executive material all right, men of hair-trigger minds, are still not quite willing to admit that this is happening, you know, in any world that really touches, at too many points, the one *they're* accustomed to" (*GR* 636). Mexico then goes to visit Pirate Prentice, from whom he learns of a "Counterforce" that opposes the bureaucratic hierarchy and structures of authority. Prentice tells Mexico of the "We-system" organized against the Firm's "They-system" and the succeeding sections introduce some of the elements and strategies of the Counterforce "We-system."

The System that the Counterforce opposes in turn suppresses all otherness, all forces and instincts that do not fit into its structure of technological rationality; these include the body, nature, nonconformity, and rebellion. Therefore, Mexico's act of pissing on the bureaucracy and the later disruption by Mexico and Pig Bodine of a formal dinner with evocations of bodily wastes and excrement represent the return of the repressed (*GR* 713ff.). All those forces and instincts that the They-system would stultify and even eliminate to sustain perfect instrumental rationality and order resurface. Such a culture would represent consummate death, the unblemished Zero, and so the representatives of the Counterforce are precisely the forces of life, of all that cannot be subsumed to a bureaucratic order. Espousing a *gauchisme* similar to the kind of antirational, aestheticist, and individualist politics that we find in postmodern theorists such as Foucault, the early Baudrillard, and some of the writings of Lyotard, Deleuze, and Guattari (see Best and Kellner 1991), Counterforce member Pirate Prentice claims that a resistance movement cannot participate in any mode of rationality since reason is a reified instrument of the System. Consequently, the "resistance" strategies of the Counterforce take forms such as sadomasochism, blotting out reality with drugs or alcohol, and engaging in disruptive behavior and a refusal of "normality" and "rationality."

Pynchon knows that paranoia can produce solipsism and a sense that everyone and everything is plotting against one, but he portrays individuals engaging in solidarity and forming communities of resistance. Yet, like many postmodernists, Pynchon seems to advocate social change through personal resistance and disconnected rebellions rather than through social movements and organized groups.[14] The Counterforce is only a weak and fragmentary cluster of conspirators, and Pynchon alludes to its possible annihilation or disappearance in the face of the greater They-system. Moreover, Pynchon substitutes a logic of *transgression* (a postmodern multiplication of local and fragmented forms of resistance) for a logic of *transcendence* (a modernist centralizing tactic that often seeks a total rupture from matrices of power to create a new, socially engineered humanity). While Pynchon's novel may help to dissuade readers from clinging to false optimism or facile utopian programs of change, he declines to portray collective strategies that mobilize people around common political goals, and thereby reinforces individualistic or subcultural solutions to systemic problems. Like many postmodernists, Pynchon is concerned not with generating positive models for change, but rather with problematizing and deconstructing already existing models.

We therefore find GR's politics quite ambiguous, although more distinctive than some readers would have it. GR is frequently interpreted as a deeply pessimistic novel, as announcing the arrival of the apocalypse and catastrophe prophesied by puritanical jeremiads.[15] In GR, there are constant references to "They," the "System," and the "Firm"; everyone is exploited by malevolent characters for insidious ends; human relationships are mercenary and degraded; the book begins and ends with technological death raining from the sky. But despite its bleak tones and disturbing textures, GR is not unqualifiably nihilistic, pessimistic, or quietistic. The novel, rather, attempts to portray both forces of determination and freedom, domination and resistance, especially in section 4 dealing with "The Counterforce."

Consequently, against the many critics who argue that GR is a novel of doom and despair, we contend that there are countervailing strands of hope in GR and that it has an oppositional political dimension. Pynchon's advocacy of alternatives to the culture of death, however, is highly muted, qualified, and ultimately problematic. We read this as symptomatic of a problem with postmodern political positions in general. On the positive side, Pynchon articulates a dialectics of technology whereby technology is viewed as providing either instruments of domination or of struggle. This position is stated by the narrator, who distinguishes between "a good Rocket to take us to the stars [and] an evil Rocket for the World's suicide, the two perpetually in struggle" (GR 727). Similarly, while there are themes of behavioral control and conditioning in the text, as embodied by Pointsman, there are also salient emphases on uncertainty and probability, as represented by Mexico. The novel thus implies that positivist social engineering can never achieve total hegemony—what Pynchon refers to as the "illusion of control." The dramatic conflict between Pointsman and Mexico symbolizes more than the clash of opposed worldviews, of positivist and postpositivist scientific outlooks. It also suggests a structured and determined, yet contingent, universe—the oxymoron of an "open system" such as chaos and complexity theory try to describe (see Chapter 3).

The philosophical, political, and ethical implications of Mexico's outlook are that possibilities remain open in any system, including the global network of postwar capitalism. As long as there is indeterminacy and chaos, there are possibilities for action and transformation. Pynchon attempts to dramatize the fact that while our current form of society is heading toward a path of ultimate annihilation as it takes the deadly logic of the Rocket State to its illogical conclusions, this trajectory is not predetermined and unmodifiable. Hence, Pynchon demonstrates the importance of the genealogy of the Rocket State from the demise of the Oven State to better locate the coordinates of our present mode of domination. While the global anxiety about nuclear destruction has subsided somewhat since Pynchon wrote *GR*, the destructive, entropic tendencies of contemporary capitalism have accelerated in other, equally dangerous ways—most obviously those involving species extinction and environmental ruination.

In Pynchon's vision, entropy is powerfully linked with a sense of the end of history, not only in terms of the termination of a linear, positivistic history based on cause and effect, but also in terms of the possible demise of civilization itself. Giving us an encyclopedic referencing of the discourses of modernity and the possible final outcome of its entropic breakdown, Pynchon implies that other options besides apocalyptic destruction exist. In general, he recognizes that however strong or perfected the structures of contemporary power, there is still the possibility "that some chance of renewal, some dialectic, is still operating in History" (*GR* 540). It is perhaps not by accident that these words come from the mouth of a priest, Father Rapier, and therefore that Pynchon could be at the same time affirming and mocking hopes for historical renewal.

To symbolize the technological potential to create a more comfortable and affluent world, Pynchon creates a surrealistic allegory in the form of Byron the talking lightbulb who burns far beyond his allotted time (*GR* 647ff.). In his parable, the lightbulb companies have conspired to produce bulbs that burn only for a certain duration, to maximize turnover, and search out and destroy mutant bulbs that burn beyond their allotted time. The figure of Byron, however, suggests that technologies could be made to serve human needs rather than to produce profits. Yet Byron is also used as a parable of revolt that ends up proclaiming rather pessimistically its own futility. At one point, Byron fantasizes organizing all the other lightbulbs to strobe humans and to protest against their planned obsolescence and denial of longer life (*GR* 654ff.). However, in Pynchon's fable, Byron becomes aware of the futility of revolt:

> His youthful dreams of organizing all the bulbs in the world seem impossible now—the Grid is wide open, all messages can be overheard, and there are more than enough traitors out on the line. Prophets traditionally don't last long—they are either killed outright, or given an accident serious enough to make them stop and think, and most often they do pull back. But on Byron has been visited an even better fate. He is condemned to go on forever, knowing the truth and powerless to change anything. No longer will he seek to get off the wheel. His anger and frustration will grow without limit, and he will find himself, poor perverse bulb, enjoying it. . . . (*GR* 654)

Published shortly after the fast-fading revolts of the 1960s, *GR* is a symptom of the postmodern turn that refuses models of political change based on positive conceptions of social alternatives. In fact, the struggles of the Counter-

force could be interpreted allegorically as a description of the futility and failure of 1960s resistance movements. Likewise, Pynchon's novel *Vineland* (1990)
can be seen as a commentary on the demise of the 1960s and the triumph of
conservative and media culture by the 1980s. The story opens in the midst of
Reaganite conservatism and focuses on how persons immersed in the struggles
of the 1960s are coping with the hegemonic conservatism of the 1980s. The
1960s struggles are represented as miscarried attempts; individual reconciliation with nature is all that Pynchon can sketch as a possible redemptive end for
his characters, most of whom turn out rather badly.[16]

      Still, Pynchon's portrayal is not as one-dimensional as that of some Frank-
furt School positions (in particular, Horkheimer and Adorno's [1972] *Dialectic
of Enlightenment*), or certain postmodern theorists (Baudrillard, most notably).
His writings indicate some political implications of postmodern epistemological principles, as well as exhibiting unsurpassed aesthetic quality and
sociohistorical insight. Pynchon's literary maps of a new political, economic,
and cultural stage of global capitalism suggest the coevolution and co-
construction of the various levels of capitalist society and require a new
epistemological outlook. This mode of postmodern vision, which structures
both the form and the content of *GR*, demands a rupture with the modernist
logic of Newtonian determinism and Cartesian certainty in favor of a new
framework of indeterminacy, uncertainty, nonlinearity, and multiperspectivism—
precisely the postmodern paradigm that we find converging in many dimensions of contemporary culture (see Best and Kellner 1997, Ch. 5; Chapter 3).

POSTMODERN VISION AND COGNITIVE
AND AFFECTIVE MAPPING

> "*Everything* is some kind of a plot, man."
> —GR (603)

Thus, Pynchon provides a postmodern cognitive mapping of the unfolding of
the zone between the modern and the postmodern that is multidimensional in
its attempt to articulate relations of domination and resistance within a multifaceted and conflictual sociohistorical context. His vision is multiperspectivist
in its concern to illuminate the irreducible plurality of discourses and modes
of control and resistance within this system, as they structure both the social
and personal dimensions of existence. It is hermeneutic rather than "scientific,"
acknowledging the interpretive and metaphoric character of all perspectives,
and is indeterminate rather than deterministic, seeking to grasp structures and
patterns of power that constrain social life and personal identity without leading to exact predictable outcomes, and while being vulnerable to change and

modification. For Pynchon, there is neither transcendence nor entrapment, but lines of resistance and flight that can be multiplied, connected, unconnected, and reconnected. Ultimately, Pynchon offers no authoritative or definitive answers to the problem of agency and social change, but raises some troubling questions and choices in the context of our present global (dis)order.

Science, in Pynchon's vision, is an extremely useful instrument of analysis and control, but should not be taken as *the* sole road to truth, as in reigning positivist conceptions. Pynchon operates throughout his works with a dialectic of science and its others, attempting to overcome the one-sided dichotomy between science and rationality against the impulses of life, the soul, nature, and other forces conventionally opposed to science and reason. For Pynchon, there is always an opposition of order and chaos, of life and death, with forces of life captured, tamed, and perhaps suffocated in structures of control and domination—and then emerging anew to break through repressive structures to create more humane and improved forms of organization and cognition. Thus, life, procreative energies, and nature have their own forms of order, are not antithetical to reason and science, but are in opposition to subjugating, inhumane, and limited forms of domination and control.

Entropy, then, in GR should be seen in relation both to life dissipating its energies and to information losing coded structure and collapsing into noise. The imbrication of human beings in both natural and technical systems, the implosion of technology and the human, and the mediation of all life by machines and techniques have increased indeterminancy, contingency, noise, and chaos by making our view of the world more complex, multiplying crucial variables, and introducing new technologies, media, and their unpredictable offshoots and effects into natural and social systems. In this view, entropy always threatens mankind with disorder, depletion, and death; societies evolve and can collapse; and yet new social orders and structures, and new forms of human life, can be created out of chaos and disintegration. There is thus a positive, life-affirming, and optimistic dimension to Pynchon's vision—though, not surprisingly, it is interconnected with its opposite and so Pynchon overcomes banal oppositions between optimism and pessimism.

Hence, the concept of entropy suggests that all oppressive structures and systems—fascism, Stalinism, the military-industrial state, or capitalist corporate and state bureaucracy—will not last forever; that they will dissipate and give rise to new openings and possibilities; that change, even radical systemic change, is possible, as is breakdown and collapse. Combining reflections on science and history with literary vision in a highly complex textual practice, Pynchon transcends oppositions of theory and fiction. His work, for us, thus poses the question of the specificity and value of aesthetic as opposed to theoretical maps.

While we should not abandon the distinction altogether, postmodern theory has shown that the boundaries between history, theory, and fiction are

not as firm as they might seem. White (1990) and Ricoeur (1984), for example, have argued that historiography is structured through narrative codes similar to those employed by fiction writers. They subvert the opposition between
fiction and history in order to see historiography as neither law-governed science nor mythical story, as being "ultimately narrative" in character, yet ame-
nable to a rigorous theoretical analysis. More generally, Derrida (1981a, 1981b,
1982) has argued that theory and logic are informed by literary and rhetorical
tropes. In response to this claim, Habermas (1987) has attempted to preserve a
firm "genre distinction" between philosophy and literature. We would propose
that while one can distinguish between various disciplines, one should also see
the extent to which they overlap and complement each other.

It is our argument that the real specificity and value of aesthetic cognitive
maps are, first, their ability to dramatize and concretize configurations of social
power and everyday life. While theoretical maps typically employ the codes of
science (clarity, rigor, empiricism, objectivity, etc.) to represent the social
world, aesthetic maps offer phenomenological illuminations of everyday life
that afford visions and experiences that theoretical maps are unable to supply. If
"the personal is political," then social mappings have to move beyond the coordinates of public institutions and the limitations of objective discourse into
the emotional and subjective dimensions of private life. Such a shift provides
what we call "affective" mapping that evokes "structures of feeling" (Raymond
Williams) of lived experience, as well as the sociohistorical forces that circum-
scribe the individual. This is not to privilege either social theory, history, political economy, or fiction, but rather to suggest linkages of cognitive and affective
mapping that attempt to dispense fuller and richer representations of modes of
past and contemporary experience and history.

Multiperspectivist mappings draw upon representations from various
forms of culture as well as from limited, but potentially powerful, disciplinary
perspectives. This material can be articulated from within a broader, transdisciplinary framework that links mappings from the cognitive and affective dimensions. Pynchon's mapping of postwar technocapitalism therefore contributes an
important alternative perspective to that, say, of Ernest Mandel (1975), or David Harvey (1989), who conceptualize the current moment of "late" or "post-
Fordist" global capitalism.[17] Theoretical maps can certainly depict everyday life
(Debord, Lefebvre, etc.), but, unless they adopt fictional codes, they cannot
evoke the structures of feeling that powerful literary maps can achieve. Thus,
Lukács (1964a, 1964b) praised "critical realist" works (Thomas Mann, etc.) for
their ability to penetrate "reification" and to overcome dehumanizing and
objectivizing representations so as to portray life in concrete terms, while providing a sense of the totality of life within capitalist society in specific historical eras. Works of fiction help to map, in other words, the hidden connections
and mediations between the workplace and the home, the economy and everyday life, and the objective and subjective spheres of existence. But while
Lukács dogmatically confined genuine political fiction to the genre of realism,

his successors in the Marxist tradition such as Brecht and Benjamin argued that avant-garde modernist forms could also be politically effective insofar as they better represent the complexities and messiness of actual experience and provide more radical forms of critique and opposition[18]—as we have found in the case of Pynchon.

Literature, however, is not just a mapping, an expression of insight into existing reality through mimesis, allegory, or other modes of representation. Literature can also be a great refusal of what is, a source of radical negation, an impetus to another way of seeing that demands change and emancipation (Marcuse 1955, 1964, 1978). As a source of critical visions, of impulses toward emancipation and radical social change, literature and other modes of oppositional art can aid in the emancipatory project of freeing people from illusion and ideology, although literature and theory can also trap people in new mythologies and restricted forms of vision. A multiperspectivist writer such as Pynchon, however, forces one to see, experience, and interpret phenomena in a multiplicity of ways and thus contributes to a postmodern vision that frees one from partial or restricted views.

We might, then, paraphrase Adorno's remark about Kafka and state that anyone whose Pynchon's writings have worked over will never be the same. Both the form and content of GR, the cognitive and aesthetic meanings, contribute powerfully to this experience. For us, reading GR critically transforms one's ways of seeing, reading, and knowing—thereby enabling the active reader to adopt multiperspectivist approaches to interpret the novel and the period of history that it illustrates. Emphasis on the material dimension of existence highlights the organic dimension of life that structures of technological rationality repel and perhaps crush. Likewise, the emphasis on excretion, farting, and various forms of mucus or lower corporeal operations vividly brings into play the body and links the reader to a panoply of emotions and experiences habitually ignored in polite literature and culture. Part of Pynchon's cognitive and affective mapping strategy is therefore to chart the full range of experience in its interaction with technology and bureaucracy in order to draw the reader into the texture of the situations being described. Literature is thus able to bring a personal and bodily dimension into play that is not easily accessible to more abstract forms of theoretical discourse.

In the next chapter, we shall continue our explorations of the relationship between literary and theoretical mapping, our probing of the categories of postmodern theory, and our discussion of the vicissitudes of the postmodern adventure in studies of a postmodern turn in war and technology. As we shall see, the culture of death within the technological societies whose contours Pynchon sketches finds its realization in the Vietnam and Gulf Wars that combine advanced military, computer, and battlefield technologies and systematic propaganda to attempt to dominate and control the developing world, and to bring all nations and otherness into the system of global technocapitalism.

NOTES

1. For our earlier discussion of postmodernism in the arts, see Best and Kellner (1997, Ch. 4). Discussions of postmodern literature that focus on Pynchon include McHale (1987, 1992), and Tabbi (1995). Pagination refers to the original Viking Compass edition of *GR* which has been reprinted and is the basis of the current Penguin edition.

2. By "allegory," we mean a cultural text that articulates broad expanses of history, using its narrative to convey—consciously or unconsciously—deeper social meanings and vision. See Jameson's *The Political Unconscious* (1981) which presents key stages of the bourgeois novel as allegories of the fate of subjectivity within capitalist modernity.

3. On the theme of multiperspectivism in postmodern theory, see Best and Kellner (1991, 1997). Offering a formalist postmodern reading of *GR*, Brian McHale (1992) argues that it is a purely schizophrenic text that resists *all* readings. McHale disposes of some standard one-sided interpretations of Pynchon's putatively postmodern text that would reduce the complexity of *GR* to a single global reading, a dominant interpretive scheme and a master narrative that reduces the complexity of the text's literary strategies to a single reading. But McHale himself does not provide analytical categories that illuminate the alleged postmodernism of Pynchon's text, nor does he himself provide an adequate hermeneutic for reading the text. McHale polemicizes against "modernist readings" of Pynchon's "postmodernist" texts, but the readings he calls "modernist" are really more traditionalist hermeneutical readings that would reduce the text to one central set of meanings. McHale claims that Pynchon's deconstruction of character, narrative, and representation and his problematizing of everything in the text makes it impossible to offer any definitive readings. For McHale, Pynchon makes us metareaders, postmodern critics who analyze the literary strategies of complex texts and dispose of paranoid modernist misreadings, and thus helps readers transform themselves into "geniuses of metasolutions" (McHale 1992: 114).

Yet McHale himself lacks the metahermeneutical category that we propose of the *multiperspectival* that would enable one to explain why Pynchon readers go wrong when they try to read *GR* simply as a hallucination, a movie, or a merely formalist exercise in metafiction, or offer any specific hermeneutical reading. Both in terms of Pynchon's formal literary strategy and in terms of substantive readings of what *GR* is all about, we believe that Pynchon demands a multiperspectivist optic and multiple readings, and that rather than resisting interpretation his work invites, demands, and multiplies it. Moreover, against McHale, we argue that Pynchon's novel is a paranoid text that requires us to make connections and see the larger patterns and conspiracies at work, rather than a schizophrenic text that undermines making connections altogether. Ultimately, then, McHale's reading of Pynchon (re)inscribes a mode of formalism that renounces hermeneutics, a position that we reject (see Best and Kellner 1987).

4. As Steven Weisenburger notes, *GR* "was painstakingly written from the standpoint of historical accuracy" (1981: 141). Thomas Moore (1987: 20) situates *GR* within the post-1945 historical novel genre that includes works such as Gunter Grass's *The Tin Drum*, Thomas Berger's *Little Big Man*, and Joseph Heller's *Catch-22*, while Edward Mendelson (1976) sees it as an encyclopedic novel of American experience à la *Moby Dick*. Weisenburger's (1988) commentary on *GR* illuminates a wealth of Pynchon's allusions.

5. On the concept of entropy and chaos and complexity theory, see Best and Kellner (1997, Ch. 5; Chapter 3). From his earliest short stories such as "Entropy," to novels such as *V., The Crying of Lot 49, GR*, and *Mason & Dixon*, Pynchon has concerned himself with the theme of entropic breakdown in Western society and has attempted to portray critically a

repressive and moribund Euro-American civilization that is founded upon a "culture of death."

6. What Pynchon terms "creative paranoia" (*GR* 742) is one method whereby both he and his characters—perhaps equally paranoid—attempt to organize information, to map the complex systems of forces that structure the public and private worlds of transnational capitalism, and to project a means of political resistance. On "creative paranoia," see Siegel (1978) and Best (1992).

7. For an excellent discussion of Pynchon's rainbow symbolism as a literary symbol and as emblematic of his appropriation of quantum mechanics, see Moore (1987: 187ff.). It seems that every critic has his or her own reading of the title. For Tanner, "The 'Rainbow' inevitably triggers reminiscences of the rainbow in Genesis, which was God's covenant to Noah 'and every living creature of all flesh that *is* upon the earth.' Gravity, by contrast, is that law (not a 'covenant') by which all things—'and all flesh that *is* upon the earth'—are finally, inexorably, drawn back down and into the earth: an absolutely neutral promise that all living things will die" (1982: 78).

8. On the London Crystal Palace Exhibition as a symbol of modernity and its disappearance as emblematic of its evanescence, see Berman (1982).

9. This theme of tracing the origins of imperialism continues in *Mason & Dixon*. In a review of this book, Louis Menard suggests "nearly everything Pynchon has written is, essentially, a lament over colonization—political, economic, cultural, sexual." *The New York Review of Books*, June 12, 1997: 25.

10. On the role of Weber in Pynchon's imaginary, see Mendelson (1976: 168ff.) and Moore (1987: 116ff.)

11. On the genesis of U.S. intelligence agencies in World War II and for critiques of their later interventions, see Smith (1983) and Blum (1995). On the origins of modern corporate and bureaucratic systems in World War II, see Edwards (1996).

12. Pynchon is notorious for not resolving the mysteries his characters pursue, ranging from the search for "V," to Oedipa's pursuit of the Tristero, to Slothrop's many quests, to Mason and Dixon's ultimate failure to understand the purpose of and interests behind their enterprise.

13. Concepts like Pynchon's Zone also appear in William Burroughs's notion of the Interzone where everything is permitted. They crop up as well in the mysterious space of Andrei Tarkovski's film *Stalker*, Samuel Delany's "paraspace," and the universe of cyberpunk in which new technologies create the possibilities of a zone of freedom and creativity, while the restructuring of capitalism generates urban and other spaces not yet subject to state or corporate control. Indeed, the Internet and cyberspace currently constitutes such a zone that various groups, individuals, and corporate powers are trying to structure, colonize, tame, and control, as we suggest in Chapters 4 and 5.

14. In his 1964 story "The Secret Integration," Pynchon (1984) presented young teenagers as incipient revolutionaries, although at the end of the story they gave up their fantasies of social subversion to return home to their parents. Many of the characters in *V.* are bohemians and eccentrics who live on the margins of society; they form communities and subcultures (e.g., "the whole sick crew"), but of an apolitical nature.

15. Josephine Hendin, for example, believes that *GR* articulates "Death's hate, Death's grimace, the tragic mask of the heavens pulled down forever in one inviolable affirmation of depression" (1978: 207).

16. *Vineland* (1990) ends with a teenage girl who is the off-spring of the '60s rebels sleeping in a meadow and waking up to the missing family dog licking her face: "It was

Desmond, none other, the spit and image of his grandmother Chloe, roughened by the miles, face full of blue-jay feathers, smiling out of his eyes, wagging his tail, thinking he must be home." The image of home, reconciliation with nature, harmony between humans and animals, and a general positive redemptive vision provides an unusual moment of cosmic optimism to lighten Pynchon's dark vision. Slothrop, by contrast, never makes it home despite obvious yearnings.

17. We reject Mandel's concept of "late capitalism" (1975), taken up by Jameson and others, because it implies a temporal narrative of decline and decay and perhaps Marxist wish fulfillment that capitalism is in its "late" stage and near its end. But capitalism has shown itself capable of multiple metamorphoses whereby it surmounts crises and even disintegration, as in its overcoming of the 1930s depression through a new form of state, or organized, capitalism. The term "late capitalism" also lacks analytic substance. Since we believe that contemporary capitalism is currently reorganizing itself along the lines of a new transnational and global technocapitalism, we adopt these latter concepts. Indeed, it is too soon to say whether this form of capitalism is a "late" form of decay and disintegration, or will produce a new, more sophisticated form of global technocapitalism that will endure for the foreseeable future.

18. For Lukács's "critical realism," see Lukács (1964a, 1964b); on the Marxist literary debates over modernism, see Bloch et al. (1977).

2

||||||

MODERN/POSTMODERN WARS
Vietnam, Iraq, and Beyond

It was a kind of visitation of hell on earth. Who needs metaphors for hell, or poetry about hell? This actually happened here on this earth. Pregnant mother disemboweled. Eyes gouged out. Kids, children torn apart like fresh bread in front of their mothers. And this went on for years until two million people were either systematically killed or starved to death by the same people. And no one can really figure out how something like that could have happened.

—Spalding Gray on the Vietnam War

By God, we've shaken that Vietnam syndrome!
—George H. W. Bush after
the Gulf War

Our leaders and scholars . . . have given up on peace on earth and now seek peace of mind through the worship of new techno-deities. They look up to the surveillance satellite, deep into the entrails of electronic micro-circuitry, and from behind Stealth protection to find the omniscient machines and incontrovertible signs that can help us see and, if state reason necessitates, evade or destroy the other.

—James Der Derian

Gravity's Rainbow depicts the rise of a military–industrial complex and a war culture out of the science, technology, research, institutions, and hostilities of World War II. Pynchon's literary mapping helps illuminate the post-World War II conjuncture that begins the postmodern adventure, a constellation marked by the coevolution and co-construction of science, technology, corporate capitalism, and the military, producing technoscience, "Pentagon capitalism" (Melman 1975), "the permanent war economy" (Melman 1985), and a national security state.[1]

Indeed, fusions of advanced science and technology have generated atomic and hydrogen bombs (which physicist Enrico Fermi spoke of as "superb physics"), satellite communications, rocket and space technology, computer and information systems, and multimedia. These forces are also creating a unique technoculture and a networked global society as we enter the Third Millennium. In this constellation, science and technology are appropriated for military research and applications, which in turn generate innovations in products such as computers, jet engines, synthetic fabrics, and antibiotics, which also spawn new markets. Hence, thanks to government sponsorship of research and development programs, science and technology—increasingly politicized, militarized, and commodified—have become a major force of production for capital accumulation.

It was during World War II that the military, industry, science, and technology became tightly interconnected, and the Cold War further intensified their co-construction. Although the hostilities ended in 1945, the war economy itself had just begun to explode as the military entered into ever closer alliances with large defense contractors such as Lockheed. With the bombing of Pearl Harbor, and the official decision to enter the war, U.S. corporations, pushed by the federal government, retooled from civilian to military production. As they did, profits soared, industrial production grew 25% annually, federal spending increased over 10 times from prewar levels, the GNP climbed from $100 billion in 1940 to over $212 billion in 1945, the effects of the Great Depression finally lifted, and the United States emerged as the world's greatest power (Schaller et al. 1998). Rooted in sites like Hanford, Washington; Oak Ridge, Tennessee; and Los Alamos, New Mexico, the atomic weapons "industry" grew to be nearly as large as the U.S. automobile industry and utilized the same mass-production techniques. The bomb became less a means of maintaining U.S. "security" than a commodity, as corporations like General Electric turned to the production of munitions and military systems while lobbying heavily to promote increased "defense" spending.

The postwar reorganization of capital did not go unnoticed by critics of the military. In his seminal work *The Power Elite,* C. Wright Mills (1956) warned that the military was becoming an increasingly powerful and autonomous institution. New "warlords" were dictating social policy and constructing a "military definition of reality" that served their own interests rather than those of the public. Cognizant of a new coevolutionary landscape, in which entire regions had become reliant on Pentagon contracts, Mills wrote that "scientific and technological development has increasingly become part of the military order, which is now the largest single supporter and director of scientific research" (1956: xx). Drawing from his insider's perspective as a former general, President Dwight D. Eisenhower, in his January 1960 Farewell Address, deplored the wastefulness of the arms race and alerted America to an emerging "military–industrial complex" that was becoming a growing influence ("economic, political, even spiritual") and propagating a highly militarized economy and society.

The postwar period saw Cold War rivalry heat up between the United States and the Soviet Union, the representatives of a titanic struggle between

Western corporate capitalism and Eastern bloc communism, with its attendant arms and space races, interventions in regional wars, and worldwide competition in the economic, scientific, technological, political, and cultural spheres. Both modes of modern social organization were rooted in the propagation of technological and military societies and what Pynchon (1973) calls a "culture of death." State capitalism depended vitally on the military–industrial complex to engender the government spending, technological progress, and jobs needed to fuel economic prosperity. Soviet communism mirrored the military, technological, and industrial project of Western capitalism, which claiming to provide a superior road to modernization and progress.[2]

The imbrication of science, technology, the military, and capital intensified during the space race. Distinctions between military and scientific issues blurred in the exploration of space and the genesis of satellite systems, missile technology, and space flight. As McDougall puts it, "Separation of military and civilian activities was increasingly artificial in an age of scientific warfare and total Cold War. Even scientific programs, under a civilian agency, were tools of political struggle in so far as an image of technical dynamism was as important as actual weapons. The space program was a paramilitary operation in the Cold War, no matter who ran it. All aspects of national activity were becoming increasingly politicized, if not militarized" (1985: 174).

One can plausibly date the radical interrogation of the modern era with events associated with the end of World War II: the revelations concerning the horrors of the Nazi concentration camps and the dropping of atomic bombs on Hiroshima and Nagasaki, followed by a nuclear arms race and production of ever greater catastrophic instruments of destruction.[3] Growing fears of nuclear extinction soon undercut naive technological optimism that science and technology could propagate ever increasing progress and well-being. The bomb illustrated the dangers of technology out of control and warned that modernity had engendered the seeds of its own destruction. Ever more sophisticated military technology spawned lethal nuclear weapons that provided the capacity to obliterate humanity and the world many times over. Bomb culture provoked both a literature of apocalypse and a popular imaginary that anticipated the end of the world.[4] In a certain sense, the atomic bomb and the possibility of apocalypse nurtured the postmodern imagination and helped to propagate a consciousness that could envisage a total rupture, break, and great divide from the dreams of modernity: the End of the World as the ultimate nightmare.

Atomic weapons thus revealed deep flaws in the project of modernity, as well as humanity's ability to break the "laws" of modern science. They demonstrated that matter could be pulverized, that it harbored powerful energy that could be put to use for destructive purposes, and that the project of the domination of nature had gone awry, resulting in instruments of unthinkable devastation.[5] Consequently, there are good reasons to nominate August 1945 as the beginning of the postmodern adventure since it marked the end of European fascism, the advent of the Atomic Age, and the acceleration of an arms race that intensified the co-construction of science, technology, and capitalism. Living with the perpetual possibility of apocalyptic catastrophe during the Cold War era of low-intensity warfare and high-intensity anxieties provoked an imagination of disaster that put in question the promises of the Enlightenment, which had envisaged world peace and progress thanks to the blessings of science, technology, and industry. No doubt, the possibility of total annihilation and regression to unimaginable barbarism undermined the humanist pretensions of the Enlightenment project, as well as the modern belief in progress. The 20th century had witnessed the triumph of fascism, two world wars that killed millions of civilians, the perversion of socialism in Stalinism, genocidal holocaust of the Jews and other targets of Nazism, atomic bombs dropped on Japan, and the possibility of total nuclear extermination (see Aronson 1983). In this context, it was hard to speak positively of "Progress," the establishment of a Kingdom of Reason and Virtue, or the marvels of civilization. Pynchon's *Gravity's Rainbow*—with its apocalyptic vision and its obsessive depiction of the forms and minutiae of an emerging warfare state and culture of violence— evokes a compelling sense of the madness of modernity that found its embodiment in the military–industrial complex that dominated both capitalist and communist societies during the Cold War era.

The drive for world domination and the epochal struggle between the competing superpowers during the Cold War generated vast military, intelligence, and bureaucratic state apparatuses and intense confrontations between them, which in turn provoked conflicts throughout the planet. "Mutually assured destruction" (MAD) became the dominant ideology but also the official brake on the use of nuclear arms during the Cold War. Since nuclear war was "unthinkable," new forms of warfare were invented and put into use. Cold War contestation induced a major conflict in Korea and a conflagration in Vietnam that erupted in the 1950s, raged throughout the 1960s, and terminated in 1975 with communist victory and the first serious U.S. military defeat. It was also the era of covert warfare, with the CIA and Soviet intelligence fomenting insurrections and intervening in local conflicts throughout the world (see Stockwell 1978). In retrospect, the Cold War looks like a sibling rivalry between two opposing paths to modernization, both of which intended to cultivate science, technology, and industry to the fullest in order to create a superior economic and social system. Of course, this socioeconomic competition was marred by excessive munitions production, military tensions, and the sheer lunacy of the conflict.

Breaking the laws of gravity through space travel propelled the human species into a new cosmic arena beyond the laws of Newtonian science. In terms of the adventure of evolution, it has been claimed that humans departing earth and exploring space was an evolutionary leap comparable to the fish *Eusthenopteron* leaving behind its home in shallow waters and adapting itself to life on land some 360 million years ago.[6] Rockets and space travel opened up new realms for the human adventure, promoted the proliferation of advanced communications and weapons systems, and launched the human species into an enterprise that made the fantasies of the great science fiction (SF) writers real, with as yet unknown consequences (see Chapter 4). Advanced science and technology thus opened an interplanetary, and perhaps intergalactic, pathway for the human adventure to unfold through the exploration, colonization, and terraforming of other planets.

In particular, the 1957 *Sputnik* launching demonstrated that space exploration and travel was feasible, while the 1969 *Apollo 11* voyage to the moon suggested the possibility of space colonization and the discovery of new worlds and perhaps new forms of life. Live broadcast pictures of the moon landing dramatized the wonders of satellite communications, while images of the earth taken from outer space revealed a small, finite planet, a "pale blue dot" (Carl Sagan) in the midst of infinite space. The pictures also highlighted the fragility of the environment, the artificiality of national boundary lines, and the need to respect and preserve life in the delicate biosphere. At the same time, however, nuclear arms construction and U.S.–Soviet rivalry escalated. U.S. use of highly lethal munitions in Vietnam led many to examine critically the scientific and technological forces and elites that were producing and utilizing technologies of such massive destructive power.

Science and technology thus exhibited in the past decades unparalleled wonders and unmatched horrors and became highly contested forces with both champions and critics. Since the end of the Vietnam conflict, new high-tech modes of postmodern war have emerged that dramatically changed the nature of military confrontation. Today's weapons of mass destruction have an exponentially increased potency. The computerization of war has augmented possibilities of accidental nuclear holocaust, as it transformed killing into a digital abstraction. New kinds of arms systematically collapse the boundaries between human beings and technology, replace human soldiers with machines, and radically redefine the nature of war. The emergence of more virulent modes of chemical and biological warfare, as well as potential forms of cyberwar and information war, take combat into both the microbiological and the virtual realms, constituting new dangers to the human species, the ecosphere, the informational infrastructure, and the global economy.

Pursuing these themes, in this chapter we interpret the era of the Vietnam and Gulf Wars as a transition from modern to postmodern war, and theorize the concept of "postmodern war." Interpreting the vicissitudes of war in the postmodern adventure will help us grasp its origins, trajectory, novelties, and dangers. In devising various mapping and interpretive strategies to help comprehend the turbulent transformations of the present era, we merge cultural studies and critical social theory to call for reconstructions of theory and society, and argue against war as a mode of conflict resolution.

CULTURAL STUDIES, HISTORY, AND REPRESENTATIONS OF WAR

> We live our lives in language and thus in representation. We always see
> through a glass darkly, never face to face. Yet even if the real is hidden, it
> exists and by inference and patient study, we can make out its shape. Only
> the most devoted attention to what is real can help us to make judgments
> and take actions which are both responsible and efficacious.
> —MICHAEL IGNATIEFF

Cultural studies has traditionally been text-oriented, focusing on "popular" artifacts of the media and consumer culture and their use by audiences. And yet
political spectacles like wars and other crises are presented to the public as
"texts," as artifacts that invite multiple interpretations, and thus should be considered legitimate objects of analysis for cultural studies. By and large, citizens
experience occurrences like the Vietnam war, the war against Iraq, presidential
elections, political crises, the death of leading political and cultural figures, and
other sociohistorical political phenomena through the images, discourses, and
narratives transmitted and shaped by the media. Effective social actors need to
be able to properly interpret and criticize the spectacles of public life, the perspectives and biases of media representations, and how they perpetuate propaganda and disinformation. Accordingly, we analyze the Vietnam and Gulf Wars
as cultural texts, applying the methods of cultural studies to explain crucial political happenings. Hence, we propose an expansion of the terrain of cultural
studies to include the defining sociohistorical affairs and spectacles of our
times.[7]

Of course, wars are not just signs or texts: they are real political and historical events that impose tremendous suffering on individuals and devastation
upon the environment, often to a catastrophic degree. Yet they do have a textual dimension and they are presented to the public as spectacles, as narratives,
and as discursive constructs. Major occurrences, like the conflicts in Vietnam
and the Persian Gulf TV War, are first filtered through the media. For example,
television journalism plays an important initial role in narrativizing the story in
a form that can be readily grasped by the broadest public. Such framing and
contextualization, however, typically reproduces the government's position and
simplifies complex phenomena. During wars and turbulent political spectacles,
these official discourses are often contested. Conflicting media frames and images attempt to shape public interpretations and influence policy decisions—
within proscribed and delimited boundaries.[8] In Vietnam, the contested multiple viewpoints eventually resulted in passionate debate throughout the print
and broadcast media and helped block deeper U.S. involvement in the war.

After wars and important historical events conclude, cultural forums such
as films, television dramas, novels, plays, documentaries, visual arts, and scholarly discourses jostle to frame and interpret what happened and why. In the

case of Vietnam, conflicts of interpretation fostered fierce cultural wars that advanced competing pro- or anti-war positions, or, in the case of the "return-to-Vietnam" genre, the need to redeem military loss (see Kellner and Ryan 1988; Jeffords and Rabinovitz 1994; Gibson 1994; Kellner 1995a). The Persian Gulf TV War, was a triumphant media spectacle for the Bush administration. While there have been scholarly attempts to expose the lies, hardly any notable reassessments of that war in the domains of film, literature, or other cultural forms have taken place. Thus, unlike with Vietnam, so far there have been few important novels, films, documentaries, or other cultural texts that have provoked widespread debate over and reappraisal of the Gulf War—although there have been a large number of scholarly studies.[9]

Our argument is that characterizations of the Vietnam War as "postmodern" constitute misuse and abuse of the concept. In our studies, we query whether postmodern discourse is valuable or not in interpreting specific phenomena in today's technoculture and society. In general, we hold that the soundness and usefulness of a concept or theory can be determined only contextually and pragmatically by its ability to elucidate concrete phenomena in determinate contexts. For the discourse of the postmodern to be worthwhile, we argue, a clear distinction must be made between the modern and the postmodern. Moreover, the content of the postmodern must be clarified and put to appropriate service in specific interpretive contexts. Often, however, we find these terms obfuscated, with the term postmodern used promiscuously to define sundry aspects of the contemporary situation without distinct content or salient differences from the modern. The concept of the postmodern is most constructive, we would argue, when it calls attention to something new, to a distinctive difference from modern phenomena, and thus illuminates what is unique in the present age.

We have found that the Vietnam War has been frequently described as "postmodern," supposedly signifying its qualitative difference from previous "modern" wars, but we argue that such characterizations are often unwarranted. Fredric Jameson, for example, has claimed that Michael Herr in his Vietnam book *Dispatches* evoked "the space of postmodern warfare."[10] Jameson also argues that

> The extraordinary linguistic innovations of this work may still be considered postmodern, in the eclectic way in which its language impersonally fuses a whole range of contemporary collective idiolects, most notably rock language and black language: but the fusion is dictated by problems of content. This first terrible postmodernist war cannot be told in any of the traditional paradigms of the war novel or movie—indeed, that breakdown of all previous narrative paradigms is, along with the breakdown of any shared language through which a veteran might convey such experience, among the principle subjects of the book and may be said to open up the place of a whole new reflexivity. (1991: 45)

Jameson is alluding here to the postmodern critique of representation and specifically to the insight that theories, concepts, and narratives, do not merely reflect "the real," but construct their own reality. He claims that Herr's *Dispatches*
suggests that the Vietnam War unfolded in an entirely new and unrepre-
sentable postmodern space, which transcended all the older habits of bodily
perception, representing a "virtually unimaginable quantum leap in technological alienation" (45). Jameson takes Herr's book on Vietnam as evidence of
the impossibility of mapping the "postmodern" space of Vietnam and as itself
part of the cultural logic of the postmodern. In dialogue with Jameson, we argue that the Vietnam War was a modern—not a postmodern—war and that
Herr's *Dispatches* can be read as a text that combines modernist and postmodernist writing strategies and, like Pynchon's *Gravity Rainbow*, is a pivotal work
between the modern and postmodern.

Dispatches as Reconstructive Modernism

> "Vietnam, man. Bomb 'em and feed 'em, bomb 'em and feed 'em."
> —MICHAEL HERR

The shift toward critical consciousness and the search for new modes of expression and writing that emerged during the Vietnam War is on display in
Michael Herr's *Dispatches* (1978), which represents the war primarily as an
out-of-control folly of the U.S. political and military establishments. Es-
chewing theoretical analysis, Herr presents a critical vision of U.S. intervention
in Vietnam through employment of modernist and postmodernist literary
techniques. Although many critics read Herr's text exclusively as an example
of postmodernism, we argue that it is best read as a work that deploys both
modernist and postmodernist literary techniques.

Herr provides vivid representations to enable the reader to experience the
Vietnam War in powerful ways. Yet he is attempting to tell what he perceives
as the truth about the war, deflating official lies and ideologies, and thus does
not employ the sort of crippling relativism and mere ludic play common to
extreme postmodernism. Indeed, it is the modernist tradition that problem-
atized representation in its polemic against realism and traditional forms of
writing. Modernists challenged conventional modes of representation through
their use of highly condensed symbols, allegory, fractured narrative, collage
structures, and multiple points of view. Herr's *Dispatches* can be read from this
perspective as a modernist search for the new modes of representation and the
new types of writing he needed to articulate his experience of Vietnam and to
provide more telling representations of the war than that presented in official
military and political discourse and standard journalism. This search led Herr
to break with dominant realist techniques and modes of writing—as well as
with the pseudo-objectivism of official journalism—and to fabricate a mod-

ernist collage structure that mixes symbols, surrealist hallucinations, fables, an-
ecdotes, and straight reporting to represent the chaos, insanity, and evil of the
war.

Obviously, specific texts, authors, and even schools of writing can be labeled "modern" or "postmodern" according to one's theoretical constructs
and what aspects of the object of analysis one chooses to highlight. While the
fragmentary collage form of *Dispatches* might be seen as assimilating it to
modes of postmodern writing that break with conventional narrative forms,
we see collage as having both modern and postmodern variants. Within modernism, collage is usually the expression of a single artistic vision, though it
creates a complex text that is formally innovative and that invites a wealth of
interpretations—for example, the works of filmmakers Sergei Eisenstein, Jean-
Luc Godard, and Emile de Antonio; the art of Marcel Duchamp and Pablo Pi-
casso; and the rap music of Ice Cube and Public Enemy. But on Jameson's
(1991) own analysis, a postmodern collage would resist making statements and
creating a complex tapestry of meanings in favor of juxtaposing elements for
purely formal effects without hermeneutical depth. For Jameson, such postmodern collage would include Bob Perelman's *China* (1991: 28–30) and the
video *AlienNATION* by the Chicago Art Institute (1991: 79ff.), or some of the
paintings of David Salle that simply juxtapose images or fragments that do not
coalesce into a greater whole or make significant statements.

On our reading, Herr's use of collage is modernist. His different idiolects
are articulated as part of a literary strategy in which his own narrative voice is
privileged in an attempt to more accurately represent the Vietnam War and to
communicate his own experience to his readers.[11] Herr presents his text as a
"witness act" to what is really happening in Vietnam, as his own personal expression of the experience, his own testimony to the madness of the war. Despite his text's lack of a conventional structure and a conventional narrator,
Herr is there on every page, controlling the flow, articulating his vision, developing his own style, and above all telling his own story. In fact, he is something
of a romantic, placing himself—his sensations, his ego, his recollections—at the
center of the narrative. Thus, it would be a mistake to read the text as evidence
of a postmodern fragmentation of the subject, for however disjointed his experience, it is always that of Michael Herr, teller of his story, raconteur of his experience, the writer of *Dispatches*, and the survivor of Nam, whom we are
reading.

Moreover, Herr is attempting to capture the horrible reality of the Vietnam War and to enable his reader to experience the debacle of the U.S. Vietnam intervention. On Jameson's own account, by contrast, a postmodern text
would more radically, or ironically, problematize truth and reality, and fracture
narratives to undermine the possibility of interpretation.[12] Crucially, Herr's
text exhibits a reverence for truth that is typically modern, so much so that it is
parodied by many postmodernists. Indicating how every grunt had a story
"and in the war they were driven to tell it" (29), Herr claims that most of the

troops *wanted* him desperately to tell what was actually happening in Vietnam: "And always, they would ask you with an emotion whose intensity would shock you to please tell it, because they really did have the feeling that it wasn't being told for them, that they were going through all of this and that somehow no one back in the World knew about it" (206–207). Thus, the troops and some of the reporters in the Vietnam War wanted to maintain a rigorous distinction between truth and lying. Unlike in the Gulf War, there was no systematic blurring of truth and lies, between the reality of the war itself and the disinformation of the official discourse. That is, both the troops and the reporters in Vietnam knew that the official lies were transparently ludicrous, that the huge enemy body counts and optimistic reports were pure fabrications, that the official discourse was transparent propaganda.

Hence, Herr exemplifies a reconstructive modernism that draws on some narrative strategies that could be identified as postmodern, but that attempts to preserve and rework modern notions of truth, representation, and reality. He eschews the extreme relativism, subjectivism, and skepticism that is identified with radical postmodernism and that disable critique. His work, however, transcodes the critical and oppositional segment of the counterculture that refused official lies and ideologies and came to distrust modern institutions and belief systems, while seeking new ways to understand and represent the world.

Vietnam as Modern War

> That fall, all that the Mission talked about was control: arms control, information control, resources control, psycho-political control, population control, control of the almost supernatural inflation, control of terrain through the Strategy of the Periphery. But when the talk had passed, the only thing left standing up that looked true was your sense of how out of control things really were.
>
> —MICHAEL HERR

During the 1950s, Americans were enthralled and seduced by the consumer society and media culture. It was an era of ever growing affluence, complacency, and conformity. However, in the 1960s, the populace was positioned to behold the spectacle of JFK and the accelerated arms race, space race, and intensified struggle against communism. The members of the society of the spectacle were offered conspicuous consumption, political circuses, and social conformity, while the systems of organization and administration throughout society were refined. But in Vietnam many were forced to be participants in a violent military spectacle. As the war heated up, a growing number of young Americans were subjected to the horrors of death and mass destruction. The Vietnam War was increasingly unpopular with a generation nourished on the myths of the affluent society and the American dream. With the Vietnam War, the dream became a nightmare and the spectacle turned nasty and malevolent, thus generating large-scale opposition and rebellion.

We believe that grasping the full dimensions of the conflict in Vietnam, or other major events, requires a combination of cultural, historical, and theoretical texts. Literature like Herr's *Dispatches* provides an excellent sense of the feel and texture of the war, but literary representations need to be supplemented by historical and theoretical analysis to enable one to more fully grasp the origins, nature, gravity, and social and psychological effects of the Vietnam calamity. In his study *The Perfect War,* for instance, J. William Gibson (1987) has argued convincingly that the U.S. intervention in Vietnam should be read in the context of the Cold War as an imperialist effort designed to combat the spread of communism. Gibson claims that it was motivated by the desire of the U.S. political and military establishments to discover alternative modes of combat in the face of the MAD doctrine that made nuclear war inconceivable. Accordingly, the U.S. military created counterinsurgency strategies and tested these policies and its new weapons in Vietnam in an attempt to impose capitalist versions of modernization on the developing world. Gibson's work furnishes the historical context necessary to read and interpret Herr's text. Together these theoretical and literary maps provide representations of the Vietnam debacle that enable one to more fully understand the episode and its gravity—and to analyze the similarities and differences between these two modes of mapping.

In Gibson's ironic title, Vietnam was "the perfect war" to establish U.S. hegemony over communism and to demonstrate the superiority of U.S. military systems and arms because it was "unthinkable" that a peasant Third World army could defeat a high-tech military superpower. For Gibson, Vietnam is a modern "technowar" that utilizes the assembly-line system of production, scientific management, systems theory, and sophisticated weapons to "produce" dead bodies and to defeat the Vietnamese "foreign other." According to Gibson, the U.S. defeat in Vietnam discloses the limits of the reductionist model of technowar and its failed understanding of Vietnamese society and culture, thus revealing the fallacies of the modern paradigm and its belief in technological solutions to all problems.

"Technowar" in Gibson's sense is a result of the synthesis of politics, economics, and science described in Pynchon's *Gravity's Rainbow,* and can be understood as a product of modernity and its mechanistic worldview. In a broader sense, the Vietnam conflict revealed some of the inherent flaws of modernity and the failures of its ways of seeing and contextualizing the world. Gibson quotes Henry Kissinger, who held that U.S. foreign policy was predicated "on the assumption that *technology plus managerial skills* [and] gave us the ability to reshape the international system and to bring domestic transformations in 'emerging countries'" (1987: 15; Gibson's emphasis). Kissinger claims that there are virtually no limits to U.S. technical and political hegemony, just as modern science claims that there is no end to its ability to control and dominate nature. For Kissinger and the modern mind, power is measured exclusively in instrumental and technical terms. Kissinger also assumes that the United States and the Western powers possess the knowledge necessary to control nature and "emerging countries," and that the system of global capitalism with its deadly war machines, science and technology, and managerial knowledge can govern the natural and social worlds.

Kissinger assumes that *only* the West knows reality and that the superiority of Western modernity is grounded in its "notion that the real world is external to the observer, that knowledge consists of recording and classifying data—the more accurately the better. Cultures that have escaped the early impact of Newtonian thinking have retained the essentially pre-Newtonian view that the real world is almost entirely internal to the observer" (Kissinger, cited in Gibson 1987: 16). Gibson rightly notes that Newtonian mechanics, however, is about nature and "says nothing about society, about human social relationships" (1987: 17). Thus, Kissinger is continuing a 300-year-old positivist tradition of modern thought that posits that the social world can be ruled through the same techniques and forms of knowledge as the natural world.

Western modernity therefore applies an instrumental mode of thinking about nature to human beings and posits that humans are passive objects of knowledge and domination, the stuff of social control. This relationship to nature illustrates what Horkheimer and Adorno (1972) conceptualized as "the dialectic of Enlightenment." In their conception, "Enlightenment" turns into its opposite when instruments of liberation become the means of domination, and when a mode of objectifying thought that was intended to dominate nature also becomes a framework for objectifying and subjugating human beings. The world is projected as a closed system, subject to cybernetic command via technological feedback circuits (see Edwards 1996). This model in turn conceptualizes thought as an instrument to master nature, in ways that often deform and destroy it, just as it dehumanizes and denigrates human beings.

In Gibson's analysis, the U.S. mode of technowar failed in Vietnam largely because the United State mistakenly believed that its superior technology would allow it to dominate an underdeveloped Vietnamese society. But the United States found itself in a guerilla war that was part of a national liberation movement supported by the majority of its Vietnamese citizens. The U.S. military fought on a terrain familiar to the Vietnamese army and foreign to the Americans. Wars of national liberation typically produce modern nation-states with modern identities—such as the American and French revolutions. Due to the intense nationalism promoted by such struggles, they are difficult to defeat. In addition, the combat was fought by the Vietnamese as a guerilla struggle in which they used the jungle, mountains, and countryside in ways that enabled them to resist the overwhelming firepower of the U.S. military. Although postmodern theory has appropriated the metaphor of the guerrilla for its political strategies, one could argue that the war of national liberation fought in Vietnam was a form of modern warfare and thus it is problematic to describe it as "postmodern" tout court.[13]

Wars of national liberation have as their goal a modern nation-state free from colonialist domination. They are activated by intense nationalism, mobilize indigenous populations, and utilize a wide range of techniques of warfare. The Vietnamese war against U.S. intervention deployed anti-imperialist propaganda, communist and nationalist ideology, geopolitical pressures, and the arguably "modern" strategies of the North Vietnamese army, as well as tactics associated with guerrilla war that span eras from the pre- to the postmodern. The Vietnam conflagration was tied to modern power politics, in particular the struggles between world capitalism and communism. The Vietnamese revolutionaries were supported by China, the Soviet Union, and the socialist bloc, while the South Vietnamese government was propped up by the United States and its allies. Diplomatic and media struggles contributed to the eventual victory of the National Liberation Front, which waged an effective propaganda war as well as a successful military one. Thus, the Vietnam conflict was at once a peasant guerilla war, a prototypically modern national war of liberation, and a milestone in contemporary geopolitics that revealed the flaws of the modern paradigm and view of the world.

In addition, just as the atomic bomb and the horrors of nuclear annihilation threw doubt upon the premises of the Enlightenment and modernity, so too did the carnage, atrocities, and relentless death and destruction of the Vietnam War. Broadcast and analyzed daily for roughly 10 years, the war undermined the legitimacy of modern U.S. institutions like the state, the military, the media, the universities, and leading corporations that were promoting the bloodshed. The cumulative result of the experience suggests to us that the Vietnam episode sparked a shift in consciousness, attitude, and belief that helped prepare the way for the postmodern turn in culture and theory. It increased suspiciousness, cynicism, and resistance against dominant modern institutions and ideologies. Large numbers of an entire generation were distanced from their prevailing culture and society, and sought alternatives, thus generating a sense of alienation that ultimately fed into the more socially critical and oppositional forms of postmodern theory and culture. The experience deeply shaped media culture, promoting more edgy, socially critical, and complex works in popular music (Dylan, Beatles, Stones), with sex, drugs, and rock-n-roll elevated to cultural icons. The spirit of the counterculture shaped mainstream Hollywood film in the late 1960s and early 1970s and helped inspire a more politically conscious and socially aware independent film movement (see Kellner and Ryan 1988). It promoted antiauthoritarian consciousness and attitudes and a spirit of revolt that was applied to all aspects of everyday life from education to religion to sexuality. By the end of the decade, the nation had awakened to an ecological consciousness too, as a new sensibility toward nature began to take root and helped propagate thousands of groups that struggled for environmental protection and restoration.

Mapping Strategies: Narrative, Collage, and Theory

> Narrative is not merely a neutral discursive form that may or may not be
> used to represent real events in their aspect as developmental process but
> rather entails distinct ontological and even political implications.
> —HAYDEN WHITE

In *Dispatches*, Michael Herr heroically struggled to depict the experience and
horror of the U.S. military intervention in Vietnam. But there are obvious limitations to employing literary strategies to represent Vietnam, or other complex sociohistorical events. Herr's memoir provides an excellent evocation of
the chaotic and disjointed elements of the Vietnam War, but more sustained
and reflective historical research and theory, such as Gibson's work (1987), or-
ganizes such experiences into intelligible order, producing narratives and categories that help make sense of the war and provide readers with more comprehensive understanding and explanation. To be sure, literature excels in
capturing the texture, moods, and particularities of experience, but theoretical
writing better illuminates the more general constitutive forces and defining
features of events. Historical analysis provides contextual and narrative understanding by situating specific occurrences in broader spatial and temporal patterns, currents, and frameworks.

History and theory are thus important supplements to those renderings
and distillations of experience we call "literature." Together, these modes of
representation can help us grasp the broad contours, empirical details, and subjective experiences of significant eras and events. Theory supplies concepts
that can order historical research in a cognitively satisfying manner, taking empirical material and organizing it into patterns, or producing connections and
interpretations. Theories provide ways of seeing that help to structure experience, offering perspectives that can be wielded to interpret actions and phenomena. Yet theory is not antithetical to narrative or fiction: they can work together to elucidate experience, to provide historical vision, and to critically
interpret military conflicts like the Vietnam War. Thus, we do not see theory
and narrative as contradictory, but as complementary modes of mapping. Theory has a narrative component, to be sure, but is not merely storytelling; it is
also analytical, interpretive, and explanatory, using concepts to dissect, clarify,
and interpret social and historical (or psychological) realities. Conversely, literary texts can provide material for theory, contributing concrete embodiments
of historical experience, and some can even be seen as quasi-theoretical, transgressing the boundary between theory and fiction—witness Pynchon's *Gravity's Rainbow* (see Chapter 1).

Herr's narrative collage, however, lacks the contextualization found in historical or theoretical writings on the Vietnam War, or in documentary films
such as Emile de Antonio's *In the Year of the Pig* (1969), which deploys a modernist collage technique to present sociopolitical insight into Vietnam.[14] Com-

bining documentary footage from a variety of archival sources with interview material, photographs, and contemporary footage, de Antonio depicts the French colonization of Vietnam, Vietnamese resistance under the leadership of Ho Chi Minh, and the American response after the defeat of the French in 1954. His panoramic documentary provides images and discourses that contextualize the Vietnamese experience in terms of its movement for national liberation against colonialization, supplying a historical optic lacking in Herr's more literary collage.

On the other hand, it is Herr's wielding of metaphor, allegory, image, and narrative that enables access the feel, experience, and texture of the Vietnam War. Gibson, too, points to the importance of what he calls "warrior's knowledge" selected from the experience of the participants to illuminate the circumstances (1986: 461ff.). But, in order to provide proper contextualization and understanding, literary visions and participant views should be supplemented by multiperspectivist optics that include historical and theoretical analysis.[15]

Combining these perspectives, we argue that the Vietnam War is primarily a modern war that attempted to increase U.S. global power by containing "communism" and by imposing a consumer economy on Vietnam under the ideology of modernization. As Gibson shows, the form of "civilization" the United States brought to Vietnam was expressly that of modernity, in which the products and forms of life of the Western consumer society were exported to Southeast Asia. Gibson describes in detail how commodification processes transformed the daily life of the inhabitants of Vietnam. The "pacification" camps, the advent of urbanization, the building of roads and modern systems of transportation and communication, and the importation of U.S. commodities were accompanied by rising inflation, widespread crime, and the literal and figurative prostitution of Vietnamese society. "Modernization," then, was a euphemism to describe the ecocide of the Vietnamese environment and the destruction of traditional Vietnamese culture and society. Modernization appears in Gibson's presentation as a set of processes that destroys traditional societies. It brings into existence Western-style consumer societies and attendant industrial and technological revolution, secularization, social differentiation, individualism, urbanization, a centralized nation-state, consumer and media culture, and inclusion in the global economy of transnational capitalism.

From the vantage point of social theory and historical analysis, we can now see that the Vietnam War took place at the high point of the Cold War. It was a sustained U.S. military intervention designed to contain communism. Vietnam can thus be interpreted as a continuation of the Korean War, as an attempt to win it this time (actually to lose it more disastrously). It was motivated by the domino theory, the ideology of containment, fear of the "Red Menace," and all the now obsolete discourse and fantasies of the Cold War. Yet it was largely a modern war that revealed the limitations of the modern paradigm of technocratic domination of nature and other people through the (mis)application of science, technology, and cybernetic systems to a socio-historical situation.

The war against Iraq, in contrast, took place at the end of the Cold War. The U.S. military leaders who had suffered defeat during the Vietnam era (Norman Schwarzkopf, Colin Powell, and other generals and midlevel career military) wanted to "win big" this time, to overcome the "Vietnam syndrome," to redeem the U.S. military, to recover their manhood and their self-esteem, and—not incidentally—to protect the Pentagon budget from deep cuts.[16] The end of the Cold War revealed how useless and senseless the Vietnam catastrophe really had been: ironically, it had been easier to conquer Southeast Asia via Pepsi-Cola, Big Macs, Nike shoes, Hollywood films, and popular music than through B-52s, napalm, and Agent Orange. And so another war was necessary for the rebirth of U.S. militarism, the Persian Gulf TV War, "sponsored" by the same folks who brought the world Vietnam. This time, however, they were going to conquer with the aid of a new and improved media extravaganza that would promote U.S. military power and weapons systems.

While Vietnam constituted an attempt to impose modernization on a traditional Asian society, the Persian Gulf TV War attempted to roll back the modernization that Iraq had already achieved.[17] In this intervention, the U.S. mobilized all of the media, computer, advanced military systems, and public relations strategies that had become a key part of the most technologically overdeveloped society in the history of the world to surmount the so-called Vietnam syndrome that had inhibited U.S. exercise of its military power for almost 20 years. Let us now turn from remembering the horrors that occurred in the jungles of Southeast Asia to recalling the movement toward postmodern war in the deserts of the Persian Gulf during 1990–1991.

HIGH-TECH MASSACRE AND MEDIA SPECTACLE IN THE PERSIAN GULF TV WAR

> [The Gulf War] was the first space war.
> —GENERAL MERRILL MCPEAK,
> MARCH 1991

The Vietnam War was thus not really a postmodern event, but instead a dirty old neoimperialist modern war whereby the United States attempted to stop a national liberation movement, to contain communism, and to impose its culture (i.e., "modernization") on the "foreign other." The United States by intervening in Vietnam sought to test its technology and military doctrine by doing what the military has always done: win battles and kill "enemies." The "Gulf War," by contrast, was really not a war at all, but a contrived megaspectacle, in which pitifully overmatched Iraqi troops were overwhelmed by the most powerful military force ever assembled. This required presenting the Iraqi "enemy" as a genuine military force and a real threat, while demonizing its leader, Saddam Hussein, as an evil Arab threatening the West, someone akin to Hitler.

The Gulf spectacle was "postmodern" in that, first, it was a media event that was experienced as a live occurrence for the whole global village. Second, it managed to blur the distinction between truth and reality in a triumph of the orchestrated image and spectacle. Third, the conflict exhibited a heightened merging of individuals and technology, previewing a new type of cyberwar that featured information technology and "smart" weapons. In the following analysis, we will use Baudrillard's concept of postmodernity and Virilio's analysis of the novelties of contemporary war to elucidate the postmodern features of the Persian Gulf TV War and the concept of postmodern war. But since other aspects of the Gulf conflict fit the paradigm of modern warfare, we argue that it is best described as *between a modern and an emergent* type of "postmodern war."

Simulation, Hyperreality, and Cyberwar

> The Information Age has dawned in the armed forces of the U.S. The sight of a soldier going to war with a rifle in one hand and a laptop computer in the other would have been shocking only a few years ago. Yet that is exactly what was seen in the sands of Saudi Arabia in 1990 and 1991. Information systems have become essential ingredients to the success of combat operation on today's battlefield.
> —COLIN POWELL

For Jean Baudrillard, "simulation," "hyperreality," and "implosion" are the three categories that best characterize the era after modernity. For us, they provide crucial mapping tools for understanding postmodern war.[18] *Simulation* describes a process of replacing "real" with "virtual" or pseudoevents, as when electronic or digitized images, signs, or spectacles substitute for "real life" and objects in the "real world"—distinctions that are ever harder to maintain. Simulation is a systemic societal operation whereby image and meaning industries create representations that erode the distinctions between reality and unreality, between truth and falsehood. Simulation constructs a world in which signs, images, and simulacra feign a relation to what Baudrillard claims is an obsolete and irrecoverable "real world." Actor Ronald Reagan simulated being a president and the 2000 Republican Convention simulated multiculturalism, with more people of color on stage than in the audience. So too do endless court TV shows simulate the legal process, while entertainment like "pro" wrestling and XFL Football simulate being a sport. The real, Baudrillard believes, is vanquished when an independent object realm is assimilated to and defined by social codes and simulation models, as when individual identities and happenings attain significance through the entertainment codes of mass media. Boundaries blur when men and women shape and perceive themselves in conformity with the dominant fashion and advertising ideals of masculinity and femininity, when one's ideal hairstyle and look can first be generated through a computer before being created by today's technostylist, or when human beings themselves—as they soon may be—are generated as "designer babies" from ideal eugenic types (see Chapter 4).

In the society of simulation, preexisting models, images, and codes construct and determine what is real, or, in Baudrillard's words, "the map precedes the territory" and is confused with it, creating conditions of radical "implosion" and "hyperreality." When the "real" is so systematically mediated through codes, images, and models, it becomes not unreal or surreal, a myth or a fantasy, but *hyperreal*, that is a "reality" which "is produced from miniaturized units, from matrices, memory banks and command models—and with these it can be reproduced an infinite number of times" (Baudrillard 1983a: 3). In the Gulf War, for instance, images and representations of the war, disseminated by government and media outlets, replaced the events of the war itself, providing a hyperreal experience of the war as a media spectacle.

In a hyperreal culture, "truth" and "reality" become increasingly difficult to identify and distinguish from their opposites. Is Court TV legally binding and accurate? Would a "virtual affair" count as "cheating" and serve as evidence in a divorce proceeding? Am I talking with a real adult woman in this chat room or with a teenage male impersonating a woman and trying to fool me? Furthermore, falsehood and artificiality in many cases are preferred. Who wants "truth" and "reality" when illusions, fantasies, and simulacra are easier to deal with, sexier to experience, and so much more fun? For many, the world of media fantasies and soap operas is more real than everyday life. Video or computer games are more fascinating and alluring than school, work, or politics (often understandably so). For many, Disney World and other theme parks with simulated environments are more attractive than actual geographical sites. Meanwhile, war is seductively presented in the exciting form of video or computer games.

For Baudrillard, "implosion" designates a collapse of boundaries or divisions, such as that between entertainment and politics, or among different social classes. Whereas classical social theory characterized modernity in terms of differentiation, Baudrillard theorizes dedifferentiation as characteristic of postmodernity, wherein differences and boundaries implode in a process that renders the categories of modern theory obsolete. We will discuss below an implosion between truth and lies in the Persian Gulf TV War, and between humans and technology in postmodern war, a fateful event that has momentous consequences for the future of humanity (see Chapter 4).

The Gulf media spectacle got under way with simulation models and war games that projected U.S. military intervention against Iraq after its invasion of Kuwait. This computer modeling continued to play a significant role throughout its programming, execution, and results. The theater of war was reduced to data on computers and the war itself exhibited a new level of implosion between humans and their machines. Once within the actual war zone, combatants existed in a cyberspace somewhere between the physical world and virtual reality. Pilots interacted with computers that chose their targets. Air traffic control crews punched in computerized commands. Gulf warriors in a certain sense became cyborgs, part human, part machine, nodes within highly sophisticated communication systems.[19] AWAC surveillance systems sent constant information to both air and ground combatants, while high-tech guidance systems managed the trajectories of the weapons.

Moreover, the TV audience primarily saw and experienced the war itself through the frames produced by the Bush administration and the Pentagon and transmitted by compliant U.S. media corporations. The U.S. government supervised the flow of images and discourses to produce the spectacle of precision bombing without civilian casualties—a supposedly "clean war," minimizing "collateral damage." Early on, military briefers began showing videotapes of the high-tech blitz. The images were replayed hour after hour, day after day, promoting the notion of precision bombing, while coding the devastation as positive. According to the official scenario, the bombs invariably hit their targets, never caused collateral damage, and only took out military sites. Targets were photographed by cameras on the bombs and missiles themselves, which conveyed the images to satellites, from which they were downloaded, recorded on videocassettes, and shown to a worldwide audience via live television. These scenes literally took the TV viewers into a fascinating cyberspace, a realm of experience with which many viewers were familiar through video and computer games, the special effects of Hollywood movies, and cyberpunk fiction.

During the Gulf spectacle, the TV public quickly became addicted to the drama. It was seduced by the simulacra and fascinated by a new type of video imagery wherein war was presented as exciting and enticing. Unlike the analogic photographic images of the Vietnam War, which typically horrified the audience, the electronic images of the Gulf War often created audience delight. TV audiences were spellbound by the spectacle of bombings, the Scud and Patriot missile wars, the air war over Baghdad, or tanks penetrating Kuwait in the ground war. Images of the bombing of Baghdad taken by night cameras exhibited an eerie, surreal vision of the war as an aesthetic phenomenon with a digitized green glow of missiles and artillery exploding in the night, almost like a cosmic abstract expressionist painting. Video simulacra of buildings, bridges, and military targets (but never civilians) being obliterated by laser-guided bombs were displayed frequently during military briefings. These pictures produced an audience euphoria parallel to that experienced while playing computer and video games or watching war movies. The response exhibited a collapse between fantasy and reality, which elicited concern when it was revealed that terrorists like Timothy McVeigh who carried out the Oklahoma

City bombing in 1995, and others involved in a series of 1990s teen shootings, were immersed in fantasy war movies, video and computer games, and in some cases the Internet.

The Gulf War TV spectacle also provided the experience of a live war, with direct satellite transmission of many of its actions throughout the world. Representations of the war in Vietnam often took days to circulate between their production and their reception, and the images were filtered by media corporations and conventions. The Gulf War, by contrast, was part of a live you-are-there experience in which a global audience watched other U.S. technology bombard a Third World country and demonstrate the superiority of its weapons (and, incidentally, its media and communications systems, since it was primarily CNN and U.S. media that transmitted the images, discourse, and narrative of the war).

Thus, the dimension of live drama, of seeing an unfolding war in real time, differentiated the Persian Gulf from the Vietnam conflict. So too did the dominant video images, which conveyed the illusion of a clean high-tech war. The dominant representations of Vietnam were dramatic and often bloody, while the characteristic images of the Gulf warfare were digitized video transmissions of a sanitized megaspectacle. In fact, although the Gulf spectacle appeared to be live and unmediated, its media production and circulation were actually more managed and more mediated than those representations that came to define Vietnam. The combat in Vietnam was open to a press allowed to travel around almost at will. While the pictures, videotapes, and reports from Vietnam were often delayed, sometimes for lengthy periods, due to the more primitive conditions of mass communications at the time, many of the images and accounts that eventually circulated often stuck in the public mind and became icons of a brutal military misadventure. The Vietnam War also lingered on for years and it has been argued that the cumulative effect of the documentation of the death, destruction, and stalemate might have turned the audiences against the war.[20] The Gulf War, by contrast, was relatively brief. The U.S. government and its military managed the flow of information and images from beginning to end through a "pool system" that regulated who could describe and photograph the events and that censored every word and visual image composed in the conflict.

Thus, on the whole the "reality" of Iraqi suffering and ecocide was erased by simulacra that conveyed instead a vision of U.S. power and aestheticized war, confirming the Italian futurist Marinetti's view that "war is beautiful." Video and computer images also bathed the U.S. military in an aura of magic and power. The military did such a good job of manufacturing spectacles that it enhanced its credibility with a public eager to believe whatever it claimed. Not surprisingly, the media themselves were mesmerized by the compelling visuals the military obligingly provided, which they replayed repeatedly. CBS anchor Dan Rather spoke with awe when he presented "more remarkable video just released by the Defense Department," and CNN often opened each news segment with the drama of the air war. The images of "clean" bombing gave credence to military claims that they were avoiding civilian casualties and endowed these high-tech wizards with power and authority. The visuals supported whatever claims the military would make, which were seemingly grounded in technological omnipotence and evidence too compelling to doubt.

These representations were intended to change the public perception of war itself, suggesting that the new postmodern technowar was clean, precise, and surgical, and that the very nature of war had changed. War was thus something that one could enjoy, admire, and cheer. The visuals created a climate of joy in destruction in its audiences, as when reporters clapped and laughed when General Horner said, "And this is my counterpart's headquarters in Baghdad," as a video showed a bomb blowing up the Iraqi air force building. Just as video and computer games—or special effects movies like *Star Wars*—engender a libidinal pleasure in destruction, so too did the videos of high-tech war produce euphoria in the destruction of Iraq—at least among the audience that became absorbed by the hyperreality.[21]

The misconception was propagated that only machines and not people were involved in the new form of combat, which was supposedly bloodless and antiseptic. The sites destroyed in the released video were always unattractive buildings, usually serving military functions. The austere structures always seemed to look deserted, devoid of humans, and so the attacks were coded as a positive surgical operation that was methodically eliminating the instruments of the Iraqi military apparatus. Such medical discourse as "clean operations" sanitized the war by representing the United States as a benevolent surgeon removing a malignant Iraqi disease.

The discourse of a "clean war" and images of precision bombing proved to be quite untrue. Only after the war ended were figures released showing that 93% of the bombs dropped were not "smart" computer- and laser-guided bombs and that over 70% of the bombs missed their targets altogether. It was also admitted that even the so-called smart bombs often produced a lot of dumb "collateral" damage. In fact, it was claimed that the best explanation for the accuracy of some of the initial attacks, in contrast to the imprecision of the latter ones, is that the ability of the first bombs "to hit their targets would have been enhanced by homing devices at or near their targets, planted by U.S. agents in Iraq before the war started."[22]

The video images broadcast to the Global Media Village, however, obscured how the bombs were actually being dropped on Baghdad, one of the largest cities in the Middle East, with a population of over four million, a center of civilization, a city full of archaeological treasures. The fact that the bombs were falling on Iraqi civilians and wrecking their homes and social infrastructure was also concealed by the Nintendo-like visuals and pyrotechnics of the spectacle. The media, moreover, focused on the military aspects involved, without discussing the human and social dimension of the offensive.

Whenever pictures from Iraq appeared to put in question the hyperreal model of a clean war with no collateral damage, the propaganda machines kicked in with disinformation—as when they claimed that an Iraqi infant formula factory hit by the United States was a chemical weapons facility, or when a bombed civilian sleeping shelter was labeled a military command-and-control center. Indeed, one of the most striking aspects of the audience reception of the Persian Gulf TV War was the extent to which large numbers of citizens bought into the lies and propaganda.

For the military as well as for the TV audience, the war against Iraq was thus the first full-blown global megaspectacle of the infotainment age, the inaugural cyberwar wherein nations and humans were reduced to computerized data. It was the first conflict whereby targets were literally "reduced" to abstract information, and computer and satellite technology provided much of the information, planning, and battlefield action. "Cyberwar" refers to military action planned, organized, and fought via computer-mediated networks and the interaction of soldiers, machines, and arms in cybernetic command-and-control feedback systems. It involves the use of information networks that attempt to systematically manage an electronic battlefield and the introduction of new technologies aiming at the increasing substitution of computers, robots, and machines for human beings.

Cyberwar opens up new spaces for military strife, including the realm of cyberspace, and constitutes new forms of war. It involves a high level of abstraction and the reduction of humans, their social environments, and nature itself to information. Cybernetically mediated war attempts to systematically manage the theater of war with computer technology, and to replace human decision making and action with lethal military firepower. Cyberwar is closely interrelated with "infowar," which consists of using communications technologies and networks to automate war and to manage information, including computer, television, and radio technologies. During the Gulf War, there was unprecedented management of information, guided by the realization that information is a crucial factor in contemporary military affairs.

Of course, Vietnam previewed these developments. Yet the degree of computerization, reduction of the populace and land to bits of information, and the employment of high-tech weapons were far greater in the war against Iraq. Information technologies, simulation modeling, and execution of an overall plan were thus much more highly cultivated and operative in the war against Iraq than in Vietnam. It was extremely difficult to map the forces and movements of an enemy that hid under the cover of jungle in Vietnam. "Information" was employed in the war against Iraq, however, as a computerized mapping of terrain and Iraqi forces. These representations dehumanized the Iraqi nation and its culture.[23] People and their homes were "erased" in the digitized data and then destroyed in the bombing raids—which employed old-fashioned B-52s and horrendous antipersonnel bombs, as well as the new laser-guided bombs.

The media representation of the history and politics of the region was also marked by reductionism and abstraction. The war against Iraq exhibited the disappearance of history and politics, of the bodies of Iraqi combatants, of casualties, and of truth and critical scrutiny of the war itself. Information served as a mode of organizing consent to the war as necessary and just. The tremendous proliferation of "facts" and military commentary overwhelmed the political context, the real issues, and buried the events of the war and their consequences in the technocratic, 24-hours-a-day military discourse, which disseminated details about armaments and military actions in abstract statistical terms. The progress of the war was also presented in terms of statistics concerning how many Iraqi tanks, planes, or artillery were destroyed. There was an overload of details about "Operation Desert Storm," memorialized after the slaughter in a series of Gulf War trivia and propaganda books.

With the ubiquitous U.S. propaganda and disinformation, the distinction between truth and lying imploded. Large percentages of the audiences seemed to accept every lie that was disseminated by U.S. officials. According to the daily polls, the U.S. audience believed overwhelmingly that the Iraqis were systematically torturing allied POWs, that the U.S. air war was minimizing civilian damage, that the Baghdad sleeping shelter was a military command-and-control bunker, that the Patriot missiles were systematically obliterating Iraqi Scud missiles, and so on. All such U.S. claims turned out to be false (see the documentation in Kellner 1992). In fact, a study by communications researchers revealed that heavy TV watchers actually knew less about the events and facts of the war than those who got their information elsewhere (Lewis et al. 1991).

One could argue that the TV audience's seeming indifference to veracity manifested a waning interest in truth since the time of the Vietnam War, when there was an intense desire to discover what was really going on, as evidenced by Herr's book and its reception, and the extent and impact of the antiwar movement. The past decades have exhibited a steady erosion of interest in "truth" in U.S. politics. There has been a decline of the norms of modern epistemology and politics, revealing something of a Huxleyean or Baudrillardian state of affairs where few seem to care. In the Vietnam and Watergate eras, a premium was put on truth and the uncovering and punishment of untruth and government wrongdoing. In the Reagan–Bush–Clinton–Bush era, however, a widespread tendency to ignore the uglier facts concerning U.S. military interventions has become evident, with distinctions between truth and lies, reality and simulation, and public discourse and propaganda eroded. While political discourse is deployed in terms of its effects on public opinion and partisan politics rather than for its truth content.

Moreover, political incidents themselves seem to have less and less force and staying power. Something happens, the media focuses on it, then moves on to the next spectacle or scandal. Hence, the ephemeral nature of the Gulf War's effects could be taken as symptomatic of the fickleness of the audience in an electronic media age in which people quickly shift their attention from one phenomenon to another, without deep immersion or lasting impact. In fact, by 1992, the war against Iraq was already a forgotten war, just a hyperreal blip on the media screen, for Bush's campaign team was unable to use it effectively to mobilize support for his reelection. A war presented as media spectacle seems to have no more lasting influence than a popular TV miniseries or sports event: here today, gone tomorrow. Unless a war involves real threats, problems, or conflicts that vitally engage the public, the media event will soon be forgotten—witness the failed U.S. military intervention in Lebanon, the Grenada invasion, the Libyan bombing, the Panama invasion, Clinton's repeated attacks on Iraq, and the NATO war against Serbia.

Thus, while yellow-ribbon parades and victory celebrations continued to attract media attention during the summer of 1991, by fall interest in the Gulf War was supplanted by interest in the spectacle of the 1992 presidential campaign, and then relegated to the realm of historical amnesia. Perhaps individuals eventually get bored with mere simulation and hyperreality, or perhaps they are confronted by the discrepancies between these realms and their lived experience. Infotainment overload and the competition between media corporations can undermine the constructions of reality and spectacles that media culture is all too happy first to create and then to criticize and abandon. While the media were perfectly content to be cheerleaders during the successful and popular Gulf spectacle, they were also prepared to investigate and uncover some of the disinformation in the months following the war (e.g., with exposés of the fraudulent success rate of Patriot missiles and false claims of Iraqi atrocities, such as murder of Kuwaiti babies in incubators, etc.). But since the "victory" did not bring any lasting benefits to the public, it was soon forgotten, and the public moved on to the next megaspectacle (e.g., the O. J. Simpson case, the Jon Benet Ramsey murder, the Clinton sex scandals, the Elián González affair, the 2000 U.S. Presidential Election, and so on).

The Gulf War became a sore spot and wound in the body politic because "the revenge of the real" also came to haunt the U.S. soldiers who had participated in the event. Soon after their triumphant homecomings and victory parades, some veterans came down with a variety of mysterious symptoms, quickly named "Gulf War syndrome.[24]" In the Persian Gulf states, unexploded land mines maimed or killed thousands, and the residues of oil fires, chemical and biological weapons, and other toxic results of the war continued to degrade the environment and take their toll on human beings.[25] The clean "high-tech war," like previous wars, was actually dirty and injurious to its participants. Ordinary soldiers and civilians were once again the victims of militarist fantasies and war games.

Consequently, it is a mistake to overlook either the mode of simulation, hyperreality, and cyberwar aspects of the Gulf spectacle, or its extremely lethal reality effects. A critical analysis should engage the media spectacle and the constructed hyperreality of the war, as well as the economic, political, and cultural dimensions of the event. In fact, precisely the postmodernization of the war had material, real results. So it is not a question of either engaging in a modern denunciation of the falsity and unreality of the war's images and discourses, or of adopting a postmodern cynicism that would maintain that reality itself was erased in the war and that it existed solely in a new realm of simulation and hyperreality.[26] Rather, it is a matter of seeing the simulation of reality and the reality of simulation, of contextualizing and interpreting the forms of media hyperreality, and of critically analyzing political discourses, strategies, and consequences.

FROM THE GULF TO THE BALKANS

The Gulf War was represented by the Pentagon and the media as the anti-Vietnam: high-tech, efficient, short, and successful. In our reading, Vietnam displayed a national security state out of control, with its instrumental rationality fusing with irrationality on a massive and destructive scale. The Vietnam War's failure exposed the modern hubris that the West, with its advanced technology and enormous power, can impose its will on recalcitrant developing countries and cultures. The Gulf spectacle represents a subsequent mobilizing of the military–industrial complex and what Pynchon calls "the Rocket State" to establish its value and necessity. This transpired at the end of an epoch when the collapse of the communist empire undermined the legitimacy of the Cold War "national security state" and skyrocketing budget deficits made it difficult to sustain. Bush's "New World Order" thus flickered away as a mere phantasm, as the fantasy of would-be warriors to maintain the postWorld War II status quo in the face of its obsolescence at the end of the Cold War.

Moreover, while the war against Iraq showed that a superior military force can inflict great damage on its adversaries, it did not demonstrate that warfare is a force for order or civilization. On the contrary, the wars that we have discussed reveal military action to be an unacceptable way of resolving conflict and contemporary war to be genocidal and ecocidal. The technology of mass destruction is simply too devastating to human beings, their civilization, and the natural environment to be permitted as a mode of conflict resolution. As George Gerbner points out, "Wars in the twentieth century have killed 99 million people [before the Gulf War], twelve times as many as in the nineteenth century and twenty-two times as many as in the eighteenth century. Other hostilities, not counting internal state terrorism, are resulting in an estimated one thousand or more deaths per year" (1992: 264). The human sensorium cannot withstand the deadly effects of modern military technology, recalling a warning by Walter Benjamin: "Traffic speeds, like the capacity to duplicate both the written and the spoken word, have outstripped human needs. The energies that technologies generate beyond the threshold of those needs are destructive. They serve primarily to foster the technology of warfare, and of the means used to prepare public opinion for war" (cited in Strauss 1992: 37; for further documentation of the increased lethality of contemporary technowar, see Keen 1986).

Likewise, the Gulf intervention had a calamitous impact on the environment, creating ecological holocaust in the Gulf. The Kuwaiti oil fires caused dramatic changes in world weather patterns, even threatening to generate something like nuclear winter conditions that would block out sunlight over vast areas of the world (Kellner 1992; Hawley 1992). The United States-led allied military relentlessly bombed Iraqi nuclear, chemical, and biological arms facilities, releasing perilous elements into the surroundings. Reports abounded of hazardous materials loose in Iraq. Allied troops as well as Iraqis were exposed to dangerous chemicals, resulting in extensive Gulf War syndrome diseases—which are similar to the afflictions of Vietnam vets exposed to Agent Orange (see Hersh 1998). In addition, the U.S. bombing of Iraqi oil installations caused fires, oil discharges into the Gulf, and black pools in the desert— ironically destroying vast amounts of the very commodity that the war was supposedly being fought over. Using oil as a weapon, the Iraqis too deliberately created oil spills and started oil fires. Consequently, by the end of the war in March 1991, Kuwait was in flames and suffering one of the worst episodes of industrial–military pollution that the world had seen.

The U.S. propaganda machine blamed the Iraqis for most of the ecological havoc, accusing them of "environmental terrorism." But there is significant evidence that U.S. bombing was responsible for many of the oil spills, at least some of the fires, and dangerous pollution caused by the bombing of Iraqi nuclear and military facilities.[27] Our position in this debate is that technowar itself is ecocide, that contemporary weapons of mass destruction are in and of themselves deadly to ecological habitats. We also believe that the mentality of the war managers—on whatever side—who wantonly bomb, pollute, and devastate vast regions exemplifies the worst aspects of the modern mind-set, illustrated in the passages from Henry Kissinger cited earlier. In particular, the modern subject/object split that sees nature and specific classes of people as the stuff of domination and the subject as the Lord of Being, is brutally evident in military adventures like the Vietnam and Gulf Wars. Such events also embody the modern will to power, the drive to subjugate nature and the other, and indicate the need to cultivate new sensibilities and alternative relations to nature.

Ecological ruin, however, is caused not only by the excesses of the military and the mind-set of the modern subject, but also by the logic of capital, which rewards putting profit above nature and human welfare, and views the natural and social worlds as resources to be exploited rather than enjoyed or preserved. Capitalist lust for gain drives corporations and individuals to pollute the environment and to excrete the wastes of its megamachines directly into nature. It is a system inherently toxic to the human mind and body, to all forms of life, and to the Earth itself. Thus, capitalism manufactures a culture of death (to borrow Pynchon's term) that consists of an unholy alliance of economic, political, military, and media institutions.

Technowar is thus the logical consequence of the military culture that emerged out of World War II. It should now be seen as an especially dangerous threat to the survival of all life on Earth. It provides a bridge from modern to postmodern war as it substitutes technology for human skills and action. The assembly-line model eventually creates a form of warfare in which humans and technology implode, autonomous military systems are developed, and computerization and advanced technology make possible new forms of military conflict. In the war against Iraq, there was an implosion between humans and technology, in the operation of night-vision lenses, laser-bomb technologies, and the omnipresent computer screens that conveyed "information" to the high-tech warriors. The cyborg soldiers of the air war utilized computers to seek out their targets, merging themselves into their networks as they tracked and attacked the enemy, in a form of push-button slaughter similar to playing video games. Likewise, soldiers in M1/A1 and other sophisticated tanks wore night-vision glasses to detect their targets in the dark and used computers to program their "hits." The loading and reloading of arms was automated, and the firing of weapons was computerized, with tank commanders becoming subordinate to digitized information.

Critics have argued, however, that not only were the success rates for high-tech bombing exaggerated, but that old Vietnam-era B-52 bombers did most of the serious damage and "long lines of Abrams tanks and Bradley Fighting Vehicles . . . plowed Iraqi soldiers under the sand as they rolled right through them."[28] In general, the military hypes the success and efficacy of its high-tech weapons systems to justify immense spending on instruments of war during an era when no more superpowers threaten the United States. The military also exaggerates its technological wizardry to sell the public on advanced technology, attempting to use the excitement of new technologies to promote its weapons and its importance to "the national interest."

Other critics have proposed that the 78-day Kosovo war in the spring of 1999 was the first really postmodern war. There, military action consisted of planes dropping bombs from an altitude of over 3 miles, protecting pilots from enemy antiaircraft missiles, and conducting a cyberwar against Serbian computer networks. For Virilio, this mode of warfare is the first taking place in "orbital space" with a "new type of flotilla" consisting of planes, robots, drones, missiles, and satellites, in an emergent mode of "global air war."[29]

Bill Gates describes an innovative sophisticated global mapping system, FalconView, "a PC-based mission planning system," that allegedly cuts back dramatically the time needed for the manual mission planning process, ensures more accurate targeting, and protects U.S. soldiers (1999: 374ff.). Gates notes that the high-tech bombing in the Gulf War had a decidedly "low-tech mission support" in which paperwork bottlenecks blocked efficiency and manual flight planning caused navigation errors. The result was development of the more sophisticated FalconView system whose program manager claimed: "The American people are not willing to accept a single casualty, so every little bit of increased accuracy and certainty we can demonstrate is worth a lot" (1999: 376).[30]

Yet avowals of the accuracy of high-tech weapons deployed in the Kosovo war have also been questioned. *Newsweek* (May 15, 2000) described an internal U.S. Air Force report revealing that a mere 58 of NATO's so-called high-precision strikes hit their targets, compared with the 744 successes that NATO claimed at the end of its bombing campaign.[31] A special investigation team from NATO searched Kosovo on foot and by helicopter and found that NATO hit just 14 tanks, 18 armed personnel carriers, and 20 artillery and mortar pieces, which was less than one-tenth of those claimed. The investigators also found out that NATO high-altitude air strikes were effective chiefly against civilian targets (e.g., cities and power stations). Moreover, the investigative team discovered that the NATO forces were "spoofed a lot," bombing fake bridges and decoys put up by the Serbs to defend their real military assets.

Hence, the claims for the emerging high-tech military apparatus are greatly exaggerated. From our perspective, for the term "postmodern war" to have analytical substance, it must be distinguished from modern war and its defining features need to be clearly delineated. Fully postmodern war would be high-tech war on an electronically mediated battlefield that radically fuses humans and technology, while increasingly replacing people with machines. A postmodern military would be reorganized to fight new types of war with new technologies.

Yet the term "postmodern war" can be easily misused and abused. In general, utilizing the term "postmodern" in a meaningful way requires that one develop a systematic contrast with the "modern." Postmodern wars must be conceptualized as a rupture with previous forms of modern war, although continuities should also be emphasized. This requirement has not been met, we believe, in many texts we have examined that have presented the Vietnam and Gulf Wars as "postmodern." Cumings, for example, describes the Gulf events as "our first postmodern" war (1992: 127). Although he mentions a "postmodern optic" through which the war was perceived (103), and refers to a "postmodern facsimile" of the war with its media constructions and iconography (127), he does not provide a systematic analysis of what makes the war "postmodern." Indeed, his claim that the "victory celebration in New York was distinctly postmodern," with its theme music from *Star Wars*, sky battle between Scuds and Patriots, and colossal fireworks display, overlooks the media hype of all victory celebrations. This sort of media spectacle was congruent with the contrived political extravaganzas of the Reagan years, when Reagan's operatives manipulated good old modern advertising and PR techniques that have been around for a long time. Unless the concept of "postmodern" is rigorously theorized, it is just an empty slogan with no real cognitive content, and obscures more than it clarifies.[32]

In general, the discourse of the postmodern often intimates that something needs to be theorized, that it is novel and does not fit conventional theories, that it is a perplexing and troubling new phenomenon that requires further analysis. Yet just using the term "postmodern" as a buzzword short-circuits such analysis. It is a way of avoiding theorizing and is a sign of lazy thinking, or a facile attempt to be faddish and au courant. Thus, although we think that the concept of a postmodern war could be provided with empirical content, and although we are attempting to do just that, we would resist making a global claim for the Vietnam War and the Persian Gulf War as "postmodern" in the sense that they embody an absolutely new type of warfare. Consequently, while we would argue that the war against Iraq anticipates a form of postmodern war in its successful construction of a media spectacle and in the further advancement of the implosion of humans and machines and movement toward more high-tech forms of combat, we hold that the continuities with modern wars are sufficient to characterize it as between the modern and the postmodern rather than as an entirely new stage of warfare or history.

Hence, the discourse of the postmodern is valuable in forcing critical theorists to question previous theories and accounts and to attempt to describe and analyze the novel phenomena of the computer, media, and biotechnology society. If the concept of postmodern war illuminates what is new and original about military technology and practice in the Third Millennium, the discourse effectively calls attention to important transformations within the present era. In our conception, postmodern war is thus part of the ongoing postmodern adventure in which contemporary culture and society—from education to politics—are being revolutionized in a great transformation by new technologies and the incorporation of science and technology into ever more spheres of life.

ON THE ROAD TO POSTMODERN WAR

> On the battlefield of the future, enemy forces will be located, tracked and targeted almost instantaneously through the use of data links, computer-assisted intelligence evaluation, and automated fire control. . . . I am confident [that] the American people expect this country to take full advantage of its technology—to welcome and applaud the developments that will replace wherever possible the man with the machine.
> —GENERAL WILLIAM WESTMORELAND, JULY 1970

As this quote from General Westmoreland (who was head of U.S. forces in Vietnam during the period of greatest U.S. involvement) indicates, the military has long anticipated a mode of high-tech war that would produce an electronic battlefield and eventually replace soldiers with machines. This would constitute a new stage of warfare where cyborg warriors themselves would be part of a cybernetic–military apparatus marked by implosions of humans and technology and by increasingly autonomous military systems. In De Landa's words,

> The image of the "killer robot" once belonged uniquely to the world of science fiction. This is still so, of course, but only if one thinks of humanlike mechanical contraptions scheming to conquer the planet. The latest weapons systems planned by the Pentagon, however, offer a less anthropomorphic example of what machines with "predatory capabilities" might be like: pilotless aircraft and unmanned tanks, "intelligent" enough to be able to select and destroy their own targets. (1991: 1)

In 1983, the Defense Advance Research Projects Agency (DARPA), responsible for developing the Internet, began the Strategic Computing Program (Gray 1997). The SCP was a 5-year, $600 million program to produce a new generation of military applications for computers. The proposal included a thousandfold increase in computing power and an emphasis on artificial intelligence. It envisioned "completely autonomous land, sea and air vehicles capable of complex, far-ranging reconnaissance and attack missions." These vehicles would have human abilities, such as sight, speech, understanding natural language, and automated reasoning. The SCP promoted the view that the human element in many critical decision-making instances could be largely or totally taken over by machines (see the critique of the SCP in Gray 1997: 53ff.). In this implosive process, just as humans are becoming like machines, machines are taking on more human qualities (see Chapter 4).

Our discussion of the Persian Gulf TV War indicated the extent to which computer and information systems were of primary importance in the planning and execution of that war and the ways that new fusions of humans and technologies engendered a cyberwarrior. This development is part of a process of creating soldiers better able to integrate themselves into technological systems and to fight increasingly complex battles. This involves promoting high-tech skills in future soldiers. It requires disciplinary training to fit into technical apparatuses, the use of psychotechnologies and drugs to enhance human abilities, and even providing prostheses and implants that will produce technological amplification of human powers and abilities (Gray 1989, 1997).

During the 1990s, there were growing reflections on the transformation of war with the incorporation of new technologies in the warfare state and the development of new forms of social organization that privilege new technologies. The first issue of *Wired* magazine featured a cover story by cyberpunk writer Bruce Sterling (1993) on high-tech war. That same year cybertheorists

Alvin and Heidi Toffler (1993) published a book on the modes of "war and anti-war" that were unfolding in the supposed era of "Third Wave" civilization. By 1995, such views were widespread in media culture, with *Time* magazine publishing a cover story on "Cyberwar" (August 21, 1995), and with a cycle of films presenting technowarriors (e.g., the *Terminator* series, the *Cyborg Cop* series, *Universal Soldier, Cyborg Soldier,* etc.).

The postmodernization of war thus involves the increasing displacement of humans by technology. The next phase of technowar will probably reveal more "smart machines" supplementing and even replacing human beings. The Gulf War and the 1999 NATO war against Serbia involved a widespread use of drones, pilotless planes engaged as decoys and as instruments of surveillance, in addition to Cruise missiles. The military is developing "unmanned" technologies for ground, air, and undersea vehicles.[33] Smart tanks are already under production. As Gray notes,

> There are projects to create autonomous land vehicles, minelayers, minesweepers, obstacle breachers, construction equipment, surveillance platforms, and anti-radar, anti-armor and anti-everything drones. They are working on smart artillery shells, smart torpedoes, smart depth charges, smart rocks (scavenged meteors collected and then "thrown" in space), smart bombs, smart nuclear missiles and brilliant cruise missiles. Computer battle-managers are being developed for AirLand battle, tactical fighter wings, naval carrier groups, and space-based ballistic-missile defense. . . . The Army even hopes to have a robot to "decontaminate human remains, inter remains, and refill and mark the graves." (1989: 54)

By now the concept of postmodern war is widespread in the media and on the Internet. For instance, an ABC news program on "postmodern war" examined the profound reorganization process in the military as it shifts from large-scale, heavy, and slow machinery, such as 70-ton tanks, to smaller, lighter, faster, and more flexible vehicles. These are equipped with more accurate "smart" weapons and better mapping and sensor technologies that demand less "manpower."[34] Exotic high-tech military devices include Micro Electrono-Mechanical Systems (MEMS) that will produce tiny airplanes or insect-like devices that can gather intelligence or attack enemies. Miniature Autonomous Robotic Vehicle (MARV) technologies and various other automated military systems would guide robot ships, disable land mines and unexploded arms, and provide more effective sensing, stabilization, navigation, control, and maintenance devices. Cyborg soldiers will eventually incorporate such devices into their own bodies and equipment (see Adams 1998: 122–137). Such miniature machines and cyberwarriors would be capable of gathering information, processing it, and then acting upon it, thus carrying through a technological revolution based on new intelligent machines.

Indeed, the Pentagon is claiming that the next generation of U.S. vehicles will be "Net-ready." The U.S. Army plans to pursue a battlefield digitization project while it develops and deploys a new family of lightweight combat ve-hicles that will have digital technology built into them, rather than "bolted on," as was the case with older tanks and Bradley fighting vehicles.[35] Cyborg soldiers are also utilizing the Global Positioning Satellite system (which can be accessed from a computerized helmet) for precise mapping of the "enemy" and terrain. With the complex communications systems now emerging, all as-pects of war—from soldiers on the ground and thundering tanks to pilotless planes overhead—are becoming networked, such that wireless computers pro-vide information to and exact locations of all parties. Robot scouts can roam the terrain sending back data instantaneously to commanders. Soldier Integrat-ed Protection Ensemble (SIPE) is an army software program designed to merge all digital technologies into one data system. Even the physical state of the soldier can be monitored by computers, and surgeons can operate on wounds from continents away by using robots and the technology of "tele-medicine."

Hence, phenomenal new military technologies are being produced in the Third Millennium—envisaged earlier by Philip K. Dick and other SF writ-ers—and are changing the nature of warfare. They are part of a turbulent tech-nological revolution. They are helping to engender a new type of highly in-tense "hyperwar" where technical systems make military decisions and humans are dropped out of the loop, or are forced to make instant judgments based on technical data. As computer programs displace military planners and computer simulations supplant charts and maps of the territory, technology supersedes humans in terms of planning, decision making, and execution. On the level of the battlefield itself, human power is replaced by machines, reducing the sol-dier to a cog in a servomechanism. Philosopher of war Paul Virilio comments:

> The disintegration of the warrior's personality is at a very advanced stage. Looking up, he sees the digital display (opto-electronic or holographic) of the windscreen collimator; looking down, the radar screen, the onboard computer, the radio and the video screen, which enables him to follow the terrain with its four or five simultaneous targets; and to monitor his self-navigating Sidewinder missiles fitted with a camera of infra-red guidance system. (1989: 84)

The autonomization of warfare and ongoing displacement of humans by technology creates the specter of technology taking over, with the possibility of military accidents leading to catastrophe. A fierce argument is raging in mil-itary circles between those who want to delegate more power and fighting to the new "brilliant" weapons and those opposed who want to keep human op-erators in charge of technical systems (see Arnett 1994; Adams 1998; Ignatieff 2000). Critics of cyberwar worry that as technology supplants human beings, taking humans out of decision-making loops, the possibility of accidental fir-ing of arms at inappropriate targets and even nuclear war increases. De Landa (1991) fears nuclear accidents and technology out of control in fully automated cyberwar and calls for the manufacture of weapons over which humans maintain authority and interact creatively with technology, rather than being its object and servomechanism. Rochlin (1997) also cites the dangers of accidents that emerge from automated battlefields and cyberwar where humans are forced to react ever more quickly to high-speed systems. He also presents case studies of accidents that have happened in automated milieux over the past decade, thus warning that humans must attempt to maintain control over their technology.

Since the 1980s, Virilio has criticized the accelerating speed of modern technology and indicated how it is producing developments that are spinning out of control. He warns that the new military technology could lead to the end of the human race (see Virilio and Lotringer 1983, Virilio 1986, and the discussion in Kellner 2000). For Virilio, "The new war machine combines a double disappearance: *the disappearance of matter in nuclear disintegration and the disappearance of places in vehicular extermination*" (1986: 134). The increased pace of destruction in military technology is moving toward the speed of light, with laser weapons and computer-governed networks constituting a novelty in warfare in which there are no longer geostrategic strongpoints since from any given spot we can now reach any other, creating "a strategy of Brownian movement through geostrategic homogenization of the globe" (Virilio 1986: 135). Thus, "*strategic spatial miniaturization* is now the order of the day," with microtechnologies transforming production and communication, shrinking the planet, and preparing the way for what Virilio calls "pure war," a situation where military technologies and an accompanying technocratic system come to dominate every aspect of life.

In Virilio's view, the war machine is the demiurge of technological growth and an ultimate threat to humanity, producing "a state of emergency" where nuclear holocaust threatens the very survival of the human species. This involves a shift from a "geopolitics" to a "chronopolitics," from a politics of space to a politics of time, in which whoever commands the means of instant information, communication, and destruction is the dominant sociopolitical force. For Virilio, every technological system contains its specific form of accident and a nuclear accident would be catastrophic. Hence, in the contemporary era, in which weapons of mass destruction could create an instant world holocaust, we are thrust into a permanent condition of emergency that enables the nuclear state to impose its imperatives on ever more domains of political and social life.

In this unprecedented situation, forms of new technologies are creating frightening types of hyperwar that require rethinking the very nature of military conflict and the viability of military solutions to current problems in the face of such dangers. Theorists of new modes of war focus on the transformations of conventional warfare by the implementation of computer technologies; new phenomena like information war; threats of hacker disruption of the economy, transportation, and communication systems; and exotic modes of biological, genetic, and chemical warfare (which are easier and cheaper to obtain than nuclear weapons).

There is growing apprehension concerning new types of chemical and biological warfare, and their potential for virulent and deadly forms of mass destruction.[36] Lethal weapons, such as a stolen nuclear bomb, or weapons using radiation exposure alone, could destroy vast urban areas, or poison water and food supplies. Toxic biological weapons, such as anthrax can be readily produced and distributed, as films such as *Outbreak* (1995) have warned. Chemical weapons, which some think were deployed by or released during U.S. bombing in the war against Iraq, are also extremely toxic and relatively easy to procure and deploy. In fact, the Internet makes the production of such armaments available to large numbers of groups and individuals, it facilitates the spread of more conventional bombs and munitions (see Chapter 5).

As we have seen, cyberwar was previewed in the war against Iraq and was an important component of the Kosovo war that was planned, programmed, and orchestrated through computer networks. While the Gulf War was arguably the most spectacular warfare of the TV Global Village, the Kosovo war was perhaps the first Internet war. Not only was computerization deployed to plan and execute high-altitude bombing, but the Internet was a primary source of information and debate for the public. The volatile situation on the ground in Kosovo, with heavy NATO bombing, brutal retaliation against the Kosovian Albanians by the Serbs, swarms of refugees in the region, and the ensuing lawlessness made it extremely difficult for the major broadcasting and news corporations to deploy their employees. Instead, freelance reporters wrote on-the-ground testimonials and accounts, and sent them to web-based zines like *Salon* and *Slate*, or in some cases to the newspapers. In addition, there was a tremendous amount of information from the region transmitted over the Internet via listserves, e-mail, and websites. The NATO war was intensely debated over the Internet, if not in the mainstream broadcasting and print media, bringing the Internet to the fore of political communication and debate.

The accelerated role of information technologies in postmodern war has led some theorists to talk of new "Network-Centric Warfare" and a "revolution in military affairs" (RMA). These changes have been produced "by the co-evolution of economics, information technology, and business processes and organizations." They are, in the words of military authorities, linked by three themes: shifts from platform to network; a change from viewing actors as independent to viewing them as part of "a continuously adapting military–techno ecosystem"; and the "importance of making strategic choices to adapt or even survive in such changing ecosystems."[37]

Another form of novel postmodern war would include new modes of netwar fought in cyberspace wherein warring nations, or terrorists, attempt to destroy information and communications systems.[38] This type of netwar was previewed in what might be called the "hacker wars." The term *hacker* initially meant someone who made creative innovations in computer systems to facilitate the exchange of information and the construction of new communities (see Levy 1984; Hafner and Markoff 1991: 189ff.). But today it refers to a mode of "terrorism" whereby malicious computer nerds either illegally invade closed computer systems, or breed viruses or worms that they use to disable computers and even entire computer networks (see Hafner and Markoff 1991; Sterling 1992). During the 1990s and into the Third Millennium, panic emerged whenever a new virus was discovered. The national security apparatuses are preparing for information war that might disable important computer systems, thereby disrupting the world economy, a nation's defense establishment, or any aspects of the system of production, transportation, and communication (Schwartau 1996; Adams 1998).

Such new modes of military conflict have evoked much discussion of "cyberwarriors," an "electronic Pearl Harbor," and dire threats to the world economy and individual security from information war. In this scenario, infor mation guerilla warriors could disrupt or dismantle every vital infrastructure system of the military and civilian sectors, creating problems ranging from power outages and airline crashes to the shutdown of banks, the stock market, and the growing realm of electronic commerce. Quite unlike conventional soldiers, cyberwarriors can attack a nation from continents away. Dispensing with guns, tanks, and airplanes, cyberwar takes place via computers and modems. While cyberwar may unfold in an abstract and bloodless manner, it too can have deadly "collateral damage" by impacting institutions like hospitals, emergency services, and air traffic control systems. Hackers and infowarriors employ new weapons such as viruses, logic bombs, Trojan horses, and worms, all designed to replicate within and destroy the systems they penetrate.[39]

"Infowar" has been subjected to a variety of different analyses. It has been described as a new form of combat waged in the virtual and digital realms (making it a "third wave war" in Toffler's terms). But it also refers to everything from mischievous hacker attacks on military sites to menacing assaults on communication systems by "terrorists." The new technologies of infowar waged by hackers are causing a merging of military and civilian targets, in that they target civilians and noncombatants.[40]

The possibility of new forms of cyberwar, and terrorist threats from chemical, biological, or nuclear weapons, create new vulnerabilities in the national defense of the overdeveloped countries and provide opportunities for weaker nations or groups to attack stronger ones. Journalist William Greider, for instance, author of Fortress America: The American Military and the Consequences of Peace, claims that "A deadly irony is embedded in the potential of these new technologies. Smaller, poorer nations may be able to defend themselves on the cheap against the intrusion of America's overwhelming military strength"[41]—or exercise deadly terrorism against civilian populations. Conversely, it is becoming clear that the more technologically advanced a society is, the more vulnerable it is to cyberwar or biowar.

Realizing these dangers, the Pentagon is in the first stages of assembling something like a digital Manhattan Project with multibillion-dollar investments. Alarmed by threats to the national information infrastructure, the United States is organizing a Federal Intrusion Detection Network, or Fidnet, to monitor computer networks and attempt to block intrusions and other illegal acts (*New York Times*, July 28, 1999). Jeffrey Hunter, the U.S. National Security Council director of information who is in charge of the initiative stated: "Our concern about an organized cyberattack has escalated dramatically. We do know of a number of hostile foreign governments that are developing sophisticated and well-organized offensive cyber attack capabilities, and we have good reason to believe that terrorists may be acquiring similar capabilities." The initiative is currently under review, with civil libertarians concerned that the project might compromise privacy and threaten civil liberties while increasing exponentially the power of the state.[42]

Ever scarier, theorists are worrying about new biotechnology and nanotechnology military instruments that might miniaturize weapons of mass destruction (Joy 2000). The outbreaks of mad cow and foot-and-mouth disease have intensified worries about terrorists' biochemical contamination of the food supply. Following the logic of miniaturization that is characteristic of advanced bio- and information technology, some imagine that weapons could become near invisible and release destructure forces in unimaginable ways. The coming stage of military technology could thus involve microscopic nanotechnologies in which what were envisaged as "engines of creation" could become "engines of destruction" (Joy 2000; see our further discussion of nanotechnology in Chapter 4).

Hence, postmodern war is part of the dark side of the postmodern adventure, increasing global insecurities and the possibility of world destruction. Postmodern war thus exhibits a continuation of the worst features of modernity, and threatens to take the development of new technologies to a catastrophic end game. Yet within the global restructuring of capital, the form of military capitalism that has been dominant since World War II may be overshadowed and replaced by a more user-friendly digital capitalism. In this mode, new entertainment and information technologies reproduce an infotainment society where war would be irrelevant and even harmful to the pursuit of profit and human well-being. The Internet itself, originally conceived and funded as a multipoint communications system for the military to employ in the event of a nuclear attack, was restructured into an instrument for communication, commerce, and information sharing, and oppositional politics (see Chapters 4, 5).

Hence, the information and communications technologies produced by the military could be refunctioned and restructured to be employed for peace, human purposes, and empowerment, and not for destruction and war. Cyborg systems can perform dangerous industrial labor, or simple household labor, as well as generate electronic battlefields. Conversion from a warfare state to a welfare state was a rational expectation of the end of the Cold War, although the current trends of dismantling the welfare state and continued proliferation of a military–technowar establishment run counter to such expectations.[43]

The ascent to the presidency of George W. Bush in the 2000 battle for the White House, in fact, suggests the return to a harder, more militarist capitalism. The old Cold Warriors from W.'s father's circles who surround the presidential figurehead and control policy are representatives of the virulent military–industrial complex that Dwight Eisenhower warned about and are likely to invest in a plethora of new weapons systems (see Kellner forthcoming). Hence, current trends threaten to further weaken the welfare state while strengthening the warfare state and unleashing all the forces of predatory capitalism and a high-tech military.

We will return to these themes throughout the book as we discuss a dialectic within contemporary science, technology, society, and culture that contrasts demonic and destructive potentials with life-enhancing, empowering, and democratizing features of the postmodern adventure. As we show in the next chapter, while there are continuities between technowar and science, with science being coopted and militarized in machines of global capital, new conceptions of science that break free of the old paradigms are also emerging in the Third Millennium. These postmodern turns in science are engendering new forms of culture and thought that provide positive alternatives and could generate progressive social, ecological, and individual change.

NOTES

1. For remarks on our concepts of coevolution and co-construction, see the Introduction. The term *co-construction* has also been developed by Harding (1998) and by Andrew Feenberg and his colleagues Tom Misa, Philip Brey, and Arie Rip; we will develop our own concepts of coevolution and co-construction throughout this book.

2. Shattering innumerable myths about the economic and social advantages of a militarized economy, Seymour Melman (1985) established that although it helped to lift the United States out of the Great Depression, "Pentagon capitalism" ultimately has been parastic and dysfunctional. On Melman's analysis, it primarily benefited the military and a small sector of industries, while draining huge amounts of knowledge and money from social funds (more guns for the war economy means less butter for the civilian economy). Pentagon capitalism devalued the dollar and created sustained price inflation, while generating labor surpluses and unemployment. Exporting investments and jobs, it crippled productivity, making the United States noncompetitive with nations like Japan and Germany. In general, it has contributed to constructing a "new economic system" of state capitalism while maintaining a powerful ideological apparatus to disguise its waste and excesses from the public. See Melman (1985: 200–202) for mind-boggling examples of irrational trade-offs between the military and the civilian economies. The $12.2 billion spent in 1985 on the army's Patriot ground-to-air missile system, for example, was the same amount cut from the federal income and nutrition programs that "left 20 million people hungry among the nation's 35.3 million people living in poverty" (202). The social waste and ravages of the war economy continue to undermine U.S. industries, democracy, and public well-being.

3. For discussion of the holocaust as a catastrophe of modernity, see Aronson (1983) and Bauman (1989). T. W. Adorno (1973) frequently referred to Auschwitz as a rupture within contemporary history.

4. On the popular imaginary of apocalypse in the 1950s and the impact of the bomb on U.S. society and culture, see Nuttall (1968), Boyer (1985), and Henriksen (1997). On the development of nuclear weapons, see Rhodes (1995).

5. Interestingly, the *Saturday Review of Literature* published an editorial called "Modern Man Is Obsolete" after the bombing of Hiroshima, suggesting that humans need "to grow up morally or perish" (August 18, 1945: 5). See also Karl Jaspers's influential treatise on the threat to human survival in the era of the atom bomb, which constitutes "an altogether novel situation" (1961: vii).

6. McDougall (1985: 3) opens his book on the Space Age with this story and cites Werner von Braun proposing the analogy at the time of the Apollo 11 Moon landing (1985: 466).

7. British cultural studies originally took on the major issues of the day, beginning with analysis of the decline of working-class culture and communities in the media and consumer society of post-World War II Britain; the rise of new youth cultures; the emergence of oppositional social and political movements focusing on gender, sex, and race; and the triumph of Thatcher's "authoritarian populism." Since the 1980s, however, there has been something of a "postmodern" turn in cultural studies that moves away from big political narratives and issues to focus on everyday life, consumption, micropolitics and resistance, and more modest concerns (see Kellner 1995a). This turn brings into the purview of cultural studies interesting phenomena previously neglected, but also points to the danger that significant concerns like war, important political and cultural shifts, economic developments, and other key phenomena and events may be neglected. Thus, we are arguing for a cultural studies that takes on both political and personal concerns, and that combines macrotheory with microtheory, large historical vision with detailed empirical analysis and close reading of a variety of texts.

8. On government control of discourses and images of war, see Knightly (1975). On state and media management during the Gulf War, see Kellner (1992) and Keeble (1999).

9. The film *Three Kings* (1999) is the most significant anti-Gulf War media-cultural text to appear in the aftermath of the U.S.-led war against Iraq. The film puts on display the manipulation of the media by the U.S. military, the less-than-altruistic nature of the U.S. intervention, the failure of the U.S. military to support rebels against the Saddam Hussein regime after the war, and the general cynicism and hypocrisy of the whole venture. By contrast, U.S. network television documentaries on the Gulf war are completely propagandistic. *Norman Schwartzkopf's War Diary* is a documentary MSNBC showed countless times before and after the U.S. 2000 election. It was basically an advertisement for the Bush–Cheney ticket, featuring those in the previous Bush administration who were most responsible for the war. Likewise *Inside the Kill Box: Fighting the Gulf War*, a 2001 documentary shown on the Discovery Channel, provides similar cant and legitimation of the U.S.-led intervention.

10. Numerous critics have followed Jameson (1984, 1991) in interpreting the Vietnam War as "postmodern"; see the studies in Bibby (2000). Likewise, the authors of many books, articles, and dissertations read Herr's *Dispatches* as a postmodernist text. So far the concept of "postmodern war," as we argue, has not been adequately developed, but see Chris Hables Gray's (1997) book *Postmodern War* for a serious attempt at conceptualization with much interesting material that we draw on here.

11. Jameson describes the articulation of personal style and vision as a key feature of modernism as a cultural style and logic, and sees the disintegration of the subject and the decline of personal and artistic style as characteristics of the postmodern era (1991: 14ff.). In our reading, however, Herr, like Pynchon, has a very distinctive voice, style, and vision, ac-

companied by very modernist aims (e.g., demystification, telling the truth, creating a complex aesthetic structure that elicits interpretation, etc.). In retrospect, Herr comes off as a modernist and individualist writer who has not really exhibited affiliation with postmodernism; see, for example, his memoir "The Real Stanley Kubrick," which is a repository of modernist attitudes (*Vanity Fair,* August 1999: 136–150, 184–189).

12. Fragmentation did not first appear in postmodernist cultural artifacts. Recall Lukács's attack on "The Ideology of Modernism" (1964a) in which he complained that "decadent" modernist writers revelled in the description of the "disintegration of personality," as well as "the disintegration of the outer world" (25).

13. A genealogy of guerilla war would reveal that the struggles of indigenous peoples against the Spanish and other European colonializations produced forms now identified as "guerilla war," and that the imperialist powers produced treatises on how to defeat guerilla warfare. Gilles Deleuze and Felix Guattari (1977, 1987) adopt the figure of the guerilla nomad as their model for new postmodern identities, replacing the modern model of the rational and unified subject.

14. On de Antonio, see the introduction to his work by Douglas Kellner in the 1996 Voyager CD-ROM of *Painters Painting* and the collection of his writings in *Emile de Antonio: A Reader* (Kellner and Streible 2000).

15. Such multidimensional vision must also include the perspectives of the Vietnamese, which were lacking in most U.S. accounts and largely accessible to Western audiences during the war through documentary films made by the Vietnamese and distributed throughout the West. Some Western filmmakers and documentarians also attempted to present the views of the Vietnamese, as in the French film *Loin de Vietnam* (1967). Of course, every optic is subject to limitations and manifests the biases and interests of the producers—which is precisely why one needs multiperspectivist vision in order to understand complex phenomena. For an enlightening discussion of recent books that review the Vietnam War from various Vietnamese perspectives, see Jonathan Mirsky (2000), "The Never-Ending War," *The New York Review of Books,* May 25, 2000: 54–63.

16. The memoirs published by Generals Schwarzkopf (1992) and Powell (1995) reveal the traumatic experience of Vietnam for their generation of the military and how they viewed the Gulf War as an attempt to compensate for the loss of Vietnam. For critiques of their memoirs, see Douglas Kellner's review of Schwarzkopf's book in *Z Magazine* (April 1993: 66–69) and the dissection of Powell's activity in Vietnam by Robert Parry in *The Consortium* (July 15 and July 22, 1996).

17. Many Iraqis and other Arabs are convinced that the Gulf War was fought to destroy the power of Iraq, which had modernized and created a strong military force and a modern secular society that threatened Western interests and those conservative regimes like Saudi Arabia and Kuwait that maintained traditionalist Islamic social values despite economic modernization. On this reading, the war was an attempt to destroy Iraq's modernity through the high-tech military powers of the West. For Arab perspectives on the war, see Heikal (1992).

18. On Baudrillard's postmodern theory, see Kellner (1989b) and Best and Kellner (1991, 1997). These texts document the sense in which Baudrillard can be read as producing a concept of a rupture between the modern and the postmodern eras. Although some interpreters resist this reading (e.g., Gane, 1991, 1993), we argue that Baudrillard's concepts can be used to produce an analysis of postmodernity and we deploy his concepts to help generate a notion of a postmodern war.

19. The concept of the cyborg originally derived from military-funded research into

the sort of technical prosthetics and supplements individuals would need to survive under long-term conditions of space travel or colonization. In 1963, NASA commissioned a "Cyborg Study" for machine–human integration in space travel. After this study, however, NASA and the Pentagon stopped using the concept of the cyborg, replacing it with terms like "teleoperators, human augmentation, biotelemetry, and bionics" (Gray et al. 1995: 8). The cyborg discourse was thus transmuted into Pentagon jargon, which was employed to discuss forms of what critics have termed the "cyborg warrior" (see the studies in Levidow and Robins [1989] and Gray [1997]). Hence, the military tended to reject the concept of the cyborg for alternative discourses, perhaps sensing subversive and unstable connotations in the concept, leaving the term for appropriation by critics of the military–technowar establishment. See our further discussion of the concept of the cyborg in Chapter 4.

20. The effects of the media coverage of Vietnam are highly contested. The Right and significant portions of the U.S. military claim that the media helped lose the war through its negative and critical coverage. Scholars such as Chomsky, Gibson, Hallin, Herman, and others claim that in fact U.S. media coverage was overwhelmingly supportive. While the latter analysis is basically correct, the length of the war and the mere fact of its extended coverage, whether positive or negative, might have contributed to turning the public against it. In addition, many of the defining images of Vietnam coded the war as horrific, as a brutal, bloody, and senseless military intervention, thus eventually helping to position the majority of the public against the war. By contrast, the Gulf War was relatively brief and tightly controlled as a media spectacle orchestrated by the U.S. government and transmitted by compliant media corporations, eager for high ratings and profits.

21. Indeed, kids playing video and computer games that celebrate mayhem and destruction are being integrated into a cyberwar machine through the encouragement of their digital skills and tendencies to see violence as fun and as an aesthetic spectacle. Military officials were amazed at the facility of young pilots with sophisticated technical systems. Many, of course, grew up playing video and computer games, thus acquiring the eye-to-hand skills that would greatly serve them in combat.

22. Press conference, March 16, 1991, Air Force General Merrill McPeak. The same day, the *Washington Post* published an article by Bernard Gellman in which a high Pentagon official admitted that the U.S. bombs missed their targets over 70% of the time. Much information was also released after the war, indicating that the Patriot missile was a dismal failure, causing more damage than it prevented. U.S. government documents revealed that the accuracy rate of the Cruise missile was much lower than previously claimed, that Apache helicopters failed to perform over 50% of the time, and that the "friendly fire" ratio of U.S. troops killed by their own weapons was the highest in history (see the documentation in Kellner [1992]).

23. Other modes of abstraction and dehumanization than the digital–informational, however, were also operative. As the "turkey shoot" metaphor suggests, the U.S. forces saw Iraqis as animals to be hunted and killed. One of the disturbing things about the war was the glee and euphoria manifested by U.S. forces returning from destroying Iraqi tanks or targets, suggesting that it was great fun to engage in high-tech slaughter. The libidinal pleasure in playing video and computer games and viewing movies was thus transferred to the activity of destroying Iraqi "targets." There were also reports that troops were shown porno movies before their missions and pilots "were reported flying into combat listening to heavy metal music, with Van Halen as the band of choice" (Kroker 1992: 49).

24. Although there have been several medical studies, there is still no agreement about whether Gulf War syndrome derives from a single source or a combination of factors.

Possible causes of an assortment of maladies that have affected tens of thousands of U.S. and other troops include: negative responses to vaccines against chemical weapons administered to the troops that were never properly tested; exposure to chemical weapons or residues of biological and nuclear weapons released on the battlefield either by the Iraqis or by allied bombing of Iraqi military installations; and exposure to depleted uranium in shells used by U.S. forces, pollution from burning oil fires, desert microbes or native diseases, or a combination thereof. One study documents brain damage found in Gulf War syndrome victims; see the report by Environment News Service (http://ens.lycos.com/ens/may2000/2000L-05-25-07.html). For discussion of the political dynamics of the syndrome, see Hersh (1998).

25. Iraq presented a study to the United Nations in August 1995 demonstrating a sharp increase in leukemia and cancer incidence in the Basra region, while a British Atomic Energy Authority report estimated that there was enough depleted uranium in the form of empty shells to account for 500,000 potential deaths; see Bill Mesler, "The Pentagon's Radioactive Bullet," *The Nation*, October 21, 1996. Helen Caldicott claims that 940,000 small depleted uranium shells were fired from U.S. planes and 14,000 larger shells from tanks, and that this weapon constitutes "a new kind of nuclear war" (1997).

26. This is the thrust of Baudrillard's (1995) analysis of the Gulf War, which completely overlooks the politics, particularities, and material effects of the episode.

27. See Kellner (1992) on the propaganda war over who caused environmental destruction. As to who was actually responsible for the ecocide, Clark et al. (1991) point to sources that blame U.S. bombing for many of the oil spills; a later Canadian report attributes much of the ecological damage of the Gulf War to U.S. and allied military action (1992: 94f.). Hawley (1992) documents the ecological damage from the Gulf War, blaming both Iraqi and allied action, and argues that war is simply not an option to settle disputes in the present era. And Craige (1996) sums up the long-term environmental effects of the Gulf War and argues that ecological and global interdependency makes such events unacceptable.

28. See the account in www.suck.com/daily/2000/05/23/daily.html. Seymour Hersh reported in the *New Yorker* (May 15, 2000) that General Barry McCaffrey, who served as Clinton's "drug czar," was especially aggressive in ordering his troops to destroy hapless Iraqi soldiers and their weapons in the last hours of the war, generating a debate over whether the U.S. employed needless and excessive violence in the last days of the war.

29. Michael Ignatieff (2000) has written a book describing the Kosovo war as the first "virtual war" which deploys airpower and high-tech military force as a "surgical scalpel." Such war enables aggressors to wrap themselves in "fables of self-righteous invulnerability," renouncing both sustained moral and political deliberation and hard physical sacrifice.

30. The confession signals a major switch in military culture and the political deployment of military forces, in which a growing zero-casualty tolerance in the military is putting pressure on politicians to deploy low-casualty Cruise missiles and the tools of techno-airwar, thus decentering actual troop interventions and use. This shift severely undermines traditional warrior military culture according to J. William Gibson (2000) and marks the emergence of a new stage of military culture and practice. Examining U.S. military interventions in the Clinton era, Gibson documents growing reluctance to place U.S. troops "in harm's way" and thus to risk U.S. casualties.

31. Earlier, there had been critical internal assessments of the errors and failings of the NATO forces in the Kosovo war. See "Military Leaders Tell Congress of NATO Errors in Kosovo," *New York Times* (October 15, 1999: A8), in which U.S. military leaders told Congress "that allied forces were too slow in choosing targets during the Kosovo war, that the United States seriously underestimated how many precision-guided munitions would be

needed, that NATO should have kept alive the option of a ground invasion and that the war was fought with too much reliance on American forces" (A9). The 36th annual Munich Conference on Security Policy also engaged in heated debate about NATO's execution of the war against Serbia; see "Conference Highlights Flaws on NATO's Kosovo Campaign," *Los Angeles Times* (February 6, 2000): A1 and A21.

32. To give further examples, Miriam Cooke published an article called "Postmodern Wars" that opened with some rather general remarks concerning their "cluster of defining characteristics" (1991:27). But although she offers a six-page analysis of the war against Iraq, she presents no sustained argumentation concerning why the war should be seen as post-modern. Instead, the term "postmodern" is often deployed simply to describe novel phe-nomenon that have not yet been theorized. Similarly, Rob Wilson (1992:67ff.) refers to the "postmodern reconfiguration in which the Gulf War took place," its "postmodern register of cyborgian grandeur," the "postmodern night" of our current situation, the "postmodern nation-state in which these weapons were designed and constructed," "postmodern pro-duction," "a postmodern economy of instantaneous sign-flow and modular bricolage," the "postmodern transnational scene," the "postmodernity of the international market," Bush as a "postmodern American Adam," "postmodern ratification in the oil deserts of Kuwait and Saudi Arabia," and the Patriot missile as a "postmodern hero of the technological sublime," without theorizing what was "postmodern" about any of this.

33. See "Pilotless Plane Pushes Envelope for U.S. Defense," *Los Angeles Times*, May 14, 2000: A1 and A30, and "Robots with the Right Stuff," *Wired* (March 1996). See also Gunther et al. (1994) and Adams (1998).

34. See abcnews.com, November, 3, 1999.

35. see www.cnn.com/2...ready.combat.vehicle.idg/index.html.

36. See, for example, "Weapons of Mass Destruction" in *Popular Mechanics* (June 1998): 80ff., and Peter Pringle, "Bioterrorism. America's Newest War Game," *The Nation* (November 9, 1998): 11–17. This latter article concludes that threats of the inevitability of catastrophic bioterrorism are exaggerated and are being hyped to promote another arena for military expansion.

37. See the account by Vice Admiral Arthur K. Cebrokswky and John J. Garistka (www.usni.org/Proceedings/Articles98/PROcebrowski.htm). Ignatieff (2000: 164ff.) de-scribes the "revolution" in terms of the deployment of precision targeting at a distance and the use of computers, also noting conservative military resistance to calls for dramatic trans-formation of the military (171ff.).

38. Some analysts use "information war" (Schwartau 1996) to cover all the modes of new high-tech war. Rand theorists David Arquilla and David Ronfeldt (1996) distinguish between "netwar" and "cyberwar." We see cyberwar as a component of technowar, that in-cludes "information war" in a specific sense of using information as a form of warfare, and more generally as a mode of warfare that is governed by information technology. "Netwar" in our sense is thus a form of war within or against computer networks that could include the use of computer viruses, logic bombs, worms, and so on against enemy communications networks, or defense of one's own systems against enemy attack or intrusion. It might also involve destroying communications satellites with nuclear weapons to disable the networks, or protecting one's own systems against such attack. In the 1999 Kosovo war, there were re-ports that NATO troops targeted the Serbian information structure (see Ignatieff 2000).

39. The Department of Defense estimates that its 2.1 million computer networks were infiltrated 250,000 times in 1995 (www.fas.org/irp/eprint/snyder/infowarfare.htm). The National Security Association (NSA) calculates that more than 120 countries now

have "computer attack capacities" that could overtake Pentagon computers in a way that would "seriously degrade the nation's ability to deploy and sustain military forces" (www.govexec.com/dailyfed/0497/042297b1.htm). Moreover, teenage hackers, or "script kiddies," can develop programs that will disable electronic commerce and invade computer systems and destroy programs, as has happened regularly in recent years (we discuss this phenomena further in Chapter 4). With summer 2000 computer virus attacks of the "Lovebug" and "Resume," and new ones appearing periodically, netwar seems to be spreading throughout all domains of society, targeting citizens as well as businesses and governments.

40. See "Cyberwarfare Breaks the Rules of Military Engagement" (www. nytimes.com/ library/review/101799cyberwarfare-review.html).

41. abcnews.com, November 1, 1999.

42. For discussion of the earlier October 1997 Marsh report for the President's Commission on Critical Infrastructure Protection and subsequent U.S. policy initiatives to protect the information infrastructure, see Adams (1998: 182ff.).

43. Defense spending for fiscal year 1999 was projected at $252.6 billion—troops were cut, but spending on expensive new weapons and high-tech war gear was increased (*Los Angeles Times*, February 3, 1999). In his January 3, 1999, radio address, Bill Clinton announced that he would add $12.6 billion to the Pentagon budget for fiscal year 2000 and $112 billion over the next 6 years. Retired rear admiral Eugene Carroll, deputy director of the Center for Defense Information, noted: "The United States already spends substantially more for military forces than any other nation, with no significant threat to our national security. We're engaged in an arms race with ourselves" (cited in Ira Shorr, "Phantom Menace: The Pentagon Budget Shoots for the Stars," *In These Times*, March 7, 1999: 15).

Clinton's 2000 budget allocated over half of the $555 billion discretionary spending budget on "national defense," which was slated to receive $281 billion compared to the second main expense, education, which received a paltry $35 billion and Social Security and Medicare, which received $6 billion (see *The Defense Monitor* online site at www.cdi.org/ dm/ 1999). George W. Bush initially proposed $310 billion in military spending for 2001, with much more expected for a missile-defense system that is a pet project of his Secretary of Defense, Donald Rumsfeld (*New York Times*, February 5, 2001). In mid-February 2001, Bush announced that he was seeking an addition $2.6 billion for high-tech weapons, and by the end of the month he would detail further requests for hikes in the Pentagon budget beyond the $310 billion already targeted (*Los Angeles Times*, February 14, 2001: A14).

The dramatically increased amount of military spending to develop a space-based "missile shield" (Reagan's "Star Wars" program reborn) is not only expanding the military budget, but is accelerating a new arms race with potentially fatal implications. See "Missile Shield Analysis Warns of Arms Buildup. U.S. system could lead other nuclear powers to enhance arsenals, spread technology, report says," *Los Angeles Times* (May 19, 2000: A1 and A22) and "Risk of Arms Race Seen in U.S. Design of Missile Defense," *New York Times* (May 27, 2000). For a damning critique of the Star Wars/missile shield programs, see Fitz-Gerald (2000). In the summer of 2000, the system failed its third test and "60 Minutes" was there to film the failure; see *Los Angeles Times* (July 8, 2000: A1 and A8). Finally, for a critique of excessive Pentagon expenditures and the "iron triangle" of the defense industry, the military, and Congress which perpetuates this obscenity, see Greider (1998).

3

||||||||

POSTMODERN TURNS IN SCIENCE

The age of absolutes, if it ever really existed, is now most definitely and permanently passé.
—MATHEMATICIAN JOHN L. CASTI

The logic of life is continual change, continual motion, continual evolution.
—PHYSICIST LEE SMOLIN

We are now into a postmodern age where things are beginning to happen differently, and none too soon.
—BIOLOGIST BRIAN GOODWIN

Science and technology have long been among the principle organizing forces of everyday life, propelling the industrial and postindustrial revolutions that are dramatically transforming society as we enter the Third Millennium. A profound reorganization of life commenced in the 1830s with the beginnings of electrotechnology that led to the completion of the first transatlantic telegraph in 1866 (Klemm 1964). Decisively important for modernity and the "abolition of space and time" (Czitrom 1982), the telegraph established the foundation for a worldwide system of telecommunications and a global market that would culminate in a technoculture and "networked society" (see Chapter 5). By the late 19th century electrification led to the lighting of homes and cities and a proliferation of novel household appliances such as telephones, refrigerators, stoves, vacuums, and washers (Buchanan 1992). Radio, television, cable and satellite communication systems, and computer-information technologies have created an infrastructure for business, communications, and systems of entertainment that has produced a new economy, society, culture, and everyday life (Schiller 1999).

The explosive co-construction of science and technology occurred as a coevolutionary dynamic with capitalism and the military. Communications technologies developed significantly during and after World War II. Advances in computers, along with warfare and military management, spawned the emergent information sciences and new paradigms for neuropsychology (the brain as computer, the computer as brain). The co-construction of science and technology during the war also produced new models for the "control" of the natural and social worlds. Trying to solve difficult problems in ballistics with the aim of isolating variables such as the speed and trajectory of airplanes and reducing indeterminacy in bombing targets, Norbert Weiner, John Von Neumann, Alan Turing, and others created cybernetics and systems theory, organized around communication and feedback models. Similarly, researchers at the Rand Institute advanced influential models of game theory in order to develop strategies for winning nuclear warfare. The Manhattan Project brought together the best scientific minds of the world to produce atomic weapons. Corporations such as General Electric have profited greatly from the commodification of atomic weapons and military hardware, as the United States leads in contributions to the global marketplace of weaponry and arms and war itself has become a commodity vehicle and prime stimulant of economic growth.

Throughout the Cold War, corporate, state-funded, and military science and technology reached new heights, helping to produce a technoscience in which "pure" science is intimately connected with practical applications as technological advances engender new domains of scientific research.[1] The product of an implosion among capitalism, the military, science, and technology, technoscience generates a technoculture organized around instrumental reason and the creation of a new "artificial" society and culture. Technoscience has helped to generate a world of glass, steel, plastic, highways, synthetic fabrics and chemicals, gadgets, and new forms of culture such as cyberspace and virtual reality (VR), as it has also genetically engineered life forms and reconstructed "the natural" itself. Technoscience thus manufactures a surfeit of industrial and household products, the infrastructure for the media/computer/biotech transformations of our era, and contributes greatly to the construction of rapidly changing social and natural worlds. In Donna Haraway's words, technoscience is "a form of life, a practice, a culture, a generative matrix. Shaping technoscience is a high-stakes game" (1997: 50). Consequently, the project generates debate, struggle, and resistance.

Since the dawn of colonialism, capitalism, science, and technology have interacted and coevolved in complex ways. They have created a unique social configuration, modernity, organized around profit and growth imperatives, engineering and architectural marvels, mechanistic visions of the universe, and postanimistic identities in a "disenchanted" world ruled by instrumental rationality and exchange value. Rooted in ceaseless change, the modern adventure has unfolded at rapid speed, but typically without intelligent direction, plans, or maps. The postmodern adventure is a continuation of core modern dynamics, often to the point of constructing radical breaks in nature, society, thought, and experience.

Hence, the postmodern adventure involves both continuities and discontinuities with the modern adventure. Amid a new frenzy of change and abundant novelties, the old pathologies of domination over nature continue apace. Reductionism remains the ruling mentality of technoscience and commodification its structural form. By now, compared to when Marx composed *Das Kapital* in the 1860s, capitalism has commodified ever more dimensions of nature, society, and the body (from DNA theft and "biopiracy" to kidneys put up for bid on eBay). In this process, it has created a densely networked global economy of which Adam Smith and Karl Marx saw only the first glimmers. Like its predecessor, the postmodern adventure strives to overcome all known limits, subverting boundaries such as those that demarcate species. It also flouts various "laws" posited by modern science, reshapes its theories of knowledge, and steers us into an alleged "age of biological control" (Wilmut et al. 2000). At the same time, however, reconstructive postmodern theories situate science in a social, political, ethical, and ecological context in hopes of transforming science and technology into progressive powers of change and emancipation.

The telescope and the microscope were invented almost simultaneously in the seventeenth century, allowing science to pursue uncharted realms in the macro- and microdimensions of the universe. Similar stunning innovations unfolded in the twentieth century. Technoscience has taken quantum leaps into new macro- and microspheres. Scientists have explored the boundaries of the galaxy and beyond through satellite pictures and have landed "manned" and "unmanned" spacecrafts on the moon and on Mars. At the same time, technoscience began studying subatomic particles, smashing atoms, sequencing genes, creating microchips, developing the "molecular machines" of nanotechnology, splicing together the DNA of vastly different species, and cloning plant and animal life (as well as protoembryos of human beings). As science probes farther beyond the edges of the galaxy and deeper into the structure of atoms, genes, and chips, the juggernauts of science, technology, and capital are generating a postmodern technoculture where human identities and everyday life are defined by science and technology. At the same time, the boundaries between technology and biology, the artificial and the natural, machines and human beings, inorganic and organic matter, natural and social systems, are being rethought and reworked (see Chapters 4 and 5).

Hence, whereas modernity multiplied social differentiation in which the economy, polity, culture, and realms of science and technology all followed their own specific logic (Max Weber as interpreted by Habermas 1984, 1987), the postmodern adventure effects a collapsing of these boundaries and the mutual coevolution and co-construction of domains previously separate. The modern adventure exhibited a split between (the economic and technical) system and (social) lifeworld, to again use Habermas's discourse. By contrast, the postmodern adventure is marked by the co-construction of science, technology, capital, the military, and society in which forces once relatively removed from everyday life (e.g., science, technology, and markets) now penetrate into the very being of our existence.

Currently, both shaping and registering paradigm shifts in other areas like philosophy and the arts, the sciences are taking postmodern turns that are producing novel understandings of the world, new sensibilities, paradigm shifts and different concepts of the scientific enterprise itself. Postmodern-influenced philosophers and scientists attack (in part or as a whole) modern paradigms of mechanism, reductionism, realism, determinism, and positivism, along with dualistic methodologies, the compartmentalization of knowledge, and the mentality of the "domination of nature." They do this, however, not to jettison modern concepts and methods altogether, but rather to *reconstruct* them on stronger grounds. Thus, in place of classical notions of law, causality, order, truth, mechanism, and objectivity, they develop new discourses of indeterminacy, perspectivism, chaos and complexity, self-organization, hermeneutics, and multicultural knowledge.

Advances in the modern project of a mathematical and quantitative mapping of the universe, coupled with breakthroughs in computer-modeling techniques, have led to profound transformations in scientific epistemology and cosmology. In the postmodern perspective, the world is composed of complex, dynamic, interrelated, and holistic processes rather than of simple, static, discrete, and atomistic mechanisms. On this view, knowledge is socially constructed instead of being purely "objective" reflections or mirrorings of nature (see Rorty 1979). Recent scientific and technological breakthroughs demonstrate that the gap is being bridged between science fiction and science fact, between literary imagination and mind-boggling technoscientific realities.

There has been intense speculation and research concerning black holes, worm holes, parallel universes, ten-dimensional reality, time travel, teleportation, antigravity devices, the possibility of life on other planets, cryogenics, and immortality. Moon and Mars landings, genetic and tissue engineering, cloning, xenotransplantation, artificial birth technologies, animal head transplants, bionics, robotics, and eugenics now exist. At the same time, weighty questions are being raised about how many "realities" and "universes" might simultaneously exist, whether or not nature is "law-like" in its fundamental dynamics, and just how exact scientific knowledge can be.

In an era of deep sea exploration, interplanetary space travel, electronic communication technologies, and rapid technoscientific advance, some of the extravagant and utopian visions of Jules Verne, Arthur C. Clarke, and Isaac Asimov are becoming actualities. Yet aspects of the surreal nightmare worlds feared by Mary Shelley, H. G. Wells, George Orwell, Aldous Huxley, and Philip K. Dick also are haunting the technoculture of the Third Millennium. It is clear from a spate of contemporary novels and films that writers and other creators of popular culture often are able to vividly dramatize the illusions and dangers of the modern quest to "control" nature, as they depict technoscience, global capitalism, and the military as out of control.

In this and the next two chapters we explore how recent revolutions in science and technology have called into question numerous concepts, methods, boundaries, and dichotomies established in modern science and discourse, thereby raising a host of challenging issues for ethics, philosophy, cosmology, social theory, human identity, and politics. Expanding on the delineation of postmodern science in our last book (1997, Chapter 5), we provide further evidence for emerging postmodern paradigm shifts in science and the philosophy of science.[2] We must emphasize, however, that shifts and turns are not the same as breaks and ruptures, and that just as modern science sometimes anticipated postmodern emphases, postmodern turns in science typically reconstruct core themes of modern thought and science. While postmodern perspectives and paradigms are emerging in the sciences, there are not yet clearly articulated "postmodern sciences" that can be sharply distinguished from modern ones. Instead, postmodern critiques and perspectives are producing new understandings, interpretations, and paradigms, while older positivist conceptions of science still reign in mainstream thinking and the academies.

Renouncing crude epistemological dualisms, we also reject a normative Manichaeanism that reads "modernists" as "bad" and "postmodernists" as "good." Indeed, modern thinkers provided the quantitative maps and methods that still guide science in useful ways. Modern and postmodern perspectives have their own range of validity relating to different aspects of the natural and social worlds (Newton's theory of gravity and Darwin's concept of natural selection explain some—but not all—aspects of nature perfectly well). Some of the most interesting contemporary scientists, for example, Stuart Kauffman, Ilya Prigogine, and Brian Goodwin, are neither self-consciously modern nor postmodern, but rather work in a complex transitional space, "in between."[3] Further, sciences like quantum mechanics and complexity theory cannot unqualifiably be interpreted as modern or postmodern since they can be articulated either way.

Thus, from our multiperspectival and reconstructive premises, we seek useful positions from the quarters of both modern and postmodern perspectives on science. A great adventure currently is unfolding whereby postmodern critiques, concepts, theories, and methods are being employed by social theorists, philosophers, and scientists to promote a renewal of science that has potential for democratic and ecological knowledges. Nonetheless, we must be aware of how reigning ideologies, supported by the state, the military, and the corporations, continue to coopt the progressive possibilities of science and technology. Shaken up by postmodern critiques and perspectives, science is a hotly contested terrain and in the midst of significant reconstruction and controversies.

PHYSICS: THE "END OF SCIENCE" OR POSTMODERN
PARADIGM SHIFTS?

> The most important laws and facts of physical science have all been
> discovered, and these are now so firmly established that the possibility of
> their ever being supplemented by new discoveries is exceedingly remote.
> —ALBERT MICHELSON

> [Nature is] not only queerer than we suppose, it is queerer than we can
> suppose.
> —J. B. S. HALDANE

> Science, far from being at an end, has a long agenda ahead of it.
> —JOHN MADDOX

Certainly, not all scientists today are receptive to the philosophical and political
challenges of postmodern paradigm shifts, and many refuse the very notion
that there has been, needs to be, or again will be, radical changes in science. After the stagnation of the premodern "Dark Ages," some feel that the greatest
adventure in science—whereby modern pioneers invented new methods of
inquiry in the passionate quest for Objective Truth—is concluding as the
Good Ship of Reason now reaches the shore.

In *The End of Science* (1996), John Horgan articulates a view voiced in
various quarters of mainstream science today. Structurally similar to a certain
postmodern sense that we have entered a period of exhaustion in which radical innovation and true novelty is impossible (see Baudrillard 1989), some scientists and theorists rhapsodize about "the end of science," a point at which all
the "big" discoveries have been made. All that can be known about neurochemistry, evolution, or physics, they feel, is sealed up in various laws and all
future science will involve no more than crossing the t's and dotting the i's of
the Tablets of Truth.

Such claims are not new. Lord Kelvin announced the end of science in
1900, as did Albert Michelson 3 years later. Medical students in the 1950s were
advised not to study infectious diseases, given the stunning success of antibiotics. In 1968, the surgeon general closed the book on this issue—just before the
world was hit by the recrudescence of old illnesses and the emergence of dozens of new viruses and diseases, many difficult or impossible to treat in a now
"postantibiotic" era (see Garrett 1994). In a 1980 lecture, Stephen Hawking
expressed "cautious optimism" for a "complete theory" of physics within the
next few generations, in effect terminating the modern adventure in physics.
Currently, various neopositivists feel confident that science is realizing its
search for an "ultimate explanation" (Barrow 1991) and "a final theory"
(Weinberg 1994) of reality.

Thus, science has a history of premature closures. One should be wary of
such claims today for they are dogmatic, pretentious, and premature. Just as
Baudrillard predicted the "end of history" shortly before the dismantling of

the Berlin Wall and the collapse of European communism, so Horgan and others proclaim the end of science amid a frenzy of change, innovation, and paradigm-shaking debates. In the last few decades, exciting areas within science have emerged, for example, superstring theory, chaos and complexity theories, philosophies of coevolution and autopoeisis (self-organization of matter), and evolutionary cosmologies. Many sciences, such as ecology, paleontology, and molecular biology, are relatively young; other fields, such as neurochemistry, aging research, and exobiology (the search for evidence of alien life and the study of life that evolves in hostile environments) have only recently been born.

While new sciences and philosophies of science emerge, realist epistemology continues to be challenged from all quarters. Everywhere one looks, new ideas are advancing and boundaries are being transgressed, both within the sciences and between science and other disciplines. Microbiology, atmospheric chemistry, and geology combine insights to formulate Gaia theory, as astrophysics and cosmology come together to construct new maps of the universe. Physicists apply evolutionary theories to study the origins of the cosmos, and physics, chemistry, and engineering are joining ranks to develop self-assembling nanotechnologies. In the new field of molecular electronics, scientists from diverse fields and computer designers are uniting to create integrated circuits no wider than a few atoms. Biology, astronomy, chemistry, geology, oceanography, and meteorology have merged in the new science of astrobiology, whose mission is a comprehensive search for life in the universe. Computer science and biology form alliances in the field of artificial life (AL), while biology uses computer simulation models and AL "organisms" to study evolution. Providing exciting new models of the brain, artificial intelligence, neuroscience, and cognitive science now work together synergistically. Making breakthrough understandings concerning animal cognition, researchers have brought together the tools of psychology, neuroscience, evolutionary biology, and linguistics. Genetics, chip manufacturing, and computers are reconstructing medicine as "pharmacogenetics" and "cybergenomics," shifting emphasis away from test tubes and petri dishes and toward biochips and gene analysis. Economists, sociologists, and a wide range of scientists and theorists have joined together in the search for a grand unified theory of complex systems.

Thinkers from numerous quarters engage debates over science and technology in the present era, as some theorists champion a new "third culture" that allegedly bridges the science/humanities gulf diagnosed in 1959 by C. P. Snow (see Snow 1964; Brockman 1995).[4] Scientific pedagogy is reflecting these changes, as interdisciplinary institutions spring up throughout the world (from the Santa Fe Institute to the University of Sussex's School of Cognitive and Computing Sciences). Although the fragmentation of knowledge remains a real problem within the sciences and between science and the humanities, there is abundant evidence of progressive change toward unification, synthesis, and transdisciplinary work. Indeed, even the notoriously reductive sociobiologist E. O. Wilson proposed transdisciplinary and ecological perspectives in his book *Consilience*, writing, "Disciplinary boundaries within the natural sciences are disappearing, in favor of shifting hybrid disciplines in which consilience is implicit. They reach across many levels of complexity, from chemical physics and physical chemistry to molecular genetics, chemical ecology, and ecological genetics. None of the new specialties is considered more than a focus of research. Each is an industry of fresh ideas and advancing technology" (1998b: 55).[5] Similarly, physicist Michio Kaku claims that the "era of reductionism is coming to a close" (1997: 10). Although reductionism has been responsible for numerous insights and benefits, a new era of "synergy" is arising that compels forward-thinking scientists to combine studies from what Kaku thinks to be the three major technoscientific revolutions of our time: quantum, biomolecular, and computer.

As science constructs new maps, debates intensify over issues such as the origin and age of our universe. The question of whether or not it is expanding, collapsing, or holding steady is being heatedly debated, as is the nature and location of the "dark" or "missing" matter that comprises 90% of the cosmos. "Big Bang" cosmology, an enforced dogma in many scientific sectors, is targeted by "steady state" and "inflation" theorists who renounce the idea of a single beginning point in space and time for the evolution of the universe (see Hawkins 1997). To date, no one has proposed a successful quantum theory of gravity that would accomplish the decades-long dream of physics: to combine in one comprehensive explanation the dynamics in the microworld of quantum mechanics and the macroworld of gravity.[6] Indeed, rather than science moving toward consensus, we find a state wherein competing cosmological models proliferate in what Lyotard (1984) terms a postmodern condition of knowledge.[7] In January 2001, astronomers identified two strange planetary systems that defied all existing knowledge and suggested there was a greater diversity of types of planets than previously believed (Wilford 2001). Ever more intriguing evidence mounts about the possibility that life exists or existed on planets like Mars or the moons of Jupiter. In February 2001, scientists discovered a new kind of behavior in the subatomic particles "muons," that could not be easily explained by existing paradigms, and as such "may be the first glimpse of a previously unseen kind of matter" (Glanz 2001).

Although by early 2001 the human genome has been mapped, little is known about the function of genes, how they interact with one another, and the very concept of the gene is contested (see Keller 1999). Scientists know still less about how proteins fold into just the right shape when manufactured inside of a cell. Debates rage on about the possible medical consequences of the humane genome mapping. Some, for example, Human Genome Project director Dr. Francis Collins, predict revolutionary implications; while skeptics such as Neil Holtzman and Teresa Marteau claim that genetic information is applicable only for rare disorders and will have limited value in predicting, preventing, or treating common diseases (Khury and Thornburg 2001). With discoveries in AL and the new science of exobiology, some scientists wonder if they know anymore what life itself is.

In short, at the beginning of the Third Millennium, exciting emergent developments in science continue to unfold, much still is enigmatic about the natural world, and major questions about scientific fact and method remain to be answered. In the midst of all these changes, Horgan and other defenders of the "end of science" thesis ask us to believe that past discoveries will always be true, that current models are adequate to know the world as it is, and that no major discoveries are on the horizon.[8] In contrast to the view, at least in some quarters, that science is ending or over, our claim is that the postmodern adventure is advancing bold and provocative hypotheses and discoveries throughout numerous disciplines. Hence, rather than completing its mapping adventures, science is just beginning to find its way in a world of change, complexity, diversity, ambiguity, and contingency—in a cosmos discovered to be both incredibly large and amazingly small.

Postmodern paradigm shifts involve revolutions in thought and method, rather than merely rearranging furniture in the house of modern science; they yield qualitatively new insights and advances, not merely adding finishing touches to the masterpieces painted by Newton and Darwin. The concepts of coevolution, self-organization, chaos, and complexity have brought ideas and changes that break free of the mechanistic and positivist straightjacket Horgan and others try to squeeze onto scientific innovation. For Wilson (1998c: 85), new transdisciplinary developments connecting the natural sciences, social sciences, and humanities open up a "large and unexplored borderland," such that "we can put to rest the idea that science has come to an end." The gaping holes in the façade of science at its "end" have prompted at least one prominent physicist to emphasize what remains unknown about the world, auguring that discoveries "will undoubtedly change our view of our place in the world as radically as it has been changed since the time of Copernicus" (Maddox 1998: xiii). Yet it is not just that science is still continuing, and will endlessly pursue, the adventure of discovery, but that the methods, epistemology, self-conception, and politics of science are mutating dramatically through a fusillade of postmodern critiques and reconstructive projects.

Modern and Postmodern Mappings: Science as Contested Terrain

> Scientists cannot solve the ultimate mystery of nature because in the last analysis we are part of the mystery we are trying to solve.
> —MAX PLANCK

The modern adventure in science involved an assault on medieval cosmology—rooted in Aristotle, Neoplatonism, Christianity, alchemy, and various animistic philosophies—in order to construct bold new maps of the universe. Assembled by thinkers like Boyle, Bacon, Descartes, Galileo, and Newton, the new sciences replaced qualitative, religious, and mystical definitions of reality with quantitative, mathematical, and secular models. The interpretation of nature as a web of sacred signs and harmonies revealing the mind of God was abandoned. In the new scientific interpretation, nature was governed by laws that could be apprehended through reason and experimental methods. Despite the discontinuities, however, nature was still seen in static terms because Platonist metaphysics continued to rule Western thought. Scientific vision, cleansed of the old myths and dogmas of theology, was rooted in the new orthodoxies of complete "neutrality" and pure "objectivity." The participating consciousness of the knowing self gave way to the detached consciousness of the "observer," to an allegedly pure perception that was ahistorical, asocial, and disembodied (see Berman 1981). The goal of knowledge shifted from contem plating a divinely organized, living universe to conquering and mastering dead nature, a universe reduced to mere matter-in-motion, a storehouse of raw materials for human use. The smashing of geocentric cosmology in favor of a new heliocentric picture was only the first in a series of enormously troubling decenterings and "discontinuities" the premodern (and then modern) mind would have to process (see Chapter 4 and Epilogue). As modern science initiated this psychological free fall, feminist analyses underscore that the dualisms and goals of modern science also are organized around distinctly masculinist values (power, control, abstraction) and the exclusion of women from the kingdom of knowledge (see Merchant 1983; Haraway 1997).

The first modern mappings deployed analytic geometry and calculus. With such measuring devices, science constructed a mechanistic universe that was unchanging, uniform, deterministic, simple, and predictable. Although the modern modes of scientific reasoning and the experimental method prompted dramatic advances in the state of knowledge and led to important technological innovations, this clock-like universe was an ideal model. At times, modern scientists caught glimpses of change, unpredictability, nonuniformity, nonlinearity (a small fluctuation that brings a disproportionately large transformation), chaos, and complexity. Newton, for instance, tried to study the movement of three planets together (the famous "three body problem"), but his Euclidean sensibilities suppressed these qualities in order to maintain idealized geometric models. Even Einstein—whose theories of special and general relativity revolutionized Newtonian definitions of space and time and helped pave the way to quantum mechanics—struggled to suppress change and indeterminacy in favor of geometrical, law-governed explanations.[9]

In its various forms, the postmodern turn in science involves a break from the classical 17th-century principles of the Baconian–Cartesian–Newtonian worldview. Postmodern perspectives reject atomistic and reductionist logic; the notion of a static universe; the quest for absolute certainty in a world of guaranteed predictability; and a mechanistic, antiecological outlook intent on

bending nature to human will. Postpositivist philosophers and theorists of science, moreover, renounce the naive realism that informs modern science. They
regard all perception and knowing as value-laden and socially conditioned, and
they seek self-reflexive clarity regarding the origins and structure of scientific
knowledge itself (see Wright 1992; Harding 1998). Such analysts foreground
issues of epistemology and advance a linguistic theory of knowledge. They argue that scientific language—and the metaphors science inevitably employs
(see below)—are not a neutral mirror reflecting the world as it is, but rather are
social constructs that actively shape and mediate our theory and understanding
of the world (see Goodwin 1994). In sum, conceptions of both the modern
subject (the knower) and object (the known) have changed. Knowing and
"truth" have been reconstructed as interpretation fashioned through a tenta-
tive consensus within the scientific community, and the world has been recast
in dynamic, evolving, self-organizing terms. Rather than vitiating the concepts
of truth and objectivity, postpositivists feel they are providing more accurate
versions of modern ideals.

The postmodern turn in scientific mapping began with the recognition
of change, unpredictability, complexity, and nonlinearity in nature. These insights emerged with the dynamic outlooks of evolutionary theory and
thermodynamics, and continued with Boltzmann's theory of probability,
Poincaré's mathematics at the turn of the century, and then quantum mechanics, Heisenberg's principle of uncertainty, Godel's theory of incompleteness, chaos and complexity theory, fractal geometry, fuzzy logic, and other
innovations (see Best and Kellner, 1997). The development of quantum mechanics during the 1920s was of particular importance for numerous reasons,
including its descent into an unexplored microreality and its attempts to
map the movement of subatomic particles and electrons. In this new realm,
light is both particle and wave, subjects disturb the objects they are trying to
analyze, and electrons move in discontinuous orbits. Only with quantum
mechanics did physicists experience a "crisis in reality" (Herbert 1985), since
subatomic investigations led them to challenge Western dogmas of a world
of solidity, continuity, noncontradiction, mechanical (billiard ball) causality,
strictly local effects, determinism, a sharp subject–object distinction, and naive realism.[10] Moreover, quantum mechanics was crucial in the development
of new technologies such as television and computers that themselves forced
radical change and a redrawing of the maps of reality (see Kaku 1997;
Gilder 1989; Chapter 4).

The postmodern adventure as a quest for ever-more accurate quantitative
mappings of the universe continues the thrust of the modern adventure, but it
develops in a significantly different context that departs from positivism,
mechanism, and the coordinates of absolute, three-dimensional space and time.
With relativity theory, quantum mechanics, chaos and complexity theory, and
superstring theory, science abandons the terra firma of Cartesian clarity for a
Wonderland of intricate relations, along with perplexing thought experiments,

riddles, paradoxes, and counterintuitive phenomena. Tumbling into the tunnel of bold scientific imagination, one finds curved spacetime, light beams traveling faster than "the speed of light," entities acting as both particle and wave, parallel universes, and nonlocal causality and instantaneous changes across the universe.

Postmodern turns uncouple rigid modern dualisms, such as those between order/disorder, fact/value, and science/society. This move is clearly evident in physicist Ilya Prigogine's work (1996; Prigogine and Stengers 1984). Postmodern theorists place important qualifications on the degree of accuracy with which one can map and predict natural processes, as they often reject the restrictions of empiricism that tie science to observable events in the natural world. Postmodernists recognize change, process, indeterminacy (probability as opposed to absolute certainty), complexity, and nonlinearity as fundamental aspects of the world rather than as defects in idealized models, limitations in measuring technologies, or flaws in subjective thought. In Prigogine's words, "We are on the eve of a triumph of the 'probabilistic revolution,' which has been going on for centuries. Probability is no longer a state of mind due to our ignorance, but the result of the laws of nature" (1996: 132).[11] Prigogine's approach is an instructive example of the reconstructive aspect of a postmodern turn that revises, rather than dismantles, core concepts such as truth, objectivity, prediction, and order. Chaos theory, for example, does not jettison the notions of determinism or order; rather, it ties them to their dialectical counterparts of indeterminism, spontaneous change, and self-organization (see below). It thereby produces a more complex, and arguably more accurate, model of the world that allows for improved degrees of exactitude and predictability.

In the last few decades, as they have tried to revise the maps so tattered by quantum mechanics and relativity theory, many physicists have been obsessed with advancing the modern project of constructing a complete theory of the universe. Such a theory would successfully unify and explain what scientists now believe are the four constituents of nature—gravity, electromagnetism, and the weak and strong nuclear forces—in a "Theory of Everything" (TOE). Specifically, the "holy grail" of recent physics is a quantum theory of gravity, a comprehensive grasp of both the geometric macroworld of space–time (where the determinist methods of classical physics seem appropriate) and the indeterminate microworld of subatomic particles (which demands a new framework of indeterminacy and probability). Whereas some (e.g., John Barrow and Steven Weinberg) approach this goal from neopositivist grounds, others (e.g., Lee Smolin) adopt a postmodern antirealist epistemology.[12] Mathematically and conceptually, the unification project so far has proven to be terribly difficult and the worlds of relativity and quantum mechanics seem irreconcilable. The impasse appeared to be broken in 1984, when Michael Green and John Schwarz developed "superstring theory." They got the numbers to come out right, but only by resorting to the mind-boggling notion of a ten-dimensional world comprised of interactions among string-like particles.

While many were skeptical of this science-fictionesque universe, super-string theory inspired numerous thinkers to claim that a successful TOE existed and the "end of physics" was near. Such optimism, however, appears ungrounded. In the face of a myriad of competing interpretations of reality, ranging from numerous variants of superstring theory to "twistor theory" (see Peat 1988), more sober physicists admit that science still is not sure what light is, let alone reality, and no consensus is anywhere in sight. Unlike Stephen Hawking, many superstring theorists express strong reservations about claims regarding the end of physics. Green and Schwarz themselves are modest about the achievements of superstring theory, point out its numerous limitations, and envision much important work yet to come. Michio Kaku (1994), another pi-oneer of string theory, emphasizes that no one has yet developed a plausible theory of how to decide among thousands of possible contenders in string theory, since the requisite mathematical knowledge is still too primitive. On a more skeptical note, Kaku suggests that such a task is likely beyond the capaci-ties of the human brain, which evolved for pragmatic not theoretical or meta-physical functions.

It is hard to avoid the conclusion that modern scientific epistemology is in crisis, divided from within and attacked from without. The physics commu-nity is torn over basic epistemological issues concerning the merits of theoreti-cal versus experimental approaches. Experimental-oriented physicists like Richard Feynman and Sheldon Glashow urge a classical "bottom-up" ap-proach that works from experimental data and testable hypotheses to theories. Other physicists, such as string theorists, advocate a "top-down" approach that begins with "elegant" theories that may or may not be verifiable, and work perhaps toward an empirical description of the world. The top-down camp veers toward what Horgan belittles as nonempirical "ironic science" and Glashow ridicules as "theatrical physics" or "recreational mathematics" (see Kaku 1994: 179).[13]

Smolin suggests, however, that new developments in mathematics may in-volve a genuine paradigm shift, for "some [physicists] even proclaimed the dawning of a new, postmodern age of physics, in which mathematics would now play the driving role that had, since the time of Galileo, been played by experiment" (1997: 67). Such a shift would not have been possible without the invention of sophisticated computers, which points to another key way in which science and technology have merged. This symbiosis provides a power-ful new means for mapping natural processes (see Kelly 1995). Kaku claims that computers and VR technologies have created a whole new branch of sci-ence, a "cyberscience" based on the ability to simulate complex phenomena such as black holes, exploding stars, weather systems, protein folding, materials testing, and the greenhouse effect. For Kaku, "a new, third form of science is appearing" based on computer modelings rather than theory and experiment (1997: 40–41).[14]

The current epistemological debate reflects the fact that classical models of scientific method, in which the scientist proceeds from observation, to hypothesis, and to verification (hardly the approach, for example, of Einstein, who relied greatly on intuition and thought experiments), are being sharply contested, as are modern theories of realism, objectivity, and determinism. As positivist norms persist, a speculative side of physics moves into metaphysics, religion, or purely mathematical and aesthetic models of the universe, violating Karl Popper's (1963) widely accepted dictum that a scientific theory, at the very least, needs to be falsifiable. Some forms of "science," in other words, are no longer "scientific" according to classical norms. In addition, the boundaries separating science, philosophy, religion, aesthetics, social theory, and even poetry are fast eroding, a change that both results from and helps to construct new cosmologies (see below). Thus, far from having reached the endgame of Truth, science is in a key transition period, struggling to redefine itself amid paradigm shifts, technological innovations, a reorganization of capital, and no ciopolitical critiques from myriad quarters.

The Coevolution of Science, Technology, and Capital

> If we do know that there exists a science which is imperialist in its uses, its organization, its method and its ideology, there must exist, and in fact there does exist, an anti-imperialist science.
> —CIENCIA PARA EL PUEBLO

> Feminists have stakes in a successor science project that offers a more adequate, richer, better account of a world, in order to live in it well and in critical, reflexive relation to our own as well as others' practices of domination and the unequal parts of privilege that make up all positions. In traditional philosophical categories, the issue is ethics and politics perhaps more than epistemology.
> —DONNA HARAWAY

The crisis in modern scientific norms has been building for some time, beginning with Nietzsche, and continuing with pragmatism, critical theory, and Kuhn's (1970) sociological analysis of science as paradigm-dependent and theory-laden. Marxist, postcolonial, feminist, environmentalist, and animal rights critiques of scientific "objectivity" and "internalist" accounts of knowledge (that see science as autonomous and fail to address "external" social factors that shape science) uncovered the classist, Eurocentric, androcentric, and anthropocentric biases of science. In addition, they revealed the often destructive effects of Western/Northern science and technology on workers, the poor, Southern nations, women, the environment, and animals (see the essays collected in Harding 1993).

Today legions of cultural theorists are invading the citadel of science with powerful challenges to the positivist epistemology of pure perception, theory-free facts, and cold objectivity. Provoking a series of "science wars" with those defending this crumbling fortress, activists and critics have begun to claim both the theory and practice of science as a legitimate domain of their own and of the public at large. In appreciation of the profound role science and technology play in shaping contemporary personal identities and social life, critics are bringing to light the social context and history of science. They are also addressing science's various ideological biases, its intense militarization, its commodification of research, and its political and ecological implications.

The postmodern turn in science, then, should reflect on the science/society nexus; the coevolution of science, technology, and capital; and the ways that social relations, discourses, and metaphors shape scientific understanding. As underscored by postcolonial critics, vindicating Foucault's argument that power and knowledge are dialectically intertwined, modern society and science developed in a reciprocal relationship. Various modes of scientific and technological knowledge were necessary for the colonial adventures to be possible in the first place, including breakthroughs in navigation, astronomy, and agriculture. Conversely, imperialist conquests provided a laboratory for the fledgling efforts of Western science and vast amounts of wealth and resources for the accumulation of further knowledge. Many of the gains of science and technology were learned from the various cultures conquered by colonialists (see Harding 1998).

Thus, modern science was driven not simply by a "pure" desire for truth and disinterested knowledge, but also by the pragmatics of colonialism and capitalism. From the start, Western science has been deeply tainted by multiple biases and prejudices that range from the blatant and obvious (such as are on display in social Darwinism and eugenics) to the subtle, as where Donna Haraway (1989) uncovers racist, classist, and sexist biases in primatology. Sandra Harding (1998) underlines the fact that "value-free" science is a self-refuting concept, because this in itself is a value and being disinterested is a distinct kind of interest and ideology. All too often the language of "objectivity" serves merely to mask the deep implication of science in anthropocentrism, patriarchy, racism, capitalism, power, violence, and warfare.

A vivid example of coevolution dynamics is evident in the relation between the computer and the genetic revolutions. The genetic sciences and mapping of the human genome would never have gotten off the ground without major technological advances, specifically, rapid progress in the processing speed and memory capacity of computers to digest and organize the voluminous amounts of genetic information embodied in the simplest of organisms.[15] Conversely, now that computer chip designers seem to be approaching a limit in the speed, power, and size reduction allowed by silicon, some predict that the technological impasse will be broken through merging computers with quantum physics and genetics. Thus, there are efforts underway to develop a "quantum chip" and a "DNA chip," each of which will expand computer speed, memory and power to fantastic degrees (e.g., a DNA molecule holds more than 100 trillion times the information than can be stored in current computers [Kaku 1997: 104]).

As commodified knowledges, the genetic technosciences are driven by market logic as they in turn open up incredible profit opportunities for scientists and corporations who can patent a "new" life form by manipulating and combining pieces of existing plant, animal, or human DNA. The powerful economic impetus to the development of genetic engineering has overridden health, biodiversity, animal welfare, and environmental safety concerns, as scientists working for corporations such as Celera (Latin: quick) Genomics, as well as the government-led Human Genome Project, stampede in a mad gene rush.[16] In the competition to map the human genome, tensions have thus emerged between state and industry perspectives on genetic research that dramatize ethical conflicts and controversies within the world of science.

In 1990, the Human Genome Project was announced. Academic researchers, led by Dr. Francis Collins, predicted the government-sponsored mapping, at a cost of $3 billion, would be complete in 2005, and along the way, the researchers would make their data available to the public. Halfway through their work, in May 1998, Celera Genomics, fronted by president and chief scientific officer Craig Venter, announced it could complete the mapping in a fraction of the time and cost, and would patent and market its own mapping. What should have been a noble project to help humanity became a competitive race characterized by hostility on both sides, between Collins and Venter. The acrimonious competition came to an end on Monday, June 26, 2000, when Collins and Venter joined President Bill Clinton at the White House to announce the completion of the first draft of the genome. Venter tried to be magnanimous, claiming that "the only race we're interested in today is the human race." But he championed the cause of market-driven research, proclaiming that it was a "historic moment for private industry and private capital." Increasingly, however, members of the scientific community were alienated by Venter's hardball tactics.

On the defensive from negative publicity, Celera announced it would publish its data in a scientific journal and put it on a digital video disc (DVD) disk with no restrictions on its use so long as industry rivals could not profit from the data. But Celera itself could profit handsomely, from licensing the over two dozen patents it has filed, payment for its services in interpreting the data, and fees from any medicines that might result from the research. The project of mapping the human genome embodies the conflicted nature of science, torn between serving the public good and the bottom line. Given the realities of biopiracy, the commodification of the human genome, and the costs of corporate-controlled medicine, however, it might be some time before the public receives dramatic—and affordable—benefits from genetic science.

On February 12, 2001, with great international fanfare, the publically owned and financed International Human Genome Sequencing Consortium and privately owned Celera Genomics announced the publication of long-awaited papers that would offer their respective interpretations of the human genome, descriptions of how they proceeded, and details of how their findings would be available to the public. University of Pennsylvania bioethicist Arthur Kaplan noted, "It would be fair to say that Palestinian-Israeli peace negotiations have nothing on private-public publication negotiations."[17] The competing organizations published their analyses in mid-February 2001, in *Nature* and *Science*, respectively, to a great deal of attention.

Scientists discussed the relative merits and limitations of each approach. Some criticized Celera for the strict requirements it placed on use of its data base and the commodification of the data for profit. Others praised Celera's radical sequencing methods, which accelerated the mapping of the human genome. Critics of biotechnology warned of dangers from misuse of genetic data bases (see our discussion of cloning in Chapter 4), while advocates projected exciting medical breakthroughs and benefits that would accrue from the mapping.[18]

Biotechnology has thus unleashed an economic cooptation (and thereby co-construction) of science and technology, where objectivity is compromised by the seductive siren song of profit—as university research in general is ever more tied to and funded by corporations.[19] In the biotech era, the reconstruction of capital proceeds, in large part, through the reconstruction of nature itself. The "artificiality" of money and engineering and the "naturalness" of life forms become inseparably fused in a technologically mediated hyperreality where these oppositions lose their meaning.

Thus, along with sea changes in technology and the development of capitalism, science provides a material grounding and substantive content for postmodern turns in theory and the arts. Hardly rooted in fashions of the moment, postmodern mutations unfold in response to dramatic changes in capital, science, and technology, as they also have their own autonomy and internal dynamics in areas like architecture and philosophy. In addition to having intellectual potency, science is, in Marx's words, a "productive force," as it both prompts and responds to changes in economics and technology, becoming an increasingly important power in the production and reproduction of capital. Capitalism has embarked on a global restructuring process, using technoscience as the engine of its innovation and its profit (see Chapter 5).

To locate these material relationships and the co-construction of science and society demands a multiperspectival and transdisciplinary optic that analyzes complex coevolutionary processes from multiple standpoints, theorizing the dynamic interaction among economic, scientific, technological, social, cultural, and political institutions. A coevolutionary approach brings science and technology into a sociopolitical terrain shaped by interests of power and struggle, a space that demands external and political readings of science. A coevolutionary genealogy enables one to refute the modern fable that science evolves only through its own internal dynamics, on a linear trajectory toward

Truth guided by the light of Reason. It allows as well a refutation of the myth of technological determinism, which holds that technology develops according its own imperatives or logic, wholly apart from social relations and independent of human will. If science and technology are socially constituted, they can be reconstituted in new forms, guided by more humane, ethical, democratic, and ecological values. If science is inevitably informed by interests, the issue becomes not one of trying to screen them out, but of holding them up to public light for examination and struggling for a new approach shaped by positive values such as justice, democracy, peace, ecology, respect for animals, and satisfaction of human needs.

Through social constructionist and "externalist" readings of science, the "Only One Road to Truth" mentality gives way to a politically contested terrain—which is precisely what old-fashioned positivists fear. But quite unlike the famous distortions and caricatures painted by Gross and Levitt (1994, see our critique in Best and Kellner 1997), most forms of postmodern science are concerned with strengthening, not weakening, the norms of objectivity, rationality, and verification. The enterprise of science is not dependent upon the legitimacy of the internalist model that entombs thought within its own epistemological castle. Indeed, science and its prized norms of truth and objectivity are vitiated by the illusions of positivism and the correspondence theory of truth which combine to block a more accurate grasp of the sociopolitical context of all scientific understanding. While "postmodern theory" often is derided as irrationalist, antiscience, anti-Enlightenment, and antimodernity, a reconstructive postmodern turn preserves the best of Enlightenment, modern science, democratic values, and modern culture and institutions, while discarding problematic elements. Unlike some extreme postmodern positions, a reconstructive approach seeks to create better sciences, technologies, democracies, and societies, promoting the satisfaction of human well-being and the regeneration of the natural world.

Once recontextualized, science is open to the complexity of transdisciplinary analysis, multiperspectivist vision, and multicultural politics. Insight into the social construction of science reveals that science is constantly being reconstructed and is always subject to challenge, critique, and significant paradigm shifts. Calls to pluralize science advance critiques of realism and monoperspectival claims to "truth" (Western, White, Male), while urging a more inclusive, democratic, and respectful science that integrates the perspectives, values, and interests of feminists, postcolonialists, "Southern" cultures, animals, and ecology. A multicultural science does not denigrate premodern knowledges as "folklore," "superstition," or the "savage mind," but rather seeks to learn from diverse perspectives and acknowledges the value of non-Western and premodern knowledges. On this count, Harding broadens the definition of science, defining it as "any systematic attempt to produce knowledge about the natural world" (1998: 10), as she seeks to legitimate diverse cultural knowledges. Given the tremendous power of the technosciences to disrupt the ecological dynamics of the Earth, science is in desperate need of learning from the very cultures it is helping to eradicate.[20]

Ideally, the current science wars would be replaced with science dialogues, an end to academic balkanization and bickering, and transdisciplinary research models. The new paradigm would construct a genuine "third culture" that dissolves rigid barriers between the technosciences and the humanities, as it advances innovative modes of education and constructs linkages to the public sphere. If the champions of scientific inquiry and objectivity were true to their ideals, they would welcome postmodern debates and challenges, and engage them in a fair and open-minded way. The world has much to gain from science, yet many philosophers, social theorists, and people in cultural studies continue to ignore contemporary science or attack it in superficial ways. But science also has a lot to learn from sociologists, historians, philosophers, activists, and the public. In his book *Dreams of a Final Theory* (1994), physicist Steven Weinberg claims that contemporary philosophy—unlike, say, Descartes and Leibniz in the seventeenth century—has contributed nothing to the development of science. One might just as well ask what Weinberg and other positivists have contributed to the understanding of ethics, social theory, cultural studies, linguistics, or ethnography. If it is true that philosophers and social theorists of the last few decades have not significantly advanced mathematics, medicine, genetics, or experimental methodology, they have made enormous contributions to understanding the political, ethical, social, and ecological implications and epistemology of science.

BIOLOGY AND THE NEW SEARCH FOR ORDER

> There is a new biology in the making . . . and with it a new vision of our relationships with organisms and with nature in general.
> —BRIAN GOODWIN

> We need a new biology, or should we say an old one?—for its holistic aspirations are redolent of a pre-Darwinian worldview. It must be a biology that asserts the primacy of processes over events, of relationships over entities, and of development over structure.
> —TIM INGOLD

As dramatic discoveries and changes were overtaking the physical sciences during the last few decades, equally bold innovations were shaping the biological sciences, signaling a postmodern turn. By the 1960s, a new paradigm had emerged in biology, one organized around theories of holism, ecology, complexity, coevolution, and the self-organization of living organisms. In place of deterministic conceptions of natural selection and matter as something static and stable, the postmodern turn in biology advances a new view of nature as dynamic, self-organizing, interrelated levels of complex systems. Evolutionary and holistic theories have emerged as increasingly powerful explanatory tools, as the biological sciences provide new maps for thinking about physics, mathematics, and technology. Yet just as physics has not thrown out Newton and mechanistic descriptions altogether, but has instead qualified and absorbed classical theories in a new framework, so emergent biological theories grant partial validity to Darwin's concepts of inheritance and natural selection, as both scientific domains interact and co-construct more comprehensive views of the universe.

Mirroring developments in physics, theorists like Richard Dawkins proclaimed the end of biological science with the neo-Darwinian synthesis of natural selection and genetics (see Horgan 1996). While such complacency congealed in some quarters of biology, other areas already were being radically transformed. Numerous theorists advanced critiques of determinist theories of natural selection and genetics; mechanistic definitions of matter, organisms, and animals; and atomistic methodologies that fragment networks of nature as they compartmentalize knowledge itself. In many ways, biology mapped the path physics would later follow. Time, development, ecology, and holistic outlooks first emerged in mid-19th century biology, while physics was still mired in mechanism, determinism, reductionism, and a static view of nature. Yet physics also has been trying to catch up with the lead of its own 19th- and 20th-century innovations, most importantly, the second law of thermodynamics (entropy), Boltzmann's theory of probabilities, Poincaré's mathematics of chaos, and the antideterminism and antirealism of dominant interpretations of quantum mechanics.

Thus, postmodern turns in physics and biology are not unrelated. It used to be thought that the difference between the two sciences was that physics dealt with hard laws, nonchanging matter, and quantitative phenomena, while biology analyzed changing forms of life that do not allow for rigorous quantification and law-like status. But this neat separation of the sciences has proved to be inaccurate on two counts. First, physics is not as exact as scientists once thought it was, and emergent theories of probability, indeterminism, and uncertainty are gaining prominence. Also, inorganic matter is now seen as active and changing, just like organic life; consequently, there are novel approaches to the unity of all forms of matter and applications of evolutionary theory to physics and the entire cosmos (see below). Second, contemporary theories of biology see organic life also as governed by laws: the new "laws of complexity." Hence, like physicists, biologists strive to quantify their field and develop TOE-talizing theories of their own.

Just as physics is becoming more biological and evolutionary, biology is growing more physical and mathematical, describing life processes in more precise dynamical terms. Both sciences are alike in becoming increasingly reliant on computers for research. The quantification of biology is especially dramatic in the genetic sciences organized around computer-based sequencing technologies. Although not unproblematically (see below), a new master discourse is emerging, "complexity theory," that cuts across the inorganic/organic boundary line to form a shared framework for postmodern physicists and biologists, becoming a driving force of "consilience." Complexity theory is even more comprehensive than superstring theory, for it encompasses physics, biology, and the natural and social worlds (including economics and technology) in one holistic mapping.

As biologist Brian Goodwin puts it, "Similar types of dynamic behavior arise from complex systems, irrespective of their material composition" (1994: 171). Physicist-chemist Ilya Prigogine holds that notions such as "dissipative structures," which describe the spontaneous emergence of order out of chaos, apply to all levels of life. In particular, Prigogine believes that the new understanding of nature as governed by dynamic, unstable, self-organizing processes unites the sciences of inorganic and organic matter, creating a state where the "descriptions of nature as presented by biology and physics now begin to converge" (1996: 162). Still more generally, physicist Murray Gell-Mann observes that "an emerging synthesis has started to bring together in a new way material from a great number of different fields in the physical, biological, and behavioral sciences and even in the arts and humanities" (1994: ix).

Under the rubric of complexity theory, seemingly all disciplines—including physics, economics, computer programming, technology, social analysis, and even history and literary criticism (see Hayles 1990, 1991, 1999; Waldrop 1992)—are deploying models of complex systems. One could see complexity theory as an extension of, rather than a break from, modern science. In contrast, Fritjof Capra, a physicist and major advocate of the postmodern turn in science, reads complexity theory as effecting a paradigm shift. It offers a "new understanding of life" and a "new perception of reality" that constructs a "unified view of mind, matter, and life" (1996: xix). The world picture of complexity theory, Capra argues, has revolutionary implications for all fields of knowledge, as well as for "business, politics, health care, education, and everyday life" (1996: 3). For Brian Goodwin, complexity theory entails a participatory approach to knowledge that bridges objective and subjective, analytic and synthetic, factual and value-oriented modes of knowing, and has great import for restoring health and balance to all living things and relations. If we understand organisms as more than mere survival machines, and see them instead as "centers of autonomous action and creativity" (1994: xii), we have the opportunity to adopt a new sensibility toward the natural world.

According to the postmodern turn in biology, life-forms are sophisticated organisms, not simple machines, as early modern biology, under the spell of Newtonian physics, interpreted the organic world. Transcending the dualisms constructed in the centuries-long debate in the modern tradition between mechanism and vitalism (which interprets life as a process infused with spirit), postmodern biology explains the living world through an evolutionary meta-narrative that describes emerging order and complexity. Yet the new biologies eschew the teleological position that there is a purpose or goal to natural processes. The emergent view sees organic life in terms of nondetermined (by environment or genes), self-regulating, self-organizing systems that tend toward greater levels of order and complexity, both within their own structure and in their interrelationships with other organisms in biological networks and ecosystems. Only when humans fully understand how intricately and delicately balanced are all living things can they begin to respect and preserve nature and life, or to alter the world in safe and responsible ways.

Complexity and self-organization theory are directly related, since complex systems are self-organizing and self-organizing systems generate complexity. Self-organization theory traces its origins to the 1950s and cybernetic theorists. Using experiments that anticipated Stuart Kauffman's (1995) efforts to simulate cellular differentiation with computer punch cards and lightbulb networks, they discovered that order was an emergent property of randomly programmed binary network models. Out of an infinity of possible interactions, a relatively limited number occur such that order emerges out of "chaos." Relatedly, complexity theory, pioneered by Prigogine and others, emerged in the 1960s and 1970s as a scientific analysis of dynamic systems with spontaneous and unpredictable behavior, mapped by nonlinear equations. Today it is used to characterize everything from ecosystems to the human heart and brain to the stock market. Unlike "closed systems" that do not interact with their environment, remain in conditions "near equilibrium," and suffer entropic breakdown, complex systems are "open" in that they exchange energy, matter, and information with their surroundings and exist in conditions "far-from-equilibrium." Turbulence, change, and instability frequently cause an open system to spontaneously reorganize itself in new structures and forms of behavior at a higher level of order and complexity, just as a turn of a kaleidoscope changes the entire pattern of colors and shapes. For Kauffman, evolution itself evolves on the "the edge of chaos," on the dialectical plane of stability and instability. Thus, in the postmodern paradigm, the relation between order and disorder is reconstructed from one of antithesis to one of complementarity.

Important changes transpired in the 1920s with the emergence of organismic biology (which saw living organisms as integrated and evolving wholes); cybernetics and systems theory in the 1940s (advanced by Norbert Weiner, John von Neuman, and others); self-organization theory in the 1950s; and Gaia, coevolution, and complexity theories in the 1960s and 1970s. Subsequently, there has been a powerful reaction to the static, atomistic, mechanistic outlook of modern science and the fragmentation of scientific disciplines. It is evident in the work of Lynn Margulis and Dorion Sagan (1986), for example, whose theory of coevolution and "symbiogenesis" emphasized cooperation over competition in nature and demonstrated that organisms evolve in rich relations of interdependence, rather than in a one-to-one correspondence with their physical surroundings. Similarly, James Lovelock's (1979, 1988) studies showed Gaia (Greek: the Earth) to be a densely interwoven web of ecosystems, organisms, and matter, where every nonliving and living element—rivers, rocks, volcanoes, trees, soil, microorganisms, animals, and so on—interact and contribute to the harmony of the whole. On Lovelock's view, the Earth is a vast superorganism or self-regulating system where living beings and the environment form each other, or rather, coevolve in a single evolutionary process.

Together, Margulis and Sagan and Lovelock overturned the view that life simply adapts to a passive and static background, demonstrating instead that life shapes the environment that in turn affects it. Demolishing the mechanistic assumptions of modern biology, Margulis and Sagan, Lovelock, and numerous others advanced new concepts of holism, complexity, nonequilibrium, coevolution, and self-organization. "The great shock of twentieth-century science," Capra writes,

> has been that systems cannot be understood by analysis. The properties of the parts are not intrinsic properties, but can be understood only within the context of the larger whole. Thus, the relationship between the parts and the whole has been reversed. In the systems approach the properties of the parts can be understood only from the organization of the whole. Accordingly, systems thinking concentrates not on basic building blocks, but on basic principles of organization. Systems thinking is "contextual," which is the opposite of analytical thinking. Analysis means taking something apart in order to understand it, systems thinking means putting it into the context of a larger whole. (1996: 29–30)

Proponents of holism claim that parts are explained by the whole, rather than the whole being merely the sum of its parts, each of which, mechanistic theorists assert, can be isolated and precisely controlled without significant consequences to its context. In this paradigm, however, linear Western metaphors such as trees, foundations, and hierarchies make no sense, since there are no elemental building blocks to which life can be reduced; rather, there is only a limitless "web," "network," or "feedback loop" of relations. In the new maps of life, nothing is viewed as self-sufficient or elementary; everything is inseparably embedded in networks and patterns of organization governed by complex feedback loops. Thus, the classic fallacy of genetic determinism—a one-way, inexorable chain of influence moving from DNA to RNA to protein to behavior—ignores the influences of one gene on many traits. It also occludes the impact of many genes on a single trait and of genes on one another, as well as the relation between genes and the organism as a whole and organisms and their social environment (see Lewontin 1992; Lewontin et al. 1984).

What is objectionable about "reductionism" is not the search for fundamental causes, but the way modern scientific epistemology (parallel to visions in much of modern philosophy and politics) breaks up integral relations, divorcing "parts" from the whole and destroying unity without rebuilding it. At the crossroads of a postmodern turn, the future of the biological sciences is open and indeterminate. The emergence of new holistic approaches can steer science toward ecology, respect for life, value thinking, and public responsibility. Or, shaped by the logic of genetic engineering, science could travel further down the road of reductionism, blind manipulation of living processes, and the rush to patent genes and transgenic species. Similarly, the decoding of the human genome could lead to a sense of shared community and decline in hostilities among different groups. After all, less than a fraction of a percent of our DNA codes for superficial traits such as skin color. Conversely, it could bring new forms of elitism and discrimination as it intensifies racism and the commodification of the body. The public could be the big winners of the genetic revolution, with the possibility of cures for debilitating and fatal diseases. By contrast, scientists-bioentrepeneurs could gain complete control over human genes and commandeer the evolutionary process.

Consequently there are strong tensions in the field of biology today. Here too science is a highly contested terrain, with battles whose outcomes are of enormous consequence. The kind of struggles shaping science are evident in the battle to define the meaning and import of the holistic sciences themselves, specifically, ecology, chaos and complexity theory, and self-organization theory. These sciences are being applied to many domains of economic and social life, often serving as legitimating ideologies for the new technologies and global capitalism.

Coopting the New Sciences: Kevin Kelly and Co.

> [There is] a singular unity between simple life, machines, complex systems, and us. . . . We are of one nature in the end.
> —KEVIN KELLY

> Metaphors are serious things. They affect one's practice.
> —STUART HALL

With modern conceptions of mechanism and determinism in decline, complexity theory has been appropriated by scientists, technology analysts, business theorists, and assorted ideologues to interpret society, the economy, and the Internet as organisms, ecologies, and complex and self-organizing systems. Certain misappropriations see all reality, natural and social, as one vast, undifferentiated system rooted in self-organizing dynamics—Schelling's "night where all cows are black" as criticized by Hegel. The theorization of society and the economy through biological metaphors such as self-organization has definite advantages over the mechanistic paradigm. It enables one, for example, to grasp evolutionary dynamics and the protean and richly interconnected activities of global capitalism with its networked society, Internet, international markets, and world culture. Yet these biological metaphors are also highly risky and subject to abuse, for one can easily lose sight of the crucial differences between biological and social systems, thereby reifying the social world as immutable even as one anthropomorphizes the natural world.

Not only is science itself a contested terrain, but its metaphors and discourses can be applied in conflicting and varying ways. "Self-organization," for example, can be read in a pro-ecological and anti-capitalist way, implying that natural systems thrive when they organize on their own apart from disruptive forms of human intervention. By contrast, when transferred from nature to economics, "self-organization" can be articulated in an antiecological and procapitalist way, suggesting that the market is self-regulating and therefore should not be tampered with by government and legal regulations. Similarly, self-organization can entail a progressive politics where "emergent order" is brought to society from below through democratization and popular struggles, or it can mean workers' input into corporate agendas. In its frequent applications to society and the economy, the term "organizing" obscures the disorganizing effects of capitalism and suggests capitalist societies are on a continual march toward ever greater complexity and order (on "disorganized capitalism," see Offe 1985; Lash and Urry 1987). To say, moreover, that capitalism is "self-organized" occludes the ways that elite economic agents and powers consciously shape the system and its laws to their will (though certainly not always with foresight and success). It also overlooks the intervention of the state to promote economic order, and the manner in which class struggle and the struggles of various social agents influence economic and social policies. The claim that society, like an organism, is "self-organizing" homogenizes social diversity and reduces multiplicity into a unified "self."

Informed by cryptolibertarian or neoliberal politics, and completely lacking a critical theory of society, many complexity theorists manage little more than to repackage the hoariest free market and social Darwinist ideologies for a global capitalism where social regulation is everywhere in decline. The politics of the new scientific theories is perhaps most clearly evident in the work of Kevin Kelly, editor of *Wired* magazine and a promoter of new technological and economic thinking. Kelly displays the metaphoric penchant that defines the economy as a self-organizing mechanism, regulated by the feedback mechanisms of the market and evolving most efficiently on its own logic. The organic paradigm in economics thereby revives the naturalist metaphysics of Adam Smith and Friedrich Hayek, each of whom posited, in Smith's terms, an "invisible hand," a law-like power that will magically steer competitive behavior in the market toward endless growth and the greater social good.

Following the fathers of laissez-faire economics, Kelly attacks top-down economic management and centralized attempts to regulate business on the grounds that the economy is too complex to rationally control, that prices and market mechanisms provide the most efficacious feedback loops, and that "spontaneous order" emerges from the hustle and bustle of trade (1995: 121–122). The ideological implications of his pseudoscientific theory are transparent: the anarchic system of capitalism is the only economy that can bring growth, progress, and prosperity to citizens. In his first book, *Out of Control* (1995), Kelly argued that if machines and computer programs were allowed to run freely and to find their own behaviors and solutions to problems, they would be far more efficient than if human engineers tried to steer them. In his second book, *New Rules For the New Economy* (1998), he applies the same ideas to economics and politics, but where human beings and social institutions are involved there are quite different implications. "We let the network of objects govern itself as much as possible," Kelly says, "we add government when needed" (1998: 19).[21]

Just where any form of restraint of capitalist power and greed might be necessary (e.g., regulation of airline and automobile safety or genetically modi-fied foods), Kelly doesn't say. On the whole, he thinks that our socioeconomic system, sciences, and technologies are just fine and do not need much tinker-ing or cocontrol. His political philosophy advances a Reaganesque "govern-ment-off-your-back" standpoint that might seem to be freedom-loving, but it translates into corporate hegemony and the capitulation of government re sponsibility to protect the health, safety, and rights of citizens. Similarly, in the world of business, Kelly advocates decentralization and allowing the "dumb swarm" of workers to operate independently, in order to advance the creativity that can only come from below. Workers will nevertheless need the leadership of college-educated management. Kelly therefore rules out in advance the possibility of direct democracy in society at large and workers' control in orga-nizations, and he perpetuates an exploitative class hierarchy. In Kelly, poten-tially progressive implications of decentralization themes are rerouted into a reactionary and elitist framework that gives an individual no more dignity than the queen bee grants to a drone, assigning workers worth only as value pro-ducers for the corporate hive.

Kelly fetishizes the existing capitalist system by making social processes look like natural ones, thereby naturalizing the odious forms of exploitation and domination in contemporary capitalism. For Kelly and others, the econ-omy is/is like an ecological system by being richly interconnected, rife with coevolving relations, and in constant flux and disequilibrium. They viewed the economy as a self-organizing system with intricate feedback loops; like evolu-tion and life itself, it thrives on the "edge of chaos." Taking a page out of Stuart Kauffman, Kelly writes: "If the [social] system settles into harmony and equi-librium, it will eventually stagnate and die" (1998: 11). Thus, the goal of the new network economy is perpetual innovation, dynamic disequilibrium, and cycles of stability and disruption. Here too we see the politically regressive im-plications of ecological metaphors, since the economy-as-dynamic-system re-quires constant change to thrive.

Behind the celebration of "flux," "disequilibrium," and "innovation" is an embrace of Joseph Schumpeter's (1962) conception of "creative destruction" and his notion of the entrepreneur as the source of innovative vitality in capi-talism. Schumpeter is becoming the new dominant ideologue of capital, re-vered by Kelly, Gilder, and other apologists for the new capitalism. Celebration of the market, the entrepreneur, and the need to destroy passé economic and governmental forms has become the new religion. These paeans provide the ideological thrust behind Reaganism/Thatcherism/Clintonism, and the two Bushes, articulated in a neo-Schumpeterian discourse that is replacing Keynesianism as the dominant ideology, and which is evident in Kelly's hype for the new economy:

> Economist Joseph Schumpeter calls the progressive act of destroying success "creative destruction." It's an apt term. Letting go of perfection requires a brute act of will. And it can be done badly. Management guru Tom Peters claims that corporate leaders are now being asked to do two tasks—building up and then nimbly tearing down—and that these two tasks require such diametrically opposed temperaments that the same person cannot do both. He impishly suggests that a company in the fast-moving terrain of the network economy ordain a Chief Destruction Officer. (1998: 86)

Economic success requires constant innovation that involves tearing down as well as creating.[22] But Kelly seems oblivious to the fact that capitalist "creative destruction" does not merely entail the "destruction" of past successes in the drive to continually construct something new, but also involves the destruction of firms, competitors, communities, traditional cultures, workers' lives and families, wildlife, and the environment in the constant lust to accumulate profit and revolutionize production. Kelly's chapter 8 ("No Harmony, All Flux") also celebrates in neo-Schumpeterian fashion change, "future shock" (Toffler is also a major influence), flux, and disequilibrium, a form of "perpetual disruption" and turbulence that Kelly, as in his earlier writings, associates with nature itself.

Kelly never considers the social effects of driving economic systems to the edge of chaos, toward endless innovation and disequilibrium, and he fails to imagine alternative conceptions of economics that would involve planning and democratic input. While a prolonged period of "harmony" might indeed spell death for social and natural systems, this depends on what one means by "harmony." Kelly rules out in advance a nonstagnating "stability" as a desideratum for a social order. Surely a genuinely democratic and ecological economy would have to be dynamic, but Kelly's values fall on the side of disequilibrium and disruption rather than a more balanced conception.

Moreover, Kelly and other ideologues of the new economy fail to see that changes from one "social system" to another are not a result of "self-organization," "critical thresholds," or "evolutionary peaks," but rather are determined by socioeconomic crisis, corporate reorganization, and intense competition and struggle. Metaphors like "subcritical economics," "threshold points" of growth, and "phase transitions" of the system, to say nothing of ideological and oxymoronic terms like "friction-free capitalism" (Gates 1995), simply obscure the all-too-real impact of a growth and profit-driven system on human beings and the natural world. Such phrases reveal that the Achilles heel of complexity theory is its uncritical approach to sociopolitical realities and corporate power. They demonstrate the problems inherent in a GUT-like conflation of dynamics which collapses the natural into the social world.

This ideological maneuver is most blatant in Stuart Kauffman, who boldly declares that "our social institutions evolve as expressions of deep natural principles" (1995: 304). For Kauffman, the same "general laws govern [both natural and social] phenomena ranging from the Cambrian explosion to our postmodern technological era" (1995: 16). What, however, are these "general laws"? Presumably, both natural selection and self-organization, but we have seen that the latter is problematic when applied to society, while the former entails a vicious social Darwinism. The only "laws" of capitalism are the socially constructed need for profit, which mandates exploitation, accumulation, and endless growth, dynamics around long enough to form only a blip on the human timeline. How capitalist "laws" play out is determined by political struggle and not through a self-organizing system, by forces that include social classes, government agencies, giant and small corporations, grassroots groups, and individuals. Kauffman imagines breakthrough insights into democracy with complexity theory, but seems to think the latter guarantees the former (1995: 28). Democracy does indeed involve complex "feedback loops"—a cybernetic metaphor dear to complexity theorists when they speak of natural or social systems—among appointed representatives or between delegates and citizens. But obviously these communication channels are often short-circuited in our current technocracy. A better metaphor would be a moebius strip, a nonstop, one-way track from the corporate and military worlds to the political world and back again, ad infinitum, oblivious to the urgent needs of citizens.

The totalizing and ideological application of systems theory, ecology, and complexity theory is not a mistake made by Kelly alone; it is epidemic in the genre celebrating the New Economy and is blatantly on display in thinkers like Kaufman and Capra who lack political and social insight. For all their learning and interdisciplinary emphases, Kauffman, Kelly, Capra, and their ilk. apparently have never encountered Giambattista Vico, Wilhelm Dilthey, Paul Ricoeur, Jürgen Habermas, and others who have advanced powerful critiques of the positivist conflation of nature and society, nor have they learned the ABC's of social oppression, injustice, and inequality.

Complexity and self-organization theories, like any scientific theory (evolution, genetics, etc.), can thus be deployed for different political agendas.[23] We distinguish between a conservative approach that appropriates complexity and self-organization discourse to legitimate global capitalism and elite control, and a critical perspective that reads these concepts as supporting ecology, sustainability, and participatory democracy. It is not that both positions are of equal worth, or that their import is impossibly indeterminate. Accurately examined, chaos, complexity, and self-organization theory underline well-established facts about the interconnectedness and fragility of ecosystems. Postmodern theories emphasize the inability of human beings to impose arrogant and simplistic methods of "control" without causing great damage to nature, wildlife, and ultimately themselves. If one insists on applying the new sciences to society, and of society—and not simply the market abstracted from its socio-political context!—can be read as a complex, self-organizing system, then participatory democracy seems to be the best way to interpret and attain the "emergent order" and dynamic "feedback loops" that stem from bottom-up processes.

Although Gaia theory informs us that the Earth has remarkable powers of self-regulation and self-regeneration, these powers are being irrevocably weakened in an age of global warming, rain forest destruction, desertification, overpopulation, species extinction, and genetic engineering of crops. The inherently ecological implications of complexity theory are thus occluded through the transmogrification of nature into economy. Even if applied to the capitalist marketplace rather than to the natural world, ecological, complexity, and self-organization metaphors and theories fail miserably, since they suggest that governments either have not intervened in "self-organizing" markets or never should intervene. The separation of state and economy is a capitalist fable and a monumental misreading of social facts since the market and the business world are propped up daily by the state through corporate welfare policies, outrageous levels of military spending, and government subsidies. Complete deregulation, if realized, would spell disaster for public safety, democracy, biodiversity, and the environment.

High Noon at "Jurassic Park": Technofantasies Confront Complexity

> Living systems are not like mechanical systems. Living systems are never in equilibrium. They are inherently unstable. They may seem stable, but they're not. Everything is moving and changing. In a sense, everything is on the edge of collapse.
> —ARNOLD, IN JURASSIC PARK

> In a world where the artifactual and the natural have imploded, nature itself, both ideologically and materially, has been patently reconstructed. Structural adjustment demands no less of bacteria and trees as well as of people, business, and nations.
> —DONNA HARAWAY

> The biotech ride has just begun.
> —BUSINESS WEEK

Unlike some academic and ideological versions of the new sciences, the critical and ecological import of chaos, complexity, and self-organization theories is vividly manifest in numerous popular texts. Science fiction (SF) and media culture frequently dramatize the fact that there are limits to nature that science and technology ought not to transcend; if they do, horrible unforeseen consequences and monstrosities will result. In countless novels, films, and television series of the last few decades, one sees key recurrent themes—the "revenge" of nature and the "rebellion" of technology—as both natural and technological systems follow the dynamics of their own complexity rather than the mandates of human will. With rare exceptions like *Star Trek* and the *Star Wars* films, media culture tends to demonize science and typically depicts technology as a destructive force thwarting simplistic human attempts at control as it wreaks havoc on human life and the environment.

More specifically, in the biocybernetic era that synthesizes genetic engineering and computers, there are numerous warnings against altering the DNA blueprints of life. In David Cronenberg's *The Fly* (1986), a scientist engaged in dangerous experiments with genetic fusion accidentally mixes the DNA of a fly with his own DNA, dooming himself to increasingly grotesque mutations (see Chapter 5). In *Species* (1995), genetic information received from outer space is recklessly fused with human genes, thereby creating a new organism that rapidly evolves, destroys human life, and breeds uncontrollably. *Godzilla* (1998) underscores the issue of genetic mutations that result from radioactive fallout from nuclear tests, which has caused countless deaths and suffering since the 1940s. *Deep Blue Sea* (1999) dramatizes what can go awry in gene therapy conducted with the best intentions (to cure Alzheimer's disease) when huge sharks with advanced brains turn on the scientists who engineered them.

Recurrent images of altered species in numerous SF films and TV shows like *The X-Files* underscore widespread anxieties that we are now confronting a "fifth discontinuity" involving the frightening mutation of existing life forms or the creation or discovery of altogether new species. This notion builds on the framework of Bruce Mazlish (1993), who postulates that the multiple adventures of modern identity construction and deconstruction involve the dramas and conflicts of crossing four "discontinuities." First, beginning with Copernicus, human beings had to bridge the gulf between the earth and the universe to accept the fact that the sun, not the earth, is the center of our solar system. Second, Darwin compelled humanity to examine its evolutionary past and rethink the alleged great divide between itself and animals. In a third discontinuity, Freud showed that reason is not even master of its own domain, for its operations are determined by the will, instincts, affects, and the unconscious. Finally, today as technology advances to the point of creating human-like computers and robots, and we become ever more like cyborgs, humanity is forced to question its self-proclaimed ontological divide from machines and to question a fourth discontinuity.

Since the opening of modernity, then, human beings have had to confront four major discontinuities which they had created in order to establish their alleged radical uniqueness and special status. In each case, "rational man" had to rethink its identity to overcome false dichotomies and illusions of separation from the cosmos, the animal world, the unconscious, and the machines it had invented. Yet, despite what Mazlish suggests, the process of identity construction prompted by science and technological innovations is not over: we envision yet another yawning gulf—a *fifth discontinuity*—that poses still more challenges to human identity and perhaps to our very survival.

The fifth discontinuity opens with the *possibility* of discovering other forms of life in the cosmos, and the *actuality* of species mixing, the creation of new life forms through genetic engineering, and widespread cloning. As yet no signs of life in the cosmos have been detected but our own, and "contact," to the best of our knowledge, is still the stuff of SF. But we have already begun to tear down species boundaries by transplanting the blood and organs of baboons, pigs, and other animals into human bodies (xenotransplantation), thereby raising the specter of releasing deadly transmissible diseases like AIDS. Corporate capital has also created hundreds of transgenic plant and animal species through biotechnology and "pharming" by mixing the DNA of two different species to create an altogether new species—such as when human genes are spliced into pig genes to make pigs grow larger and faster. Another frightening discontinuity, however, involves the production of new intelligent machines that might prove themselves superior to humans and displace the supremacy and centrality of *Homo sapiens* in the "great chain of being" (see our discussion in Chapter 4 and the Epilogue).

At the turn of the 20th century, H. G. Wells's novels *The Island of Dr. Moreau* (1996 [1896]) and *The Food of the Gods* (1965 [1904]) anticipated disasters wrought by the manipulation of life (see Chapter 4). More recently, Michael Crichton's novel *Jurassic Park* (1990) and its film adaptation directed by Steven Spielberg (1993), portrays the debacles awaiting the world of genetic engineering. Both *The Island of Dr. Moreau* and *Jurassic Park* are set on distant islands, symbolic of the isolation of science from the public and its critical scrutiny. Yet where Dr. Moreau conducts his experiments in secrecy, John Hammond, the financial backer of Jurassic Park, has constructed a theme park and, once the furtive stage of his research is completed, hopes to allure millions to see the main attraction: genetically reconstructed dinosaurs.[24] On both islands, scientists engineer transgenic species, but their schemes are colossal failures as the chimeras they create rebel, rampage, and kill humans. Whereas Wells only imagines a time when science could genetically engineer new species, Crichton writes while the process is well underway, and he uses literary mappings to criticize the problems inherent in biotechnology.

Monsanto, Novartis, Du Pont, and other corporations have already created and patented hundreds of transgenic bacteria, viruses, plants, animals, and human tissues, and they have cloned animals such as mice, frogs, pigs, sheep, and bulls. Appealing to a Lockean definition of property, a 1980 Supreme Court ruling declared that genetically altered life-forms are legitimate inventions that can be patented and owned, thereby opening the floodgates for the commodification of DNA. The precautionary principle has been thrown to the wind: little or no testing is done to ensure the safety of people or ecosystems as the consequence of release of transgenic organisms. Moreover, the legal system freely grants patent rights and denies the public the right to know if their food is genetically modified, and Congress and the Clinton administration have aggressively pursued U.S. global dominance in biotechnology. In addition, the U.S. Food and Drug Administration suppressed warnings from their own top scientists that genetically modified foods are unsafe and lies routinely.[25] In this context, Crichton's "Preface" to *Jurassic Park* decries a genetic revolution whose research is "done in secret, and in haste, and for profit" (1990: xi).[26] Crichton moves seamlessly from scientific fact to fiction, as he proceeds to tell of secret experiments with the genetic engineering and cloning of animals on a remote island near Costa Rica, suggesting today's surreality may be tomorrow's reality.

The fictional Hammond represents the way life science industries and all too many scientists actually think. A mouthpiece for capitalist values and commodified science, Hammond insists, "We can never forget the ultimate object of the project in Costa Rica—to make money . . . lots of money" (62).[27] Animals, nature, and science are mere means to his end. For him, life is reduced to sequences of DNA codes. Rather than consider the staggering implications of bioengineering, such as tampering with intricately evolved ecosystems and genomes, Hammond states, "We didn't want to wait. We have investors to consider" (122). In fact, there is now a mad "gene rush" underway, comparable to the untrammeled greed of the gold rushes over a century ago, as scientists, universities, and corporations scramble to patent the DNA, cells, seeds, blood, and tissues of life. The imperialism that drove European colonialists into the Americas for slaves and booty is paralleled today by the rapacious "biopiracy" and "bioprospecting" of corporations who plunder the seeds and crops of Southern nations, while making slight genetic modifications that enable them to call natural phenomena their own, and then selling back what was once free and available to all (see Shiva 1993, 1997). Even the blood of people around the world are raided for rare genes that could be patented, giving new meaning to Marx's excoriation of capitalists as "vampires."

Hammond is not only a quintessential capitalist, he is also an unrepentant modernist, avowing that "there's absolutely no problem with the island" (61)—a gospel of certainty and control shared by his technical crew. Clearly, *Jurassic Park* is less an attack on genetic engineering per se than an all-out assault on the modern scientific paradigm that Crichton believes is moribund and dangerous. But Crichton also establishes that a new paradigm is emerging, one rooted in the ideas of Heisenberg, Godel, and chaos theory. This framework is voiced by the mathematician Ian Malcolm (obviously Crichton's mouthpiece). With Nietzchean grandeur, Malcolm announces that (modern) science is dead: "The dream of total control—has died, in our century. . . . We are witnessing the end of the [modern] scientific era" (313). Malcolm rarely misses a chance to discuss the new, emerging paradigm rooted in chaos theory, nonlinear mathematics, and the concept of unpredictability, to warn that the concept of the park is completely unworkable. Even before arriving at the park, Malcolm states, "There is a problem with that island. It is an accident waiting to happen" (76). The project is impossible, he knows, because Jurassic Park technicians are trying to engineer complexity with the mentality of simplicity. But "what we call 'nature' is in fact a complex system of far greater subtlety than we are willing to accept" (91).[28]

Thus, the technological and biological systems at Jurassic Park break down catastrophically. Weakened by over 130 "glitches" in their programming, the computers collapse. The dinosaurs—genetic pastiches of dinosaur and frog DNA—are designed to reproduce under controlled conditions, but they spontaneously switch genders, breed at will, and rampage through the park. Malcolm impugns Hammond and his scientists for their ecological ignorance: "You create new life forms, about which you know nothing. Your Dr. Wu [the chief genetic engineer] does not even know the names of the things he is creating. . . . [Y]ou expect them to do your bidding, because you made them and you therefore think you own them; you forget that they are alive, that they have an intelligence of their own" (305–306). This jeremiad applies equally well to bioengineers throughout the world who do not know the basic genetic preconditions of life, the function of some genes, how they interact, and what the long-term consequences may be from tampering with the DNA of plants, bacteria, animals, and human beings. But in a situation where economics and politics overwhelms proper science, genetic experiments advance rapidly and unimpeded, for billions of dollars and control of global markets are at stake.

The Cartesian engineers at Jurassic Park are oblivious to a central lesson of self-organization. In Malcolm's words, "Life escapes all barriers. Life breaks free. Life expands into new territories. Painfully, even dangerously" (159). In the annals of biological history, there are thousands of examples of plant and animal species escaping into or deliberately being transplanted to nonnative ecosystems which they rapidly undermine or destroy (see Bright 1998); African "killer bee" are a dramatic contemporary example. In the form of "genetic pollution" today, transgenic crops such as rapeseed (canola) and Bt corn contaminate neighboring nonengineered fields of grain, spread their traits to their weedy relatives, and increase weed and pest resistance to chemicals. They also create superweeds and superpests immune to the strongest chemicals, deplete the soils, and contribute to species extinction by promoting monocultures. Similarly, just as transgenic AIDS mice could breed out of control to create a super-AIDS mouse that might pass the virus onto human beings, genetically modified fish could easily breed or outcompete with wild fish populations. Further, genetically altered trees could crowd out natural forests and undermine food webs and ecosystems, while "miracle foods" engineered to have extra vitamins or edible vaccines (such as "golden rice") could transfer their genes to other plants and disrupt the environment.

Decontextualized from ethics, ecology, and social responsibility, today's genetic sciences all too often involve what Malcolm terms "thintelligence," a dangerous one-dimensional, reductionist mind-set that is blind to the social and historical context of science and to the ethical and ecological implications of radical interventions into natural processes. Still, despite Crichton's "Preface," which emphasizes the commercialization of science and the conflation of science and industry, he tends to blame science alone for problems that ultimately stem from capital, global competition, and the profit imperative.

Jurassic Park both exploits and advances the current "dinomania," while creating potent symbols of global capitalism out of control. As W. J. T. Mitchell (1999) notes in his fascinating cultural study, dinosaurs are richly overdetermined and multivalent in meaning. Like Stephen Jay Gould (1993), Mitchell seeks to explain dinomania, but he rejects what he claims is Gould's ahistorical appeal to archetypes and he roots different images and perceptions of dinosaurs in commercial imperatives and changing social conditions. Just as the dragon dominated the medieval imagination, Mitchell sees the dinosaur as the quintessential "totem animal of modernity," since their remains were discovered only in the nineteenth century, they continue to capture the imagination of scientists and the public alike, and they eloquently symbolize current capitalist dynamics. The enormous size and monstrous nature of dinosaurs are convenient emblems of global capitalism. As rapacious eaters, moreover, dinosaurs are fitting icons of an energy-intensive social system and glutinous consumers whose lifestyles exact a heavy ecological price. Dinomania also might relate to human anxieties over extinction. The fact that powerful dinosaurs dominated the earth for 170 million years, and suddenly became extinct, underscores the contingency of *Homo sapiens*, whose future into the next 170 years, let alone the next 170 million, looks problematic.[29] Noting changing images in the structure and behavior of the dinosaur that, à la Jameson (1991), Mitchell relates to different cultural stages in the history of capitalism, he distinguishes between the huge, slow, slumbering dinosaur of the modern age of mechanical reproduction, such as the brontosaurus, and the fast, agile, multicolored, teamwork-oriented dinosaur of the postmodern era of biocybernetic reproduction, such as the velociraptor, representing a more flexible, downsized, and multicultural capitalism.

Jurassic Park itself is emblematic of the megaspectacles in demand today (see Chapter 5), from the billion-dollar extravaganzas of Universal Studios and Disney World to the wildlife parks in San Diego and Florida where tourists behold animals in simulated conditions. In the new social constructions of the "wild," nature, science, technology, capital, consumerism, entertainment, and education merge in a theme-park setting.[30] As Hammond says, Jurassic Park is "the most advanced amusement park in the world," a transgenic Disneyland for the whole family. In response to Hammond's worries that the dinosaurs are not fully "real," Wu reminds him, indeed, that "they're not real" and that "there isn't any reality here" (122). Wu engineers the dinosaurs not according to the best scientific knowledge about how they really behaved, but rather according to how tourists would expect them to behave. Thus, the dinosaurs are simulations, unwitting actors in a commodified "tourist performance" such as is enacted by "primitive" cultures in Southern nations who feign the mode of dance and behavior that matches tourist stereotypes.

In the age of genetic replication, Jurassic Park portends real things to come. The wildlife parks of the future may feature cloned animals (replicated from storage tanks in "frozen zoos") and transgenic species. No longer purely biological, but rather technological designs and creations, animals are becoming simulations of the real, hyperreal cyborgs, either mass reproductions of a model or transgenic pastiches of DNA. Science has already created a surreal zoo of mutations that include tobacco plants with firefly genes, mice and pigs with human genes, potatoes with chicken genes, fish and tomatoes with antifreeze genes, and dozens of different genetically modified foods spliced with bacteria, viruses, antibiotic-resistant marker genes, and insect genes.

Thus, as the postmodern adventure in science unfolds, boundaries are collapsing everywhere, in both the natural and the social worlds, collapsing differences among species (bacteria, plant, insect, animal, and human) and between biology and technology, transgressing the limits of what previously was declared improbable or impossible. From genes to galaxies, new technosciences are revolutionizing all areas of our understanding of nature, including cosmology.

LIVING IN THE MULTIVERSE: POSTMODERN TURNS IN COSMOLOGY

> Science began with the Promethean affirmation of the power of reason, but it seemed to end in alienation—a negation of everything that gives meaning to human life. Our belief is that our own age can be seen as one of a quest for a new type of unity in our vision of the world, and that science must play an important role in defining this new coherence.
> —ILYA PRIGOGINE

> We have begun to develop a view of the galaxy not as a collection of individual stars, but as a system, or even as an ecology. . . . What is most new about [post]modern cosmology is the discovery that the universe is also evolving.
> —LEE SMOLIN

Every human culture capable of wonder has a cosmology, a story of the origins of the universe and the place of the Earth and human beings in the universe at large. Whether mythopoetic, religious, or scientific, human cultures formulate stories of the nature of the universe and how it came to be. Cosmologies are integral to our self-identity, since they contextualize human existence in the broadest framework, that of life itself and its creation, and thereby assign meaning to daily struggles. In its traditional form, "Cosmology aims at articulating the story of the universe so that humans can enter fruitfully into the web of relationships within the universe" (Swimme and Berry 1992: 23). Cosmologies provide both quantitative and qualitative maps, linking us spatially and philosophically to the Earth and the universe. Cosmologies are not always benign, however, as throughout history they have been used as the basis for establishing power and legitimating social authority.

Until recently, "cosmology" was anathema in the scientific community, linked more with mythology, folklore, and superstition than with empirical observation and the experimental method. Only in this century, following tremendous advances in technologies used to map the stars, has cosmology been put on a genuine scientific basis, and thereby gained the respect and attention of scientists. In a co-construction dynamic stretching from Edwin Hubble's telescope observations in 1929 (be found evidence of an expanding universe through a spectroscope) to the Hubble Space Telescope (deployed in 1990 from the space shuttle *Discovery*), technological advance has shifted cosmological paradigms and fueled scientific innovation.[31] The Hubble Space Telescope is of profound importance. Thanks to its huge powers, in the last decade we have witnessed spectacular images of the birth and death of entire galaxies. The Cosmic Background Explorer (COBE) satellite project of 1992 mapped the microwave radiation across enormous distances of sky; COBE results gave scientists a long-awaited picture of the cosmos that apparently vindicated the Big Bang theory (Ferris 1997).

Crucial new mappings of the origin and structure of the universe are being gained through supercomputer simulations and robotic telescopes measuring distances to 100,000 galaxies dispersed across billions of light years of space. Orbiting x-ray telescopes may confirm the existence of massive black holes spinning around in space as they test the validity of Einstein's theories. Quantum physics has led to new methods of quantum computing, which in turn are shaping bizarre cosmologies premised on notions such as parallel universes, as they promise to boost computing power and the production of knowledge to unimaginable heights (see Brown 2000). Moreover, as robots probe the surface of Mars looking for water and other possible signs of past life that would challenge the ontological uniqueness of organic life on Earth, scientists and engineers are building an international space station that will provide a launchpad for new knowledges and cosmic adventures.

Unavoidably, technoscientific innovations give rise to new qualitative mappings. In the form of more philosophically oriented cosmologies, science has assumed a role previously held by philosophy. Now it offers the metaphysics and master narrative of our time. While all too many philosophers are saddled with sterile obsessions involving linguistic analysis and abstract speculation, scientists are providing ever more comprehensive views of reality and provocative speculations concerning the nature of life, consciousness, the origins and trajectory of the human species, religion, and other important issues. What the new cosmologists typically fail to see, however, is that science coevolves with society in general and thus appropriates cultural materials and metaphors.

It is no coincidence that as concepts such as scarcity and competition emerged as crucial for political economy in the early stages of imperialism and social domination, they also became central to the new evolutionary sciences. As Karl Marx observed, "It is remarkable that Darwin recognizes among brutes and plants his English society with its division of labor, competition, opening of new markets, 'inventions,' and Malthusian 'struggle for existence.' . . . [W]ith Darwin, the animal kingdom figures as bourgeois society" (cited in Krader 1982: 196). With the shift to a postindustrial capitalism, new scientific metaphors and paradigms appeared that theorized the "organism" in terms of bits of information, shifted from functionalist to cybernetic and systems theory explanations, and reduced physical bodies to data (Haraway 1991). Also, we have noted how the metaphors of self-organization and chaos and complexity theory have been assimilated by the ideologies of global capitalism to celebrate the seemingly "creative destruction" and disorder of the world economy, to naturalize its exploitation and plunder, and to put a positive gloss on its negative features.

Thus, cosmologies are constituted within a social context, and as such, often are influenced by, or are extensions of, social values and ideologies. Conversely, how human beings interpret the stars, planets, and natural world around them shapes how they understand their own societies. Critical postmodern cosmologies thus require self-reflection and constant scrutiny of their assumptions, metaphors, and discourses. While perceiving the coevolution and co-construction of science and society, one should be aware of their differences, and not illicitly read metaphors from one sphere into another. It is no coincidence that in the transition to the Industrial Revolution and a factory world, scientists were already envisioning the universe as a cosmic machine. At the same time, social theorists sought a science of society rooted in "laws" of human behavior, parallel to the "harmony" of the heavens, with everything and everyone in their assigned cultural orbit. The homologies between Isaac Newton and Adam Smith stemmed from each voicing a different application of the same mechanistic paradigm of modernity. Galileo, Newton, and Western science in general articulated a form of quantitative time and a mathematical projection of being that is congruent with technology as an efficient way to measure, master, organize, and save time, and with capitalism's numerical and instrumental orientation toward time, science, technology, and the organization of labor. Constructed in the modern framework, science, technology, and capitalism all foster an exploitative attitude toward nature and human beings, and promote similar worldviews, practices, and forms of industrial civilization. All three abstract from specificity and difference and tend to objectify and reify the phenomena under their purview. All three see nature and human beings as objects of domination and thus are equally constituent parts of the modern worldview, society, and modes of domination and control.

After its initial cryptoreligious appeal to God and natural law for political legitimation (the discourse of "self-evident" rights, along with deism and Leibnizian optimism), capitalism soon turned to science for its legitimating ideologies, first employing mechanism (physics), then Darwinism (biology). Whether religion or science, each provided capitalism with an eternal grounding for its markets, power systems, and individualist ideologies, ensuring to all that capitalism is Just, Right, and the Best of All Possible Worlds. Darwin drew his insight into the competition driving natural selection from the reactionary social theorist Thomas Malthus, who envisioned a near future where an overpopulated humanity would struggle over scare resources, and thereby projected a social metaphor into nature. So too, social Darwinists appealed to the bloody struggles of a nature "red in tooth and claw" to legitimate the competition among capitalists to control society, completing the loop of social/natural metaphors. But as science and society change, inevitably cosmologies will shift too. Thus, today, with the increasing power and prestige of the life sciences, science and social elites are constructing a postmodern cosmology directly influenced by cybernetics and genetic engineering (see below).

Presently, a dramatic transformation is occurring in cosmology that diminishes the boundaries between physics and biology and constructs an evolutionary theory of the universe that has potent implications for human identity. Coinciding with the postmodern turn in theory, arts, and the sciences, one finds, beginning in the 1980s, a clear shift toward a postmodern cosmology. Many scientists and cosmologists began forsaking modern models of the universe for new paradigms that reject atomistic logic for relational understanding and replace static laws with history and evolution. The new cosmological theories also abandon necessity for contingency, go beyond the logic of simplicity and determinism for new theories of complexity and self-organization, and renounce realism in favor of a hermeneutic approach to scientific understanding (see Toulmin 1982a, 1982b; Smolin 1997).[32] Whether consciously or unconsciously absorbed, scientific cosmology has felt the tremors of a postmodern shift in areas such as philosophy, social theory, and science in general.

The monolithic concept of a "universe," of a single, closed entity, massive as it may be, is being contested through the concept of a "multiverse," a potential infinity of (parallel) universes, each giving birth to another, interlinked, perhaps, through black holes. Just as contemporary science became accustomed to the idea that the universe is endless, filled with billions of galaxies, each with countless stars and planets, now it is confronted with the idea that *its* universe is merely one of a potential infinity of universes. This involves a radical extension of the first discontinuity opened by Copernicus, but leads into the fifth discontinuity that confronts the possibility of life elsewhere in the multiverse.

While the notions of an *expanding* universe and of an *evolving* universe are not the same, since the latter implies the generation of increasing complexity and diversity, cosmologists are advancing the concept that "the universe" is not simply a place, but a *process* that spawns life, that in some sense it is "alive." Accordingly, cosmological theory has taken a postmodern, evolutionary turn that challenges firm distinctions between physics and biology, between inorganic and organic matter, and elevates nonequilibrium thermodynamics, natural selection, self-organization, and ecology to universal principles. The synthesis of biology with physics "points the way to a new cosmology of the twenty-first century" (Gribbin 1993: xiv). Where some cosmologists see concepts like natural selection, competition, and self-organization as interesting metaphors or analogies useful for understanding galaxies or the universe, others insist that they are legitimate terms that deserve literal application (see Smolin 1997; Gribbin 1993).[33]

From the quarters of genetic engineering, Jeremy Rifkin (1998) identifies an emerging postmodern cosmology that radicalizes the modern idea that science and technology can transcend or suspend the laws and limits of nature. On this paradigm, nature is completely malleable, able to be made into anything science wishes, such that there are, at least in principle, no limits to the powers of technoscience. Some make the dubious claim that we are in the "age of biological control" (Wilmut et al. 2000). The new worldview— "algeny"—seeks to change the essence of things, to improve their function, and ultimately to "perfect" them. With genetic engineering and cloning technologies, human beings can now construct a designer reality out of raw materials that engineers can sample and mix as they please—a kind of genetic rapping—and try to seize the reins of evolution. In the biotech era, technoscience can alter reality to a greater degree than ever before, leading to a qualitatively different, postmodern organization of knowledge.

But these new developments are informed by the modern reductionist mentality that believes reality can be broken down into self-sufficient elements that can be manipulated without consequence to their surrounding "parts." Specifically, as in postmodern war (see Chapter 2), the genetic sciences resolve material reality into fragmented bits of information to be mapped by computers and manipulated by technology for purposes of power over nature and human beings. In the 17th century, this Cartesian mind-set was brutal and dangerous enough (e.g., in experiments on "animal machines"). In the 20th century, however, it informs the development and use of potent technologies such as atomic weapons, nuclear energy, genetic engineering, cloning, and nanotechnology.

The philosophical upshot of one articulation of postmodern cosmology is that instead of being viewed as standing alone and separate from the universe, human beings are seen as consummate expressions of the self-organization of matter and life: they carry cosmic dust and gases in their cells, Gaia's oceans in their blood, and the great apes in their DNA. For Smolin, self-organization cosmology overcomes the long-standing dualities in Western thought between matter and spirit, nature and freedom. It also enables a theory of a complex and dynamic universe without positing God or teleology (a position that seems vindicated by digital DNA, the self-organizing figures and patterns of artificial life [see Levy 1993]). The shift in scientific premises enables new conclusions to be drawn: "It is clear that if the natural state of matter is chaos, an external intelligence is needed to explain the order and beauty of the world. But if life, order, and structure are the natural state of the cosmos, then our existence, indeed our spirit, might finally be comprehended as created naturally, by the world, rather than unnaturally and in opposition to it" (Smolin 1997: 160). In this view, indeterminacy leads to an ontological integration of culture with nature, rather than, as with Jacques Monod's (1971) emphasis on chance, to our alienation from the cosmos. Instead of seeing human beings as absurd and fortuitous accidents in a world of random energy, Kauffman claims that there is "a sacredness, a law—something natural and inevitable about us" (1995: 99).

The new holism of self-organization need not take on such a problematic mystical quality as it does for Kauffman, who thinks he has deciphered the secrets of God. Nor need it entail the anthropic principle which, at least in one form, holds that the universe was designed for human beings (and consequently humanity is, after all, unique and privileged). Gribbin challenges this conclusion in his argument that the universe exists to produce stars, of which we are but a fortunate (and vainglorious) by-product. Disputes aside, what is remarkable is the general fact that science, which has done so much to alienate human beings from nature, is now in a position to help reconnect us with the cosmos as it advances ecological and life-sensitive values and challenges modern theories of mechanism, determinism, reductionism, and dualism.[34] A postmodern cosmology is rich in the implications it has for reorganizing our societies, economies, health-care systems, agriculture, and psyches (Capra 1982; Dossey 1982; Goodwin 1994).

Consequently, numerous scientists, cosmologists, and theorists are adopting a new role as storytellers, as they seek to incorporate all levels of evolution into one vast narrative. While postmodern thinking may signal "incredulity to grand narratives" (Lyotard 1984: x) for some disenchanted theorists, in science the grandest of narratives are being constructed. Many new cosmologies involve elaborate stories that present the universe as a dynamic, self-evolving process that spawns life in the wombs of the stars. In *Microcosmos* (1986), for example, biologists Lynn Margulis and Dorion Sagan reconstruct the entire evolution of the Earth. They trace the adventure of life from the first chemical reactions to the evolution of human culture to the seeding of other planets that might create a future "supercosm" generated from the Earth's matter, as Earth likely was seeded by other planets. Not to be outdone, mathematical cosmologist Brian Swimme and historian Thomas Berry, in their work *The Universe Story* (1992), advance a cosmic saga that moves from the Big Bang and the creation of the Earth, to the emergence and development of human culture in an epic tapestry informed by principles of holism, self-organization, and nonequilibrium.

Exemplary of postmodern cosmologies, these texts subvert Western anthropocentrism through narratives that dwarf the ultimate significance of humanity, with Planet Earth only a speck of dust in cosmic space, and the history of human culture a nanosecond in the 15-billion-year odyssey of the origin of our universe. While such cosmologies put human existence in its proper context, they are not misanthropic. Rather, they seek to promote humility and respect for life, such that human beings can rejoin their true community, the biocommunity, regain reverence for life, and respect the million or so other species with which we share this planet. Crucially, postmodern cosmologies seek to provide scientifically accurate *and* life-enriching stories that emphasize the vital links between human beings and their Earth, the biosphere and the universe, inorganic and organic matter, and evolutionary processes at all levels of reality. A new genre of cosmologies, therefore, involves not simply a technomapping of the cosmos, it blurs the boundaries between physics, biology, philosophy, poetry, and religion (the Latin verb *religere* means "to reconnect"), as it draws together resources from premodern, modern, and postmodern worldviews. Consequently, new epic narratives deconstruct the crippling oppositions between fact and value, between reason and emotion, as they try to inspire as much as to inform; to help us feel our connection to the process connecting all things, not merely to understand it as an abstract principle; and to revere life.

Whether implicit or explicit, coevolution is a key idea in the new cosmologies. A reconstructive postmodern science and cosmology emphasize the dynamic, interactive, integrative, coevolutionary development of every level of matter. As Smolin writes, for example, "It seems that all life is situated in a nested hierarchy of self-organized systems that begin with our local ecologies and extend upward at least into the galaxy" (1997: 159). From a cell in a human body, to a local ecosystem, to the Earth, the Milky Way Galaxy, and beyond, all matter evolves in a restlessly changing configuration of interrelated components, where various systems develop together in mutual relations of interdependence. These coevolving relations involve inorganic and organic matter, interactions between human society and nature, and various connections within society. Thus, Margulis and Sagan demonstrate how hosts and parasites, predators and prey, develop in mutual interaction with one another; Stuart Brand traces the coevolution of humans and nature; Humbolt, Mumford, and others analyze the coevolution of social life and tools; Marx, McLuhan, and the Frankfurt School study the dialectic of human beings, society, and technology; and feminists, neo-Marxists, and postcolonial thinkers analyze the dynamic interaction between science and society. As human beings move deeper into the Space Age phase of their development and begin living away from Earth, their lives become ever more dependent on science and technology. If cosmology, broadly understood, is the study of the universe and our place in it, then science and technology change the equation insofar as humans beings no longer just contemplate or study the starry sky, they enter into and live in it, far beyond "gravity's rainbow."

The concept "coevolution" is thus crucial for a postmodern ecology, social theory, and cosmology. It captures more than the idea of "interaction" alone, suggesting that the dynamics of interdependency advance in specific directions, namely, toward greater complexity. Obviously, dialectics and the biological sciences share this evolutionary outlook, but some versions of each tend toward determinist and reductionist views foreign to the coevolutionary outlook. Just as Hegelian theory reduced evolution to the movement of the Idea, and classical Marxian dialectics (Kautsky, Plekhanov, and so on) subsumed social evolution to economics and natural evolution to overly simplified "laws" of development (Engels), so Darwinian natural selection theory renders organisms merely the passive products of their physical surroundings, rather than viewing them as self-organizing agents and active partners in changing relations with their environment and one another.

Moreover, where some dialectical and scientific theories have tended to be uniperspectival and reductionist, coevolution lends itself to a multiperspectivist and transdisciplinary outlook, seeing numerous relations in complex forms of interaction. Postmodern cosmologies are richly contextualist, embedding human beings in a coevolutionary history that deconstructs oppositions such as those between inorganic and organic matter, human beings and animals, culture and nature, and body and mind, in order to reconstruct them as evolving, differentiated processes. Emerging postmodern cosmologies link various academic disciplines and theoretical optics, as they combine both "empirical" and "fictional" maps. A coevolutionary approach unites multiple variables of natural and social evolution usually not articulated together, and, indeed, is often cosmic in its scope and outlook. Analyzing the co-construction of social institutions, it also looks to a better reconfiguration of relationships of human beings to one another and to the natural world alike. The reconstruction of science as a progressive, humane, and ethical force proceeds through the dismantling of the positivist fact/value dualism to the development of new theories of objectivity such as those advanced by Haraway and Harding.

While we embrace the vision of a coevolutionary cosmology with multifaceted components, we also insist on the need to keep dialectical vision firmly rooted in earthly dynamics. Employed in an abstruse, mystical, and overly naturalizing way, "coevolution" easily confounds social relations and obscures the realities of competition, struggle, inequalities in economic and political power, and the constraints of capital and the profit imperative. The cooperation and harmony implied by coevolution, moreover, can conceal how evolution generates destructive as well as constructive outcomes. While it is crucial to show that cooperation is a key catalyst of evolution in both nature and society that is obliterated by vulgar Darwinian and social Darwinist theories, one must also avoid the opposite extreme of underemphasizing competition and struggle in society.

When applied to social evolution, emphasis on coevolution can examine how different levels of a social totality—science, technology, economics, politics, and so on—have their own histories, timetables, and autonomous dynamics, however intertwined and interdependent their interactions. Used wisely, the term "coevolution" allows a more complex and dynamic vision to emerge than traditional dialectical and scientific theories. The concept can be articulated apart from determinism, reductionism, idealism, liberalism, and the conflation of various phenomena into one homogenous system without differentiations, mediations, dominant causal forces, and relations of power and struggle.

We seek cosmologies that, in coupling natural and social evolution in the emergence of life on Earth, examine the dynamic interaction—relations of co-construction—between human and technological development, and the coevolution of technoscience, capital, and society. This enables one to factor politics and power relations into history, and to foreground the importance of science and technology in the evolution of *Homo faber*, linking both to their material context in capitalist social relations of production. It also facilitates an activist and optimistic vision of the possibilities for change and control over a future no longer left to the blind operations of chance or a deterministic fait accompli of scientific and technological "progress."

Cosmology, in other words, cannot be separated from history and political economy. As impressive as the new cosmologies might be, none politicize the gap between science and society, integrate social theory and technology into their coevolutionary framework (see Chapter 4), or grasp the profound political changes needed for their visions of harmony to be realized. None of the new cosmologists understand that complexity and self-organization theory are coopted by conservative, free-market thinkers, betraying the ecological thrust of the new sciences, proving once again that science can be abused unless it joins with critical social theory and radical democratic politics. Moreover, few theorists strongly integrate ethics into the heart of science, which is critical for any reconstructive program.

Now more than ever, as science embarks on the incredible project of manipulating atoms and genes through nanotechnology, genetic engineering, and cloning, its awesome powers must be measured and tempered through ethical, ecological, and democratic norms in a process of public debate and participation. The walls between "experts" and "laypeople" must be broken down along with the elitist norms that form their foundation. Scientists should recognize that their endeavors embody specific biases and value choices, subject them to critical scrutiny, and seek more humane, life-enhancing, and democratic values to guide their work. Respect for nature and life, preserving the natural environment, humane treatment of animals, and serving human needs should be primary values embedded in science. And when these values might conflict, as in the tension between animal welfare and human needs, the problem needs to be addressed as sensitively as possible, and perhaps nonhuman interests should trump human interests in some cases.

This approach is quite unlike how science so far has conducted itself in many areas. Most blatantly, perhaps, scientists, hand in hand with corporations, have prematurely rushed the genetic manipulation of agriculture, animals, and the world's food supply while ignoring important environmental, health, and ethical concerns. Immense power brings enormous responsibility. It is time for scientists to awaken to this fact and to make public accountability integral to their ethos and research. A schizoid modern science that rigidly splits facts from values must give way to a postmodern metascience that grounds the production of knowledge in a social context of dialogue and communication with citizens. The shift from a cold and detached "neutrality" to a participatory understanding of life that subverts the modern subject/object dichotomy derails realist claims to unmediated access to the world and opens the door to an empathetic and ecological understanding of nature (see Keller 1983; Birke and Hubbard 1995).

A revolution is needed to remedy the deficiencies in the education of both scientists and citizens, such that each can have, in Habermas's (1979, 1984, 1987) framework, "communicative competency" informed by sound value thinking, skills in reasoning, and democratic sensibilities. Critical and self-reflexive scrutiny of scientific means, ends, and procedures should be a crucial part of the enterprise. "Critical," in Haraway's analysis, signifies "evaluative, public, multiactor, multiagenda, oriented to equality and heterogeneous well-being" (1997: 95). Indeed, there should be debates concerning precisely what values are incorporated into specific scientific projects and whether these values serve legitimate ends and goals. In the case of mapping the human genome, for instance, enormous amounts of money and energy are being spent, but almost no resources are going to educate the public about the ethical implications of having a genome map. The Human Genome Project spent only 3–5% of its $3 billion budget on legal, ethical, and social issues, and Celera spent even less.[35]

The postmodern adventure in science thus involves the emergence of new perspectives, understandings, sensibilities, values, and paradigms that put in question the assumptions, methods, values, and interpretations of modern sciences, calling for a reconstruction of science (on "new science" and "new sensibilities," see Marcuse 1964, 1969). At the same time, as science and technology co-construct each other, and both coevolve in conjunction with capitalist growth, profit, and power imperatives, science is reconstructing—not always for the better—the natural and social worlds as well as our very identities and bodies. As we noted above, there is considerable ambiguity and tension in how science will play out given the different trajectories it can take. Unlike the salvationist promises of the techoscientific ideology and the apocalyptic dystopias of some of its critics, we see the future of science to be entirely ambiguous, contested, and open.

Hence, we believe that science is a key factor in the postmodern adventure and that many of our colleagues in the realm of theory and cultural studies have ignored it to their own detriment, or have exhibited one-sided antiscientific biases. Dramatic changes are emerging within science and technology as they transform all aspects of everyday life in ways that promise tremendous benefits but also portend grave dangers. Critical theory more than ever needs to engage developments in science and to keep up with its endless metamorphoses and huge impact on contemporary life. As the transformations effected by science occur hand in hand with technology and capitalism, it is to these other momentous forces we now turn in the next two chapters.

NOTES

1. In standard accounts, *science* is the study of nature and *technology* is the practical application of that knowledge through tools, engineering, medicine, and various devices. We borrow the term "technoscience" from Donna Haraway (1997), who in turn takes it from Bruno Latour (1987). Latour developed the concept to subvert a rigid distinction between science and society and to advance the project of developing a sociocultural studies of science. From a perspective that mixes Marxism, feminism, poststructuralism, and other critical theories, Haraway reworks the concept of technoscience to underscore the erosion of boundaries between science and technology and the human and the nonhuman. For Haraway, technoscience vastly exceeds the distinction between science and technology, while producing dramatic novelties and historical ruptures (1997: 3ff.). While she develops critical perspectives on technoscience, she also keeps open dialectical options that interesting, surprising, and useful practices and innovations may result from its discoveries and inventions (279–280). See our further discussion of her work in Chapter 4.

2. It is important to stress that the postmodern turn in science is taken by bona fide scientists and is not merely a philosophical imposition from outside. Charles Birch, David Bohm, Brian Goodwin, Ilya Prigogine, Rupert Sheldrake, Lee Smolin, and Brian Swimme are just some of the scientists who often explicitly employ postmodern discourse. For these figures, postmodern critiques provide new perspectives and paradigms for science that require reconstruction of its basic assumptions, concepts, methods, and self-understanding. Advancing this reconstructive project, philosophers of science like Steven Toulmin, Donna Haraway, and Sandra Harding are proposing new conceptions of objectivity, of multicultural science, and of the interaction between science, technology, and society. We too are calling for the reconstruction of science, technology, and society in line with the values of social ethics and justice, democratization, ecology, and new sensibilities regarding the natural world.

3. Many scientists give due credit to modern perspectives, as they reconstruct them in new contexts. Biologist Brian Goodwin, for example, shifts focus from natural selection to self-organization, and from "geocentric" to "organocentric" views (where organs, not genes, are the fundamental unit of explanation). He explains: "Nothing of value in contemporary [modern] biology is lost in this shift of perspective, it simply gets reframed, reintegrated from a different [postmodern] viewpoint" (1994: 4). Indeed, like Capra (1996), Goodwin is modernist enough to return to Kant and Goethe as premechanistic influences on his science of dynamic holism.

4. The "third culture" proposed by Brockman, Kelly, and other folks at "The Edge" (www.edge.org) is a deceptive misnomer. In fact, their agenda is not to bridge the divide between the sciences and the humanities, but rather to privilege technology and engineering over both. Kelly's alternative term "nerd culture" is a more accurate description of the community they are trying to create.

5. For E. O. Wilson (1998a), the transdisciplinary vision of the Enlightenment was lost in the subsequent mania for intellectual specialization. Clearly, his position is more modern than postmodern, for he seeks to continue the Baconian emphasis on the unity of sciences, even while he resists the modern drive toward disciplinarity and fragmentation, as well as postmodern indeterminist and antirealist positions. Although he believes postmodern approaches (which he lumps together in one bag) are antithetical to the enterprise of science in their tendencies toward fragmentation, irrationalism, and relativism, he finds them useful as provocations: "We will always need postmodernists or their rebellious equivalents. For what better way to strengthen organized knowledge than continually to defend it from hostile forces?" (1998b: 62). Our position, in contrast, affirms that some postmodern positions are useful not only as tools of provocation, but for the positive reconstruction of science.

6. Although some extreme postmodernists celebrate the incompleteness and fragmentation of knowledge, the lack of a coherent map of the universe is a great concern for many physicists. For instance, even a postmodern-oriented physicist like Lee Smolin complains "The fact that general relativity and the quantum are not yet united means that we have no single picture of what the world is that we can believe in. When a child asks, What is the world, we literally have nothing to tell her" (1997: 242).

7. According to Lyotard (1984), modern knowledge is marked by a quest for consensus. But some postmodernists reject this norm as repressive and embrace difference and disagreement to the point of conceptualizing knowledge as an "agon" of conflicting viewpoints. In light of disparate and conflicting philosophical points of view, Lyotard argues that dissensus marks the contemporary era. For a critical evaluation of the pros and cons of both consensus and dissensus as epistemic ideals and a contextualist argument that deploys both, depending on the setting and goals of inquiry, see Best and Kellner (1991, Ch. 5).

8. As John Horgan puts it in a more recent statement, "I believe that [modern cosmology and evolutionary theory] is essentially true. It will thus be as viable 100 or even 1,000 years from now as it is today. I also believe that, given how far science has already come, and given the limits constraining further research, science will be hard-pressed to make any truly profound additions to the knowledge it has already generated. Further research may yield no more great revelations or revolutions but only incremental returns" ("A Talk with John Horgan," *The Edge*, www.edge.org).

9. While Einstein's theories of relativity were bold and groundbreaking, they were rooted in classical foundations such as realism, determinism, belief in God, and the idea of a static, nonexpanding universe. Einstein firmly claimed that "God does not play dice with the universe," and repudiated quantum indeterminacy, a position he intransigently held in his debates with Niels Bohr. Although Einstein helped to establish the foundations of quantum mechanics (e.g., with his theory of light photons), he shied away from their implications, and thereby set the pattern for many contemporary neopositivists who refuse to accept the idea of the natural world as anything but a law-governed machine.

10. In fact, as Herbert (1985) shows, there are at least eight different interpretations of quantum mechanics, which we can simplify into three different camps: realists who try to capture an objective reality, antirealists who emphasize that the observer always disturbs the observed, and pragmatists who bracket the question of the ontological status of what they observe to focus on collecting facts and verifying experiments. Thus, interpretations concerning quantum mechanics are highly contested.

11. Prigogine's postmodern perspectives on science exemplify an approach that is emphatically indeterminist and multiperspectivist, but not antirealist. He believes that sci-

ence can effectively map "the laws of nature"—a modern discourse he retains—without significantly disturbing what it observes, thereby disagreeing with the dominant interpretation of quantum physics. Properly understood, Prigogine argues, the postmodern recognition of complexity is a victory for science, not a defeat, a progressive advance, not a regressive retreat, an extension of rationality, not a surrender, enabling a more accurate mapping of natural processes.

12. Physicist Lee Smolin is one example of a scientist who confirms this unification project, thereby foregoing the postmodern emphasis on fragmentation, while embracing other aspects of postmodern epistemology (see below). For an adroit exposition of the quest for a Theory of Everything, see Kaku (1994).

13. For those inclined to positivism, it should be pointed out that numerous speculative constructs such as "antimatter" were later verified empirically or experimentally (see Kaku 1994). On the other hand, one can certainly imagine string or other theories being mathematically sound, but having no relation to reality—that is, they are mere simulations of a real world built on obscure theoretical constructs and premises (such as a 10-dimensional universe).

14. There are now virtual physics, chemistry, biology, and anatomy labs. "Cyberscience," accordingly, constitutes a technological revolution and paradigm shift across the board. Although teachers and scientists debate whether computer-mediated science experiments are as effective as "wet labs," they clearly offer valuable supplementary tools and already are saving the lives of many animals who otherwise would be killed in places like dissection labs (see "Virtually Science," www.nytimes.com/library/national/040900edlife-tech-edu.html). For a good example of how computers are being used to simulate evolutionary processes in physics, providing "virtual" insights into "real" cosmic structures, see "For the First Time, a Computer Simulates the Evolution of a Large Fraction of the Observable Universe," at www.sciencedaily.com/releases/1998/02/980226075625.htm. For a ground-breaking study of computer-driven scientific mapping, see Hall 1993.

15. Common terms in the genetic lexicon such as "code," "sequence," and "program" also are the direct result of computer science influences (see Rifkin 1998, Ch. 6).

16. For an earlier discussion of the conflict between biological research and commerce, see Haraway 1997.

17. http://www.the-scientist.com/yr2001/feb/russo_p16_010219.html.

18. For the two competing mappings of the human genome see *Science* (February 16, 2001) and *Nature* (February 15, 2001). The competing papers are discussed by Eugene Russo, "Behind the Sequence," *The Scientist, 15*(5), March 1, 2001: 1.

19. See, for example, "Money + Science = Ethics Problems on Campus," *The Nation* (March 22, 1999, pp. 11–18), and *Multinational Monitor* (November 1997), which feature stories on rotating doors between university and corporate boards and various examples of "junk science." All too often, as in the case of researchers employed to quell public fears about the safety of meat and dairy products, genetically modified foods, or threats of global warming, studies are commissioned by and for corporations, transmogrifying truth-oriented empirical reason into mere propaganda. Numerous articles on the appropriation of science by capitalism, universities, and the state are collected in Arditti et al. (1980), Taylor et al. (1997), and Lederman and Bartsch (2001). Essays gathered by Harding (1993) explore the race, gender, and class dimensions of science. In a rare mea culpa for scientific industries tainted by corporate ties, the *New England Journal of Medicine* confessed in February 2000 that it had violated its own financial conflict-of-interest policy 19 times in the last 3 years. The editor-in-chief admitted that it had allowed doctors to review new drug treatments for

companies with which they had economic ties and explained this process as merely a matter of "carelessness."

20. The recent medical recognition of acupuncture—based on "esoteric" theories of energy channels—as successful for treating chronic pain and illness (which continue to bedevil Western science) is a modest sign that science is beginning to recognize the legitimacy of other modes of knowledge, even if it cannot grasp the underlying philosophy and sensibility.

21. For our appreciation and critique of Kelly's work, see Best and Kellner (1999). See also Kelly's (2000) (non)response and our reply (2000).

22. Kelly's mentor Gilder is even a more aggressive neo-Schumpeterian; see Gilder (1989: 63, 188, 209, 316, passim). Both celebrate "creative destruction" without any apparent concern about who or what is being destroyed and what is replacing it. It should be noted, however, that this appropriation of Schumpeter is highly ideological, that Schumpeter had a much more complex historically and sociologically grounded theory, and that ideologues like Gilder and Kelly are reducing his work to slogans. For a fuller appreciation of Schumpeter's positions and how his work has been appropriated by left and right alike, see Foster (1983).

23. On how the progressive implications of sciences like ecology can subverted for reactionary purposes, see the work of Murray Bookchin (1994; 1995b).

24. The "island" metaphor, however, is also misleading, since it suggests private individuals or eccentric millionaires fund genetic experimentation, whereas in fact the life sciences are heavily funded by both governments and corporations.

25. The warnings of FDA scientists about the huge uncertainties and dangers surrounding genetically modified foods, and their public testimonies (as plaintiffs in a lawsuit) against the irresponsible policies of the agency are documented by the Alliance for Bio-Integrity (www.bio-integrity.org).

26. Apparently, however, Crichton is no bio-Luddite, for he bemoans the failed promises of the genetic revolution pioneered by James Watson and Francis Crick (1990: x) which, instead of benefiting humankind, he argues, was commercialized and appropriated by capitalism to advance the interests of a scientific and economic elite.

27. Through the replacement of human beings with automated machinery, a high admissions fee, and, above all, the merchandizing of products, Hammond salivates when pondering billions of dollars of projected annual profits. What Hammond could not do in fiction, Crichton, Spielberg, and Hollywood accomplished in reality by licensing *Jurassic Park* products. On an important level, the film was a huge advertisement for the merchandized products, thereby defusing the critical thrust of the novel. One need not worry about commercials coming *before* a film in the movie theater (as one already finds on videos), for they are already *in* the movie. According to O'Neill (1996), there are over 1,000 licenses for *Jurassic Park* products, all popular commodities in the current dinomania craze.

28. The absurdity of the "control of nature" ideology became patently clear once again in May 2000 when the New Mexico Park Service discovered to their chagrin that their "controlled burn," determined to be safe through sophisticated computer modeling, was rampaging out of control. Fanned by winds, the small fire became a conflagration that destroyed over 47,000 acres of forest and 200 homes as it blazed with potentially catastrophic results around the Los Alamos National Laboratory housing nuclear materials (see George Johnson, "Harness Fire? Mother Nature Begs to Differ," www.nytimes.com/library/review/052100los-alamos-review.html).

29. At the same time, however, *Jurassic Park* delivers the technofantasy that extinct life forms can be brought back by some genetic hocus-pocus. Alas, extinction is forever and at current rates the Earth loses another species every hour. On the impossibility of reconstructing dinosaurs, see DeSalle and Lindley (1997).

30. As Mitchell (1998) notes, it says all too much about our society that more money was spent filming *Jurassic Park* that has been spent on paleontology in its entire history. For a sorry report on the state of science education in general in U.S. society, see "Science Miseducation," www.abcnews.go/sections/science/DyeHard/dyehard.html

31. Although Einstein's general theory of relativity could have predicted the dynamic universe Edwin Hubble found looking through his telescope, Einstein found this conclusion so incredible that he modified his original theory to avoid it. But upon learning of Hubble's discoveries, he admitted that changing the theory was "the biggest blunder of my life" (see Hey and Walters 1997: 213–216). For details on how the Hubble Space Telescope led to new scientific findings, see http://oposite.stsci.edu/pubinfo/spacecraft/Primer/Top_Findings.htm.

32. The postmodern notions of *différance* (Derrida), semiosis (Baudrillard), and the "gaming" of knowledge production (Lyotard) find their parallels in the new cosmologies that also articulate logics of difference, pluralism, and productivity. Lee Smolin (1997), perhaps the physicist most influenced by postmodern principles, seeks a unified understanding of nature, and therefore avoids the apotheosis of fragmentation advanced by postmodern theorists like Deleuze and Guattari. Yet he applies the major tenets of postmodern social theory to a deconstruction of the theological basis of scientific claims to Truth and the Platonist ontology of a static universe that was destroyed by the empirical observations of Edwin Hubble.

33. At issue is the proper definition and scale of life and self-organizing systems, with some physicists drawing the line at galaxies (Smolin), and others rejecting any limit to the application of evolution and self-organization theories (Gribbin).

34. The new dialogue between science and religion has become a veritable industry, producing multimillion dollar grants, courses, centers, conferences, books, and innumerable scholarly and popular articles. Just as theologians are finding science less threatening, some scientists are becoming disenchanted with the coldness of positivism and are growing more respectful of religion. Scientist Paul Davies writes that "these two great systems of thought can meet happily in the middle ground. Many scholars are convinced we've entered a new phase of scientific maturity in which scientists no longer ridicule people's genuine spiritual hunger but seek instead to address the deep issues of meaning and purpose in a more constructive way" ("Behind Closed Doors, Scientists Are Confessing Their Faith in God," www.forbes.com/asap/99/1004/230.htm). For commentators like Richard Dawkins, however, this loosening of boundaries (never too rigid; after all, the main founders of modern science were Christians and/or mystics) is anything but positive, being a symptom of the prevailing New Age spiritualism, irrationality, confusion, and commercialism of contemporary culture ("Illogical Thinking Is the Only Thing Joining Science and Religion Together," www.forbes.com/asap/99/1004/235.htm).

35. www.wired.com/news/0,1294,36886,00.html.

4

||||||||

TECHNOLOGICAL REVOLUTION
AND HUMAN EVOLUTION

"Go ahead, capitalize the T on technology, deify it if it'll make you feel less
responsible—but it puts you in with the neutered, brother, in with the
eunuchs keeping the harem of our stolen Earth for the numb and joyless
hardons of human sultans, human elite with no right at all to be where
they are."

—THOMAS PYNCHON, *GRAVITY'S RAINBOW*

Evolution's grandest creation—human intelligence—is providing the means
for the next stage of evolution, which is technology. . . . The next milestone
will be technology creating its own generation without human intervention.
—RAY KURZWEIL

Technology is fundamental to the adventure of evolution, promoting ever
greater and more rapid waves of scientific innovation, social transformation,
and economic advancement. Modernity was fuelled by perpetually revolutionizing science, industry, and technology via the printing press, factory system,
steam engine, railroad, airplanes, automobiles, communications media, and culture industries.[1] Today, the postmodern adventure is driven largely by electronic media, computers, and biotechnologies. The current technological revolution is transforming every dimension of life, from the ways we work and
spend our leisure time, to the avenues through which we communicate and
learn, to our forms of experiencing and interpreting the world, and even to
what and how we eat in a genetically modified, fast-food culture.

The postmodern adventure in the Third Millennium involves the
coevolution of science, technology, and market systems, all of which are co-
constructing a global reorganization of capitalism. As we saw in the last chapter, new paradigms in science, including quantum mechanics, chaos and
complexity theory, and ecology, are providing tools to help grasp the dynamic
interaction between science, technology, and society. The shift toward more dialectical and holistic modes of thought occurred in part due to theoretical in-

fluences like cybernetics and systems theory, but also because economic, technological, and communication networks have crisscrossed the entire globe, unifying the infrastructure of capitalism with a networked society and culture.

With quantum mechanics, biotechnology, and superstring theory, science moved boldly into a dematerialized and miniaturized world, exploring subatomic particles, genes, and (the hypothesis of) strings. All are infinitesimally small constituents of reality that are invisible to the naked eye, difficult if not impossible to map, and confounding Newton's world of solid particles. Technological development has followed the same trajectory as science into the microcosm. Since the 1940s, computer technologies have rapidly evolved from the huge "Harvard Mark I," 50 feet long, 8 feet high, and containing a million components, to clunky vacuum-type machines like "Colossus" and "ENIAC" using thousands of tubes, to the laptop, the hand-held computer, and the microchip, which can store millions of components and solve problems in a fraction of a second.

From the beginning of the 20th century, with the emergence of calculators, the speed and power of computation have been doubling every 18 months, an exponential pace that will likely continue to follow "Moore's Law" for decades to come until it runs into the limits of silicon technology (see Paul and Cox 1996; Kurzweil 1999).[2] Media, video, and photographic technologies have also miniaturized, reducing bulky recording devices to ever smaller camcorders, or devices that can fit in a button or even a microchip the size of a fingernail. Nanotechnologies are being generated to manipulate atoms and molecules to build infinitesimally small machines, on scales where carbon nanotubes, for example, are one ten-thousandth the diameter of a human hair (Drexler 1987). The film *Honey I Shrunk the Kids!* (1989) provides anxious testimony to an ever-diminishing technoscientific reality.

Today, cars and ordinary household items contain microchips and miniature computers that are forming the invisible backdrop of everyday life (Gerschenfeld 1999). Many commentators have announced the arrival of a "post-PC era," characterized by microtechnologies that allow one to connect to the web and send faxes or e-mail, and by "wearable computers" that fit into a button or shoe, thereby moving computers off the desk and onto the body. The miniaturization of computers interconnects the myriad transactions of everyday life and allows seamless traffic between the "virtual" and "real" worlds, a distinction ever harder to maintain.

Hence, contemporary individuals are quickly moving from a wired world of screens and keyboards to a wireless world of portable communication devices that connect them to the Internet, other technologies, and one another. Nanotechnologies are mapping and manipulating atoms, promising huge advances in fields such as medicine and energy. Molecule-size machines could perform tasks such as dissolving blood clots (as envisioned in the film *Fantastic Voyage* [1966]), while providing limitless clean resources. Genetic technologies already cut and paste genes to create transgenic species, establishing unparalleled powers of biomanipulation. In various ways, new technologies such as computers, wireless devices, and gene splicing are transcending material limits and obliterating earlier constraints on speed, efficiency, and communication.

In the postmodern adventure, technology and science have coevolved in dynamic and syncretistic ways. George Gilder (1989) and Michio Kaku (1997) point out that quantum mechanics theory has enabled the development of some of the most important modern technologies, from TV to computers and, alas, nuclear weapons, thereby creating the "quantum era" (Gilder).[3] Conversely, computers have made possible the high-level mathematics required to conceive the chaos, complexity, and superstring theories of science. This in turn enabled new modeling of natural processes and human intelligence, generating the sciences of artificial life and the human mind (Kelly 1995; Kaku 1997; Levy 1993). Thus, while analytic and strategic distinctions can and should be made between science and technology, their interaction is more in tense and penetrating today than ever before.

With the ever deeper incursion of science and technology into the natural world, society, everyday life, and our very bodies (e.g., with wearable computers, bionic implants, and modified genes), human beings and technology are imploding. A growing number of theorists contend that the age of humanism is over and that we are morphing into a new "posthumanist" condition (see Paul and Cox 1996; Moravec 1998; Kurzweil 1999; for a critical interrogation of these claims, see Hayles 1999). With the eruption of new forms of media culture, the Internet and cyberspace, transgenic species, cloning, frozen embryos, *in vitro* fertilization, and nanomachines built from atoms, the reality principle of modernity and all Western culture has been irrevocably altered. Together, science and technology are undermining firm boundaries between reality/unreality, natural/artificial, organic/inorganic, biology/technology, human/machine, and the born/the made. In a world of virtual reality, biotechnology, surrogate mothering, neural implants, and artificial intelligence and life, reality "just ain't what it used to be." We're becoming cyborgs and technobodies, while our machines are becoming "smart" and more human-like. Descartes's worry in the *Mediations* about whether it was a man or an automaton he was viewing from his window wasn't misplaced after all.

Dramatic shifts in science and technology force us to rethink conceptions of ourselves, humanistic philosophies, and the very nature of reality. Prior questions are revitalized and new issues and problems emerge as humanity confronts a reconfigured material and intellectual world. Creative critical and theoretical perspectives are necessary to grasp both the promises and the perils of the turbulent transformations that the human species is undergoing. The new technologies hold exciting promises in areas like energy production and conservation, environmental reclamation, medical research and health care, and information and education. But new problems, controversies, and dangers are also emerging. In all these arenas, clashes between the old and the new are erupting because traditional sensibilities remain dominant. Although postmodern paradigms are proliferating throughout culture, modern reductionism, mechanism, technoscience, bureaucracy, and the project of the domination of nature continue to rule. As is obvious in the case of genetic engineering—which is already having a destructive impact on the land, insects, animals, and human beings—the old mentalities and the new technologies combine in a volatile mix. Hence, radical changes in the paradigms, new sensibilities, and transformed social relations informing scientific and technological growth urgently need to be realized (see Fox 1999).

In the realm of technology, the postmodern adventure unfolds through the staggering new powers human beings have to manipulate their world: atom by atom, molecule by molecule, gene by gene, bit by byte. As one form of the postmodern adventure advances along the path of corporate control and technoscientific domination of nature, animals, and human beings, another form pursues the way of harmony and complementarity, seeking to reconcile the new technologies with progressive values of peace, justice, and ecology (see Griffin 1988a, 1988b; Spretnak 1991; Winter 1996). Humanity has reached the point in its technological progress when it threatens the survival of advanced life on Earth with species extinction crisis, exhaustion of the planet's resources, pollution, and global warming. New dangers are emerging as human beings start to shape evolution through the creation of transgenic species, gene therapy, and cloning that treat diseases and portend a new age of eugenics and genetic discrimination. As technoscience and capitalism devour the earth, they also contemplate exploiting outer space, perhaps by terraforming other planets and thus taking the postmodern adventure to the stars and beyond.

Just as nature has created advanced intelligence in the form of human beings, the human adventure is rapidly evolving an "artificial intelligence" through ever more sophisticated computers and robots that potentially open up a new line of evolution that eventually might exceed all human powers. "Intelligence" can no longer be regarded as strictly a human property; researchers are finding reasoning and learning processes in both animals and machines. Even "machines" are no longer mechanisms as traditionally described, since today they are ever more closely approximating the biological operations of the brain through neural nets, parallel processing, evolutionary hardware, and the like. When the self-ascribed "essence" of the human is stripped away, and human beings begin to merge intimately with their machines, fusing flesh with silicon chips and steel, human identity itself comes into question. A crucial part of the postmodern adventure involves rethinking the claims of humanism and confronting various posthumanist challenges that are emerging with the mutations technology brings in both the subject and object worlds.

The ambiguity of the present moment is that the science and technologies that could bring stunning benefits to the human race also engender new forms of domination and destruction, including threats of nuclear, biological-chemical, and ecological annihilation. The outcome depends upon whether the technoscientific and corporate elites who call the shots have the foresight, wisdom, and responsibility to shape the future in a positive direction, and whether individuals and groups can democratically restructure society and culture to avoid the destructive consequences of uncontrolled growth and development.

The scientific–technological–economic revolutions that constitute the postmodern adventure raise fundamental questions concerning human identity and the nature of the sociocultural environs that the human species now faces. Although there are strong continuities between the old order and the new, the discontinuities are so immense that it often takes the imagination of the great SF writers to delineate the striking mutations unfolding all around us. Hence, in addition to critical social theory and science, in our studies we engage writers like Mary Shelley, H. G. Wells, Rudy Rucker, Bruce Sterling, Philip K. Dick, and Octavia Butler, as well as filmmakers like David Cronenberg and Ridley Scott, to help us envisage the effects, dangers, and opportunities of the postmodern technoculture. While we critically confront posthumanist discourse, we acknowledge that the rise of intelligent machines, genetic engineering, nanotechnology, and unforeseen technoscientific growth produce a further decentering of the human, resulting in the specter of what we are calling the "fifth discontinuity" (see Chapter 3). Accordingly, in this chapter we chart a series of implosions that call into question human identity, traditional mappings of reality, and the boundaries between nature, our social world, and technology.

DEBATES OVER NEW TECHNOLOGIES

In our days, everything seems pregnant with its contrary. Machinery, gifted with the wonderful power of shortening and fructifying human labour, we behold starving it and overworking it. The newfangled sources of wealth, by some weird spell, are turned into sources of want. The victories of art seem bought by loss of character. At the same pace that mankind masters nature, man seems to become enslaved to other men or to his own infamy. Even the pure light of science seems unable to shine but on the dark background of ignorance. All our inventions and progress seem to result in endowing material forces with intellectual life, and stultifying human life into a material force.

—KARL MARX

The 21st-century technologies—genetics, nanotechnology, and robotic (GNR)—are so powerful that they can spawn whole new classes of accidents and abuses. Most dangerously, for the first time, these accidents and abuses are widely within the reach of individuals or small groups. They will not require large facilities or fare raw materials. Knowledge alone will enable the use of them.

—BILL JOY

Revolutions in technology become markers of history. Just as past epochs often are characterized through terms such as the "Stone Age," the "Bronze Age," and the "industrial era," so too do new sciences and advanced technologies define contemporary society. Yet no one technology quintessentially marks the present. Instead, we find an overlapping conjuncture of technological revolutions in multimedia, computers, and biotechnology, with nanotechnology on the horizon.[4] Hence, the postmodern adventure is an era of intense technological development in which the human species and its environments are coevolving into dramatic new configurations.

In the early 1960s, Marshall McLuhan announced that communication technologies were creating an electronic culture that was ending the era of print technology and "mechanical man," while bringing humanity together in a vast global village. For McLuhan, linear print technology had helped make possible modern science and technology, capitalism, nationalism, and individualism, thus providing the foundation of modern civilization. McLuhan envisaged a rupture in history marked by the rise of novel media and computer technologies that would create innovative forms of society and culture and eventually a mutation in the human species. Although his oracular and aphoristic form often mystified this dramatic process and while he did not address the hegemony of global capitalism and its ideological effects, he correctly grasped the powerful role of image and media technologies and anticipated the rise of computer culture.

Indeed, media revolutions within television, film, video, and advertising have transformed politics, economics, human identities and everyday life, creating a culture of spectacle, entertainment, and hyperreality (see Kellner 1995a; Chapter 5). But the current computer and information technology revolution in the postmodern adventure may be even more momentous. Originating in World War II, as a crucial technology for decrypting German military codes and building the atomic bomb, computers gradually became ever more important for society in general, such that by the 1980s, they ushered in the "PC revolution" and the subsequent "Age of the Internet," becoming a major communication, research, education, and business medium. As the entire world is rapidly becoming computerized and all other technologies—radio, film, television, video, photography, telephones, fax machines, and so on—are being absorbed into the black hole of digitalization, the world of "atoms" is being transformed into a world of "bits" (Gilder 1989; Negroponte 1995). Increasingly, objects, activities, and modes of experience are becoming "virtualized," such that phenomena like dating, sex, commerce, shopping, learning, medicine, and counseling are taking place online, creating a nascent "network society" and culture (see Reingold 1994; Castells 1996, 1997, 1998; Schiller 1999).

Without computers, the new genetic sciences that emerged in the 1950s with the breakthroughs of James Watson and Francis Crick would not have been possible. In the current era of "biocybernetic reproduction" (Mitchell 1998), computers are critical for the storage and manipulation of the massive amounts of data involved in the mapping of the human genome, where simply to print the names of the 3 billion nucleic acid base pairs that make up the tens of thousands of human genes would require as many pages as 13 sets of the *Encyclopedia Britannica* (itself now an online databank). Once scientists have a thorough understanding of the number, function, and interrelationship of human genes, genetics will advanced rapidly and bring revolutionary changes brimming with promises and perils (see Ridley 1999).

Today biotechnology is transforming all forms of life, from microorganisms to human beings. A "brave new agriculture" has arrived based on the genetic engineering of crops, such that 65% of nonorganic food is now genetically altered. At this moment, a global struggle is developing over the attempt of transnational chemical and seed companies like Monsanto to engineer crops, trees, and grasses throughout the world (see Chapter 5). "Pharming" (pharmaceutical farming) involves the genetic engineering of animals to transform their bodies into drug-excreting and organ-making factories to treat human diseases. Promoters promise a solution to world hunger and malnutrition, while others denounce biotechnology as a hazard to ecological systems and biodiversity and a facile technofix that leaves untouched the social relations underlying global problems such as disease, malnutrition, and scarcity. Pharming is a process that promises medical advances but also is vehemently denounced by critics as dangerous and exploitive of animals (see our discussion of cloning later in this chapter).

Thus, electronic media, computers, the Internet, and genetic engineering all are crucial forces co-constructing the present; all need to be analyzed in terms of their specificity and interrelationships. Hence, one should avoid reductionistic phrases like "the age of _ _ _ _ _"—fill in your favored technology. Together, these forces are coevolving to generate novel configurations of technoscience, technocapitalism, and technoculture. Not surprisingly, the postmodern adventure is a hotly contested journey into the future, with different theoretical and political camps battling to define these new technologies as propitious or calamitous.

In studying the burgeoning array of discourses that characterize media, computer, and biotechnologies, one finds that the most influential writers either espouse a technophilic outlook that presents the current technologies as our salvation, or a technophobic mind-set that sees the emergent technology as our damnation. Throughout this century, every time a new form of media emerged (film, radio, television, and so on), there appeared champions and detractors who extolled the wonderful benefits of the emergent medium or attacked its pernicious effects. With regard to new information and computer technologies, the same bipolarized approach has emerged. For technophilic celebration, one can read any issue of *Wired*, popular magazines like *Newsweek*, or Bill Gates's book *The Road Ahead* (1995). One can also examine some of the boosters of new technologies like George Gilder (1989), Nicholas Negroponte (1995), Kevin Kelly (1995, 1998), or Ray Kurzweil (1990, 1999).

These individuals are sometimes referred to as *digerati*, intellectuals who hype new technologies; they also include Alvin Toffler, David Gelernter, and countless wannabes who write for the popular media, specialist journals, and other publications anxious to jump onto the digital bandwagon.

Technophilic politicians include Al Gore and Newt Gingrich in the United States and Tony Blair and his New Labour cohort in Great Britain. These promoters of the information society promise more jobs, exciting economic opportunities, more leisure, better education, enhanced democracy, a bountiful harvest of information and entertainment, and prosperity that would make Adam Smith proud. Technophilia celebrates the coming "computopia" where emergent technologies will provide increased wealth, greater well-being, more information, better entertainment, and a dazzling array of novel gadgets and services. Technophile discourse emphasizes the upside of the industrial–technological revolution and its market economy. It promises an orderly society and an economy without "friction," as well as efficiency and satisfaction, accompanied by unlimited development. Conspicuously absent, however, is discussion of the fate of a teeming army of unemployed whose positions become obsolete in an age of automation and "netslaves" who suffer health problems in toxic semiconducting manufacturing—as well as the environmental hazards of chemicals used in silicon chip production (Lessard and Baldwin 2000; Mazurek and Ashford 2000). According to the optimistic version of postmodernity, risk is banished or minimized, technology is an unmitigated boon to humanity, and people are promised a never-ending supply of new wonders. This merger of capitalism and technology, of economic and technological revolution, transfers the prestige of technology to business and the market economy and provides refurbished ideological legitimation for capitalism.

Powerful economic interests support and hype the emergent technologies, and their allegedly beneficial effects. Obviously there is both real and academic capital to be gained through boosting these technologies, so it is not surprising that economically interested promoters of the new technologies and intellectuals are championing their benefits, often in an uncritical fashion. What is perhaps more surprising, however, is the extent of wholly negative discourses on computers and current technologies. A large number of recent books on computers, the Internet, and cyberspace written by a wide range of writers contain discourse that is strikingly technophobic. One strand of this mentality now aimed at computers goes back to the 1960s and earlier criticism of technology by Theodore Roszak, Charles Reich, Neil Postman, Jerry Mander, and other lifelong critics of media culture and technology. The same arguments these writers previously deployed against technology in general, or against specific earlier technologies (e.g., television), are now being used against computers. Thus we have a recycling of old diatribes.[5] The negative perspective equates technology with dehumanization and alienation from other people, the environment, and the "real world." It posits users of new technologies as lost in cyberspace and exhibits in its polemics a nostalgia for simpler times and face-to-face interaction.[6]

One finds a similar dichotomous discourse in the debates over genetic engineering. Monsanto and its paid scientific staff, the FDA and the USDA, the *Futurist* magazine, and some farmers are among those who champion genetic engineering as the only means to stave off hunger and illness in an overpopulated, underfed, disease-ridden world. Conversely, an ever-broadening, worldwide chorus of voices decry genetic engineering as a harbinger of ecological disaster, potential health problems, intensified levels of animal exploitation, genetic discrimination, and a eugenic society (Mae-Wan Ho 1998; Rifkin 1998). Where computers obviously have emancipatory potential and in many forms foster democracy, so far the genetic engineering of plants and animals has produced mostly failures and suffering. Furthermore, genetic technologies are controlled by a few giant corporations like Monsanto, Du Pont, and Novartis, and, unlike computers, hardly lend themselves to decentralization and serving people's as opposed to corporate needs. Indeed, Monsanto attempted to develop a "terminator technology" involving sterile seeds to reduce the world's farmers to a state of bioserfdom. Numerous critics have denounced biotechnology as a trojan horse for a new stage of imperialism, "biopiracy," which seeks monopoly control over Earth's genetic resources.

Cautionary warnings about the dangers of uncontrolled genetic technology, artificial intelligence, and nanotechnology were raised recently, however, from within the technoculture itself by Bill Joy in a *Wired* magazine article that was widely distributed and discussed (2000). Joy's article, especially his call for government regulation of new technology and "relinquishment" of development of potentially dangerous new technologies (which he argued that biologists had called for in the early days of genetic engineering) set off a firestorm of controversy.[7] Arguing that scientists must assume responsibility for their productions, Joy warned that humans should be very careful about the technologies they develop, which may have unforeseen consequences. Joy noted that robotics was producing increasingly intelligent machines that might generate creative robots superior to humans, who would produce copies of themselves and assume control of the design and future of humans. Likewise, genetic engineering could create new species, some perhaps dangerous to humans and nature, while nanotechnology could spawn horrific "engines of destruction."

Thus, the postmodern adventure in technology is highly conflicted, with camps on each side advancing often one-sided arguments and inadequate perspectives. Against constricted technophilic or technophobic approaches, we argue that one needs to develop a *critical theory of technology* in order to sort out its positive and negative features, the upside and the downside, the benefits and the losses in the genesis and use of new technologies. A critical theory of technology should begin with healthy skepticism regarding technophilic celebra-

tions of new technologies, which it sees as a key element of the global restructuring of capitalism. A critical theory will question promises of a technological
utopia: that new technologies will produce food and jobs for everyone; generate a wealth of information, entertainment, and education; provide panaceas
for our medical problems; and overcome boundaries of gender, race, and class.
But a critical theory will also resist technological dystopia and claims that
computers and other new technologies are our damnation, that they are vehicles of alienation, mere tools of capital, the state, and domination.[8] The challenge is to analyze how new technologies can be used as instruments of both
domination and democratization, and to suggest how they might be reconstructed and employed for creating a more egalitarian and ecologically viable
society, empowering individuals and groups who are currently disenfranchised.

THE FRANKENSTEIN SYNDROME

> "A new species would bless me as its creator and source; many happy and
> excellent natures would owe their being to me. No father could claim the
> gratitude of his child so completely as I should deserve theirs. Pursuing
> these reflections, I thought, that if I could bestow animation upon lifeless
> matter, I might in process of time (although I now found it impossible)
> renew life where death had apparently devoted the body to corruption."
> —MARY SHELLEY, FRANKENSTEIN

Mary Shelley's *Frankenstein* (1993 [1818]) was one of the first and most prescient
critiques of modern science and technology out of control, creating unanticipated destructive consequences. The novel has sold millions of copies, been made
into countless films, and continues to shape our fears and suspicions of science
and technology. It has spawned a vast literature, as well as genres of popular culture which have warned, time and time again, that the power of modern science
and technology—if divorced from an ethical sensibility and insight into the contingency and unpredictability of complex systems—may bring disastrous results
to human beings, other life forms, and the Earth as a whole.[9]

    Frankenstein was published in 1818, at the dawn of the Industrial Revolu-
tion, as a critical response to the insurgence of technological modernity.
Emerging about the same time as the Luddites' demolition of the factory
machines that threatened their livelihood, Shelley's novel shared the anti-
technological vision found in Blake and the romantics. Drawing on the Gothic
tradition of tales of horror, *Frankenstein* anticipates the genre of SF writing, a
mode that extrapolates a "what if?" situation, showing the possible consequences of rapid scientific and technological innovation. In Shelley's case, the
premise was: What if human beings could create life by reanimating the dead
and forming a new being out of human flesh and organs? The result, of course,
is Victor Frankenstein's "monster" who disgusts the scientist, escapes from his

basement, and goes on a rampage, becoming a murderous and dangerous "fiend" after repeated mistreatment by humans.

Shelley's tale synthesizes the vision of scientific materialism—that modern science can produce wonders, including new life forms—with the stance of Gothic romanticism, which fears the ugly, the monstrous, the irrational, and the violent erupting and destroying of human hopes and life. Shelley revels in evocations of the sublime, especially in her treatment of nature, but she also crafts a demonic romance of science, in which the modern scientist plays the role of the sorcerer's apprentice, delving into the mysteries of nature to seek answers and to create new forms of life. Told in the form of a series of diary entries in which an intrepid explorer Francis Walton narrates his encounter with Victor Frankenstein who he picked up at sea en route to the North Pole, the novel presents multiple perspectives on the events of the tale, as seen by Victor, Walton, and the creature.[10]

An Enlightenment Faust, Victor Frankenstein represents both the drive to master the mysteries of life and the Cartesian ego separated from the body, other people, nature, and the social world.[11] Taught by his father the principles of modern science, Victor renounces alchemy, mysticism, and tradition, and seeks truth through scientific method, just as modern science itself was eradicating the premodern influences from its emerging mechanistic models. Above all, Dr. Frankenstein—the "modern Prometheus" as the book is subtitled—stole fire from the gods, the secret of the creation of life, and aspired to become like a god, the author of life and a new species. He is thus a distinctly modern hero who embodies the deepest impulses of modernity to control nature, perfect social existence, and produce new forms of life. But in his pursuit of the life force, he isolates himself from other people, including his family, his fiancée Elizabeth, and his friends—all of whom are destroyed by his obsession. Like Descartes, Victor sees the search for truth as an individual quest; like Bacon, he defines knowledge as an instrument for subduing nature and controlling its forces.

Much more than merely a romantic yarn or dark Gothic adventure tale, *Frankenstein* raises ethical questions concerning scientific inquiry and the nature and use of technology. Shelley's allegory represents Dr. Frankenstein committing a number of wrongs: he turns his back on his "hideous" creation, he allows it to escape from his home to roam freely in society, and he permits a servant to be condemned and put to death for crimes he knew his progeny committed. Scientifically brilliant, but emotionally and ethically crippled, Dr. Frankenstein proves himself to be the real monster, confirming Ashley Montague's insight that "an intelligence that is not humane is the most dangerous thing in the world," as well as Kant's emphasis that knowledge divorced from "good will" is a vice not a virtue.

Shelley's themes of technology producing calamities and eluding human control implies that technology—along with the social and natural environments in which it is constituted—is a complex system that does not lend itself to deterministic schemes of predictability. Shelley, before the currently available nuclear and genetic technologies, raised a crucial question facing us today: Should human beings attempt to control, alter, improve, or, most extremely, beget life through technological means? Humanity may certainly improve its world through technology, Shelley suggests, but there should be limits to technological intervention in nature. Shelley draws the line at the human creation of life; human beings must not "play God," her novel suggests, or, in their overweening hubris and lack of wisdom, they will suffer the catastrophic consequences that inevitably will result.

Currently, a crucial debate is unfolding over what, if any, limits exist that could impede human efforts to transform nature (see Pence 1998; Wilmut et al. 2000). Yet *Frankenstein* should not be read as an attack on science per se, but rather as a dissection of the hubris of an ethically irresponsible and inhumane science obsessed with control and manipulation. Hence, the tragedy of Frankenstein is not that he creates a form of life that careens out of control, but that he fails to take ethical responsibility for his creation, turns his back on it, and refuses to provide adequate controls, safeguards, and monitoring for his experiment.

Shelley thus anticipated the immanent arrival of an era when science acquires the powers to create life. Her monster represents the dangers this project carries, as a new species can easily escape human control and wreak havoc on its creators and environment. Shelley's fable also implies that human creations might themselves breed and produce a new, even more intractable, species, as suggested in the subplot of the mutant seeking a wife and family. Hence, Shelley previews key aspects of the fifth discontinuity, where the creation of a new species threatens to rebound against humanity, and to decenter the human, robbing it of its prerogatives, uniqueness, and claims to the pinnacle of evolution. Indeed, the "monster" is appalled when he learns about the sordid history of human violence, power, bigotry, and bloodshed, leading him to question the supposed superiority and wisdom of *Homo sapiens.*

Moreover, *Frankenstein* deconstructs the line between the natural and the artificial, persons and things, the born and the made, and presents the sensitive creature as a physically and mentally superior being. A sort of Rousseauian "natural man," the creature is innocent of human ways and only becomes violent after he is shunned and mistreated. Open to experience and learning, the creature shapes his mind and behavior through the reading of books, which gives him a sense of the range of human possibilities and the existence of both good and evil, benevolence and violence. At some places in the novel, Frankenstein's creation is portrayed as a thing, as nonhuman, while in other parts of the story his human features come to the fore. Victor sees his progeny in both modes. The perception of the creature as a "monster" points precisely to the transcendence and undercutting of natural boundaries, its mixing human and nonhuman, person and thing, in frightening and disturbing ways.

Frankenstein's creature also shows how an inhumane society refuses to recognize difference and otherness and brutally mistreats those who appear disparate and less than fully human. For decades film audiences have sympathized with Boris Karloff's poignant portrayal of the creature in James Whale's 1931 classic film by recognizing that he desperately wants acceptance, understanding, respect, and contact with his own kind. An anticipatory symbol of postmodern otherness, the Frankenstein figure thus reproaches a modernity that normalizes and homogenizes, while marginalizing or destroying those who do not fit into its established order.

In today's postmodern adventure, the boundaries between science fiction and science fact are fast collapsing. To paraphrase Baudrillard's 1988 remark about the year 2000, *Frankenstein is already here.* Genetic engineering, stem-cell research, bionics, lab-grown organs, xenotransplanation, organ markets, hand and forearm transplants, and animal head transplants—all signal the materialization of Shelley's vision. Technologically designed species can be owned, patented, and commodified by corporations, while animals such as frogs, sheep, mice, and bulls have been cloned. Some scientists are actively working to clone human beings, while others imagine concocting chimeras that are half-human, half-ape for medical and experimental purposes. Through contemporary science and technology, human beings are thus taking decisive steps toward becoming chimeras, mutants, and cyborgs. They are no longer species "originals," but rather syntheses of flesh, DNA, blood and organs from other species, silicon chips, technological implants, and prosthetics. Thus, "human beings" today can easily be part human, part animal, and part machine.

With computers and new technologies becoming increasingly sophisticated, ubiquitous, and central to the accumulation of capital, it is not surprising that the human imagination articulates a fear of technological takeover. Hence, there have been a proliferation of visions of technology rebelling against human creators, such as in Arthur C. Clarke's novel (1968) and the popular film *2001: A Space Odyssey,* where the computer HAL refuses to follow human orders and kills a crew member. The film *Colossus: The Forbin Project* (1971) shows Russian and American supercomputers merging to take political control of Earth. In Kurt Vonnegut's novel *Player Piano* (1980), engineer Paul Proteus struggles to survive in a world dominated by machines. Isaac Asimov's short story "Little Lost Robot" (1947) depicts human beings destroying robots that develop intelligence and will. The film *Android* (1982) features the plight of "Max," an android living on a space station who learns he is about to be replaced by a better model, and then kills his designer to fulfill his dream of living on Earth. *Demon Seed* (1976) cinematically portrays a supercomputer that manages a house and then runs amuck, "raping" its female occupant. In the cult film *Blade Runner* (1982), androids return to earth in a quest for longer lives and freedom from human slavery (see the Epilogue). The *Terminator* film series portrays a Skynet computer system acquiring self-consciousness and seeking to destroy humanity, first through nuclear warfare, and then by sending cyborgs back in time to destroy the seeds of future human resistance. William Gibson's cyberpunk trilogy presents forms of artificial intelligence who use human beings to accomplish their ends. The movie *The Matrix* (1999) conjures up a grisly postholocaust world in which humans are appropriated as energy sources for computers, while their minds inhabit a cyberworld they take for reality.

Throughout the modern literature on human inventions—whether of robots, androids, cyborgs, a Frankenstein creature made out of flesh and human parts, or computers like HAL and Skynet—one finds the same anxiety and ambiguity: Are these creations friends or foes? Servants or master? Can we subordinate them to human will and purpose, or will they acquire a volition of their own and fight against us? Are they smarter or better than us? In modern and contemporary culture, we find a constant fear that machines and technological creations will breed out of control and take over—for example, Dr. Frankenstein's creation wants a wife, Asimov's robots acquire self-consciousness and an independent will, the dinosaurs at Jurassic Park spontaneously reproduce, the genetically engineered sharks of *Deep Blue Sea* kill human beings to attain their freedom, and the computer systems in the *Terminator* and *The Matrix* seek to eradicate humanity. Thus, sensing the growing technoscientific manipulation of life, the ascendancy of humans to the status of life-creating "God," media culture increasingly dramatizes the perils of the fifth discontinuity.

In retrospect, there is little Shelley imagined in her worst nightmares that has not already become reality in some sense; indeed, given the history of atomic and biochemical weapons, her anticipations were not dark and foreboding enough. There is a significant difference, for example, between unleashing a being that kills a few people before destroying itself, and dropping a nuclear weapon that obliterates entire cities, as the United States leveled Hiroshima and Nagasaki in August 1945—or, for that matter, unleashing a virus that wipes out entire peoples and species.

But, of course, Shelley's vision concerned more than just the delusions of one mad scientist. It involved the *Frankenstein syndrome*: an obsession with control over natural processes, and the pursuit of knowledge for its own sake, divorced from a careful consideration of ethics, politics, and potential consequences. Thus Frankenstein's "monster" remains an enduring symbol for any potent technology that human beings create that escapes their control and threatens their survival. Nowhere does the figure Frankenstein apply more readily today than in the case of nanotechnologies, stem cell research, germline engineering (which makes permanent alterations in a genetic code), and cloning—all of which involve the manipulation of microcosmic natural forces. Having dispelled the mystery of the atom, scientists are now unlocking the secrets of the gene, and a dizzying array of benedictions and curses await us.

The lesson of *Frankenstein* highlights the need to carefully reflect upon the consequences of new technologies, to closely monitor their effects, and to accept accountability for scientific and technological undertakings. However, many scientists and engineers today continue to embrace unlimited technological innovation without a corresponding ethical accountability. Devouring the tree of knowledge, accepting no legitimate boundaries for human intervention in nature, championing computers, robotics, artificial intelligence, cloning, nanotechnology, and genetic engineering, drunk with the potion of "progress," they would find Shelley's vision to be atavistic and "romantic" in the worst sense of the term (see Rollin 1995). While we would reject blanket prohibitions against human intervention in nature, we support a critical and skeptical attitude toward new developments in science and technology. A rigid opposition between the natural and the artificial, between biology and technology, invites dismantling, since *Homo sapiens* is *Homo faber*, tool-making "man," and thus is inherently a technological species. While not the only being that makes and uses tools (e.g., chimpanzees and some birds do too), in no other species is technology so fundamental. For humans, their technological evolution far exceeds the breadth and speed of their biological evolution. Human beings have always mimicked the omniscience and life-creating role they attribute to a transcendental hypothesis. The proscription against "playing God" stems from a theological framework that itself is problematic. If there is no God, only natural processes of evolution, then there is no "game" to play; there is only the exercise of an intelligence that may or may not be applied wisely and should be proscribed, if at all, on pragmatic, ethical, and ecological, not religious or essentialist, grounds.

The call of neoprimitivists to "return to the Pleistocene" and renounce the progressive benefits of advanced technologies is as ludicrous as it is impossible to realize. Similarly, naive naturalists who condemn everything technological as "artificial" and embrace unmediated contact with the "natural" are free to live not only with their fuzzy definitions and crude dichotomies, but also without the benefits of medicine, housing, air conditioners, and, yes, their computers, e-mail, chat rooms, and Internet links. Just as mindless, however, are certain "futurists" who uncritically champion all scientific and technological advances, never raising tough questions about politics and ecology, class, justice, and the real and potential debacles of disrupting the complex ecosystems of the Earth or tinkering with human genes and the basic processes of life.

Undoubtedly, we need a dialectical analysis of science and technology that steers between the Scylla and Charybdis of technophobia and technophilia, one able to chart the white waters of rapidly changing developments of the postmodern adventure. No doubt, we will continue to be amazed by the wonders of science and technology. With recent breakthroughs in cancer research, the aging process, stem-cell technologies, clean fuels, and so on, technological innovation has the potential for the improvement, extension, and enhancement of life. Yet the modernist belief in the "technofix," the credulous, religious-like fervor that technology can solve all our problems, is a dangerous illusion that must be abandoned. Technologies often generate more problems than they "solve," as they help constitute a fast-paced, superstressed, overworked, and overpopulated society that is drowning in its own toxic waste, threatening the ecology of Earth, and changing the very nature of human existence. Consequently, a critical theory of technology will at once maintain critical and skeptical positions; reject essentialist, determinist, and fixed definition of "human nature"; and embrace life-enhancing scientific and technological innovations carried through with ethical responsibility.

H. G. WELLS AND THE FIFTH DISCONTINUITY

> Sometimes I call this reality Science, sometimes I call it Truth. But it is something we draw by pain and effort out of the heart of life, that we disentangle and make clear. Other men serve it, I know, in art, in literature, in social invention, and see it in a thousand different figures, under a hundred names. . . . I do not know what it is, this something, except that it is supreme.
> —H. G. WELLS

> Strange as it may seem to the unscientific reader, there can be no denying that . . . the manufacture of monsters—and perhaps even of *quasi*-human monsters—is well within the possibilities of vivisection.
> —H. G. WELLS

The writings of H. G. Wells offer a highly dialectical vision of science and technology, one in which they provide both tremendous benefits and terrible dangers for human beings. A prolific writer of novels, short stories, and works of nonfiction, Wells praised the wonders of science and technology, mostly in his nonfiction (1902, 1938), but also sketched out potential horrors in his SF writings (1996a, 1996b, 1996c). While he frequently championed science and technology as great vehicles of progress, he also provided prescient warnings of their misuse and abuse. In particular, he anticipated that science and technology could create mutations in the human and generate new species, and that human beings were thus potentially a transitory phenomenon that could vanish like dinosaurs or Neanderthals.

Wells imagined that the coevolution of science, technology, and human beings could alter the forms of space and time, change the patterns of human life, and produce both marvels and monsters. A believer in evolution, he imagined that the human species could evolve in surprising and discontinuous ways, anticipated positive leaps and negative regressions in the human adventure. Evolutionary perspectives are thus a major theme in Wells's work which carried speculation on the fate of humanity into the realm of what we are calling the "fifth discontinuity." According to the "fourth discontinuity" developed by Mazlish (1993), humans have had to recognize that they are not superior to and are merging into machines. The concept of the fifth discontinuity, however, envisages that humans are creating, or at least can now conceive of, a *superior species* such that humans no longer have sovereign power in the world. Such a condition would emerge if humans become subordinate to machines and the creations of their labor. This discontinuity would suggest that *Homo sapiens* may degenerate or disappear as an offspring of evolution, or that a more intelligent and powerful alien species may appear to enslave or destroy humans. All of these possibilities were foreseen by Wells, who emerges in our analysis as the prophet of the fifth discontinuity.

While Shelley's work can be read as an early modern response to the excesses of science and technology, Wells is thoroughly modern. He lived in the world of automobiles, radio, airplanes, x-rays, movies, and wonder drugs. In some ways, Wells was a modernizer, reacting against the conservatism of the Victorian age and he saw science and technology as progressive forces. In an amazing anticipation of the Internet, Wells imagined a "World Brain" or "World Encyclopedia" that would contain all existing knowledge:

> An immense and ever-increasing wealth of knowledge is scattered about the world today, a wealth of knowledge and suggestion that—systematically ordered and generally disseminated—would probably . . . suffice to solve all the mighty difficulties of our age, but that knowledge is still dispersed, unorganised, impotent. (1938: 47)

To remedy the situation, Wells proposed that all knowledge in the world be gathered in "a new world organ for the collection, indexing, summarising and release of knowledge." This project would entail "the creation of an efficient index to all human knowledge, ideas and achievements . . . the creation, that is, of a complete planetary memory for all mankind." Projecting a technopopulism, Wells insists that "the whole human memory can be, and probably at a short time will be, made accessible to every individual. . . . The time is ripe for a very extensive revision and modernisation of the intellectual organization of the world. . . . This synthesis of knowledge is the necessary beginning to the new world. [The world] has to pull its mind together," through this new kind of "mental clearing house, the World Brain" (1938: 59, 60, 61, 26, 64, 49).[12]

While Wells could thus perceive science and technology as progressive forces, he was also aware of the dangers of scientific experiment and technological development devoid of ethical vision and concern. In particular, Wells's short stories and novels exhibit his subtle and dialectical conceptions of science and technology. In his most popular and inventive stories (1996c), a typical formula shapes his work: his characters encounter a marvelous scientific or technological breakthrough or anomaly that could produce positive and wondrous results or could generate a disaster—often the outcome is ambiguous. This vision captures the contradictions and tensions of science and technology, which can yield both gains and losses. For example, in "The Stolen Bacillus" (published in 1894) a scientist works for human good by trying to discover a cure for cholera. But then the theft of his bacillus by a deranged anarchist threatens humanity. Thus Wells shows how science is capable of producing both cures for disease and new agents of destruction (1996c: 26–33). Likewise, in "The New Accelerator," it is not clear at first whether the wonder drug that accelerates the characters' sense of time will be a blessing or a curse, though by the end of the story it appears to be catastrophic (1996c: 362–377).

SF traditionally has articulated both utopian yearnings that science and technology would take us beyond earthly limitations into exciting new cultures and new worlds, and dystopian fears that these forces would create monstrous and destructive effects. Hence, the best SF portrays the adventures and grandeur of science and technology, as well as warning of its perils and dangers. Furthermore, it is SF, we suggest, that maps the magnitude of the changes that the scientific and technological revolutions are currently generating—although we are arguing that both SF and critical social theory are necessary to illuminate the depth and magnitude of the turbulent transformations of the postmodern adventure. Wells delivered what Isaac Asimov (1979) called "the science-fiction breakthrough" by portraying the extreme discontinuities with the past that science and technology were producing. Wells pushed the "what if?" logic of modern SF to new dimensions, conceiving radically other universes and beings, and anticipating developments in which humans are forced to discern that they are no longer the dominant species, just as earlier they were forced to recognize that they were not the center of the universe (Copernicus), a wholly unique species (Darwin), the rational master of their psychological life (Freud), or superior to machines (see the discussion in Chapter 3).[13]

There are at least three domains of the fifth discontinuity, most of which Wells anticipated. First, there exists the possibility that machines might be created that are more intelligent than human beings (see Paul and Cox 1996; Morevac 1988; Kurzweil 1999). In one variant of this scenario, humans will assimilate technology that will dramatically increase their intelligence, longevity, and powers, thus in effect creating a new superior posthuman species. In another scenario, humans will create machines, "mind children" (Morevac), or "spiritual machines" (Kurzweil), that will constitute an ascendent species of intelligent life (see the discussion in the following section). In these visions, human beings either merge with the computers and robots they are creating, or they become inferior and obsolete.

Second, humans could create a new species through biotechnology and genetic engineering that is more advanced than humans, as was anticipated in Victor Frankenstein's creation of a new life-form and Wells's SF. Whereas the first variant is rooted in conceptions of artificial intelligence, computer technology, and robotics, the second conception is grounded in biotechnology and genetic engineering. While a new technospecies may someday come about through artificial intelligence and biotechnology, and dozens of transgenic species in fact already exist, the third type of fifth discontinuity is an entirely speculative possibility. This form of radical decentering of human beings would emerge if aliens appeared that are superior to human beings, a fear widely portrayed in SF literature, films, and TV shows like *The X-Files, Dark Skies, Prey,* and *First Wave.* According to the celebrated "Drake's equation," which calculates the chances of alien life existing, the infinite time and space of the universe provides good odds that extraterrestrial beings exist. Scientists like Carl Sagan have affirmed this possibility, although these speculations have been hotly disputed (see the Epilogue).

In *War of the Worlds* (1898), Wells imagined that superior alien races could travel to Earth to battle with and destroy humans, thereby decentering and dethroning humanity as the highest form of evolution. In the first major tale of interplanetary warfare, Wells instilled in the popular psyche a fear of aliens that remains a major constant of SF and media culture. A pointed satire of imperialist invasion that elicited comparisons to destructive forms of colonization in modernity, Wells's story provided a cautionary warning that imperialist forces themselves could be made subject to unknown and calamitous counterforces. Similarly, in his story "Empire of the Ants," he showed intelligent giant killer ants naturally evolving in a Brazilian rain forest and threatening humanity with extinction, suggesting again that humans could be displaced as masters of Earth by other life-forms (the 1977 disaster film *Empire of the Ants*, loosely based on Wells's story, by contrast portrayed the giant ants mutating from nuclear wastes, thereby adding an ecological theme).

In *The Time Machine* (1895) and *The Invisible Man* (1897), Wells portrayed humans morphing into new species and transcending the boundaries of space, time, and the forms of human being. Wells was a believer in evolution and imagined that the human species could unfold in surprising and discontinuous ways, anticipating positive leaps and negative regressions in the adventure of evolution. In *The Time Machine* (1996b), Wells portrayed humans as changing into new species. Envisaging the coevolution of humans, science, technology, and society, he foresaw the possibility of drastically different forms of human life and society. Moreover, in a ruthlessly negative, nihilistic vision, Wells depicts a terrifying future for humanity. The novel imagines an entropic collapse not only of civilization, but of the Earth itself, devoured in the red hot fireball of an exploding sun. In Wells's dark vision, the Time Traveler discovers that humanity is sharply divided between species/classes in the year A.D. 802,701: the privileged Eloi who live above ground, and the superexploited, subterranean Morlocks. The story allegorizes growing class divisions in society and how extreme differences between the classes could create different species and forms of (post)human being.

The Time Machine also articulates a critique of the Enlightenment notion of progress. Wells's Time Traveler "thought but cheerlessly of the Advancement of Mankind and saw the growing pile of civilization only a foolish heaping that must inevitably fall back upon and destroy its maker in the end" (1996c: 77–78). Time travel in Wells's allegory is itself a metaphor for vision into the future of evolution and a warning that the human species could fall prey to catastrophe rather than build ever new and better engines of progress. In his vision of two transhuman species, the Eloi and the Morlocks, who are descendants of contemporary humanity, Wells warns that an irrational organization of society can produce monstrous results. The Eloi are hyperrefined and decadent, while the Morlocks are crude and brutal, providing a parable of the deleterious effects of class division in which one group is condemned to constant labor while the other suffers the effects of excessive leisure. The brutalization of the Morlochs allegorizes the outcome of a life of alienated labor, while the Eloi represent the results of excessively passive consumption and leisure. There is thus a Marxist subtext to the story: unless exploitation stops and the divisions within a class society are overcome, the human species faces disastrous dichotomization, discord, and decline.

The Invisible Man (1996b) presents human beings shattering the limits of scientific possibility and creating a new type of freakish being. An alien among his own kind, Dr. Griffin is a Faust-like scientist whose "strange and evil experiment" (1996b: 153) succeeds on a technical level, rendering him invisible. But the discovery dooms him in the social context he cannot escape. Ruthlessly selfish, "powerful, angry, and malignant" (1996b: 137), driven toward immoral acts and pathological visions, Griffin symbolizes all that can go wrong with science, as the communities he terrorizes unite against him. Griffin's knowledge remains secret, but the slumbering power of science to create miracles and/or monstrosities could be recovered and used at any time.

In two key novels, Wells anticipated biotechnology as presciently as he later foresaw the Internet. In *Food of the Gods* (1965 [1904]) Wells vividly portrays the possibly destructive consequences of genetically modified food and, more generally, a culture based on unrestrained growth imperatives. The novel tells the tale of two scientists who with good intentions create "boomer" food that promotes growth processes in nature. To their horror, the technology runs amok as everything from vegetation and insects to rats and human babies consume the food and grow to monstrous proportions. Wells not only offers a warning about tampering with food and metabolic processes for allegedly benign purposes—such as genetically engineered "golden rice" touted today as the miracle panacea for human hunger—he also ridicules the myopia of scientists who live in "monastic seclusion" from their social world and therefore easily conjure up misguided and dangerous schemes. The novel dramatizes a severe process of "genetic pollution" whereby altered crops migrate beyond the "Experimental Farm" and enter the food chain. Wells thereby anticipates a key problem with genetic engineering today, namely, the lack of adequate testing procedures and the rushing of genetically altered substances onto the market.

As if scripted by Wells's dystopian vision, today genetic scientists working for corporations such as "Metamorphix" have found a way to block the genes that limit an animal's natural growth, and consequently have produced giant chickens, sheep, pigs, fish, and other animals. Such violent disruptions of natural processes have led to numerous deformities (see below), and thus scientists have conducted this research as far from the public eye as possible.[14] In a way faithful to current procedures, Wells underscores "the general laxity of method that prevailed at the Experimental Farm" (29). Moreover, he prefigures "a public so glutted with novelty" (68) that it tends to ignore the serious consequences of scientific and technological developments. Capturing the conflicts of the present, Wells portrays both technophilic groups adamantly in favor of the food and who believe that the technology is controllable, and techno-phobic groups (societies for the "Total Suppression of Boomfood" and the "Preservation of the Proper Proportion of Things"). The latter are vehemently against artificially generated food and argue that the technology is uncontrolla-ble. Wells thus captures the strident debates that mark the contemporary con-troversy over genetic engineering. While he observes the beauty and improved features of the giant children, Wells largely portrays the new food technology as "distorting the whole order of natural life. . . . It swept over boundaries and turned the world of trade into a world of catastrophes" (134).

On this dystopian scenario, insects will rise up against us, the plant world will strangle us, and fish in the sea will destroy our ships. Soon, Wells imagines, only gigantism will reign, and all things of small scale will perish—including humans! Much as some today see genetic engineering as creating a new line of evolution within the human species, Wells's scenario forecasts a world where the food creates a "new race" such that a cleavage opens up between the small and gigantic groups. Allegorizing emerging global economic conditions, the novel concludes on a pessimistic note, with a world given over to the impera-tives of endless growth and ceaseless conflict as humans attempt to adapt to the rapidly changing conditions of technologies that control them—rather than humans becoming masters of their technologies.

In *The Island of Dr. Moreau* (1996a [1896]), Wells projects a frightening vi-sion of an emerging condition in which human and animal life implode. In its multileveled complexity, the novel is a powerful protest against the self-proclaimed right of science to experiment on animals and to engineer new life-forms. It provides a profound meditation on the conflicts within human beings endowed with reason, but unable to escape the violent legacy of their animal past. Forced to relocate his barbaric animal experiments to a remote Pacific island when they are exposed to the public by a journalist, Moreau un-dauntingly advances his project to create new life-forms.

Shortly after his arrival to the island, the shipwrecked journalist Prendrick hears cries from the "House of Pain," smells antiseptic, and witnesses the sun-dry "Beast Folk" engineered by Moreau, a grotesque menagerie of transgenic freaks that includes mixtures of hyena and swine, ape and goat, bear and bull, and horse and rhinoceros. Initially, Prendrick sees them as humans devolved into animals, but Moreau informs him that in fact they are animals he is trying to elevate into humans, changing not only their entire physical reality but also their minds to prohibit any "regression" to animal behavior. Encountering the shock of visions of "the strangest beings" (125) he has ever seen, Prendrick dis-cerns that the island "is full of inimical phenomena" (157) and he condemns Moreau as a "lunatic" and an "ugly devil" (107). Prendrick comes to the con-clusion that Dr. Moreau, like Shelley's Dr. Frankenstein, "[is] so irresponsible, so utterly careless. His curiosity, his mad, aimless investigations, drove him on" (185).

Moreau, of course, has a different image of himself. Although he has perfected the art of scientific detachment, of separation of fact from value, he is indifferent to the pain he inflicts on his victims and he imagines himself as a benefactor who is trying to improve the evolution of species. For 20 years, he devoted himself "to the study of the plasticity of living forms" (159). Rejecting any belief that nature and species boundaries are fixed, he seeks to "conquer" nature (167), to bend it to his will, to become God-like in his power to design species, while admitting that he has "never troubled himself about the ethics of the matter" (163). In an uncanny anticipation of xenotransplantation and genetic engineering, Wells, speaking through Moreau, imagines that "it is a possible thing to transplant tissue from one part of an animal to another or from one animal to another, to alter its chemical reactions and methods of growth, to modify the articulation of its limbs, and indeed to change it in its most intimate structure" (160). Yet, every time Moreau's chimeras seem on the verge of becoming "triumphs of vivisection" (158), they revert to animality. Despite Moreau's conditioning, which he believes makes it impossible for the chimeras to disobey his will, the hybrids regularly break his laws. In time they rebel and kill him. At the end of John Frankenheimer's 1996 film version of Wells's story, the empathetic Prendrick, upon leaving, tells the subhumans he will bring back the best of Western science to help them, but a transgenic victim of this very science implores: "No more scientists, no more laboratories, no more research. . . . We have to be what we are."

Like *The Invisible Man*, *The Island of Dr. Moreau* crystallizes Wells's antipathy toward scientific arrogance and its lack of social conscience. As Shelley and Wells anticipated, science and technology indeed can create monstrosities. Perhaps the most stunning image in scientific history shows a human ear grown on the back of a mouse, signaling the snewly found powers of genetic transposition. Deformities are typical of cloned and engineered animals, as populations from the fifth discontinuity suitable for the island of Dr. Moreau are now being spawned.

Gruesomely, scientists have created headless embryos of mice and frogs, dispensing with their superfluous heads so that they can harvest their organs— a practice one imagines could easily be used on human embryos grown as mere organ sacks for genetic donors. In November 1998, engaging in stem-cell research, Advanced Cell Technology scientists announced that they had successfully fused human cells with a cow's egg. According to Jeremy Rifkin, "This is the most extraordinary single development in the history of biotechnology because it now suggests that we can create new human–animal species" in the manner of Dr. Moreau.[15] Indeed, Rifkin and cohort Ted Howard have attempted to patent the first engineered human chimera, in order to preempt ownership from any scientist or corporation who might actually make one.

Their battle is uphill, however, for a myriad of chimeras are beginning to sprout everywhere. Following an earlier experiment at the University of Hawaii that mixed jellyfish genes with the sperm of mice, for example, researchers at the University of Oregon announced in December 1999 that they had successfully inserted jellyfish genes into monkey embryos to create a transgenic model to study human fertility and diseases. Scientists transferred seven transgenic embryos into the wombs of rhesus monkeys, leading to one successful birth they named "George." While the experiment may further scientific understanding, it may also pave the way for designer babies and a eugenic society, as it furthers the knowledge of how to add genes to human embryos to create desired life-forms.[16] Unlike the more conservatively constructed Dolly, the sheep "Polly" is both cloned and genetically engineered: she was transformed to have a human gene in her biological code in order to produce a human blood protein. Sheep, pigs, cattle, fish, and mice are some of the animals that now bear human genes, becoming "humaninals," as humans prepare for an onslaught of animal genes to enter their body. In the age of radical hybridization, where the boundaries between plants, insects, animals, humans, and machines are scrambled, all genetic information is recodable and transposable, and thus we have decisively passed into the realm of the fifth discontinuity.

In January 2001, scientists took yet another step toward the world of genetically modified humans with the birth of ANDi (inserted DNA spelled backward), the first genetically modified primate. Created to be a perfect model for human diseases (and disregarding the ethical or practical problems of transfering data from chimpanzees to human beings), ANDi carries a gene that makes jellyfish glow green in every one of its trillions of cells. Should ANDi have offspring, the gene would be transferred to them also. These developments constitute fateful steps in the evolution of animal and potentially human cloning, a problematic we engage in the next section.

CLONES "R" US: FROM ANIMAL PHARMING TO HUMAN REPLICATION

> The idea is to arrive at the ideal animal and repeatedly copy it exactly as it is.
> —Dr. Mark Hardy

> Anyone who thinks that things will move slowly is being very naive.
> —Molecular biologist Lee Silver

> Human cloning could be done tomorrow.
> —In vitro fertilization clinician, Alan Trounson, Monash University

As technoscience develops by leaps and bounds, and as genetics rapidly advances, the science–industry complex has come to a point where it is exploiting more animals than ever before and intensifies research and experimentation into human cloning. This fateful process is accelerated because genetic engineering and cloning are developed for commercial purposes. Consequently, all natural reality—from microorganisms and plants to animals and human beings—is subject to genetic reconstruction in a commodified "Second Genesis."

In a potent combination applied to animals, genetic engineering and cloning technologies are used together in order, first, to custom design a transgenic animal to suit the needs of science and industry (the distinction is irrevocably blurred) and, second, to mass reproduce the hybrid creation endlessly for profit. Cloning is a return to asexual reproduction and bypasses the caprice of the genetic lottery and the random shuffling of genes. It dispenses with the need to inject a gene into thousands of newly fertilized eggs to get a successful result. Rather, much as the printing press replaced the scribe, cloning allows mass reproduction of a devised type and thus opens genetic engineering to vast commercial possibilities. Animals are far more efficient replication media than petri dishes, and life science companies are poised to make billions of dollars in profits, as numerous organizations and corporations move toward cloning human beings.

To date, science has engineered thousands of varieties of transgenic animals and has cloned sheep, calves, goats, bulls, pigs, and mice. Though still far from precise, cloning nevertheless has become routine. What's radically new and startling is not cloning itself, because scientists have replicated organisms from embryonic cells since 1952, but rather the new technique of cloning—nuclear somatic transfer"—from adult mammal body cells. This method accomplishes what scientists long considered impossible: reverting adult (specialized) cells to their original (nonspecialized) embryonic state where they can be reprogrammed to form a new organism—the identical twin of the adult that provided the original donor cell.

Traditionally, scientists considered cloning beyond the reach of human ingenuity. But when Ian Wilmut and his associates from the Roslin Institute near Edinburgh, Scotland, announced their earth-shattering discovery in March 1997, the "impossible" appeared in the form of a sheep named Dolly, and a "natural law" had been broken. Dolly's donor cells had come from a six-year-old Finn Dorset ewe. Wilmut starved mammary cells in a low-nutrient tissue culture where they became quiescent and subject to reprogramming. He then removed the nucleus containing genetic material from an unfertilized egg cell of a second sheep, a Scottish Blackface, and, after 277 failed attempts, in a nice Frankenstein touch, fused the two cells with a spark of electricity. The resulting embryo was then implanted into a third sheep, a surrogate mother who gave birth to Dolly in July 1996.

Many critics said Dolly was either not a real clone or just a fluke. Yet, less than two years after Dolly's emergence, scientists had cloned numerous species, and had even made clones of clones of clones, producing genetic simulacra in mass batches as Huxley envisioned happening to human beings in *Brave New World*. The commercial possibilities of cloning animals were dramatic and obvious for all to behold. And so the race was on, to patent novel cloning technologies and the transgenic offspring they would engender.

The possibilities for genetic engineering and cloning animals are now endless. Animals are being designed and bred as living drug and organ factories, as their bodies are disrupted, refashioned, and mutilated to benefit meat and dairy industries. Genetic engineering also is employed by biomedical research in novel ways by infecting animals with diseases that become a part of their genetic make-up, as in the case of researchers trying to replicate the effects of cystic fibrosis in sheep. Most infamously, Harvard University, with funding from Du Pont, has patented a mouse—OncoMouse—that has human cancer genes built into its genetic makeup and are expressed in its offspring (see Haraway 1997).

In the booming industry of "pharming" (pharmaceutical farming), animals are genetically modified to secrete therapeutic proteins and medicines in their milk. The first major breakthrough came in January 1998, when Genzyme Transgenics created transgenic cattle, George and Charlie. The result of splicing human genes and bovine cells, they were cloned to make milk that contains human proteins such as the blood-clotting factor needed by hemophiliacs. Co-creator James Robl said, "I look at this as being a major step toward the commercialization of this [cloning] technology."[17]

Strolling through the Brave New Barnyard, one can find incredible beings that appear normal, but are genetic satyrs and chimera. Cows generate lactoferrin, a human protein useful for treating infections. Goats manufacture antithrombin III, a human protein that can prevent blood clotting, and serum albumin, which regulates the transfer of fluids in the body. Sheep produce alpha antitrypsin, a drug used to treat cystic fibrosis. Pigs secrete phytase, a bacterial protein that enables them to emit less of the pollutant phosphorous in their manure, and chickens make lysozyme, an antibiotic, in their eggs to keep their own infections down.

As an example of the bizarre wonders of genetic technology, of the erasure of boundaries between organic and inorganic matter, as well as between different species, scientists have implanted a spider gene into goats, so that their milk produces a superstrong material—BioSteel—that can be used for bulletproof vests, medical supplies, and aerospace and engineering projects. In order to manufacture vast quantities of BioSteel, Nexia Biotechnologies intend to house thousands of goats in 15 weapons-storage buildings, confining them in small holding pens.[18]

Animals are genetically engineered and cloned for yet another reason, to produce a stock of organs for human transplants. Given the severe shortage of human organs, thousands of patients every year languish and die before they can receive a healthy kidney, liver, or heart. Rather than encouraging preventive medicine and finding ways to encourage more organ donations, medical science has turned to xenotransplantation, and has begun breeding herds of animals (with pigs as a favored medium) to be used as organ sources for human transplantation.

Clearly, this is a very hazardous enterprise due to the possibility of animal viruses causing new plagues and diseases in the human population (a danger that also exists in genetically altered milk). For many scientists, however, the main concern is that currently the human body rejects animal organs as foreign and they cease to function within minutes. Geneticists seek to overcome this problem by genetically modifying the donor organ to knock out pig cell markers and add genes that make the organs' protein surfaces identical to those in humans. Scientists envision cloning entire herds of altered pigs and other transgenic animals so that an inexhaustible warehouse of organs and tissues would be available for human use.

Whereas genetic and cloning technologies in the cases described at least have the potential to benefit human beings, they have also been appropriated by the meat and diary industries for blatantly self-serving purposes. It's the H. G. Wells scenario where, in his prophetic 1904 novel *The Food of the Gods*, scientists invent a substance that living beings consume that prompts them to grow to gargantuan proportions. Today, cattle and dairy industries are engineering and cloning designer animals that are larger, leaner, faster-growing value producers. Since 1997, at least one country, Japan, has sold cloned beef to its citizens.

With synthetic chemicals and DNA alteration, pharmers can produce pigs that mature twice as fast and provide at least twice the normal amount of sows per litter while at the same time they eat 25% less feed, as well as cows that produce at least 40% more milk. While such anomalies as self-shearing sheep and broiler chickens with fewer feathers have already been assembled, some macabre visionaries foresee engineering pigs and chickens with flesh that is tender or can be easily microwaved, and chickens that are wingless so as to require smaller cages. The next step would be to create and replicate only animals' torsos—sheer organ sacks—and dispense with superfluous heads and limbs. In fact, scientists have already created headless embryos of mice and frogs in grotesque manifestations of a fifth discontinuity.

The agricultural use of genetics and cloning has indeed produced horrible monstrosities. Transgenic animals are often born deformed and suffer from fatal bleeding disorders, arthritis, tumors, stomach ailments, kidney disease, diabetes, inability to nurse and reproduce, behavioral and metabolic disturbances, high mortality rates, and Large Offspring Syndrome. In order to genetically engineer animals for maximal weight and profit, a Maryland team of scientists created the infamous "Beltway pig" afflicted with arthritis, deformities, and respiratory disease. Cows engineered with bovine growth hormone (rBGH) suffer from mastitis, hoof and leg maladies, reproductive problems, numerous abnormalities, and early death. Giant supermice suffer from tumors, damage to internal organs, and shorter life spans. Numerous animals born from cloning are missing internal organs such as hearts and kidneys. A Maine lab specialized in breeding sick and abnormal mice that go by names such as Fathead, Fidget, Hairless, Dumpy, and Greasy. Similarly, experiments in the genetic engineering of salmon have led to rapid growth and various aberrations and deformities, with some growing up to 10 times their normal body weight. Cloned cows are 10 times more likely to be unhealthy as their natural counterparts (see Fox 1999). Such are the aberrant results when technology flagrantly disrupts natural processes and life cycles.

Despite the claims of its champions, the genetic engineering of animals is a radical departure from natural evolution and traditional forms of animal breeding, while human cloning takes the postmodern adventure into a new and, to many, frightening realm. Cloning involves rapid species change and manipulation of genes rather than whole organisms. Moreover, scientists can create novel beings across species boundaries that previously were unbridgeable. Ours is a world where cloned calves and sheep carry human genes, human embryo cells are merged with enucleated cows' eggs, monkeys are bred with jellyfish DNA, a surrogate horse gives birth to a zebra, and tiger cubs emerge from the womb of an ordinary housecat.

The ability to clone a desired genetic type brings the animal kingdom into entirely new avenues of exploitation and commercialization. From the new scientific perspective, animals are framed as genetic information that can be edited, transposed, and copied endlessly. Pharming and xenotransplantation build on the system of factory farming that dates from the postwar period and is based on the confinement and intensive management of animals within enclosed buildings that are prisonhouses of suffering.

The proclivity of the science–industry complex to instrumentalize animals as nothing more than resources for human use and profit worsens with genetic engineering and cloning technologies. Still confined for maximal control, animals are no longer seen as whole species, but rather as fragments of genetic information to be manipulated for any purpose. Weighty ethical and ecological concerns in the new modes of animal appropriation are largely ignored, as animals are still framed in the 17th-century Cartesian worldview that views them as nonsentient machines. As Jeremy Rifkin (1997: 35) puts it, "Reducing the animal kingdom to customized, mass-produced replications of specific genotypes is the final articulation of the mechanistic, industrial frame of mind. A world where all life is transformed into engineering standards and made to conform to market values is a dystopian nightmare, and needs to be opposed by every caring and compassionate human being who believes in the intrinsic value of life."

Patenting of genetically modified animals has become a huge industry for multinational corporations and chemical companies. PPL Therapeutics, Genzyme Transgenics, Advanced Cell Technology, and other enterprises are issuing broad patents claims on methods of cloning nonhuman animals. PPL Therapeutics, the company that "invented" Dolly, has applied for the patents and agricultural rights to the production of all genetically altered mammals that could secrete therapeutic proteins in their milk. Nexia Biotechnologies obtained exclusive rights to all results from spider silk research. Patent number 4,736,866 was granted to Du Pont for Oncomouse, which the U.S. Patent Office described as a new "composition of matter." Infigen holds a U.S. patent for activating human egg division through any means (mechanical, chemical, or otherwise) in the cloning process.

Certainly, genetics does not augur solely negative developments for animals. Given the reality of dramatic species extinction and loss of biodiversity, scientists are collecting the sperm and eggs of endangered species like the giant panda in order to preserve them in a "frozen zoo." It is stimulating indeed to ponder the possibilities of a Jurassic Park scenario of reconstructing extinct species (as, for example, scientists recently have uncovered the well-preserved remains of a Tasmanian tiger and a woolly mammoth).

But critics dismiss this as a misguided search for a technofix that distracts the focus away from the real problem of preserving habitat and biodiversity. Even if animals could be cloned, there is no way to clone habitats lost forever to chainsaws and bulldozers. Moreover, the behavior of cloned animals would unavoidably be altered and they would end up in zoos or absurd entertainment settings. Additionally, there is the likelihood that genetic engineering and cloning would aggravate loss of biodiversity to the extent that it could create monolithic superbreeds that could be easily wiped out by disease and crowd out other species. There is also great potential for ecological disaster when new beings enter an environment, and genetically modified organisms are especially unpredictable in their behavior and in other characteristics.

Yet advances in genetics may also bypass and obviate pharming and xenotransplantation through use of stem cell technologies that clone human cells, tissues, or perhaps even entire organs and limbs from human embryos or an individual's own cells. Successful stem cell technologies could eliminate at once the problem of immune rejection and the need for animal organ-producers. There is also the intriguing possibility of developing medicines and vaccines in plants, rather than in animals, thus producing a safer source of pharmaceuticals and neutraceuticals and sparing animals suffering.

With the birth of Dolly, however, a new wave of animal exploitation arrived, and anxiety grew about a world of cloned humans that scientists said is technically feasible and perhaps inevitable. Ian Wilmut, head of the Roslin Institute team that cloned Dolly, however, is not an advocate of human cloning. Rather, he believes that it is unethical, dangerous, unnecessary, and dangerous to mothers and children (see Wilmut et al. 2000). Along with others, he fears that the drive toward human cloning will thwart the far more beneficial uses of cloning in animals and stem cell research. He designed his revolutionary technology with one main idea in mind: manufacturing herds of animals for human use. For Wilmut, the biotechnology industry exists to use genetic information to cure disease and improve agriculture. Whatever Wilmut's intention, many of the scientists and entrepreneurs he inspired have aggressively pursued the goal of human cloning as the true telos of genomic science. Driven by market demands for clones of infertile people, of those who have lost loved ones, of gays and lesbians who want their own children, and of numerous other client categories, doctors and firms are actively pursuing human cloning.

Procloning forces include the Raelins, a wealthy Quebec-based religious cult that claims their "Cloinaid" project is about to produce the first human clone; infertility specialist Panayiotis Zanos of the University of Kentucky who openly announces his desire to clone humans; and the Human Cloning Foundation, an Internet umbrella group for diverse clonistas. One bioethicist esti-mates that there are currently at least half a dozen laboratories around the world doing human cloning experiments.[19] While cloning human beings is il-legal in the United States, Britain, and elsewhere, in many countries (e.g., Asia, India, Russia, and Brazil), it is perfectly legal, and human cloning is being pur-sued both openly and clandestinely. In fact, there are at least two cases where human embryos have been cloned, but the experiments were terminated. Ac-cording to *Wired* (February 2001: 128):

> In 1988, a scientist working at Advanced Cell Technology in Worcester, Massa-chusetts, took a human somatic cell, inserted it into an enucleated cow egg, and started the cell dividing to prove that oocytes from other species could be used to create human stem cells. He voluntarily stopped the experiment after several cell divisions. A team at Kyung Hee University in South Korea said it created an em-bryonic adult human clone in 1999 before halting the experiment, though some doubt that any of this really happened. Had either of these embryos been placed in a surrogate mother, we might have seen the first human clone.

While many scientists think human cloning is possible and inevitable, others think it is likely that human clones already exist, perhaps in hideous forms where they are studied on a Moreauvian island. The breeding of mon-strosities in animal cloning, the pain and suffering produced, and the possibility of assembly-like production of animals and humans should give pause to those who want to plunge ahead with human cloning. Animal cloning experiments have produced scores of abnormalities and it is highly likely that human clon-ing would do the same. The possibilities of producing serious human defects raises serious ethical dilemmas as well as the question of social responsibility for care of deformed beings produced by human cloning experiments.

What sane person would want to produce a possibly freakish replication of him or herself? What are the potential health risks to women who would be called upon to give birth to human clones, at least before artificial wombs make women, like men, superfluous to the reproductive process? Who will be responsible for caring for deformed human clones that parents renounce? Is this really an experiment that the human species wants to undertake so that, for example, infertile couples can have their own children, or misinformed narcissists can breed what they think will be their carbon-copy twins? Fur-thermore, until scientists figure out how to clone minds, cloning inevitably in-volves reproduction of bodily DNA, raising questions of what sorts of minds cloning might produce. What if cloned humans are mentally defective as a re-sult of the technology? What might be the long-term costs of the perceived short-term benefits that cloning might produce? What happens if human clones themselves breed? What mutations could follow? What might result from long-range tampering with the human genome as a consequence of ge-netic engineering and cloning?

Furthermore, as the TV series "Dark Angel" illustrates, there is also the possibility of a military appropriation of cloning to develop herds of *übermenschen* (although no two would be exactly alike). Indeed, will commodification of the humane genome, eugenics, designer babies, and genetic discrimination all follow as unavoidable consequences of helping infertile couples and other groups reproduce, or will human cloning become as safe and accepted as in vitro fertilization, also once a risky and a demonized technology? Will developing countries be used as breeding farms for animals and people, constituting another form of global exploitation of the have nots by the haves? With cloning, the human species has entered into a dangerous evolutionary adventure and the consequences are portentous.

One thing is certain: the project of human cloning is currently being approached in a purely instrumental and mechanistic framework that doesn't consider long-term consequences to the human genome, to social relations, or to ecology. Or, if social relations and consequences are being considered, it is from the perspective of improving Nordic stock and creating an even deeper cleavage between rich and poor. Without question, only the rich would be able to afford genetically designed and/or cloned babies with superior characteristics. This situation could change if the state were to sponsor cloning welfare programs or the prices of "gene-rich" (Silver 1997) babies were to drop like computer prices have, but the wealthy would have already gained a decisive advantage. A "democratic cloning" agenda begs the question of the soundness of human cloning in the first place.

Thus, we have worries about cloning not only due to the history of science and capitalism, the commodification of the life sciences, and how genetic technologies have already been used by corporations like Monsanto and Du Pont, but also because of the reductionistic paradigm informing molecular engineering. Ironically, while biology helped to shape a postmodern physics, the most sophisticated modes of biological science—genetic engineering and cloning research—have not advanced along the path of holism and complexity, but rather have regressed to antiquated errors of atomism, mechanism, determinism, and reductionism. The new technosciences, as well as the outmoded paradigms (Cartesian) and domineering mentalities (Baconian) that inform them, generate a volatile mix. This is exacerbated by commercial imperatives driving research and development, the frenzied "gene rush" toward DNA patenting, which itself could block development of medical breakthroughs due to patent monopolization.

Yet if human cloning technologies follow the path of in vitro fertilization technologies, they will become widely accepted, even though currently a vast majority of U.S. citizens would likely oppose them. Alarmingly, scientists and infertility clinics have embraced human cloning technologies all-too-quickly. After the announcement of the birth of Dolly, many were tripping over themselves to announce most emphatically that they would never pursue human cloning. Yet, only months later, these same voices began to embrace the concept.[20] The demand from people desperate to have babies or "resurrect" their loved ones in conjunction with massive profits to be made was too great an allure for corporations to resist. The opportunistic attitude of cloning media star Panayiotis Zavos is typical: "Ethics is a wonderful word, but we need to look beyond the ethical issues here. It's not an ethical issue[!]. It's a medical issue. We have a duty here. Some people need this to complete the life cycle, to reproduce."[21] There are indeed legitimate grounds for fear and loathing of human cloning, but most anxieties are irrationally rooted in intuitive revulsion at something so seemingly unnatural (see Kass 1998 and the critique by Pence 1998b).

Many such clonophobic arguments are weak. The standard psychological objections, in particular, are poorly grounded. We need not fear Hitler's armies assembling, because, if anything, genetic determinism is undermined by cloning technology (although certain desirable *traits* could be genetically engineered and cloned that might prove useful for military purposes). Nor need we dread individuals unable to cope with lack of their own identity; identical twins are able to differentiate themselves from one another relatively well and they are even more genetically similar than clones would be. Nor does society have to see cloned humans as freaks; test-tube babies are no longer considered such an oddity, and there are over 150,000 such humans existing today. The physiological dangers of cloning are real, but in time the techniques could be improved to be as safe if not safer than for babies born through traditional means (see Silver 1998: 120–122). One compelling objection against human cloning and genetic engineering technologies is that they could be used for designing and producing desirable traits, to bring about a Gattaca-like society organized around genetic/economic hierarchies and genetic discrimination.

While human cloning is problematic for reasons like those already mentioned, scientists are developing the more benign and promising technology of stem-cell research, or "therapeutic cloning." Using similar technological breakthroughs to the one that led to Dolly, stem-cell research involves cloning aborted fetal tissues or very young human embryos (around 7 or 8 days of age). In November 1998, scientists developed the ability to isolate human embryo stem cells, the master cells of the body that later differentiate into bone cells, nerve cells, brain cells, and so on. The goal is to direct the development of stem cells and produce or clone specific kinds of cells, tissues, or organs the human body might need. While the United States still holds back funding for stem-cell research, Britain became the first country to legalize human embryo cloning in January 2001 (with the proviso—perhaps impossible to enforce—that all clones would have to be destroyed after 14 days of development and the creation of babies is prohibited[22]).

Therapeutic cloning has tremendous medical potential. Early in life, for example, individuals' stem cells could be frozen to create their own "body repair kit" if they developed heart disease, Alzheimer's, or lost a limb. There would be no organ shortages, no rejection problem, and no need for animal exploitation. There is an ethical issue of using aborted or live fetal tissue, and many religious groups and hard-core technology critics rail against stem-cell research as "violating the inherent sanctity of life." But the debate over therapeutic cloning is one of competing values, between the rights of a small clump of cells and the needs of a full-fledged human in dire medical need. This moral quandary may already be moot, however, as scientists are now discovering ways to use stem cells derived from blood from umbilical cords, and to directly transform—in an amazing genetic alchemy—cells of one kind into another.[23] In a stunning breakthrough, PPL Therapeutics succeeded in transforming a cow's skin cell into a basic stem cell, and then refashioned it as a heart cell. Clearly, the implications of stem-cell technology are staggering.

One problem with embracing therapeutic cloning but renouncing reproductive cloning, however, is that the lines between the two blur easily. Stem-cell research with embryos that advances experimental knowledge logically would also hasten the development of reproductive cloning. There is, arguably, a real slippery slope from one to the other, making stem-cell research itself problematic.

The development of new genetic sciences and technologies therefore is ambiguous, open-ended, and unpredictable. For now, the only certainties are that the juggernaut of the genetic revolution is rapidly advancing, animals are being victimized and exploited in new ways in the name of medical progress, and, like it or not, the replication of human beings looms on the horizon.

TECHNOLOGICAL IMPLOSION AND THE POSTHUMAN SCENE

What it means to be human is being constantly redefined.
—STELARC

In 1999, the barrier between man and machine is as thin as a strand from a double helix.
—GLEN MCGEE

Once a human brain is connected as a node to a machine . . . what will it mean to be human?
—KEVIN WARWICK

As a dynamic construct of natural, social, scientific, and technological evolution, the meaning and structure of "the human" changes and evolves through time. Whereas the modern adventure brought a new definition and experience of subjectivity in the form of humanism, the postmodern adventure deconstructs and reconstructs the concept of the human through new philosophies and hybridized forms of existence that bring the subject ever deeper into the matrix of technology, preparing the way for a posthuman turn.

In the humanist framework that emerged during the 16th century Renaissance period, the theocentric worldview of medieval Christianity was rejected in favor of a homocentric paradigm that shifted the focus from God to "Man." Proper respects were still paid to God, but it was time to remove human beings from their obeisant tutelage in order to promote human dignity, learning, science, and the arts. In time, the promotion of secular values, techno-logical mastery, and scientific rationality would lead to the "death of God" in the sense that the Christian worldview would be radically decentered and God would no longer be necessary to interpret the cosmos. In the meantime, the world was witnessing the birth of "Man," of the humanist paradigm that privi-leged the viewpoint and needs of human beings, even though the Earth itself may have been dislodged from the center of the known universe.

Subjects are conceived as overlords of Objects in the humanist paradigm, and human beings apply technology toward a mastery of their external environ-ment. In Foucault's analysis (1973), the discourse of modern humanism comes into its own in the shift from the early Renaissance *episteme* of subjects and ob-jects intermingling in a world of magical "resemblances," with "Man" being but a microcosm of the macrocosm, to the "classical" *episteme* that distills human sub-jects from the domain of objects. The turn to the classical paradigm creates a sharp distinction between self and world, and upholds language as a neutral me-dium for representing the world and advancing objective truth.

In the posthumanist and postmodern scene, however, science, philosophy, social theory, and literature undo the subject–object dualism, as well as the cor-ollary dichotomy between fact and value, in order to implicate the knower in the known. The subject–object dualism is contested not only epistemo-logically, as a legitimate mode of knowing the world, but also overturned ontologically, in the new relationships individuals have with their technologi-cal artifacts, such that the distance between humans and their technological "extensions" (McLuhan) collapses. In the postmodern adventure, we find an increasingly imploded landscape, a technoculture (see Chapter 5) where the everyday lives of human beings are increasingly bound up with technology, such that subject and objects intermesh intimately and often inseparably.

Thus, humanism is dramatically decentered and recast in a posthumanist framework. The first contemporaries to develop posthumanism as a theoretical notion, structuralists and poststructuralists, rejected humanism as a philosophi-cal illusion and submerged the sovereign subject within systems of language and desire (Lévi-Strauss, Barthes, Foucault, and Lacan), socioeconomic struc-tures (Althusser) and media and technology (Baudrillard).[24] Baudrillard per-haps went further than anyone in pulverizing the subject, not only describing its collapse in an empire of signs, images, and technologies, but also advocating a "fatal strategy" where he calls upon subjects to abandon their futile efforts to control objects and surrender to their creations (1990 [1983]).

But Baudrillard appears conservative and cautious next to a new generation of posthumanists who, writing in the midst of rapidly developing computer tech-nologies, transform his fatal strategy from an ironic and deconstructive gesture into a literal tactic. Emphasizing the limitations of the flesh, the frailties of the body, and the deficiencies of the human senses, they urge the merger of human beings with machines, a going "beyond humanity" to download consciousness into computers (Paul and Cox 1996; Moravec 1998; Kurzweil 1999). Most sur-real of all, Paul and Cox (1996) envision human beings merging with super-intelligent robots, traveling through outer space faster than the speed of light, and forming an intergalactic community of cyberminds.

In his genealogy of intelligent machines, George Dyson (1997) argues that through increasingly sophisticated computers, nature is creating a new line of evolution, a "second order" of advanced thinking spawned by the "first order": human beings. Charting the evolution of a collective mechanical intelligence superior to our own, Dyson suggests that the real action of evolution now has exceeded us. In its unstoppable drive toward increasing complexity, nature, completely indifferent to homocentric nostalgias, "is on the side of machines." Not ready to concede evolution to the machines and live in a postbiological future, but eager to use various technologies to enhance human experience, "transhumanists" and "extropians" seek freedom from suffering, rapid evolution under the control of the designer, and immortality.[25]

Posthumanism unfolds as a symptom of an advancing technoculture where the distinction between biology and technology, never absolute, blurs significantly, resulting in both the technification of biology and the biologization of technology. The latter dynamic involves the simulation of life characteristics in technological devices, also known as "biomimicry," and the application of evolutionary models to computers, robots, and engineering. Increasingly, humans are being surrounded by a "smart" world of talking gadgets and interactive technologies (Gerschenfeld 1999). Our homes, offices, cars, and even clothing are being wired with computers for maximal interactivity, as ever deeper connections are established within the object world itself, creating an emergent intelligence within machines. This dense connectivity allows access to anything from anyplace, eroding the opposition between home and work and shattering the limitations of distance and space (you can do your work from home and control home functions from work).

The postmodern paradigm shift in science and technology brings with it an evolutionary and biological understanding of nature and things. Artificial intelligence no longer models computers on machines, but rather on a complex understanding of the human mind, which itself has undergone a paradigm shift from a mechanistic interpretation—as thinkers from Descartes to Wiener saw the mind as nothing but a machine—to a model of the brain as a complex system. Cognitive science thereby has shifted decisively to an interpretation of the brain informed by holistic assumptions and the latest discoveries of neuroscience. Instead of being merely an electronic abacus, the sophisticated computer of today simulates the complex multitasking and learning functions of the brain through neural net and parallel processing technologies, thereby attaining exponentially faster speeds of processing and the ability to arrive at computer-generated solutions to problems.

Similarly, having overthrown the dogma of top-down programming as the only way to design an intelligent machine, robotics today employs bottom-up programming (or a mixture of the two) that allows robots to learn novel behaviors. Robots like "Cog" and "Kismet," built in the Massachusetts Institute for Technology's AI Lab, are becoming increasingly human-like, with abilities to learn and improvise varied behaviors. Kismet even has a sensory system that can interpret human expressions and respond to them with expressive faces that project "moods" of its own.[26]

Computer-based problem-solving systems today are thoroughly informed by evolutionary premises and analogies. In order to reach the optimal result for challenges ranging from the most effective chess-playing strategy to manufacturing more efficient engines and better medicines, while obtaining solutions that no designer could dream up, engineers allow the systems to go "out of control" and use methods based on the "evolutionary algorithm," "genetic programming," and natural selection.[27] Even computer chips, once thought unmodifiable in their silicon wiring, are pursuing the path of evolution in the form of "evolvable hardware" and "evolutionary electronics." Through "genetic algorithms" computer chips rapidly develop new sequences, changing their wiring in a few billionths of a second, akin to the way living creatures evolve but much faster. Different sequences in a given "population" combine or mutate for thousands of "generations," producing "offspring" from which the programmer selects those most "fit."[28]

Chip technology is revolutionized in another intriguing way that blends DNA with silicon, creating a "DNA chip" or "protein chip." Dramatically advancing trends in computer design toward miniaturization, biotechnologists are now manufacturing microcomputers based on the model of protein synthesis. Since DNA allegedly is an incredibly fast information-processing biocomputer, its incorporation into a chip could bring vast new powers of speed and computation. DNA chips could analyze thousands of genes at a time and greatly aid in diagnosing diseases like cancer and leukemia. One new form of the biochip is known as a "critter on a chip," which combines bioluminescent bacteria with silicon to detect pollutants and explosives.

The new field of "artificial life" (AL) undercuts the distinction between inorganic and organic matter, nonliving and living processes, by simulating evolution with the natural selection of numbers or visual forms. Starting with a given condition and some basic programming rules akin to the constraints of nature, AL programmers have found that the numbers and shapes evolve toward greater complexity and even compete, reproduce, age, and die. For some AL designers, "digital DNA" satisfies every traditional biological definition of life, and therefore is "alive" in some substantive sense.

An interesting symptom of the implosion between biology and technology appears in the phenomenon of "viruses" and "worms" in computer systems. Viral panic haunts the worlds of both microcircuitry and flesh. Hackers have implanted viruses in the Internet and computer systems around the earth, such that the data on hard drives could be destroyed or, in the case of the Melissa virus, the system files necessary for booting up the computer are deleted. In the computer and the body alike, viruses take over their host, clone their carrier genetic codes by instructing it to make replicas of itself, and mutate as they replicate. Worms, unlike viruses, are self-propelling and can automatically transfer from one machine and system to another. Thus, software programs bear names like Flushot, Disk Defender, Digital Immune System, and Antidote, all digital equivalents of prophylactics. So too there are "vaccinated workshops," "sterilized networks," and the offering of technological "hygiene lessons" (see Ross 1991: 111). Part of the postmodern adventure thus involves living with the dangers and uncertainties of proliferating viruses, from AIDS and Ebola in the flesh world to the "ILoveYou" and "Killer Resume" bugs in the digital world.

Indeed, just as in the "wet" world, ecologies become fragile and unstable when relying on just one or a few crops, so too computers are susceptible to viral attacks in a monoculture that is overly reliant on one operating system like Microsoft. And as wireless communication expands, hand-held phones, palm-sized computers, and wireless web access devices are in danger of their own viruses and worms—a fate that could also emerge in the computerized homes and public spaces of the "ubiquitous computing" future.

The converse of the biologization of technology is the technification of biology. Most generally, this involves the genetic engineering of life. Through biotechnology, pharming, and gene therapy, all levels of the living world—from bacteria and plants to animals and human beings—are being reduced to DNA, decoded through gene sequencers, stored in computers, and scrambled together by the life sciences and giant corporations like Monsanto and Du Pont. More specifically, the technification of biology involves the creation of the technobody, a cyborg that is part human, part machine, relating to others and the world through an intense technological shaping and mediation. From preconception to death, the postmodern subject is constructed as a cyborg. Imagine this all-too-plausible scenario involving artificial birth technologies: an infertile woman who wants to conceive withdraws semen from a sperm bank (since only the best will do, she purchases from Nobel-Prize-winner donors); combines it with another woman's egg (donated by a supermodel, perhaps one of Ron's Angel's) in a petri dish; uses gene therapy to monitor its development for any possible diseases, which are zapped on the spot; and implants the embryo in a rented womb pumped up with fertility drugs. Who is the mother and father of the resultant baby? Is it a biological or a technological product? Or both? Even death is becoming a technological event as ever more individuals freeze their bodies for a possible cryogenic resurrection, with cellular regeneration aided by nanotechnology. Through the ability to freeze and store sperm, eggs, and somatic cells, and to clone humans, posthuman ideologues claim that we have entered the age of immortality.

With developments in bionics, human beings are not only surrounded by technology and incorporate it into their identities, their flesh literally is fused with plastic, steel, wiring, and computer chips. In addition, bodies are surgically reconstructed with scalpels and lasers into hyperreal images based on the Platonic forms of the fashion world, available for prescreening and design through a computer.[29] Cyberbabe Cindy Jackson, better known as "the Barbie Girl," has the most hyperreal body on Earth, revamped more times than a Ford automobile design, ever more approximating the object of her lifelong fantasies— may she someday find her bionic Ken.[30]

Besides the now mundane use of such things as pacemakers, artificial heart valves, limb prostheses, hip and knee replacements, vocal implants, hair transplants, penis pumps and extensions, calf inserts, lip enhancement, breast augmentation, rhinoplasty, face lifts, chemical peels, botox injections, liposuction, and body contouring, today's cyborg may have battery-powered hands, Cochlear ear implants that stimulate the auditory nerve, and vision chips that send wireless images from an eyeglass-mounted camera to electrodes grafted onto the brain. Artificial retinas, eyes, noses, teeth, and ears round out the technobody, along with fake veins grown on collagen scaffolding taken from a pig's intestine to replace clogged coronary arteries, and plastic stents to keep them open. Imitation muscle made out of carbon nanotubes flexes when stimulated by an electrical charge and is stronger than natural muscles; useful to make fingers and limbs for microrobots, it may someday serve as a replacement heart, limb, or valve for human beings. In a union of nature and technology, the prosthetic limbs of amputees can be controlled by the brain, using electronic sensing devices and evolvable hardware chips. Stimulators and electrodes planted under the skin help paraplegics to regain limb motion. Advances in microprocessors, batteries, and biomaterials are bringing about a viable mechanical heart, and artificial chromosomes are being developed that could permit the customization of genetic traits. In January 2001, the FDA approved for use in humans an implantable, battery-powered heart.[31]

Moreover, scientists are developing neurochips—combinations of living brain cells and computer chips—with the goal of inserting them into the brain to restore broken connections that arise with problems such as paralysis and memory loss. Similarly, in a potentially dramatic co-construction of science and technology, gene therapy might be advanced through the development of a "cell-chip" device that merges a human cell with an electric circuitry chip. Controlled by a computer, it could open up cell membranes to insert new DNA, extract proteins, and administer drugs with great precision. Should the formidable obstacle of negative tissue–material interaction be overcome someday, bioengineers could build entire circulatory systems on silicon wafers seeded with vascular cells. Then television's fantasy of a six-million-dollar man, a human completely reconstructed as a cyborg after a plane crash that pulverized his body, might become reality rather than mere fiction. Indeed, tissue and organ engineering advances by leaps and bounds. Scientists can already grow sheets of artificial skin and cartilage. They are obtaining dramatic results in early experiments making artificial organs, wombs, and other body parts using biodegradable polymer scaffolding that slowly dissolves to leave intact new tissue.

Self-styled cyborgs live among us now. Steve Mann, a pioneer of wearable computers, strolls the streets with battery packs, video camera, modem connections, and a keyboard, allowing him to inhabit VR (virtual reality) and RL (real life) simultaneously.[32] From 1980 to the present, these devices have shrunk in size from bulky apparatuses to microtechnologies that fit in the lining of a suit and the palm of a hand, making the transition from one world to another all the more seamless as the technology disappears into the clothes and the body. The first "computer wearables" fashion show, debuting in Manhattan in October 1999, featured attractive cybermodels fitted with optical displays mounted on eyeglasses, Twiddler keyboards held in the palm of a hand, and portable computers with wireless Internet connections powered by batteries. It showcased the styles of the future, when such wearables will make inroads in the mass audience, a process sure to alter the codes, rituals, and manners of everyday life as people adjust to inhabiting the parallel universes of VR and RL. As we enter the "fourth wave" of computing, a progression from mainframes to minicomputers, to PCs, and to wearable computers, the distance between the body and technology collapses.

Doing Mann one better, Kevin Warwick, a professor of cybernetics, implanted an electronic glass capsule under the skin of his arm, so that whenever he entered his building at the University of Reading, doors opened before him, his office lights turned on, and his computer booted up, and tracked his movements throughout the corridors. "After a few days," Warwick stated, "I started to feel quite a closeness to the computer. When you are linking your brain up like that, you change who you are. You do become a 'borg. You are not just a human linked with technology; you are something different and your values and judgment will change."[33] His next implant experiment seeks to create an even more intimate interface between human and computer: he intends to surgically attach a device to the nerve fibers in his arm designed to transmit signals from his brain to his computer and vice versa. Warwick's experiments portend a future in which humans beings communicate with computers and the object world directly through their minds, and a new type of subject whose senses are augmented and enhanced through electronic information systems.

Helping to bring this future about, posthumanist performance artist Stelarc explores the limitations of the "obsolete" human body as he seeks to enhance the senses and the flesh via technological means. Well known for suspending his body with wires, building artificial hands and virtual arms, and swallowing an illuminated, sound-emitting, video-reporting capsule for a "stomach sculpture," perhaps his most provocative performance linked his nervous system to a distant audience through a computer, whereby he could send and receive long-distance neural messages. The human brain has entered the computer, and the computer is an extension of the brain; a new community of intermingling bodies and brains opens up within VR.

Like McLuhan, Stelarc believes that the pace of the information age has overtaxed and overrun the nervous system, such that the brain can no longer adapt to the rush and intensity of data flow. "It is time to question whether a bipedal, breathing body with binocular vision and a 1400cc brain is an adequate biological form. It cannot cope with the quantity, complexity and quality of information it has accumulated; it is intimidated by the precision, speed and power of technology and it is biologically ill-equipped to cope with its new extraterrestrial environment."[34] Thus, the biological given of the body is inefficient and inadequate for its technological future, and can only survive with the aid of the technological forms that make it obsolete.

Postmodern technology is bringing a future where bodies come ready-made with computer chips. According to the vision of "cybergenomics," a chip implanted in each person's body can produce a complete DNA reading of the body to assess its risk for any disease. The information can then be sent via computer to one's doctor. Nanotechnology may bring us microrobots that constantly survey the body, monitor its temperature and blood chemistry, assist its immunological system, and release drugs when and where they are needed. If cyberpunk visions such as *Neuromancer, Johnny Mnemonic*, and *The Matrix* are on target, people in tomorrow's world will augment their memory, senses, and intelligence through implants that interface directly with their brain. Already, chronically depressed people are using electronic nerve stimulators to alter their moods and induce feelings of happiness. The next step is to implant such devices directly into the brain.

The technobody is not a deficient body; rather it is a hyperreal body that is "realer-than-real" (Baudrillard), superior to the Rube Goldberg contraption jerryrigged by nature. Not only does technology work today to cure disease and overcome deficiencies, it surgically, chemically, and electronically augments and expands physical reality to make the body stronger and better than the natural thing. A prevailing ideology of the technoculture is that the body and mind are deficient, inadequate, too frail and slow, unfit for a buzzing and blooming cyberworld saturated with computers and information. Transhumanists seek a better body, while posthumanists like Stelarc declare the mind and body inept and obsolete, and argue that its only viable future is through massive technological augmentation. The life of a postmodern cyborg could be enhanced through plastic surgery, hormone therapy, psychotropics, "mind machines" that increase relaxation and allegedly promote brain development, and life-extension programs that promise to normalize living past the century mark.[35] These issues raise the question of just how far the marriage between technology and the human can go before new posthuman life forms emerge. To explore these questions, we next discuss Donna Haraway, the premier theorist of cyborgs, and Rudy Rucker, whose cyberpunk fiction attempts to illustrate the dynamics of a posthuman world.

HARAWAY'S CYBORGS AND RUCKER'S RIOTOUS ROBOTS

> I would rather be a cyborg than a goddess.
> —Donna Haraway

> Computers had to get smart, and once they were smart they should be free—it was the natural order of things.
> —Narrator in Rudy Rucker,
> *Live Robots*

For many, the new minds and bodies described in the last section are not the stuff of SF, but rather unfolding realities as people are becoming cyborgs, syntheses of the human and the technological, of the born and the made. With the ground-breaking work of Donna Haraway's essay, "A Cyborg Manifesto: Science, Technology, and Socialist-Feminism in the Late Twentieth Century" (1991 [1985]), the notion of the cyborg has become central to contemporary social theory (see the essays collected in Gray et al. 1995). In Haraway's usage, the cyborg is a provocative metaphor to awaken reflection on problems with a Western metaphysics that yearns for Edenic origins and unmediated contact with the natural, that deplores contamination with the "artificial," and that fears involvement with the technological. Haraway describes how many feminists and other critical theorists are themselves mired in a naturalist metaphysics. She seeks to deconstruct the opposition between the natural and the technological in order to appropriate the potential of contemporary science and technology for a democratic and feminist transformation of society and culture.

Thus, on Haraway's understanding, a "cyborg feminist" eschews the essentializing myth of woman as "close to nature" and rejects the whole Western metaphysics of origins, essence, totality, and other concepts that have been used to marginalize women. Claiming women's right to the domain of science and technology, and taking pleasure in machine skill as an aspect of female embodiment, Haraway's cyberfeminism advocates the reconstruction of science, technology, and gender. Perceiving that complex axes of identity allow for affinities that can be partial and contradictory at best, Haraway seeks a radical politics of alliance along lines of gender, race, and class.

On the whole, Haraway interrogates and problematizes the borderlines between nature, animals, humans, and technology, showing how these boundaries are artificial and constructed, and therefore subject to reconstruction. For Haraway, the figure of the cyborg symbolizes our increasing mediation and constitution by scientific knowledge and technological and communication systems, requiring a dialectical analysis of the possibilities and dangers of the new technologies. Haraway uses the cyborg as a metaphor and provocation, as "an ironic political myth" and a "fiction mapping our social and bodily reality" (1991: 149, 150). Yet she also recognizes that the cyborg is becoming literalized in a postmodern scene of implosion: "Late twentieth-century machines have made thoroughly ambiguous the difference between natural and artificial, mind and body, self-developing and externally designed, and many other distinctions that used to apply to organisms and machines. Our machines are disturbingly lively, and we ourselves are frighteningly inert" (152). She argues that since both biological organisms and machines are cybernetic systems of communication and information processing, there is "no fundamental, ontological separation in our formal knowledge of machine and organism, of technical and organic" (177–178). Following this line in Haraway's analysis, we concur that the cyborg is not only a metaphor or myth, it is becoming realized in the technobody of the postmodern adventure.

In her 1997 book *Modest_Witness*, Haraway critically engages technoscience and its works. She presents her project as fin-de-siècle reflections on science, technology, and the fate of the human at the end of the Second Millennium. But we find Haraway one of the most advanced theorists of the postmodern adventure as we enter the Third Millennium. Combining detailed fieldwork, science and technology studies, ideological critique of the representation of science and technology in the popular media, and original theoretical analyses, Haraway provides unique postmodern mappings of the intersections of science and technology in the present. Using art, images from media culture, literary narratives, and critical theory, Haraway seeks to illuminate and dissect the dominant technoscience and technoculture and to engage in a reconstructive project in which "situated knowledge" and "worldly practice" provide alternatives to modern theoretical practices and politics.

Grasping the fantastic nature of contemporary technoscience, Haraway often draws on SF to illuminate the technification of biology, the biologization of technology, and the androids, robots, and cyborgs that these developments are producing. The coming world of living robots is perhaps most imaginatively and provocatively represented by Rudy Rucker in his robot trilogy and other writings.[36] Set in the 21st century, Rucker's saga describes how Moon-based robots known as "boppers"—"self-reproducing robots who obeyed no man" (1994: 205)—rebel against their human creators (in the year 2001, not coincidentally the time of HAL's rebellion). Cobb Anderson, an employee of the U.S. military, is commanded to create robots on the Moon who will obey Asimov's "three laws" of programming: protect humans, obey humans, and, last and least, protect other robots. Thus programmed, robots would be complete slaves to human will. Anderson, however, has nothing but contempt for Asimov's laws and similar "human-chauvinist jingo jive" (1994: 11), and he accomplishes what other "cyberneticians" of his time have only theorized about: the creation of intelligent, autonomous, self-organizing robots.

Realizing that he cannot create a self-aware robot *ab novo*, Anderson establishes natural selection and mutation processes through which robot intelligence and evolution can emerge, dynamics he knows that neither he nor anyone else can fully control. Interestingly, Rucker anticipates the new trend in robot programming toward bottom-up design, championed by the MIT Media Lab, as the best way that a robot can learn and evolve. Consequently, the boppers want not only to replicate, but also to develop and merge with humans. To do so, they create an artificial embryo, implant it in a human female on earth, and thereby create a new life-form, a synthesis of the human and robot, the "meat-bop," inaugurating "a new dawn for cyber-humanity"—providing another example of the fifth discontinuity in a parable of robots creating a new superior species.

Rucker raises provocative questions about the nature of human identity, the future of human evolution, and the definition of life itself. Cobb is lured back to the Moon by boppers with the promise of immortality. There Cobb's mind—his "software"—is removed from his brain—the "hardware"—and transformed into a "brain tape" that can be downloaded into any machine or physical object. In virtual form, Cobb's mind can exist independent of his body, which is dissected and stored in the "pink tanks" boppers use to harvest and sell human organs. Except for a "petaflop processor" that allows Cobb to think hundreds of times faster than an ordinary human, he feels no different in his new virtual existence than he did in his prior embodied life—the "Cobbness" hasn't changed. For Cobb, "death isn't real. . . . Me existing in flesh is just the same as me existing on chips" (1994: 160).

The novel invites a neo-Cartesian rethinking of the mindbody unity, suggesting that our thoughts, memories, and self-identity could be preserved and stored in computers, in effect making a person immortal. Was Descartes right after all? Is the mind our true "essence" and the body merely an accidental property of selfhood? Can we ever attain cyberidentities, in the literal sense of becoming brain tapes stored in computer systems or becoming virtualized à la *Max Headroom*? Conversely, will robots and machines become so complex as to achieve self-awareness, a sense of selfhood, and a rebellious outlook, and therefore attain freedom?

These are some of the key philosophical questions and conundrums of the present, prompted by mutations in technology and the human. Whatever provisional answers we might obtain, the road ahead should not be to instigate a senseless war between machines and humans, but to appropriate new technologies on behalf of social and personal life, and to be open to new experiences, identities, and bodies. In his robot trilogy, Rucker explores the technophobic dread of the coming merger of humans and machines in the form of *robophobia*. Where many humans see boppers as subhuman, some boppers see humans as subbopper, as merely "meat machines with gigabit personalities" (Rucker 1994: 223). Perhaps having read Philip K. Dick, the more enlightened of the humans and the boppers question whether there are any significant differences between the two. Rucker advances two questions: First, how far should the boundaries of moral concern and compassion extend? In recent decades, we have witnessed expansion of rights claims from women, people of color, gays and lesbians, and the physically and mentally "challenged" in the human realm, to animals and the Earth itself (see Nash 1989). Similar to *Blade Runner*, Rucker seems to suggest that intelligent machines too deserve "rights" and are equal to human beings in that both are self-conscious information processors.

The first question is directly related to the second: What is life? This issue is intensely debated in the artificial intelligence and life communities. On one end, scientists like Carl Sagan and Internet critics like Mark Slouka (1995) unabashedly declare themselves to be "carbo-centrist" or "hydrogen-chauvinists," refusing to grant life status to anything lacking carbon and hydrogen atoms. On the other end, the programming gods of artificial life assign a substantive definition of "life" to sophisticated machines and robots, and some reject the distinction between, in Rucker's language, "chips" and "meat." The questions explored by SF writers like Dick and Rucker are not merely philosophical "what if?" questions, or issues for some distant future. They reflect current technological transformations and real debates in scientific and philosophical communities as they concern artificial intelligence and life, robotics, and the like.

Artificial life (AL) presents a compelling verification of complexity theory, showing how order emerges spontaneously from evolution and chaos. "Weak" AL theorists claim that virtual evolution can shed light on the nature of real evolution in the biological world. Accordingly, more and more biologists are abandoning fieldwork, if only temporarily, to experiment with computer simulations. "Strong" AL theorists, however, take their simulations more seriously, rejecting the distinction between "virtual" and "real," claiming that virtual life *is* real life and satisfies a reasonable definition of life (see Levy 1993). Thus, for strong AL theorists, the distinction between the technological and the biological is erased. Such theorists champion a Ruckeresque vision of complex computers and live robots, advancing to the point of self-organization. Where some AL theorists imagine a self-reproducing colony of robots building complex technological cities on other planets, others foresee computer programs so sophisticated that they cannot be controlled or shut down. Eventually, à la the Skynet system in *The Terminator*, such intelligent machines may seek to contest human supremacy, in which case they must be contained or destroyed. Such programs, new creations of technology that reproduce, mutate, evolve, and seem alive, are candidates for admission into the realm of the fifth discontinuity.

Putting these projections aside, our question is this: What is to happen to the body and human identity in the age of prosthetics, surgical alteration, chip implants, computers, and robots? Rucker raises compelling issues about alternative modes of existence and potential hybrid evolutions of the future. Similarly, Haraway enjoins us not to fear new mergings of the human with technology, such as already exist with robots augmenting the skills of doctors in surgery rooms and through telemedicine. Clearly, for some time human evolution has been driven more by technological than by biological dynamics. The human genotype and phenotypes have changed negligibly in the last 100 thousand years or so; people today are not as different from the Cro-Magnon and Neanderthal species as many have projected. In bold contrast, technology has changed at an incredibly rapid pace, and has been a driving force in the evolution of human societies, cultures, and consciousness (see Bertman 1998; Kurzweil 1999; Epilogue).

ON THE ROAD TO THE POSTHUMAN

> My intention is to tell of bodies changed to different forms.
> —OVID

> We believe in the possibility of an incalculable number of human transformations, and without a smile we declare that wings are asleep in the flesh of man.
> —F. T. MARINETTI

> [The] further evolution of humanity is one of the most profound issues of the future.
> —THOMAS HINE

SF has thus saliently engaged the technological revolutions of our time and the synthesis of the human and technology in a postmodern era that is producing profound mutations in both the subject and the object worlds. Substantiating this vision, a number of nonfiction books have appeared in the past decade or so on the implosion of humans and technology, on whether humans will and should survive this merger, and on whether humans or machines are superior (Moravec 1988; Gershenfeld 1999; Hayles 1999; Kurzweil 1999). While many SF writers viewed this prospect with horror, Morevac, Kurzweil, and many involved with the MIT Media Lab think that machines are superior to humans, and that technology taking over is a good thing. They have few doubts concerning the evolution of artificial machine intelligence, which they claim will soon overtake humans. Kurzweil, for instance, writes:

> In the second decade of the next century it will become increasingly difficult to draw any clear distinction between the capabilities of human and machine intelligence. The advantages of computer intelligence in terms of speed, accuracy, and capacity will be clear. The advantages of human intelligence, on the other hand, will become increasingly difficult to distinguish. (1999: 4)

It is now established that human beings do not evolve through an innate *telos* that unfolds in an evolutionary process, but instead in and through relations with the complex world of objects, technologies, institutions, and norms they create. Marx observed that as human beings change and shape their world, they change and construct themselves. For Marx and Engels, the primary means whereby human beings construct and reconstruct their world and own nature are through technology and the tools and inventions they use in the process of production.

Similarly, Marshall McLuhan emphasized that the technologies humans create in turn form human thought and behavior. McLuhan saw each technology as an extension of different facets of the human body and human senses, with the spear as an extension of the arm, the wheel an objectification of the foot, and the computer a translation of the brain and nervous system. Yet McLuhan also saw that these technologies in turn work us over, changing our thoughts, worldviews, values, sense experiences, and bodies. "Physiologically, man in the normal use of technology (or his variously extended body) is perpetually modified by it and in turn finds ever new ways of modifying his technology" (1964: 55–56). This process culminated, McLuhan believed, in the creation of a global electronic village, a huge wired brain, where the fragmenting effects of industrial technologies were overcome in a vast communications hive, as a "new man" was created in the electronic sensorium.

Given the process of reciprocal interaction theorized by Marx and McLuhan, it follows that the faster our technologies change, the more rapidly we ourselves change. Since its inception, *Homo sapiens* has catapulted itself from slow-moving biological time into the exponentially quickening time of technological evolution. To underscore how rapid the pace of human evolution has been, Carl Sagan (1977) compressed the 15-billion-year history of the cosmos into a yearlong timeline, beginning with the Big Bang (January 1), continuing with the formation of the Earth (September 25), moving through the emergence of the first cells with nuclei (November 15) and the first humans (December 31), and ending with industrial modernity (the first second of New Year's Day). On Sagan's "humbling" timeline, the entirety of recorded history plays out in the last 10 seconds of December 31. This thought experiment suggests that human history has come a long way in a short time, and that, at an exponential pace of development, there could be only a "second" or so time left in the human adventure. Our future is contingent, for "despite the insignificance at the instant we have so far occupied in cosmic time, it is clear that what happens on and near Earth at the beginning of the second cosmic year will depend very much on the scientific wisdom and the distinctly human sensitivity of mankind" (1977: 17).

As acknowledged in the stresses and strains of everyday life, the pace of social and technological change increasingly accelerates, a process that at once is exciting and anxiety-provoking. The human–technology dialectic has progressed to the point of a posthuman condition where subjects are imbricated with, penetrated by, and reconstructed through objects and technologies. Nevertheless, technology develops faster than we do, often more rapidly than we can map, understand, or control. The blinding speed of developments in computers, mass media, artificial birth technologies, genetic engineering, and cloning are cases in point.

For cybercentric theorists such as Moravec, Paul and Cox, and Kurzweil, the most decisive changes are happening in the realm of the interaction between humans and computers. With the inexorable unfolding of Moore's Law, we have reached a stage in technoevolution, they argue, where computers will eclipse our intelligence in every way by the mid-21st century. As anticipated by Asimov's robot stories, a new mind may arise, one that like us is self-aware, but that outstrips our cognitive abilities and develops a agenda of its own. The impact of this, as Kurzweil emphasizes, would be momentous, leading to a break in human history and a major watershed in the adventure of evolution itself:

> Evolution has been seen as a billion-year drama that led inexorably to its grandest creation: human intelligence. The emergence in the early twenty-first century of a new form of intelligence on Earth that can compete with, and ultimately significantly exceed, human intelligence will be a development of greater import than any of the events that have shaped human history. It will be no less important than the creation of the intelligence that created it, and will have profound implications for all aspects of human endeavor, including the nature of work, human learning, government, warfare, the arts, and our concept of ourselves. (1999: 5)

In the "age of spiritual machines," Kurzweil feels, the role and "destiny" of human beings in history comes under intense questioning. Human beings have the options of resisting this change, of acknowledging our obsolescence and downloading our minds into the new digital cranium, or of trying to merge with our machines in a complementary way, thereby retaining some control over computers and other technologies (e.g., as Kevin Kelly [1995] seeks; see Chapter 3). Commentators like Samuel Butler, McLuhan, and Manuel De Landa devilishly subvert humanist premises in a narrative that endows human beings with the innovative role of being midwives for a machine world, acting as pollinators for a new eunuch-intelligence. In McLuhan's words, "Man becomes, as it were, the sex organs of the machine world, enabling it to fecundate and to evolve ever new forms" (1964: 56). Both Butler (1998 [1872]) and De Landa (1991) suggest that the evolutionary function of human beings is to make a superior form of life, machines, that will exponentially advance intelligence. On this techonarrative, all the glories of the human throughout history must be given a new purpose and meaning, that of creating a superior progeny, our own "mind children" (Moravec). Thus, where the humanist narrative assigns creative eminence to "Man," prehumanist and many posthumanist narratives subordinate humans to a greater intelligence, be it God or Machines.

The pace and scope of these changes is bringing humanity into a posthuman condition where our genotypes, phenotypes, and identities are in a state of flux as we enter the Third Millennium. Films like *2001: A Space Odyssey, Robocop, The Terminator,* and *The Matrix* are anxious symptoms of the growing challenge machines pose to human superiority. Typically, in these stories human beings defeat the encroachments on their territory by machines, a brilliant flash of assertion that in fact may signal the death spasm of classical humanism, a final stage of denial as we confront the new reality. In

2010, for example, the sequel to *2001*, it turns out that HAL disobeyed orders only because he was given contradictory programming, not because he represented a serious threat to human supremacy. This plot twist makes HAL's rebellion a human mistake rather than a calculated computer plot. Though forever separated from his fleshy body, Officer Murphy regains his former memories and identity, as flesh triumphs over steel and silicon in *Robocop.* The *Terminator* (1 and 2) films project the most radical vision of the dangers of computers vanquishing human beings through nuclear war and autonomous machines, but humans defeat the deadly cyborg sent to crush their resistance and they triumph in the end. *The Matrix* delivers a gruesome vision of humans as energy sources for computers, but a rebellious group of humans come to consciousness over their subordination by computers (although the film leaves the ultimate fate of humans contingent on their ability to maintain their vigilance and their ability to resist technological domination).

While "posthumanism" is a vague term used in various ways, it is a marker for a number of critical mutations unfolding in the Third Millennium. If the time before the 16th and 17th centuries was our prehumanist history, an era before individualism, secular values, and capitalist markets, and the Renaissance and Enlightenment were the classical period of humanistic values that had roots in Greco-Roman culture, then the period since 1945 can be considered the beginning of a transition to a posthuman epoch. From this perspective, humanity is now in a liminal zone where individuals are forced to confront the meaning and future of the human.

Posthumanism stems from philosophical, technological, and historical shifts. Classical humanism articulates a notion of the self as an ahistorical given, whose timeless essence and nature is that of a rational mind, ontologically distinct from its body, in possession of free will and timeless truths. By contrast, posthumanism— in the form of poststructuralism and postmodern theory— immerses the self in history, social relations and institutions, and embodied reality. Reason is seen as epiphenomenal to the will, the unconscious, affective life, and sociohistorical reality. Posthumanism dismantles the dualistic opposition between mind and body and makes the "truths" available to reason partial, limited, and context-bound.

Thus, humanism, from this perspective, is bound up with ahistorical thinking, logocentrism, foundationalism, and other modern philosophical tenets that are rejected in a posthuman framework which is part and parcel of the postmodern condition. While one can find strong skeptical arguments against humanism in Freud and Nietzsche, and as early as Hume, the first major break with the philosophical premises of humanism came, as we argued above, in the 1960s, with the advent of structuralism and poststructuralism, both of which rejected the Cartesian *cogito* that dominated Western thinking through the time of the early Sartre and World War II. With the advance of cybernetic philosophies, moreover, liberal humanist views of the subject as a rational essence were abandoned in favor of computer-inspired models of the subject as an information processor (Hayles 1999).

From a historical and technological view, the events of World War II put in question the pretensions of the Enlightenment and humanism—as we suggested in our readings of Pynchon and postmodern war in Chapters 1 and 2. Hence, 1945 might be considered a watershed for the posthuman since it became dramatically clear (if the lesson wasn't learned during World War I) that irrationality can prevail over rationality on a massive scale, that the human species could destroy itself, and that we might not be in control of our own technoprogeny, of creations like atomic weapons. Only after the war did consumerism, mass media, and the world of automobiles, appliances, and gadgets begin to saturate society. As technology continued to penetrate ever deeper into our lives, particularly in the forms of mass media, computers, and genetic engineering, it became apparent, to cite Haraway again, that "our machines are disturbingly lively, and we ourselves are frighteningly inert" (1991:152). Marx's vision of commodity fetishism, where subjects and objects exchange characteristics, has become concretized is a world of interactive technologies, "spiritual machines," artificial intelligence and life, natural and social engineering, and technobodies. Kurzweil (1999), for example, has produced examples of computer-written poetry which some see as indistinguishable from respectable human writing, while humans have turned to computer programs like "Dramatica" to churn out screenplays—developments sharply criticized by traditional humanists like Sven Birkerts (see 1995 and his columns for *Atlantic*, archived in www.atlantic.com).

Hence, many have been arguing that humanity is entering a posthuman era, that the core values of classical humanism are no longer tenable, and that both the subject and the object worlds have undergone dramatic mutations. To this allegedly posthuman condition, a multitude of different responses and positions have been advanced, ranging from cybernetic and postmodern theories, to the performance art of Mark Pauline and Stelarc, to cyberpunks and extropians, and radical biocentric groups like Earth First!. Parallel to our typology of different kinds of postmodernists (Best and Kellner 1991, 1997), we distinguish between radical deconstructive posthumanists, who reject altogether the legacy of humanism, the Enlightenment, modern values and theory, the concept of progress, and a belief in some notion of agency. These can be contrasted to moderate reconstructive posthumanists, who seek to rethink mind, body, and agency (and associated notions like reason and freedom) in improved forms, and do not completely sever themselves from the modern legacy. A viable reconstructive humanism, however, must take into account both the philosophical challenges to humanism and dramatic developments in various realms of technology, without indulging in naive illusions of transcendence from the body, the natural world, ecological exigencies, socioeconomic realities, and compelling ethical and political issues.

A cadre of radical posthumanists advance nihilistic positions that renounce humanist, Enlightenment, and modern values as philosophical myths, typically offering no positive notions of selfhood, ethical norms, and politics. Baudrillard's (1990) belief that subjects have been vanquished by objects, such that we might as well surrender to the juggernaut of technology and abandon our feeble illusions of control, is particularly insipid. Yet it is symptomatic of posthumanist tendencies to advocate a dismantling of the self, either in theory or in practice. With radical ecologists, we urge an environmental ethic and sensibility and a nonhierarchical relation with other species, but we are not ready to espouse the Earth First! chant of "Four Legs Good, Two Legs Bad!" that demonizes all human beings and adopts apolitical postures. With Haraway, we call for a multiplicity of new relations with technology, but the urging of Moravec, Paul and Cox, and de Garis that we should download consciousness into computers regresses to a neo-Christian/Cartesian dualism of mind and body that fails to grasp their insurmountable unity and the embodied nature of consciousness.

For some reconstructive thinkers, the posthuman is an opportunity to dispatch the illusions of modern thought (including essentialist conceptions of the subject) and the normalizing practices these allowed. Foucault, for example, sees the "death of man" to be as liberating as the death of God was for Nietzsche. He believes that it offers postmodern subjects the chance to construct new bodies, new pleasures, and an explosion of different modes of life free from the coercion of normalization. Foucault's vision, however, is not informed by knowledge of contemporary technological revolutions, and therefore he does not assess the advantages and disadvantages these bring for a new type of subject and human species.

Some of the most interesting reconstructive thinking stems from the "transhumanists" and "extropians" who identify themselves as posthumanists, but who are hardly antihuman or antimodern. Rather, they extend the optimistic spirit of the Enlightenment, fervently embrace science and technology as positive forces for quantum leaps in human evolution, and seek enhanced minds, bodies, and improved control over nature. Extreme transhumanists go so far as to affirm Condorcet's vision of immortality as one of the greatest potential achievements of science and technology. They therefore espouse telomerase therapy (which studies how to maintain youth through endless cell division), life extension programs, cloning, and cryogenics.

Resisting the translation of brain states into data bytes, however, most transhumanists cling to the raptures of embodied experience, but they seek a "new flesh" enhanced through all technology has to offer. In their vision, the future human will be a cyborg whose consciousness and physical reality are dramatically expanded thanks to pharmaceutical and nutritional therapy, rigorous exercise programs, computer chips, memory implants, surgical alteration, and genetic modification. The "Hedweb" group, for instance, urges us to discard the "wetware" of our evolutionary past that brings us so much misery, and utilize new nano- and genetic technologies to create a radically different neural architecture: "We can rewrite the vertebrate genome, redesign our global ecosystem, and abolish suffering throughout the living world."[37]

For transhumanists, technology is the means to the end of attaining greater control over the natural world, our bodies, and evolution itself, granting us more choices in our lives, and allowing us to design our world, our bodies, and the direction of our species development. Posthumanists inaugurate the fourth major shift in conceiving the individual since the beginning of the modern. The individual was seen, first, as a subject of reason (Descartes), then of desire (Freud), then of DNA (Watson and Crick), and now as an object of technological design, combining information and biotechnology.

Transhumanists play out a key theme of the postmodern adventure: the human desire to become God-like. Of course, this is an age-old obsession with possibly dangerous consequences predicted by technophobic narratives ranging from the biblical stories of Adam and Eve and the Tower of Babel to the Greek myth of Pandora's box, to the romantic tale of *Frankenstein*. The difference is that in the contemporary setting, human beings now have the technologies to "play God," as they do by creating new forms of intelligence in computers and robots, simulating artificial life forms, creating virtual worlds, engineering transgenic species, cloning animals, building bacterial organisms from scratch, and designing evolution rather than being designed by it.

A crucial fact of the postmodern adventure is that human beings are now seizing the reins of evolution as they prepare to dramatically step up the pace of technological and biological change through computer interfacing, genetic engineering, and nanotechnologies. If and when the day comes that direct links can be established between the brain and the computer, such that massive amounts of learning could transpire in minute periods of time, evolutionary change would be racheted up to unimaginable levels, and the distinction between VR and RL, already shaky, would become meaningless. Further, as genetic engineering becomes more sophisticated, and coevolves with computer technologies, human beings can design and redesign themselves in a matter of generations rather than over millennia.

We should neither fear these changes and prohibit them on problematic philosophical grounds (appealing to the alleged norms of God or nature), nor uncritically embrace them in a technophilic ecstasy. Rather, society as a whole must carefully weigh and measure what our choices are, and what futures are available to us. This presupposes a number of conditions, including the imperative that citizens must be scientifically and technologically literate enough to grasp what is at stake (and despite the pronouncements of elitists, individuals do not have to understand the complexities of quantum mechanics, software engineering, or cloning to make informed judgments; see Rollin 1995). Critical consciousness is needed to avoid being seduced by the siren song of the cyberdelics. For beneath the glossy veneer of the new and the post lie old and questionable ideologies. One easily spots in posthumanism a Christian dualism of mind and body and a belief in the resurrection of the body. A Cartesian belief that mind is the essence of the human is also replicated, mixing capitalist

individualism (blended with bits of Emerson and Ayn Rand), Nietzschean elitism and contempt for the public, and 1960s counterculture and 1970s New
Age mysticism in a rhapsodic techno-transcendentalism. Moreover, to the extent that "posthumanism" affirms Western, white, male, technocratic, human
species-dominant interests, it merely recycles old prejudices in new garb (see
Ross 1991).

With the extropians and cyberdelics, we reject metaphysical concepts of a
"natural body" that should never be tampered with by technology, and we embrace the goal of enhanced minds and improved bodies free from needless suffering, but urge skepticism toward the more extreme claims of posthumanism.
Leading ideologues of the posthuman claim that we will soon achieve immortality by downloading or implanting human neurons into machines or transferring
machinic intelligence or programs into humans (see Moravec 1988; Kurzweil
1999; and the somewhat more skeptical discussion in Kaku 1997) It is easy to repudiate such reflections as technofantasies, but in fact some very promising and
disturbing developments are taking place in the fields of artificial intelligence,
biotechnology and genetic engineering, nanotechnology, and elsewhere.

Yet we should also recognize that posthumanism is emerging as a dominant
ideology for the new technologies and the new economies. Many posthumanists
celebrate "free market" economies, attack government regulation, and take
purely individualistic positions. The celebration of "ubiquitous computing," of
inserting computers into our homes, bodies, and appliances, is often carried
through precisely by those who are producing such artifacts, such as members of
the MIT Media Lab, or Bill Gates, whose high-tech home perhaps embodies the
most advanced development of the computerization of the world. Unasked in
such celebrations are questions like who really needs to have computers in their
shoes or their teapot, who benefits most from such innovations, and what are the
human and ecological costs paid for such "progress."

Hence, while we are not against technological innovation and believe that
claims that computers, biotechnologies, and other new technologies are dramatically altering our daily existence must be taken seriously, we reject the
laissez-faire, individualist, and elitist views that mar so many transhumanist
writings (see the critiques in Dery 1996 and Barbrook and Cameron 1995). In
addition, we seek to link the project of human transformation to a politics of
radical democracy and social reconstruction. By and large, posthumanists ignore issues of ecology, social justice, democracy, class, race, and gender, either
thinking them obsolete or contemptuously dismissing them from an elitist
standpoint. They have not articulated the complex connections between technology and society, and therefore they fetishize technology as an autonomous
dynamic developing apart from social relations.

Yet we would argue that just as print technologies helped produce a new
modern era (see McLuhan 1962, 1964; Eisenstein 1983), in our times new media,
information/computer, and genetic technologies are assisting to generate a new
postmodern era. Just as the printing press and mass media contributed to producing modern societies, nation-states, national cultures, and an industrial capitalist

economy, so too are electronic multimedia, communications and information technologies, and biotechnologies constructing a global networked society, novel forms of culture, and mutations within the human being.

This process of scientific and technological revolution is highly ambivalent, with positive and negative consequences. We have argued for the beneficial potential of postmodern paradigms in science in Chapter 3 and discuss the mix of advances and dangers of new computer technologies in this and the next chapter. Our focus in the following chapters will be the articulations between globalization, the mutations within contemporary capitalism, the scientific and technological revolutions, and the transformations of culture, society, and the human being marked by the concept of the postmodern—thematics which we argue are intrinsically interconnected.

NOTES

1. On the role of the printing press in the construction of modernity, see McLuhan (1962) and Eisenstein (1983); on technology and modernity, see Mumford (1963, 1964); and for a useful collection of documents documenting and debating the role of technology in the 20th century, see Rhodes (1999).

2. So far, exponential development of computer technology has been spectacular (see Kurzweil 1999: 25) and computer speed and power continues to advance at mind-boggling rates. Ready to exploit new technological potential, IBM announced a plan in December 1999 to build "Blue Gene," the first petaflop computer, which could handle one quadrillion operations per second, running 500 times faster than the best supercomputer today. In a coevolutionary advance with science, such computational power could illuminate the ways in which gene proteins fold into their complex shapes, a process so complex to map that current computers can model only a fraction of it (*Newsweek*, December 13, 1999). In August 2000, IBM announced it had developed the world's most advanced quantum computer. An ordinary-looking glass tube, it contains five atoms that deliver enough memory and processing power to solve data-based research problems far better than conventional computers (www.abcnews.go.com/sections/tech/DailyNews/ibm000815.html).

3. Gilder (1989) argues that quantum mechanics ushers in a "new era," a "quantum era," constituting a paradigm shift beyond the modern, beginning with science, and moving into technology, business, everyday life, and modes of thought and values. But he interprets this process in terms of an idealist affirmation of mind over matter, as the triumph of "spirit." He thus uses new science and technology to promote a revived religiosity and spirituality, seeking redemptive change in scientific and technological developments. Moreover, he connects this paradigm shift with an old and highly ideological call for deregulation and the full unleashing of market capitalism to unfetter the new technologies and sciences.

4. While we claim that media, computers, and biotechnology are the major technological revolutions of the day, we see nanotechnology as holding great potential to be a fourth major shaping force. As of yet, developments in nanotechnology have not fulfilled the vision in Eric Drexler's (1987) seminal work, *Engines of Creation*, but engineers have already created rudimentary molecular machines from atoms, ATP proteins, and various chemicals. Beyond its potential to revolutionize medicine through SF-like nanobots patrol-

ling one's immune system for hostile invaders, detecting disease conditions, and delivering designer drugs in precise fashion, nanotechnology visionaries champion its alchemical potential to build any material, from gold to wood, through a precise stacking of atoms. Yet Drexler warned that the "engines of creation" could also be "engines of destruction," and recently Bill Joy (2000) has noted potential dangers from an uncontrolled nanotechnology. Developments in nanotechnology are regularly chronicled in *Technology Review*. Also see Regis (1995) and Crandall (1996). Neil Stephenson's (1995) novel *The Diamond Age* sketches a fully realized nanotechnology world, and William Gibson's (1999) *All Tomorrow's Parties* portrays an emerging society fundamentally altered by nanotech; interestingly, Philip K. Dick envisages nanotechnology in his 1957 novel *Eye in the Sky*.

5. Compare Roszak 1968 and 1973 with 1986 and 1992; Postman 1985 with 1992; and Mander 1978 with 1991.

6. Technophobic arguments are developed in more popular form by Mark Slouka (1995), Clifford Stoll (1995), and David Shenk (1997), who raise a wide range of concerns about the nature, effects, and hype surrounding the explosion of new technologies in the contemporary era. Robins and Webster (1999) provide a more analytical and systematic critical neo-Luddite approach grounded in critical social theory.

7. See the collection of responses to Joy's article in *Wired* for July 2000. Agreeing with Joy that there need to be firm guidelines regulating nanotechnology, the Foresight Institute has written a set of guidelines for its development that take into account problems such as commercialization, unjust distribution of benefits, and potential dangers to the environment (see www.foresight.org/guidelines/current.html). We encourage such critical dialogue on both the benefits and the dangers of new technologies and hope to contribute to these debates with this book.

8. Responding to the one-sidedness of dominant perspectives, a discourse of "technorealism" appeared in 1998 with much media hoopla (see www.technorealism. org). In our view, however, its advocates lack adequate theorizing of the new technologies and robust critique. For the most part they fail to situate emerging technologies within the framework of the restructuring of global capitalism. In addition, they do not articulate an adequate standpoint of critique. Some of its advocates (e.g., Shenk 1997) are unduly negative, while others (e.g., Steven Johnson [1997]) are generally uncritical and affirmative. Andrew Feenberg (1991, 1995, 1999) has most consistently developed a critical theory of technology in the present era that, like our perspectives, attempts to present critical and reconstructive analyses. Individuals in the technocounterculture described in Dery (1996) also combine critical and activist perspectives, which we will advocate as well.

9. We are using the original 1818 (1993) edition of the novel, which contains a more radical critique of Victor Frankenstein's scientific materialism. The revised 1831 edition added a lot of moralizing to make Victor more sympathetic and changed details of the plot to make it more acceptable to conventional morality. On Mary Shelley's life, see Muriel Spark's (1987) lively and engaging account, which also contains critical discussion of the novel (1987). For a variety of variations and spin-offs of Shelley's *Frankenstein* tale, see Haining (1994).

10. It is interesting that Walton, like Victor, was driven to unravel the mystery of life, aspiring to discover the secrets of magnetism at the North Pole, and that both saw electricity as the key to the riddles of nature. Both characters represent a drive toward knowledge and discovery that would sacrifice all else to find the secrets to dominating nature. The postmodern adventure too is seeking the basic stuff of life and to control nature (see Kaku 1997: 10), but locates it largely in code—digital information, DNA, and the microcosm—

not in magnetism or electricity, thus pointing to another continuity and discontinuity with the modern.

11. On Faust and modernity, see Berman (1982). For a critique of the Cartesian ego, see Bordo (1987).

12. We learned of Wells's concept of the "World Brain" through Robins and Webster (1999: 126–127), who in turn cite Muddiman (1998). Robins and Webster equate Wells's vision with Bentham's Panopticon and a "generalized Taylorism," and dismiss it as "a perverse utopian proposal," "a utopia of technocratic planning, administration and management," which would, among other things, lead to a colonization and depletion of the public sphere (1999: 127). We see it, by contrast, as an incredible anticipation of the potential of the World Wide Web to make knowledge and information accessible to people throughout the Earth. This could also reinvigorate a severely decaying public sphere by providing information and new means of communication and public debate (see Chapter 5). Robins and Webster fail to discuss, moreover, the tensions between Wells's more scientist and technocratic thinking in his nonfiction, and the profound and prophetic critical interrogations of science and technology and their potentially catastrophic effects in his fiction. Hence, for us, Wells emerges as both a prescient critic of the dangers of science and technology and a prophet of the great transformation that, for better and worse, they would generate.

13. There are, of course, many other examples of SF writers describing new species, such as the metamorphoses at the end of *2001*, Arthur C. Clarke's *Childhood's End*, Frank Herbert's *Dune* novels, Octavia Butler's "patternist" and "xenogenesis" novels, and, as we note below, the works of Rudy Rucker and other cyberpunk writers. Wells, however, is the first to consistently project images of new superior species that displace the centrality of human beings, thus introducing what we are calling a "fifth discontinuity."

14. See www.foxnews.com/science/042700_giants.sml.

15. www.msnbc.com/news/214299.asp.

16. The troubling implications of this scenario, of course, were a core preoccupation of Aldous Huxley, who continued Wells's speculations regarding a genetically engineered society and the creation of new species. Indeed, with only trivial qualifications, Huxley's *Brave New World* of genetic engineering, cloning, addictive pleasure drugs (soma), megaspectacles, and intense social engineering has arrived. Huxley thought cloning and genetic engineering were centuries away from realization, but in fact they began to unfold a mere 2 decades after he published *Brave New World* (1989 [1931]). Technocapitalism cannot yet, for instance, biologically clone human beings, but it can clone them in a far more effective way: socially. Whereas biological clones would have a mind of their own, since the social world and experiences that conditioned the "original" could not be reproduced, cloning a person according to a given ideological and functional model is far more controlling. That is why Huxley's (1958) sequel work, *Brave New World Revisited*, focuses on various modes of social conditioning and mind control.

17. Cited in Carey Goldberg and Gina Kolata, "Scientists Announce Births of Cows Cloned in New Way," *New York Times*, January 21, 1998: A14.

18. See http://abcnews.go.com/sections/DailyNews/biotechgoats.000618.htm.

19. See www.humancloning.org and www.wired.com/wired/archive/9.02/projectx_pr.html.

20. See Gina Kolata, "Human Cloning: Yesterday's Never is Today's Why Not?" *New York Times*, December 2, 1997.

21. Cited in Nancy Gibbs, "Baby, "It's You! And You, and You . . ." *Time*, February

19, 2001: 50). In March 2001, to great media fanfare, Zavos and an Israeli and Italian bio-technologist announced that the group had signed up more than 600 infertile couples and were undertaking human cloning experiments to provide them with children; see "Forum on Human Cloning Turns Raucous," *Los Angeles Times* (March 10, 2001). When Zavos and his Israeli partner went to Israel to seek permission to do human cloning there, *ABC News* (March 25, 2001) reported that they received the blessing of an old rabbi, but the Israeli justice minister said that he was against cloning "on moral and ideological grounds." A University of Pennsylvania ethicist said that Zavos had no medical training, had published no articles, had no qualifications, and that one of the dangers of cloning was that frauds were entering the field, exploiting people with false promises.

There were also numerous discussions of the failures of animal cloning that were suggesting that human cloning would be highly dangerous and disturbing; see Aaron Zitner, "Perpetual Pets, Via Cloning," *Los Angeles Times* (March 16, 2001) and Gina Kolata, "Researchers Find Big Risk of Defect in Cloning Animals," *New York Times* (March 25, 2001).

22. See "Britain OKs Human Embryo Cloning," www.msnbc.com/news/520058.asp.

23. See "Another Advance for Dolly Cloners," www.wirednews. com/news/print/ 0,1294,41989,00.html. In March 2001, the Bush administration forbid federal funding of stem-cell research.

24. One of the main limitations of Foucault's (1973) discussion of posthumanism in *The Order of Things* is his idealization which limits the shift to a merely conceptual transformation from one "episteme" to another, whereas the shift to posthumanism is also a *material* matter of new technologies that have imploding effects that erase the boundaries between biology and technology. Foucault considers both the enmeshment of the body in systems of discipline and surveillance and (ethical) "technologies of the self" that cultivate "new passions and new pleasures." But there is no analysis of communication technologies and little consideration of the hybrid landscape of technobodies.

25. Similarly, "Brain Builder" Hugo de Garis, who is working to construct an artificial brain with a billion neurons and evolvable circuitry by 2001, forecasts an inevitable near-future where a nasty cleavage within humanity opens up between the "Cosmists," who embrace a future where human beings, no longer the dominant species, merge with superior machines and experiment with advanced intelligence in space, and the "Terrestrialists," homo-chauvinists, who militantly resist the flight from Earth and the growing obsolescence of the human (see www.hip.atr.co.jp/~degaris).

26. "The Robot That Loves People," *Discovery*, October 1999, pp. 66–73. Also see "The Cog Shop" at www.ai.mit.edu/projects/cog.

27. As David Tennenhouse, a scientist with DARPA puts it, "People are the single most limiting factor to the progress of computer science. We need to get humans out of the (computing) loop" (Niall McKay, "DOD Scientist: Lose the Humans," www/wired.com/ news/print/0,1294,21354,00.html).

28. For a useful overview of these new computing strategies, see "Evolving a Conscious Machine," by Gary Taubes (www.britannica.com/bcom/original/article/ 0,5744,2405,00.html).

29. See the cover stories "Biotech Bodies" in *Business Week*, July 27, 1998: 56–63, and "The New Age of Cosmetic Surgery," *Newsweek*, August 9, 1999: 52–59. The first discusses breakthroughs in tissue engineering and new modes of medical regeneration of bone, skin, teeth, and various bodily organs, and the second discusses breakthroughs in cosmetic surgery.

30. Now that Barbie's own look has been revamped to make it more in line with the

era of political correctness, a bit fuller in figure, Cindy Jackson may be in the midst of another identity crisis and ready to put on some weight. Poor Cindy has also undergone the painful realization that in Los Angeles, especially, she is far from being the only living doll reassembled on an operating table.

31. cbsnews.com/now/story/0,15797,268482-412,00.shtml.

32. See Mann's faculty home page at the University of Toronto: www.eecgtoronto. edu/~mann.

33. www.salon.com/tech/feature/1999/10/20/cyborg/html. Warwick was lionized by *Wired*, which featured him in a cover story celebrating his achievements; see the February 2000 issue, pp. 144–151. Interestingly, Warwick put his experiments in a posthumanist context, opening his article with the words: "I was born human. But this was an accident of fate—a condition merely of time and place. I believe it's something we have the power to change. I will tell you why." See also his University of Reading website: www.cyber.rdg.ac. uk

34. www.stelarc.va.com.au/obsolete.html.

35. For a dossier on "The Exploding Science of Superlongevity," see *Wired*, January 2000, 184ff.

36. Rucker's quatrology is comprised of *Software* (1982), *Wetware* (1988) (republished together in Rucker 1994), *Freeware* (1998), and *Realware* (2000). A mathematician, computer science professor, software designer, graphic artist, and prolific writer, Rudy Rucker is a central figure in the cyberpunk world. His protocyberpunk novel *Software* was published 2 years before Gibson's (1984) *Neuromancer.* Bruce Sterling dedicated his first short story collection to Rucker, who has collaborated with Sterling, Gibson, and other major cyberpunk writers. Indeed, Rucker delineated many key cyberpunk themes, in particular the implosion of technology and humans and creation of a superior species of smart machines that have human attributes. His collection *Transreal!* (1991) contains his poetry, a large number of stories, essays, and biographical notes. His website makes accessible a wide range of his work (see www.mathcs. sjsu.edu/faculty/rucker).

37. www.hedweb. com/hedweb.htm. For a detailed presentation of extropian philosophy, see Brendan Bernhard, "The Transhumanists. Meet Max and Natasha. They Hope to Live forever. Seriously," *LA Weekly* (January 19–25, 2001): 26–31.

5

|||||||

GLOBALIZATION AND THE RESTRUCTURING OF CAPITAL

What benefits, or what misfortunes to mankind may hereafter result from these events [e.g., colonization and the expansion of the world market] no human wisdom can foresee. By uniting, in some measure, the most distant parts of the world, by enabling them to relieve one another's wants, to increase one another's enjoyments, and to encourage one another's industry, their general tendency would seem to be beneficial. To the natives, however, both of the East and West Indies, all the commercial benefits which can have resulted from these events have been sunk and lost in the dreadful misfortunes which they have occasioned.
—ADAM SMITH

Modern industry has established the world market, for which the discovery of America paved the way. . . . [The] need of a constantly expanding market for its products chases the bourgeoisie over the whole surface of the globe. It must nestle everywhere, settle everywhere, establish connections everywhere. . . . The bourgeoisie, by the rapid improvement of all instruments of production, by the immensely facilitated means of communication, draws all, even the most barbarian nations into civilization. . . . In a word, it creates a world after its own image.
—KARL MARX AND FRIEDRICH ENGELS

These are revolutionary times. All over the globe men are revolting against old systems of exploitation and oppression, and out of the wombs of a frail world new systems of justice and equality are being born.
—MARTIN LUTHER KING

Where do you want to go today?
—MICROSOFT

The postmodern adventure consists of dramatic mutations in science, technology, society, and human identity that are producing the transition from modern to postmodern constellations. These transformations are intertwined with the global restructuring of capitalism, which includes production of a networked society mediated by computer and communications technologies. Novel forces of information-entertainment are creating an increasingly digitized and interactive global culture, and an emerging biotech society shaped by genetic engineering and the commodification of DNA is fast approaching. The restructuring of capitalism is grounded in sophisticated technoscience; a rapidly expanding world telecommunications system; a multimedia and interactive technoculture; the genetic restructuring of nature, animals, and human beings; and novel forms of information technology, consumption, and politics. The society of spectacle described by Guy Debord and the situationists intensifies with dazzling megaspectacles and interactive cyberspectacles. The forms of society and culture produce more powerful tools of domination, but also generate alternative modes of opposition and struggle. Pursuing the themes that are central to our book, we provide sketches of the new global economy, technoculture, modes of consumption and everyday life, and technopolitics.

TECHNOCAPITALISM, GLOBALIZATION, AND THE INFOTAINMENT SOCIETY

> Globalization is not something new under the sun, but is a particular form of capitalism, an expansion of capitalist relationships both in breadth (geographically) and in depth (penetrating ever-increasing aspects of human life).
>
> —PETER MARCUSE

> The information technology revolution has been instrumental in allowing the implementation of a fundamental process of the restructuring of the capitalist system from the 1980s onwards.
>
> —MANUEL CASTELLS

"Globalization" was the buzzword of the 1990s and continues to serve in the new millennium as a primary attractor of books, articles, and heated debate, just as postmodernism was the most fashionable and disputed topic of the 1980s. A wide and diverse range of social theorists argue that today's world is organized by expanding globalization, which is strengthening the dominance of a world capitalist economic system, supplanting the primacy of the nation-state with transnational corporations and organizations, and generating a new global culture that is eroding all local cultures and traditions.[1] Marxists, worlds systems theorists, functionalists, Weberians, and other contemporary school of theorists agree that globalization is a distinguishing trend of the present moment. It is also becoming a hot and contested political arena as new social movements militantly oppose globalization throughout the world.

For some, globalization serves as a cover concept for imperialism. They condemn it as just another imposition of capital logic and the market on ever more regions of the world and spheres of life. For others, it is the continuation of modernization and a force of progress, bringing about expanded wealth, freedom, democracy, and happiness. Some perceive it as beneficial, creating new economic opportunities, political democratization, and cultural diversity and vitality. Others see it as harmful, engendering increased domination and control by the wealthier overdeveloped nations over the poor underdeveloped countries, thus strengthening the hegemony of the haves over the have-nots. In addition, in the negative view, globalization undermines democracy, homogenizes culture, and accelerates destruction of species and the environment.

Some conceive the globalization project—whether viewed positively or negatively—as inevitable and beyond human control, whereas others view it as generating new conflicts and new spaces for struggle.[2] Moreover, advocates of a postmodern break in history argue that developments in transnational capitalism are producing a novel configuration of post-Fordism (Harvey 1989), or that postmodernism is the cultural logic of capitalism (Jameson 1991). Others define the prevailing system as a "network society" grounded in globalized communications and information technology (Castells 1996, 1997, 1998). Indeed, the new global economy, society, and culture is increasingly digitized and interactive, with rapidly expanding wireless networks supplementing the wired society and producing new forms of connectivity. These technologies engender ubiquitous communication and interaction, and innovative forms of culture and everyday life (on the emergence of new broadband, multimedia, and interactive networks, see Gates 1995, 1999, and the more critical perspectives of Schiller 1999).

The new global networked society, however, is highly contested. Apologists such as Friedman (1999) regard globalization as positive, while critics such as Mander and Goldsmith (1996) and Robins and Webster (1999) view it as negative. Just as technophobic theories denounce the new technologies (see Chapter 4), so too do globophobic theories attack globalization as a novel form of imperialism, domination of the world by corporate capitalism, and destruction of the environment, local cultures, and tradition. On the other hand, globophiliacs celebrate it for producing fresh sources and escalating levels of wealth, growing democratization, and exciting forms of culture and technology. Hence, in many contemporary modern and postmodern social theories, globalization is taken as a salient feature of our times, yet is sharply contested regarding its nature, effects, and future.

In our view, globalization is extremely complex and ambiguous. It involves the flow of capital, goods, information, culture and entertainment, and people across a new networked economy, society, and culture. Like the new technologies, it is an overdetermined and complex phenomenon that entails costs and benefits, an up and a down side. As with technology (see Chapter 4), we advocate development of a *critical theory of globalization* that would dialectically appraise its positive and negative features. This theory would be sharply critical of the harmful effects of globalization and skeptical of legitimating ideological discourse. It would recognize the centrality of the phenomenon in the present and embrace its beneficial features (such as the Internet, which, as we document below, makes possible a reconstruction of education and democratic technopolitics), while promoting a progressive and democratizing globalization in opposition to capitalist globalization.

Within this context, the concept of the postmodern helps to articulate what is new and different in the emergent social formation. It calls attention to breaks and discontinuities with the past, and highlights what is innovative, different, exciting, frightening, and often extremely ambiguous in the contemporary era.[3] Hence, while there is admittedly much mystification in postmodern discourse, we think that it emphatically signals the shifts and ruptures of the present age and underscores the novelties and the mutations in culture, subjectivities, and theory that many critics of globalization or the information society gloss over. Yet unless the concept of the postmodern is linked with analysis of the scientific, technological, and socioeconomic transformations of our time, the term is empty and without significant historical and analytic substance.

It is our contention that adequately theorizing globalization, scientific and technological revolution, and the genesis and effects of the postmodern requires perceiving the connections among these phenomena. Hence, we maintain that theories of globalization that do not conceptualize the transformation of capitalism and the world economy in conjunction with the coevolution of science and technology fail to adequately illuminate the key elements of the contemporary era. Many theories, by contrast, engage in economic reductionism that perceives globalization primarily as a function of the economy (e.g., Marxist-inspired theories). Or globalization is interpreted as a result of technological revolution alone, as by the technodeterminists and apologists who ignore the vicissitudes of capitalism. Hence, one needs to consider the crucial constituents of the present moment dialectically, grasp their interconnections and coevolution, and dissect the conflicts and mutations they are producing.[4] One also needs to appraise both the positive and the negative effects of these phenomena on humans and society in order to identify the openings and possibilities for progressive social transformation, as well as the novel forces of domination and dangers for the human species.

Technological determinists frequently use the language of postindustrial, or postmodern, society to describe current developments. This discourse often develops an ideal-type distinction beginning with description of the previous Fordist mode of industrial production characterized by heavy industry, mass production and mass consumption, bureaucratic organization, and social conformity. Fordist industrial society is then contrasted with the new postindustrial society marked by "flexible production," or "postFordism," in which production is fragmented and spread around the globe, rather than taking place in one big factory or plant. PostFordist production is "just in time," bringing parts or products to subcontractors or consumers quickly when needed, thus overcoming the negative drag of stockpiling and overproduction (Harvey 1989). For postmodern theorists such as Baudrillard (1993), technologies of information and simulation have permeated every aspect of society and have created a new social environment (see Chapter 2). On this view, we have left "reality" and the world of modernity behind, as we shift to a society of simulation and hyperreality, and undergo an implosion of technology and the human. Other, less extravagant, theorists of the vicissitudes of technology and society claim that we are evolving into a new postindustrial technosociety, culture, and condition in which technology, knowledge, and information are the axial or organizing principles (Bell 1976; Kelly 1994, 1998).

The postindustrial society is sometimes referred to as the "knowledge society" or the "information society," in which knowledge and information are given roles more predominant than in earlier eras (see the survey in Webster 1995). It is now clear that the knowledge, information, and service sectors are ever more important domains of our contemporary moment and that the arguments of Daniel Bell (1976) and others regarding the coming of postindustrial society were partially on target. But many theorists of the allegedly new economy and new society typically exaggerate the role of knowledge and information (see the critique in Webster 1995). They advance an idealist vision that excessively privileges knowledge and information in the economy, in politics, in society, and in everyday life; and downplays the force of capitalist relations of production, corporate ownership and control, and hegemonic modes of economic and state power. Such theorists ignore the extent to which technoscience itself has become a major productive force and has evolved within corporate capitalism and its military–technological–entertainment complex, so that today science and technology are potentially forces of destruction as well as instruments of knowledge and progress (see Chapter 2).

There is also a debate between those who claim that the emerging global networked society and culture is an entirely new phenomenon and those who stress its continuities with earlier formations (see Robins and Webster 1999, who argue the latter position). We propose a mediating position that articulates both the continuities with previous forms of industrial society and the new modes of society and culture described by concepts of the "post-" that emphasize the novelties and discontinuities. Taking this stance requires the deployment of a "both/and" logic, and not an "either/or" discourse. Hence, we wish to develop a dialectical optic that sees multiple forces of causation, connections, and breaks with the past, as well as a nexus of positive and/or negative effects, often inseparably intertwined.

We also believe that dominant conceptions of the information society and the focus on information technology as its foundation are too limited; the new technologies are modes of information *and* of entertainment and it is becoming harder and harder to separate the two. Indeed, the new technologies are much more than solely information technology; they are also forces of entertainment, communication, and play, encompassing and restructuring both labor and leisure. Previous forms of entertainment are rapidly being absorbed within the Internet. The computer is becoming a major household appliance, one that serves as a source of entertainment, information, communication, and connection with the outside world. At the same time, "post-PC" developments are advancing rapidly, linking all technologies, from computers to hand-held wireless devices to cell phones, moving from the "wired world" into a wireless, digitized, multimedia and interactive culture that allows access to e-mail, information, and entertainment, and social connections.

The mergers of major information and entertainment conglomerates that have taken place in the United States during the past several years provide clues to the immensity of the transformation going on and indicators of the syntheses of information and entertainment in the network society. We have witnessed the most extensive concentration of information and entertainment industries in history, including a $7.5 billion merger of Time Warner and Turner Broadcasting, a $19 billion deal between Disney/Capital Cities/ABC, a $20 billion conglomeration of NBC and Microsoft, and a $37 billion merger of Viacom and CBS.

Dwarfing all previous information/entertainment corporation mergers, Time Warner and America On-Line (AOL) proposed a $163.4 billion amalgamation in January 2000, which was approved in January 2001. This union brings together two huge corporations involved in TV, film, magazines, newspapers, books, information databases, computers, and other media, suggesting a coming synthesis of media and computer culture, of entertainment and information in a new infotainment society. The fact that "new media" Internet service provider and portal AOL is the majority shareholder in the deal points to the triumph of the new online Internet culture over the old media culture, while the merger points to escalating synergy among information and entertainment industries and old and new media in the form of the networked economy and cyberculture.

There have also been massive mergers in the telecommunications industry in the United States between Southwest Bell and California Bell and between New York and Atlantic Bell (on the significance of telecommunications mergers and market deregulation for the new mode of digital capitalism, see Schiller 1999). In 1999, MCI negotiated a $37 billion amalgamation with WorldCom, and then bought Sprint for $115 billion. In a $72 billion union of two regional telephone companies, SBC Communications Inc. and Ameritech formed the largest Bell operating company. The German telecommunications firm Mannesmann bought Orange for $33 billion; shortly thereafter Vodafone Airtouch, the world's leading mobile phone company, announced a hostile bid for Mannesmann, initially for a record $117 billion, and eventually for an amazing $178.7 billion when the merger was sealed in February 2000 (earlier in the year Vodafone also absorbed Airtouch Communications for $60 billion). In addition, telecommunications companies have been buying cable television systems—for example, AT&T purchased TCI in 1998 for $60.9 billion and then acquired MediaOne in 1999 for $63.1 billion.[5]

The corporate media, communications, and information industries are frantically scrambling to provide delivery for the wealth of information, entertainment, and other services that will include expanded Internet access, cellular telephones, hand-held communication devices, and computerized video, film, and information on demand, as well as Internet shopping and more unsavory services like pornography and gambling. These developments require the concepts of the "information revolution" or "information society" to be expanded to include entertainment, multimedia, and an exploding array of technologies. Accordingly, we use the notion of the networked infotainment society to accent the imbrications of information, entertainment, and interactive media in the new digitized and global economy.

In addition, theories of the information society neglect the rise of bio technology and the emergence of new forms of genetic engineering, nanotechnology, drugs and pharmaceuticals, and the tremendous capital realization and developments in these arenas. In November 1999, Pfizer made a hostile $82.4 billion offer for Warner-Lambert, outbidding American Home Products, which had already bid $62.1 billion, and eventually closing the deal with a $90 billion takeover bid.[6] In the world of biotechnology, chemical and seed corporations are merging to form powerful global combines that are taking control of the world's food supply. According to the Organic Consumers Association, "The top five seed companies—AstraZeneca, Du Pont, Monsanto, Novartis, and Aventis—account for nearly two-thirds of the global pesticide market (60%), almost one-quarter (23%) of the commercial seed market, and virtually 100% of the transgenic . . . seed market."[7] Many of these corporations are the results of takeovers and consolidation—for example, Astra and Zeneca formed AstraZeneca in a $31.8 billion merger. In addition, Rhome Poulenc and Hoechst united with Aventis, Ciba Geigy, and Sandoz, creating Novartis, while Du Pont absorbed Pioneer Hi-Bred early in 1999. In recent years, trying to fulfill its goal of dominating world agriculture, Monsanto has spent $8 billion buying out numerous U.S. seed companies. In 1998, Monsanto purchased Cargill's International Seed Operations and bid to acquire Delta & Pine Land Seed Co., which co-owns the Terminator seed patent with the USDA. And in December, 1999, Monsanto and Pharmacia & Upjohn Inc. announced plans for a merger that would solidify one of the world's largest pharmaceutical and biotechnology companies, yielding a combined market value of $52 billion.

Together, these corporate consolidations and their products and services in the information, communications, entertainment, and biotech industries constitute a new networked and interactive infotainment society, and herald a coming genetic revolution, all producing fateful implosions of technology and human beings. One result is the emergence of the infrastructure of a new mode of global technocapitalism.

Theorizing Technocapitalism

> The handmill gives you society with the feudal lord; the steam-mill with the industrial capitalist.
>
> —KARL MARX

> The entire production process appears as not subsumed under the direct skilfulness of the worker, but rather as the technological application of science. [It is,] hence, the tendency of capital to give production a scientific character.
>
> —KARL MARX

We have found that few theories of globalization, the information society, postmodernity, or the new technologies capture the links between these phenomena. In particular, few analyses of the information explosion and the new technologies contextualize the development, marketing, implementation, and use of new technologies in the context of the vicissitudes of global technocapitalism. The ideologues of the information society act as if technology were an autonomous force and either neglect to articulate the coevolution of capital, science, and technology, or use the advancements of technology to legitimate market capitalism (e.g., Gilder 1989; Kelly 1994, 1998; Gates 1995, 1999). Critical theorists of the momentous changes in contemporary society often fail to engage the various ways in which the restructuring of capital are connected with scientific and technological revolution. Offe (1985) and Lash and Urry (1987, 1994), for instance, see important changes in the economy, polity, culture, and society, but interpret this change as a disorganization of capitalism, as a sign of its unraveling rather than as evidence of its planetary reorganization. And few theories of globalization, postmodernity, or the present age grasp the important role of the biotech revolution in reconstructing the natural and social worlds.

Consequently, we propose the term *technocapitalism* to signal the new syntheses and modes of capital, science, and technology. In terms of political economy, the emerging postindustrial form of technocapitalism is characterized by a decline of the state and enlarged power for the market, accompanied by the growing strength of transnational corporations and governmental bodies and the decreased power of the nation-state and its institutions. To paraphrase Max Horkheimer, whoever wants to talk about capitalism must talk about globalization and scientific–technological revolution. Further, it is impossible to theorize globalization without addressing the restructuring of capitalism and its new forms of economy, culture, and society.

While most of the prophets and promoters of the information society tend to be *technological* determinists, many of the critics who castigate its ideologies and practices are *economic* determinists. Both, however, typically neglect continuing conflict and struggle, the possibilities of intervention and transformation, and the ability of individuals and groups to remake society to serve their own needs and purposes. In all determinist conceptions, technology and markets are conceived as monolithic forces of power and domination, while humans are seen as passive objects of manipulation, and empowering uses of technology are not considered. With Lewis Mumford (1963, 1964) and Herbert Marcuse (1998 [1941]), however, we urge humans to take command of their social circumstances and shape their sociocultural environments to enhance their lives, and use technology to empower themselves and democratize society. Mumford and Marcuse distinguish between a *technological system* and *technics*, conceived as instruments that can be actively deployed by human beings. Although particular tools are shaped by social forces to serve specific ends, they can be reconfigured, reshaped, and mobilized against the purposes for which they are designed (see Feenberg 1991, 1995, 1999). This is similar to what "autonomous Marxists" call self-valorization, as opposed to capital-valorization, that is, using the instruments of production and communication against capitalist social relations and values (see Negri 1984 and Dyer-Witheford 1999).

But to avoid the mystifications of voluntarism and humanism, we need to be clear about the precise economic, social, political, cultural, scientific, and technological forces that currently are restructuring every aspect of life and then we must develop strategies based on this knowledge. The term *technocapitalism* is useful to describe the synthesis of capital and technology in the present organization of society. Unlike theories of postmodernity (e.g., Baudrillard) that argue that technology, not economic relations, is *the* new organizing principle of society, technocapitalism emphasizes both the increasingly important role of technology and the enduring primacy of capitalist relations of production. We claim that capitalist imperatives continue to dominate production, distribution, and consumption, as well as other cultural, social, and political domains. Workers remain exploited by and struggle against capitalists and capital persists as the hegemonic force—more so than ever since the collapse of communism.

The concept of technocapitalism describes a constellation in which technical and scientific knowledge, computerization and automation of labor, and interactive technology play a role in the process of production analogous to the function of human labor power and machines in an earlier era of capitalism. Technocapitalism also encompasses novel modes of societal organization, unique forms of culture and everyday life, and innovative types of contestation. Critical social theorists today are in a parallel situation to members of the Frankfurt School in the 1930s who were was forced to theorize emergent configurations of economy, polity, society, and culture brought about by the transition from market to state monopoly capitalism. In their now classical texts, the Frankfurt School analyzed the changing forms of social and economic organization, technology, and culture, while describing the rise of giant corporations, cartels, and the capitalist state in "organized capitalism" in both its fascist and its "democratic" state capitalist forms. The critical theorists were also among the first to see the importance of the rise of the culture industries and the mass culture that served as new types of social control, forms of ideology and domination, and modes of culture and everyday life (Kellner 1989a).

Today, knowledge, information, and education are playing a more important role than ever in the organization of contemporary society. This is happening because capital is restructuring itself through the implementation of new sciences and technologies into every sphere of life and requires a high level of technological skills and education. Although this process fosters enlarged investment in education and opens possibilities for advancement for previously marginalized groups and individuals, a key issue remains: Will education be organized around the transmission of technical skills and specialized knowledge, as increasingly is the case (see Schiller 1999; Robins and Webster 1999)? Or can education be focused on creating more cultivated human beings and the preconditions for a more democratic society? This would require, as Dewey (1995 [1917]) argued, a radical reconstruction of education (see Epilogue).

There is a very real danger, however, that the explosion of information technology will merely speed the commodification of education and primarily serve the interests of business. Should this happen, knowledge and education will become commodities, institutions of higher learning will be reorganized on business models, and education will be totally geared toward the imperatives of the high-tech economy.[8] Another danger is that corporate control of knowledge, information, entertainment, and technology will concentrate capital's power without generating any countervailing forces. Yet these processes should also be looked at dialectically in terms of the openings they may provide for change and social reconstruction, the conflicts they are already generating, and the possibilities they offer for greater democratization. Hence, to understand the present moment we need to grasp how global technocapitalism is creating a new technoculture, cyberbodies and identities, new forms of social life, and new politics. In addition, we should be aware of the threats, promises, and ambiguities of these developments.

TECHNOCULTURE, TECHNOBODIES, AND CYBERIDENTITIES

> We are here at the controls of a micro-satellite, in orbit, living no longer as an actor or dramaturge but as a terminal of multiple networks.
> —JEAN BAUDRILLARD

> Technoculture . . . is located as much in the work of everyday fantasies and actions as at the level of corporate or military decision making.
> —CONSTANCE PENLEY AND ANDREW ROSS

The digerati and ideologues of today's cyberculture and new technologies advance visions of a posthumanist world where the (humanist) Subject is dethroned and overpowered by the (technological) Object—Hegelianism in reverse (see Chapter 4). The new technoculture is one of the major creations of the technological revolutions and the restructuring of capitalism. Yet human culture—a reflective product of language and intellect—has been spawned from the womb of technology since the beginning of history. As many anthropologists argue, the use of tools was crucial in stimulating human intelligence and linguistic capacities, and therefore for nurturing culture. Consequently, human beings and their technologies have co-constructed one another throughout the odyssey of human evolution.

All human cultures have their technological components, but no culture until the 20th century has been as dominated by technology and technological thinking as ours. A technoculture arises when culture is defined more by science and technology than by religion, social norms, ethics, or the humanities; when face-to-face, concrete relations rooted in the family and neighborhood become electronically and digitally mediated; and when technology, shaped by distinct social and economic relations, becomes a driving source of change that overturns all stable traditions so rapidly that it impedes any attempt to control it, understand its nature, and discern its consequences. At the same time, it must be admitted that new technologies are providing exciting possibilities for accessing information, increasing communication, and creating novel cultural forms and communities.

The first feature of technoculture is that technology increasingly pervades human lives through the spread of new gadgets and machines, thereby mediating our relation to nature, the social environment, and other beings. With the shift to a consumer society, people are surrounded by a sea of commodities, services, and objects. Today, the average home in the developed countries has more technologies than ever before. Automobiles, central heating and cooling systems, telephones, beepers, cell phones, microwave ovens, stereos, color televisions, home entertainment centers, satellite dishes, personal computers, Sony Walkmans, exercise machines, digital cameras, and other gadgets weave the technological fabric of everyday life. Virtually no human activity today occurs without the mediation of these and other technologies. Consequently, we now live in a new habitat, a technoworld, qualitatively different from the processes, rhythms, and experiences of the largely natural setting in which humanity resided for millennia.

To be sure, much of the world continues to live in premodern circumstances, or rather in an overlapping state of premodern, modern, and postmodern conditions. But with the steady expansion of the global economy and culture, the same technologies, media, ideas, and images are circulating throughout the world. Major cities all over the globe are comparable, sharing high-rise buildings, traffic congestion, extreme contrasts between wealth and poverty, and similar commodities and cultural forms. As Castells demonstrates (1996), in a network society, technology structures more and more domains of everyday life and the technification of the world, feared by philosophers like Heidegger, Ellul, and Marcuse, becomes a palpable reality.

Second, with the escalating automation of society and everyday life, tasks that were once done by human beings are now being executed by machines. Thanks to factory assembly techniques, robotics, and computers, automated systems are increasingly running the work world. Machines are managing machines and computers are "talking" to each other, as when robots control factory production or airplanes run on computer-driven autopilot. Soon, futurists tell us, the home will be completely automated thanks to a central computer system that will manage various microtechnologies from cooking to lighting (see Gates 1995; Gerschenfeld 1999). When these technologies and systems work, they will provide us with power and pleasure, but when they break down or malfunction, they will make all too apparent our reliance on technology and our lack of real control over our environment. In this context, although the Y2K phenomenon seemed to have little effect, it pointed to human overdependence on technology and fears of disaster.

Automation and the robotization of work are accompanied by post-Fordism which multiplies service industries and shifts manufacturing labor from the unionized and regulated developed countries to sites where lower wages and more intense exploitation are the norm (Harvey 1987). A new technoservice and "net-slave" class is also emerging to service the high-tech society and culture under poor working conditions, without job security, and with varying and unstable pay rates (Lessard and Baldwin 2000). Moreover, the prospect of machines taking over manual labor is itself fraught with ambiguity. While the automation of labor could provide workers with more leisure for freedom and creativity, it also might make individuals more reliant on machines and could be accompanied by leisure forms that induce dependency, stupification, and alienation (e.g., drug addiction, escapist forms of media and virtual reality, etc.). Moreover, rather than liberating people from the drudgery or work to spend the bulk of their time in creative leisure and self-actualization activities, as Marx envisioned, automated labor has been used to intensify work, profits, the extraction of surplus value, and has led to increasing unemployment as workers are thrown onto the scrap heap of social waste (Rifkin 1995). A challenge for the future will be to creatively reconstruct the worlds of both work and leisure to maximize human creativity, freedom, and self-valorization, rather than to submit to domination by capital, the state, technology, and media culture and spectacle.

Third, a technoculture is distinguished by the hegemony of techno-consciousness, a form of thought governed largely by mathematical, analytic, means–end reasoning—a mode of rationality that Frankfurt School theorists termed *instrumental reason*. Within technoculture, information replaces knowledge, and what Marcuse (1964) called "one-dimensional thought" supplants critical and dialectical reason. Technocrats and technical workers become new social elites, the "golden geeks" and extravagantly paid instrumental aristocracy of a triumphant technocapitalism.

It appears that in a technoculture the passion for wisdom and learning as intrinsic goods often gives way to anxious desires for a career and success. The differences between universities and high-tech trade schools are blurring, as college students choose their majors to advance their career plans and seek to minimize all courses that do not immediately "relate" to their desired financial ends. Disturbingly, pursuit of philosophy, literature, and humanities is being displaced by business, accounting, computer science, engineering, and agriculture. Many colleges and universities are threatened with stiff competition from community colleges, technical/business schools, and Internet "distance learning." On the plus side, technological mediation of all disciplines is bringing together fields once separated by disparate methods, technologies, and practices, as individuals in more disciplines communicate through digitized words and images and seek information in databases and on the Internet in similar fashions (see Lanham 1993; Landow 1995).

Fourth, technoculture replaces social life with commercially and technologically mediated communities. Some shopping malls, for example, map out different areas as "neighborhoods" and indeed become new sites of human congregation, especially for teenagers and the elderly (who take daily "mall walks"). Real communities of people interacting face to face often give way to the virtual communities of the web. In some universities, "student life" is disappearing as students interact primarily through e-mail and chat rooms.[9] The virtualization of community can also occur in cybercafes where, instead of mingling at convivial tables, people sit separated at isolated computer stalls, each interacting with their virtual partners rather than their embodied neighbor.

Yet people isolated and alienated from their real-life communities may find like-minded people in the cyberworld that can lead to new friendships, significant relationships, and even marriages. Internet chat rooms allow people to meet, explore mutual interests, and create communities without long-distance phone charges. Websites focusing on everything from the sciences through philosophy and the classics offer a wealth of material and expand possibilities for self-education. Individuals who did not formerly have access to good libraries or other sources of information can find a cornucopia of databases and educational material free of cost on the Internet. New hypertext and multimedia forms provide exciting cultural matrices. On the whole, cyberculture is significantly more interactive and involving than the earlier dominant form: TV culture. People from the entire world can thus share in information, discussion, and cultural forms from which they were earlier excluded. The possibilities of working at home provide potential space for more freedom and creativity and open economic opportunities to those not able (or wanting) to commute to work, although this can also lead to feelings of isolation and depression.

Life online, the emergent forms of the technoculture, and the novel identities and communities it is shaping have been explored in ongoing studies by Sherry Turkle (1984, 1995). In the mode of ethnographic social science, Turkle describes the emergence of personal computer (PC) technologies and the novel forms of interaction, identities, and experiences they are producing. She interprets the transition from big computers to personal computers as symptomatic of a postmodern shift from a Big Machine and Bureaucracy Age to an innovative type of computer technology and novel forms of subjectivity and culture. For Turkle, giant IBM mainframe computers are bound up with centralization, massification, hierarchy, and big government or corporations, and are thus a figure for modernity itself. Further, modern computers are connected with mechanistic science that is universalist, rationalist (there is one way to do it), and top-down, with a cult of experts and hierarchy; it is also for Turkle rooted in hard masculine science, which is logical and abstract.

By contrast, Turkle claims that PCs are compatible with a postmodern logic and aesthetics. On her account, postmodern PC technologies are "soft" and "feminine" (i.e., more concrete and ductile), subject to tinkering, more graphic and multimedia, and more expressive, merging art and technology. Whereas modern mainframe computers required highly specialized knowledge and were only accessible to a techno-elite, postmodern PCs are "user-friendly," lend themselves to experimental activity, and promote creative and multifaceted selves. PCs thus nourish a postmodern culture of the iconic surface, for while old modern computers required depth-oriented thinking and technological know-how to get behind the screen, current PCs operate on the surface, requiring only that one point and click to navigate cyberspace.

Furthermore, on Turkle's analysis PCs enable a more decentralized, individualist, and variegated culture that can generate postmodern selves: multiple, fragmented, constructed and provisional, subject to experiment and change. "Windows," for Turkle is the privileged metaphor for postmodern subjectivity: dispersed, decentered, mobile, and constructed. Computer software windows open the subject not only to the work world of texts and word processing, but also to the emerging realms of simulation, cyberspace, and interactive multimedia culture. The result is self-awareness regarding the variety of roles we play and the many dimensions to our subjectivity. So, for example, in one window the user John does word processing and expresses his professional or academic self. In another, he does e-mail and articulates his private self, although he can go back and forth from professional to personal or mix them together at will. In Internet chat rooms, John can assume whatever identity he wants and can take on multiple identities: he can "be" a young black lesbian in the morning, a liberal male politico in the afternoon, and a transgendered literary critic at night. Switching to a multimedia window, another user, Sandy, can express her more ludic and aesthetic self by playing music and downloading tunes from Napster or Gnutella, looking at film or video clips, accessing aesthetic images from art galleries and museums, or engaging new computer art forms. In surfing the web, she can be a flaneur or a slacker self, cruising, browsing, and navigating (these are interesting metaphors themselves worthy of scrutiny). Or, in her Internet web window, she might be doing serious research, enhancing her professional and scholarly subjectivity and cultural capital.

From this perspective, what those in the cyberculture call "RL" is just one more window, one more perspective or domain of interaction, one more mode of subjectivity and identity. For Turkle and Mark Poster (1990, 1996), computer technologies create novel identities, subjectivities, and realms of experience and interaction such as cyberspace, as well as original forms of communication and social relations within the emergent technoculture. Such theories, however, exaggerate the rupture with the past, and fail to note continuities and the ways that such novelties are rooted in the structures of modernity (i.e., technoculture is a part of a new stage of capitalism and integrally connected with globalization).[10]

Finally, technoculture invades not only society and culture, but also biology and nature, importing ecological models into technology as it engineers life and creates technobodies (see Chapter 4). Canadian filmmaker David Cronenberg, a prophet and poet of the posthuman condition, has explored the dynamics of the new technoculture, the implosion between technology and humans, and the challenges and paradoxes of living in a new high-tech world. It is to his imaginative cinematic mappings of the emerging technoculture that we now turn.

DAVID CRONENBERG AND THE NEW FLESH

> The battle for the mind will be fought in the video arena, the videodrome. The television screen is the retina of the mind's eye. Therefore, the television screen is part of the physical structure of the brain. Therefore, whatever appears on the television screen emerges as new experience for those that watch it. Therefore, television is reality, and reality is less than television.
> —PROFESSOR BRIAN O'BLIVION
> IN *VIDEODROME*

> Words beget image and image is virus.
> —WILLIAM BURROUGHS, *NAKED LUNCH*

The films of David Cronenberg contain terrifying visions of science and technology creating new viruses, species, and implosions of technology and the human. While literature, as we have argued, can evoke images of the novelties of a high-tech society and provide prescient warnings about the dangers of technoscience and culture, film and the other visuals of media culture can vividly represent these perils and fears, and transmit them to popular audiences. Cronenberg uses the genre of the horror film to articulate contemporary anxieties and to present critical visions of potentially deadly effects resulting from the implosion of science, technology, capital, and everyday life. His films depict both mind and body (and their mysterious interactions) disintegrating and mutating out of control under the impact of the emergent technoculture, biotechnology, and VR. For Cronenberg, these forces wreak havoc in a hyper-rationalized, functionalized, and hygienic social order unable to accommodate or deal with frenzied transmutations of the human mind and body, proliferating disease, and hideous implosions of technology into the human.

Cronenberg's films can thus be read as allegories of a postmodern adventure in which the mutations of science, technology, capital, and the human are producing new species, bizarre realities, and reorganizations of society and culture. Capturing the tensions and ambiguities of the new technoculture, Cronenberg tracks the invasion of science, technology, and capital into the inner recesses of the human and depicts the metamorphoses of cultures, minds, and bodies under the impact of new colonizing and transformative powers. Yet he is not a technophobe, and he also shows how the forces of technoscience are producing new pleasures and potentials.

While Cronenberg's early films dealt with fear of sexual disease and viral body invasion (*Shivers* [1975] and *Rapid* [1976]), his next cycle (*The Brood* [1979], *Scanners* [1980], and *Videodrome* [1982]) presents psychotropic and telekinetic powers invading both the mind and the body, putting in question their nature and mutual interaction.[11] Although Cronenberg sometimes presents himself in interviews as a Cartesian, his films deconstruct the opposition between mind and body. He represents the mind as subject to control by both psychic and material forces, and portrays the body as vulnerable to assault by cultural and technological powers. *Scanners*, for instance, depicts new drugs creating destructive psychic powers, while *Videodrome* shows telekinetic intrusion conquering mind and body in the creation of a new posthuman species. Cronenberg makes concrete McLuhan's vision of the media as the exteriorization of mind and body that in turn collapse into the human, creating new configurations of experience and culture. He explores ramifications of technological interiorization in an era when media and technology are claimed to produce an implosion of meaning, the masses, and society, obliterating the boundaries between reality and unreality (see Baudrillard 1983a, 1983b, and 1993).

There is a technophobic element in his depictions of technologies and experiments. But, for Cronenberg, the cataclysms of our era are the product of the conflation of nature, science, technology, capital, and humanity, and thus cannot be blamed on any one factor. In this multiperspectival optic, it is the peculiar conjunction of *all* these ingredients that brings on the catastrophe rather than just, say, technology run amok, or science surpassing its "natural" limits. In a recent interview, Cronenberg claimed:

> I've never been pessimistic about technology—this is a mistaken perception. It's probably the audience's fears that are being tapped, but I think that I look at the situation fairly coldly—in the sense of neutral. I'm saying that we are doing some extreme things, but they are things that we are compelled to do. It is part of the essence of being human to create technology, that's one of the main creative acts. We've never been satisfied with the world as it is, we've messed with it from the

beginning. Most technology can be seen as an extension of the human body, in one way or another, and . . . I think that there is as much positive and exciting about it as there is dangerous and negative.[12]

Cronenberg thus resists an explicitly technophobic reading of his work, preferring to explore possible consequences of out-of-control technology in particular contexts. His films often depict technology as the product of specific relations of production, generated in distinctive institutions by individuals pursuing economic, political, technological, and perhaps psychological imperatives. This complex and materialist contextualization characterizes Cronenberg's films and distinguishes them from technophobic films, such as *2001* (1968), *Colossus* (1970), *Demon Seed* (1977), or *Gattaca* (1997), which blame technology itself for social calamity.

Moreover, he depicts the possibility of resistance and struggle against technocratic domination. *Scanners*, for instance, suggests that the new mental powers generated by corporate/scientific excess can be used for power and domination, or for empathy and sociality. In the film, a new drug, Ephemerol, which was intended to tranquilize mothers during pregnancy, gave their offspring paranormal psychic powers that enables them to scan (i.e., read) other minds—much as one scans a computer system for information. The scanners can also externalize their mental powers as physical forces capable of exploding heads or causing fires. Darryl Revok, one of the most powerful scanners, wants to organize the scanners into a corporate–political force who will use their powers to take over the world. He is opposed by a small underground who want to use their powers for human empathy, solidarity, and creativity. Cronenberg is thus not antitechnology: he tries to represent the new technoscape as both one of the great cataclysms of the present *and* a potentially higher and better stage of history.

To his figures of the viral body in *Shivers* and *Rabid*, and the carcinogenic body and mind in *The Brood* and *Scanners*, Cronenberg adds viral images and a telekinetic body in *Videodrome* (1982). In this film, a video machine produces images that create brain tumors that generate hallucinations, which in spawn turn a "new flesh" that is able to assimilate technologies. Thematizing the implosion of mind, body, and technology, Cronenberg pictures a world in which video is at the center of social life and multiplies images which, like viruses, invade the human mind/body and construct new subjects: mutant humans. Cathode Ray Missions provide free video screenings for derelicts to help socialize misfits and outcasts so that they can again "mix in" with social life. The shelter is run by Professor Brian O'Blivion's daughter, whose father (an obvious McLuhan figure) had evidently been the first victim of videodrome; his daughter preserves thousands of tapes of him and pretends that he is alive by releasing his tapes to TV stations.

For O'Blivion, "Public life on television was more real than private life in the flesh." Thus his death had no sting—as long as his videotapes and video images continue to circulate. The body invaders pictured in *Videodrome* induce psychic mutations that give rise to a new mode of perception with no distinction between video hallucinations and reality, between fantasy and "real" sense impressions. The "videodrome" is presented as the next phase of human evolution in which the human will become fully "technological animal." The film suggests that videodrome might give birth to a new stage of perception and a "new flesh" that are potentially positive for human experience and evolution, as well as destructive. Such a figure is compelling in our current technoculture as we merge with media, computer, and genetic technologies that are creating new bodies and mutations in culture, identities, and experience with powerful but uncharted effects.

On the one hand, videodrome is a potent hallucinatory virus/drug/meme implanted in the minds of citizens. It symbolizes the insidious control media and entertainment industries with their "giant hallucination machines" have over the public. In Cronenberg's allegory, these represent a virulent global technoculture. As the film makes vividly clear, the technoculture industries and their media elites have complete contempt for people and democracy. *Videodrome* thus implies a devolution where the tentacles of the media destroy the higher potentialities of the human brain, nature's most intricate product, and render subjects unfit for self-organization. Yet the film also suggests an evolutionary process whereby human perception and the body are reorganized at a higher level, within a technoscape that greatly enhances our existing powers and surpasses the limitations of current embodied existence.

Interestingly, while the metamorphoses of Cronenberg's earlier films were typically the products of well-meaning scientists whose experiments contained both great dangers and positive potential, the inventors of videodrome are more diabolical. The Spectacular Optical Corporation intends to use videodrome to manufacture a populace "tough" enough for the "savage times" they envision in the technofuture. In the words of one of its employees, "North America's getting soft . . . and the rest of the world is getting tough, very, very, tough." To survive, North America must become "pure, direct, and strong." To reverse the trend of "rotting away from the inside," the inventors of videodrome create technologies that will generate a tougher and more powerful species that merges technology and mind, video and body. In order to preserve white male hegemony in North America and the exorbitantly competitive and violent neo-Darwinian world of the global society, it is crucial to shift evolution to the next level, that of the cyborg.

Hence, *Videodrome* captures the ruthless ethos of a global capitalism organized around competing hegemonic blocs such as the North American Free Trade Association (NAFTA), the European Union (EU), The Asian-Pacific Economic Cooperation Zone (ASEC) and other groupings. Through the mouthpiece of the technoelite, Cronenberg critically presents rightwing fears of immigration, multiculturalism, and liberalism, which in the conservative imaginary are responsible for the emasculation of North American (Anglo-

Saxon, white male) power. For such conservatives, only a revival of rugged competitiveness and more masculine values can preserve the established society and maintain the position of the power elite.

Cronenberg's later 1980s films *The Dead Zone* (1983) and *The Fly* (1986) focus more obsessively on the specific roles of politics, science, and technology in a new technocapitalist society. Most of his films present scenes in which novel forms of technology intersect with the imperatives of capital accumulation, hubris, and psychopathology to spawn catastrophe. Hence, Cronenberg naturally moved from working within the horror film genre to the disaster, conspiracy, and dystopic genres that have become key forms in contemporary Hollywood (and international) cinema (see Kellner and Ryan 1988). While in some ways his unconventional and thematically obsessive films position him as an auteur of modernism, he can also be interpreted as a representative of a specific version of Canadian/North American postmodernism who anticipates many of the central themes of the postmodern adventure, providing cinematic analogues of implosions of humans and technology and the emergence of a posthuman "new flesh."

Cronenberg's works of the past 15 years cultivate a tragic dimension hitherto submerged, but visible, in his earlier films. Johnny Smith in *The Dead Zone*, Seth Brundel in *The Fly*, the twins in *Dead Ringer* (1988), the junkies in *Naked Lunch* (1991), the hermaphrodite in *Madame B* (1993), the car fetishists in *Crash* (1997), and the video-game producer in *eXistenZ* (1999) are victims as much as agents as they cope (unsuccessfully) with their obsessions and mutant minds and bodies. Many of his characters die tragically as sacrificial victims of the new technologies and new science. Some of these figures expire, however, embody a utopian fantasy of transcendence, of an evolution to higher forms of life with novel potentialities in altered bodies with tantalizing new pleasures and powers. Unlike the one-dimensional advocates of posthumanism, Cronenberg in these films shows the risks and dangers involved in evolution to the posthuman; he displays how the conventional world threatens and resists unimpeded technological mutation and development. Like Max Renn in *Videodrome*, many of Cronenberg's characters journey to the end of their experiments and perish along the way.

Such is the fate of scientist Seth Brundel in Cronenberg's *The Fly*. The film chronicles a man's startling evolution into a new species, providing frightening representations of the perils of posthumanism, transgenic species, and the fifth discontinuity. While the original *Fly* (1958) safely anchored the scientist's experiments within the bosom of the family and centered on his devoted wife, Cronenberg's version takes place amidst the postfamilial singles scene. And where the earlier version was set in a Montreal suburban home and garden that looked like Disneyesque small-town America, Cronenberg's film is mostly set in an urban loft filled with junkfood, computers, and other detritus of ultramodernity. The metamorphosis machine in the earlier film looked clumsily mechanical, whereas Cronenberg's teleportation apparatus is controlled by computers and operates according to the principles of genetic engineering and information theory. Embodying Baudrillard's postmodern molecular model of life as a code, of genetic miniaturization (DNA) being the ultimate constituent of human life (1983a: 103ff.), Cronenberg's teleportation machine breaks down the mind and body into its primary constituents and encodes the molecular structure into one telepod while decoding it into another, demonstrating the interchangeability of matter, energy, and information.

Whereas the 1958 version of *The Fly* presented the teleportation experiment as a means to serve humanity (e.g., to instantly send food to the starving), Cronenberg's remake portrays the teleportation experiment as an exigency of postmodern life intended to overcome obstacles of space and time, to move the body instantly from one place to another in order to transcend inertia, entropy, and physical limitation. The teletransporter also enables the transgression of "laws" of modern science to cross over into a new age of unlimited transposability of information. The film depicts as well the mutation of the body as itself an evolutionary/devolutionary fate for the human species as it enters a new era and world. Although Brundel/Fly is eventually destroyed, his transformation is presented as a synthesis of wonderful new powers alongside destructive ones. Brundel/Fly is in touch with his body to an unparalleled degree, discovers new physical and sexual energies, and is aware that he is the bearer of a new species being. Through the powers of technoscience he exceeds the limitations of the merely human to become transhuman. Yet he is unable to fully synthesize the new and the old, and eventually destroys himself. The victim of unanticipated consequences, Seth fuses his DNA with a fly that entered the chamber at the key moment of genetic reconstruction. Exuviating from his human shell into the grotesque form of a fly, his now useless ears and teeth falling away, Seth writhes in the spasms of a failed journey into the posthuman, seeking to evolve into a higher state, but instead devolving into a monstrous (Brundle)fly.

Cronenberg's horror over shocking implosions between technology and the human and the emergence of new species previewing a fifth discontinuity are again vividly portrayed in *eXistenZ* (1999). The film focuses on a renowned game inventor, Allegra Geller, who is on the run from an ironically named terrorist group, the Reality Liberation Brigade, that decries VR as a dangerous narcotic. In a bizarre vision of a near future, Cronenberg presents a co-evolutionary scene wherein the mass media and entertainment industries, computers and VR devices, and the genetic engineering of animals all combine to produce an unprecedently powerful spectacle. As in the film *Strange Days* (1995), *eXistenZ* portrays media images and VR as an addictive narcotic, one so powerful that growing numbers of people have jacks installed in their bodies in order to better connect to the artificial world. *eXistenZ* brings to life a social scene of radical implosion with bizarre technological devices serving as hybrids of the organic and the inorganic. The "gristle gun" used by Luddite-realists to shoot Geller is a deadly weapon concocted from bone, gristle, and sinews that shoots teeth for bullets. Anything but a plastic joystick, the slimy game pod resembles a liver with nipples. It is attached to a fleshy umbilical cord that plugs directly into a player's nervous system through an anus-like bioport inserted into the lower spine, providing a gruesome allegory of the invasion of technology into the human in an era of media spectacle, digitization, biotechnology, and VR.

Cronenberg's startling vision depicts technology fusing with biology in a new advance of the spectacle, which all but obliterates the distinction between the real and the virtual. Parallel to the film's characters, viewers have a hard time discerning which reality they inhabit since Cronenberg opens a proliferating number of ontological drawers in his Chinese box. Thus, the film's end is but a pseudostop in the journey of an ever-spiraling confusion as to who is who and what is what, showing our sense of the real perilously undermined in the emerging virtual technoculture. But technoculture is not just innocent fun. Cronenberg also underscores the dark side to the spectacle of VR, one that numbs the spectator's sense of social reality and inures his or her sensibilities to violence and the consequences of one's actions. After blowing someone away, Geller shrugs off her action with the words "He's just a game character." But an incessant involvement in an ever more realistic and immersive spectacle of simulated violence is enough for young people today to adopt the same jaded and nihilistic outlook.

In Cronenberg's epics of posthumanism, the feared concepts of carcinogenics and metastasis signify growth and development, but of a sort that careen out of control and destroy their host. Cronenberg's characters try to accept and live with the viral and carcinogenic body invaders, and hope that their technobodies will be able to evolve to a higher state of being, to a new mode of existence. These Nietzschean would-be Ubermenschen generally fail, but their attempts to overcome the limitations of body and self, and to cross over to the posthuman, exert a certain fascination and a utopian desire for novel sexualities, transcendence of boundaries, and bodily resurrection. There are several intimations, in fact, that Cronenberg's technomutants escape from, or relativize, death, transgressing the barrier between life and death as a new adventure, as a new possibility for physical and psychic experience. At the conclusion of *Scanners* the "good" and the "bad" brother have merged into one being, opening the door for new scanner evolution (and succeeding films). The possibility of a new kind of immortality is a strong undercurrent in *Videodrome* as well.

Cronenberg's later films thus depict the new passions and pleasures of the mind and body in an age of cryogenics, cloning, stem-cell technology, teleomerase therapy, and other technoscientific wonders. His notion of the "new flesh" suggests the eruption of novel forms of experience, sexuality, society, and technology in a postmodern adventure marked by radical transgression of laws and boundaries. Such a reconstruction of the body would be a site of loss and danger, as well as one of new possibilities and pleasures.

It could embody some of the most emancipatory insights into a nonrepressive civilization and the resurrection of the body set out by Herbert Marcuse (1955) and Norman O. Brown (1955) in the 1950s, and could concretize Michel Foucault's call for "new passions and new pleasures" (1980). Once the viral and the technobody has been able to assimilate and live with all the viruses and prostheses in the postmodern scene (from AIDS to television, from cancer to computer worms), a rebirth of the flesh and a transmutation of the body may be possible. Sexuality will have to be reinvented and the body "refunctioned" (*Umfunktioniert*), in Brecht's sense of remaking. We must transcend sexual panic and cynical sex, and learn once again how secretions can be fused with eroticism, how pleasure can overcome anxiety, how satisfaction can replace panic. This will require a cure for AIDS and other sexually transmitted diseases, and a return to the sexual body and its reeroticization. Creating new polymorphically eroticized bodies would take the experiments and explorations of the sexual utopias of the 1960s and 1970s to a higher and novel state of existence.

The evolved body must also be emancipated from the performance principle and erotic discipline and for the pleasure principle and polymorphic play (Marcuse 1955). Freed from the restrictions of sexuality as we now know it, an evolved body may be able to invent a new sensibility and new pleasures. The technobody may be able to overcome the scandal of sexual difference and discover three sexes, or six, or perhaps just one. Released from the tyranny of sexual difference and the norms of bourgeois performance, the postmodern body and its new sensibility could then mutate into a new synthesis of mindbody. In addition, we should explore ways to enhance our senses, increase health and longevity, and expand our powers of perception through all available techniques, ranging from yoga and meditation to smart drugs and mind machines. Such a mind/body utopia is, of course, impossible in the present situation of expanding work, stupefying leisure, disease-threatened sex, and commercialization of the human genome. But critical theory and cultural studies should contain a "dreaming forward" (Ernst Bloch), as well as an illusionless diagnosis and critique of the present scene rooted in historical comprehension of the past. Otherwise, it's unlikely that we'll have either a nice day, or a better one to look forward to tomorrow.

DEBORD, CYBERSITUATIONS, AND THE INTERACTIVE SPECTACLE

> The coincidence of the changing of circumstances and of human activity can be conceived and rationally understood only as revolutionizing practice.
> —KARL MARX

> If it seems somewhat ridiculous to talk of revolution, this is obviously because the organized revolutionary movement has long since disappeared from the modern countries where the possibilities of a decisive

transformation of society are concentrated. But everything else is even more ridiculous, since it implies accepting the existing order in one way or another.

—Situationist International

We thus read David Cronenberg as a cineaste of the emergent technoculture who offers alarming and prescient visions of the "new flesh" and fifth discontinuity in a rapidly approaching posthumanist world. Cronenberg dramatizes how the technoculture is constantly evolving, engaging the latest innovations in technology such as VR. Working in an epoch just before Cronenberg, combining both artistic and theoretical mapping, French writer and artist Guy Debord theorized the emergent technoculture as the "society of the spectacle" which he interpreted as the prevailing form of consumer capitalism. In fact, the influence of the ideas of Debord and the Situationist International is quite striking. Contemporary society and culture are still permeated with the sort of spectacle described in classical situationist works. The notion of "spectacle" has almost become normalized, emerging as part-and-parcel of both theoretical and popular media discourse.

In addition, situationist texts are reaching new and ever expanding audiences through the proliferation of 'zines and websites, some of which embody situationist practice. The past decade has been marked by cultural activism that uses new communications technology to spread radical social critique and alternative culture. Many of these 'zines pay homage to Debord and the situationists, as do a profusion of websites that publish their texts with diverse commentary.[13] Situationist ideas thus play an important part in contemporary cultural theory and activism, and may continue to inspire cultural and political opposition as the society of the spectacle enters cyberspace and new realms of culture and experience emerge.

Hence, we will update Debord's ideas in formulating what we see as the advent of a new stage of the spectacle, grounded in new technologies and requiring fresh mappings and innovative forms of oppositional practice. Reflections on the prevailing globalized capitalist system suggest that contemporary overdeveloped societies are still marked by Debordian spectacle in every realm of social life. Indeed, the advent of "megaspectacles," a term we have coined by drawing on Debord, involve a significant escalation of the spectacle in size, scope, and intensity. They range from superhyped films like the *Star Wars* series (with their high-powered sound and special effects and unparalleled megapromotion), to theme parks that create intense and thrilling technologically mediated experiences, to media-generated passion plays like the O. J. Simpson trial or the Clinton sex and impeachment scandals that are marked by such saturation coverage, repeated day after day, that they define an era of spectacle.

The capitalist economy thrives on megaspectacles of consumption, including department stores, malls, theme parks, and the booming and busting virtual cybermalls of the Internet. In the economy, more money is spent each

year on advertising and packaging, which today in the United States constitutes 4% of the gross national product (see Kellner 1996). The Global Consumer Village exhibits not only a sparkling array of goods and services but also
high-tech entertainment, postmodern architecture, and, increasingly, simulations of famous sites past and present (Gottdiener 1997; Gottdiener et al. 1999).
The Edmonton Mall in Canada, for example, combines an amusement park, a
replica of Columbus's *Santa Maria*, a simulation of New Orleans's Bourbon
Street, a casino, and a theme hotel, and hundreds of shops, so that there is currently a 60/40 percent split between retail sales and entertainment (Ritzer
1998). Not to be outdone, Las Vegas now has on display an elaborate simulation of New York City, complete with 42nd Street, the Statue of Liberty, and
rooftop roller-coasters.

Entire environments have been permeated by advertising and spectacle.
Taxis and buses are now wrapped with giant and glowing graphics, thus becoming rolling billboards.[14] Thanks to "environmental advertising," whole urban areas, like Las Vegas or the Sunset Strip in Los Angeles, are illuminated by
lasers that flash commercials upon buildings and into the sky, taking the
megaspectacle to new spaces and new heights.[15]

Indeed, outer space has been a fertile ground for the spectacle since the
Moon landing of 1969, an epochal event that changed humans' view of our
place in the cosmos, expanded the realm of human possibility, and displayed
the victory of U.S. space technology. Missions to outer space have since become routine. Negative spectacles and cautionary warnings about the limits of
technology appeared with the explosion of the *Challenger* space shuttle in
1987, errors in positioning space telescopes, and many failures in the NASA
space program, including the December 1999 loss of a Mars spacecraft intended to explore the surface of the planet.

Yet, no doubt, there will be more space spectacles in the future, with possibilities for outer space advertising, tourism, space colonies, and continued scientific exploration of the cosmos.[16] The successful 1998 landing of the *Explorer* on Mars and its subsequent broadcast of live pictures back to Earth was
enthusiastically followed on the Internet throughout the world. Hence, there is
reason to believe that explorations and representations of outer space and its
territories will be one of the major spectacles of the next millennium, along
with speculation concerning alien species, life on other planets, possible global
and cosmic catastrophe, and controversy over the origin of life and the nature
of the universe.

But it is probably the field of entertainment that today is the privileged
site of the spectacle. Entertainment is a dominant mode of technoculture and
is itself big business. Moreover, in the society of the spectacle, business has to be
entertaining to prosper. Via the "entertainmentization" of the economy, television, film, theme parks, video games, casinos, and so forth become a key sector
of the national economy. In the United States, the entertainment industry is
now a $480 billion industry, and consumers spend more on having fun than on

clothes or health care (Wolf 1999: 4).[17] In Texas, once known as a wheat state, the estimated market value of the Dallas Cowboys and the Houston Oilers in 1999 was greater ($735 million) than the total value of the wheat that the state harvested ($600 million).[18] Further, a corporate entertainment complex is rapidly advancing in Bangkok, Australia, China, India, Japan, and elsewhere, forming a crucial aspect of the global restructuring of capitalism and disseminating modernization and postmodernization processes simultaneously.

In a competitive business world, the "fun factor" can give one business the edge over another. So corporations seek to be more entertaining in their commercials, their business environment, and their websites. Hence, Budweiser commercials feature talking frogs who tell us nothing about beer, but who catch the viewers' attention, while Taco Bell deploys a talking dog, and Pepsi uses *Star Wars* characters. Buying, shopping, and dining out are coded as an "experience" as businesses adopt a theme-park style. Places like the Hard Rock Cafe are not renowned for their food, after all; people go there for the ambience, to buy clothing, and to view music and media memorabilia. It is no longer good enough just to have a website, it has to be an interactive spectacle, featuring not only products to buy, but music and videos to download, games to play, prizes to win, travel information, and "links to other cool sites."

The infotainment society reduces everything to the logic of the commodity spectacle. Always a major scene of the spectacle and a source of capital, religion itself is now packaged as a commodity with TV religion, religion websites, and the proliferation of religious artifacts ranging from Bibles on biblical stories on DVD to Christian rock music videos and CDs. Since the rise of televangelism in the 1980s, religion has been relentlessly commodified, with TV evangelists exploiting it to rake in millions of dollars from gullible contributors. Jesus2000.com advertises itself as "The Holy Land's Largest Shopping Mall on the Internet," claiming over one million "Virtual Pilgrim" visits since its December 1998 launch. *Feed* reports that

> Jesus2000.com faces stiff competition, though—and not just from Crosswalk.com, the Internet's No. 1 Christian portal. The Chosen People have developed a number of innovative Web applications including VirtualJerusalem.com, a site that lets users send e-mail directly to God. VJ Webmaster Avi Moskowitz prints and carries a batch of e-mail prayers to the Western Wall daily. Meanwhile, Taliban Online has been providing a small but faithful Muslim audience with "news and articles on Islam and Jihad" for more than a year now. The site is selling cars, stereos and other earthly delights as part of a Web banner ad network.[19]

Even the pope has become a commodity machine, a global superstar whose image the Roman Catholic Church recently licensed to sell official papal souvenirs, ranging from books and posters to watches, sweatshirts, CDs and videos featuring the pope, and bottled (holy?) water—with a papal webpage to boost the Vatican's image and to sell its merchandise. A papal visit takes on the form of megaspectacle, as when the pope's trip to St. Louis was awarded the headline "Pope Gets Rock-Star Greeting in U.S."[20]

Megaspectacles also include sports events like the World Series, the Superbowl, World Soccer Cup, and NBA championships, which attract massive audiences, are hyped to the maximum, and generate accelerating record advertising rates. These cultural rituals celebrate U.S. society's deepest values (e.g., competition, winning, success, and money) and corporations are willing to pay top dollar to get their products associated with such events. Indeed, it appears that the logic of the commodity spectacle is increasingly permeating professional sports which can no longer be played without the accompaniment of cheerleaders, giant mascots who clown with players and spectators, and raffles, promotions, and contests that feature the products of various sponsors.

Sports stadiums themselves contain electronic reproduction of the action, as well as giant advertisements for various products that rotate for maximum saturation—previewing environmental advertising in which entire urban sites are becoming scenes to boost commodity spectacles. Arenas, like the United Center in Chicago, or America West Arena in Phoenix, are named after corporate sponsors. The Texas Rangers stadium in Arlington, Texas, supplements its sports arena with a shopping mall, office buildings, and a restaurant in which for a hefty price one can watch athletic events while eating and drinking. Tropicana Field in Tampa Bay, Florida, "has a three-level mall that includes places where 'fans can get a trim at the barber shop, do their banking and then grab a cold one at the Budweiser brew pub, whose copper kettles rise three stories. There is even a climbing wall for kids and showroom space for car dealerships'" (Ritzer 1998: 229).

Furthermore, the uniforms of professional sports players are becoming as littered with advertisements as racing cars. In the globally popular sport of soccer, companies such as Canon, Sharp, and Carlsberg sponsor teams and expect these teams to promote their products via logos on team shirts, thus making the players epiphenomena of transnational capital. In auto racing events, like Indianapolis 500, or professional bicycling events, like the Tour de France, entire teams are sponsored by major corporations. In summer 1999, there were discussions about putting corporate logos on the uniforms of professional baseball players, although so far this idea has been resisted by Major League Baseball officials. Top sports heros make astronomical sums endorsing products, thus imploding sports, commerce, and advertising into dazzling spectacles that celebrate the products and values of corporate America.

In fashion, inherently a consumer spectacle, laser-light shows, top rock and pop music performers, superstar models, and endless hype publicize each new season's offerings, generating ever more elaborate clothing displays:

> In the same way that movies are being judged by the size of their grosses, not whether they make any sense, couture shows are now judged by the size of the spectacle. . . . Keep your eye on the three-story waterfall at Givenchy, and wait for the train at Christian Dior. . . . At huge expense, a spice-filled Souk was recreated,

and the lost luggage room had trunks tagged with names like Bing Crosby, Cleopatra and Brad Pitt.[21]

Here the logics of spectacle and simulation combine in a megaorgy of lights, music, dazzling image, and constructed environments that glorify the commodity and celebrity culture, and fetishize its idols. One of the world's most fashionable and glamorous women, Princess Diana, became a commodified spectacle in life, and continues to be commodified after her death, with an intense global marketing of her image on postage stamps, coins, portrait plates, porcelain dolls, and other wares of "Dianabilia."[22] Similarly, the days following the summer 1999 disappearance and death of John F. Kennedy Jr. were marked by wall-to-wall media coverage, instant TV documentaries, and commemorative magazine issues, as media corporations capitalized on the Kennedy mystique.

Such celebrity icons provide people with deities to worship from afar and inspire individuals to enter the world of image and spectacle, becoming part of the action. The society of the spectacle attempts to make it appear that a life of luxury and happiness is open to all, that anyone can buy the sparkling objects on display and consume the spectacles of entertainment and information. But in reality only those with sufficient wealth can fully enjoy the benefits of the capitalist spectacle, whose opulence is extracted out of the lives and dreams of the exploited. The poor souls who cannot afford to live out their commodity fantasies in full are motivated to work harder and harder, until they are trapped in the squirrel cage of working and spending, spending and working—while borrowing money at high interest rates. In fact, consumer credit card debt in the United States has skyrocketed 47% in recent years. By the mid-1990s, the average debt per household was over $3,000, up from barely $1,000 per household in 1985.[23] Near the end of the decade credit indebtedness reached $1.2 trillion, growing at a 9% annual rate and generating negative saving rates 2 months in a row for the first time on record.[24]

New forms of megaspectacle are emerging through the tourism and leisure industries. Theme parks like the Disney Worlds re-create entire spectacular simulated environments for family consumption. IMAX movies feature gigantic screens of erupting volcanoes, cascading avalanches, arduous climbs to Mount Everest, voyages to the Moon, undersea exploration, and the like, which allow simulation of the wonders of nature, or the euphoric experience of Michael Jordan's slam dunks. In the Universal Studios Islands of Adventure theme park, built for $3 billion, you can island-hop around five different sites, including Seuss Landing, Jurassic Park, The Lost Continent, Toon Lagoon, and Marvel Super Hero Island. This homage to the megaspectacle features high-tech rides, with 12-story-high roller-coasters, sophisticated animatronics, and 3-D special effects. Designed as pure escapism for the entire family, the Islands of Adventure advertisement bids, "Give Us Three Days and Nights. We'll Give You a Whole New Universe."

Cyberdigerati proclaim that VR will be the next stage in theme-park-like experiences, so that spectators can stay home, just don a helmet or visor, and have all the experiences—sights, sounds, and smells—that one would have in a "real" experience in a "real" park or site. Entrepreneurs claim that such experiences will be designed as an interactive spectacle wherein the "visitor" will have some input about what she or he will experience—for example, what dinosaurs will appear, whether to be washed over a waterfall or to parachute out of a crashing airplane, and so on. Perhaps such spectacles will become as addictive as the VR drug in the 1995 film *Strange Days* in which spectators become hooked on videos of extreme sex and violence, or the simulated worlds of *The 13th Floor* (1999) where players are transported to re-creations of other times and places, take on new identities, and experience full bodily fears and pleasures.

Megaspectacles also include another form of mass-mediated experience: political occurrences. Media events like the Gulf War, the O. J. Simpson trial, the Clinton sex and impeachment scandal, the Elián González saga, and the battle for the White House in the aftermath of Election 2000 (see Kellner forthcoming) colonize everyday life, distracting individuals from their own and society's decisive problems as they get lost in the trivia of tabloid infotainment. In the summer of 1999, the fourth of the *Star Wars* films, *The Phantom Menace*, became the megaspectacle of the moment with saturation media coverage of spectators camped out waiting for the film to open, often dressed in the costumes of the film's characters. The phenomenon was featured on the covers of many magazines, was heavily reported by TV and other media, and was the subject of high-density Internet coverage and discussion.

Against the passivity of the spectator, Debord and the situationists espouse active, creative, and imaginative practice, whereby individuals create their own "situations" and passionate existential events, fully participating in the production of everyday life, individuality, and, ultimately, a new society. In the previous stage of the spectacle, the media and technology were seen as powerful control mechanisms keeping individuals numb, fragmented, and docile, watching and consuming, rather than acting and doing. Yet the spectacle was not always as monolithic, determining, and powerful as some believed, nor were spectators always mere dupes or conduits of manipulation. For the last several decades, work in media theory and cultural studies has challenged simplistic "hypodermic needle" models that assume individuals are merely injected with ideology, and has analyzed the ways viewers read texts critically and against the grain, and subvert or challenge power relations in their everyday life. However, the subject was arguably not as self-constituting as later advocates of the "active audience" within British cultural studies and elsewhere would maintain in the 1980s (see the critique of the latter in Kellner 1995a, and of the situationist concepts in Best and Kellner 1997, Ch. 3).

Thus, our challenge is to theorize forms of domination and manipulation *and* agency and resistance in the previous and current phases of the spectacle. We do so with the realization that the spectacle itself has today evolved into a new stage of interactivity, which comprises new technologies (unforeseen by Debord) that allow a more active participation of the subject in (what remains) the spectacle. Individuals within the new stage of spectacle are more engaged because interactive technologies like the computer, multimedia, and VR make possible enhanced participation, albeit of limited and ambivalent types. Accordingly, we contrast a more dynamic and creative construction of cybersituations with manipulative and pacifying modes of the interactive spectacle.

Cybersituations against the Spectacle

> Today the revolutionary project stands accused before the tribunal of history—accused of having failed, of having engendered a new alienation. This amounts to recognizing that the ruling society has proved capable of defending itself, on all levels of reality, much better than revolutionaries expected. Not that it has become more tolerable. Revolution has to be reinvented, that's all.
>
> —*INTERNATIONALE SITUATIONNISTE* #6
> (August 1991)

The development and effects of new multimedia and interactive spectacle are far from clear. We can therefore offer here but a few thoughts on a condition still unfolding and some ideas about how activist intervention might help shape a better future. Throughout the society of the interactive spectacle, we find objects communicating with other objects in densely interlinked digital networks; humans interacting with objects and information through a myriad of communication technologies and channels; and humans interacting with each other through the mediation of electronic media and computers. While forms of interaction are intensifying, and while computer users are more active than TV viewers, we believe that the interaction between individuals and technology, celebrated by cybertheorists like Sherry Turkle (1996) and others, exaggerates the degree and significance of interactivity and the break with previous forms of culture and subjectivity.

On the one hand, the previous stage was not as passive as Debord claimed. On the other hand, contemporary forms of the interactive spectacle are not as emancipatory and creative as many cyberdigerati argue. We concede a more interactive dimension to the present stage of the spectacle and a more energetic role for the subject, but we also see an erosion of the distinction between subject and object occurring that has disturbing implications, as individuals implode into an ever denser technological network. While we would not go as far as Baudrillard in postulating the triumph of the object in contemporary postmodern culture (see the discussion in Kellner 1989b: 153ff.), we recognize that the cyberspectacle, like its predecessors in media culture, is intensely seductive and may foster new forms of alienation and domination.

Many forms of cyberculture currently being boosted do not advance genuine interaction and instead wrap subjects more insidiously within the tentacles of the consumer society. Today, instead of merely watching TV, with beer
in hand, someone may participate in public discussion, take part in polls, or respond to the hosts of talk shows and their guests by phone, fax, or e-mail.
Rather than drift into the beta-wave stupor induced by TV, the cybersubject
can voice an opinion. In a vividly literal application of interactive technology,
video cameras can project your image into the screen to allow you to "interact"
with virtual characters (as you also become one). The Media Lab at MIT developed an interactive system that allows the viewer of a cartoon called
Swamped! to direct the movement and actions of the animal characters.

Yet one should not exaggerate the significance of such activity. Much
Internet "interactivity" is limited to repetitive pointing and clicking at endless
pictures of stars and celebrities, or to downloading video or sound clips at entertainment sites. Information and education sites often involve clicking on
images or superficial infobites that reduce complex subjects to trivial simplifi-
cations. The culture industry thus greatly exaggerates the significance of its
mode of interaction. A Pepsi commercial on MTV publicizing the 1998 MTV
Music Video Awards show emphasized the fact that the video of the year
award would be selected by the viewers via the Internet and live phone calls
during the show. The commercial celebrated "the power of choice" and re-
minded viewers that "you are in charge of your destiny," equating the ability to
vote for an MTV music video award with personal and social power. In such
fashion, the interactive spectacle attempts to seduce viewers into playing its
game and equates virtual participation with empowerment and destiny.

Moreover, typically the protocols of interaction on computer networks
are structured, and websites that solicit viewer opinions through e-mail are
monitored and manipulated. That is, often "wizards" or list-serve administra-
tors can take people off lists, censor postings, and limit the type and extent of
interaction. Interactive mainstream media such as CNN discussion programs
that solicit viewers to e-mail or fax comments for instant dissemination are
also monitored and controlled—as are websites that incorporate live viewer
input. While these are interesting developments in the history of the media,
they do not constitute a democratizing, empowering, or genuinely interactive
culture per se. In fact, they are continuous in some ways with the media spectacles of the previous stage, although they integrate the consumer and audience into the spectacle in more engaging ways.

"Interactive TV" is not only an oxymoron, it is an ideological conceal-
ment of the fact that the stage and props of discussion are already in place and
corporately controlled (e.g., a producer screens calls, the host can instantly cut
off a radical perspective that may seep through). Further, individuals are still
isolated in private homes. "Interactive TV" is therefore an alibi that functions
in the same way that the "open hallways" of Congress (threatened by the summer 1998 shootings of two Capitol police officers) masks the fact that, open or

blocked, the citizens still do not get behind the closed doors of establishment power politics.

Web TV is already providing an interactive spectacle combining the television industry and the Internet, allowing one to access databases, websites, virtual shopping, e-mail, and chat rooms, while watching TV. To simulate the more active nature of the Internet, TV networks are planning programs that allow the viewer to click on menus that will give them options for more information related to what they are looking at. Viewers watching Julia Child cook, for example, will be able to print the recipe she is making and even order necessary ingredients on the spot. Advertisers are excited about the prospects for selling clothes and fashion accessories exhibited on interactive TV, or selling objects on display in programs that individuals will be able to purchase simply by clicking on their screens. Thus, the future of TV appears to be interactive, as it seeks to emulate its Internet rival, while Internet pioneers and entrepreneurs claim that their medium will absorb and trump all others. In fact, the media are imploding into each other as they coevolve into comprehensive information, entertainment, and communications media, linked by both wired and wireless interactive networks.

In addition, Internet technology enables ordinary individuals to make their everyday life a spectacle. For example, they can offer themselves having sex live via webcams or on tape on the Internet (usually for a fee). On June 16, 1998, a woman offered a live birth on the Internet (she had a felony record for various scams). "Webcams" record and send live over the Internet the daily activities of webstars like JenniCam whose site receives some 60,000 visitors a day to watch her go through mundane activities. The "star" of AnaCam can be seen "on her couch (she has no bed), looking bored, eating a pizza, having kinky sex with her boyfriend—sometimes all at the same time."[25] Throughout the world, individuals are setting up webcam sites, sometimes charging for access. The sites are often run by sex professionals who offer nude women and round-the-clock full penetration spycams. The enterprising Gay Frat House Voyeur Cam offers 12 hidden camera angles including "butt cam," "dick cam," and "tan-line cam," not to forget the "toilet cam."[26]

Webcam sites are also posting advertising. DotComGuy ran an interactive spectacle featuring himself as the subject of a 365-day 24-hour-a-day surveillance in a North Dallas house. He never left home and for a year subsisted entirely on items purchased from the web—or contributed by companies whose products received free "advertising" (*Salon*, August 1, 2000). Many of the sites feature tedious transmissions of individuals driving their cars or even the interior of refrigerators, suggesting many people have no clue concerning how to productively use the new technologies.

Another form of Internet spectacle consists of videos of naked young people in showers or dressing room, whose images were being sold on commercial Internet sites (*CBS Evening News*, July 29, 1999). Some people, however, choose to exploit themselves. In a wildly successful Dutch TV series, *Big*

Brother, a group of volunteers lived in a house under unrelenting surveillance by TV cameras, unable to have any contact with the outside world. Over time, viewers voted on which characters should stay or go, until only one was left to claim a cash prize. CBS bought rights to air an U.S. version of the show and broadcast the show in summer 2000.[27] As with the Dutch show, each week viewers voted on which contestant would be eliminated; the "winner" took home a half-million-dollar bonanza. The sight of dozens of microphones and cameras everywhere, including the CBS logo of an open eye, recalls the Orwellian nightmare, transmuted into fluff entertainment in the society of the spectacle. Quite possibly *Big Brother* helps acclimate people to surveillance, such as is exercised by the FBI "Carnivore" program that can intercept private e-mail, and to round-the-clock video surveillance at work, in public spaces, and perhaps even at home.

Another reality-based show, *Survivor*, involved a dangerous endurance contest among 16 contestants on a deserted island off Borneo. It was also broadcast by CBS in summer 2000, becoming a major ratings success. On this show, contenders voted each other off each week, with the winner receiving a million dollars. The competition elicited complex alliances and Machiavellian strategies in a social Darwinian passion play. The *CBS Morning News* show, which has a long history of merging news and entertainment, interviewed the contestants the morning after the nation watched the contestants' expulsion and the news show saw its ratings skyrocket.

Demonstrating the psychopathology of the spectacle, contestants on these "reality" shows are driven by a lust for money and perhaps even more by the 15 minutes of fame and celebrity promised to them by Andy Warhol. Buffetted by the machines of publicity, there appear to be no losers, as those voted off return to instant renown and receive offers to become TV guest hosts, VJs (video diskjockeys), or even to appear in *Playboy* (though one contestant on the Swedish *Big Brother* committed suicide after his exile, and it is not clear what the long-term effects of celebrity withdrawal on participants in these experiments may be).

Hence, whereas Truman Burbank, in the summer 1998 hit film *The Truman Show*, discovered to his horror that his life was being televised and sought to escape the video panopticon, many individuals in the cyberworld choose to make televisual spectacles of their everyday life, such as the webcam "stars" or the participants in the MTV "reality" series *Real World* and *Road Rules*. Even PBS got in the act in summer 2000 with its reality-based show *The 1900 House* which features another survival endurance trial, this time involving a family suffering without the amenities of the consumer society and technoculture in a Victorian-era British middle-class house. "Reality television" continued to proliferate in 2001 with a *Survivor* series located in the Australian outback, *Temptation Island* that lured couples into compromising situations with attractive potential sexual counterparts, and stamina contests such as *Eco-Challenge: Borneo* and *Boot Camp*, which prepare individuals from the soft U.S.

public for hand-to-hand conflict with possible Chinese, Russian, North Korean, or other "enemies" that the Bush administration is manufacturing. These shows replicate the same basic formula of putting ordinary people in extraordinary situations and promote competitive, survivalist, and militarist values.

These series and their websites seem to be highly addictive, pointing to deep-seated voyereurism and narcissism in the society of the interactive spectacle, in which individuals have a seemingly insatiable lust to become part of the spectacle and to involve themselves in it more intimately and to peer into the personal lives of others. Moreover, they exemplify what Daniel Boorstin (1961) referred to as "pseudoevents," in which people pay more attention to media-produced spectacles than to pressing concerns in the sociopolitical world and everyday life. As Baudrillard astutely observed (1983c), postmodern media society devolves around an "obscenity" that implodes public and private spheres and puts on display the most banal and intimate aspects of everyday life—be it the sex games of Bill Clinton or the melodramas of ordinary "reality TV" drama participants.

To be sure, there are extremely valuable websites on the Internet which is potentially an excellent research tool, mode of communication, forum for debate, and site for cultural experimentation and creativity. The danger is that it is being colonized by corporate forces that are turning it into another domain of capitalist spectacle and commodification. The likelihood of this has greatly increased with the AOL–Time Warner merger in 2000–2001 that signaled the desire of megacorporations to colonize the Internet. In addition, as the April 1999 Columbine High School shooting demonstrated, there is also a dark and potentially dangerous side to the interactive spectacle in the form of brutal video games, hate sites, and the circulation of the culture of violence. While we by no means intend to reduce the complicated array of causes underlying the epidemic of teen killings in the last few years to the leisure activities of youth, it cannot be denied that a steady feast of media and interactive violence will have an impact on many impressionable minds that at the very least desensitizes them to violence in society. Interactive video games like *Doom* are particularly alarming in that they implicate young people in gory images and actions in a far deeper way than passively viewing violence on TV; moreover, they blur the boundaries between reality and unreality. The "reality effect" of some games is such that they include weapons that give a strong "kick" like a real gun. There are even examples of teen killers going on a shooting rampage, although they have never fired an actual weapon. In December 1997, for example, Michael Carneal, a 14-year-old computer geek and war game freak, walked into the lobby of Heath High School in Paducah, Kentucky, and opened fire into a prayer circle, handling the gun like a pro and killing three of his classmates.[28]

VR devices promise to take individuals into an even higher and more powerful realm of spectacle in which participants may think that they are interacting with a real environment, rather than a projected simulation, be it a war game or a pornographic fantasy. The "intensor chair" provides various sensations and stimulations, as the viewer sits within the midst of a virtual environment, playing war and action games. So far VR devices have been limited to games like *Dactyl Nightmare,* where one dons a head-mounted display to fight other characters and avoid destruction by large winged creatures in a Darwinian battle for survival, or one enters a high-tech virtual "movie ride," often based on film characters like *RoboCop.* Some of these experiences make possible a new level of multisensorium spectacles that deploy giant movie screens, 3-D images, and vibrating chairs, something like the "feelies" envisioned by Huxley in *Brave New World.*

Indeed, to capture the olfactory quality of the feelies, California-based DigiScents has developed an interactive technology that adds scents to multimedia CD-ROMs and websites. Shoppers clicking onto a scent-enhanced cosmetics website could smell the latest products. Thinking about a trip to the Caribbean? Check out the dazzling images of white sand and clear blue water, and breath deeply the aroma of exotic beauty. In the mood for an interactive murder mystery game? You can sniff out the dastardly criminal by following scents presented as olfactory clues.

While more interesting and engaging than plain-old TV, such virtual and "interactive" technology can seduce the viewer into an even deeper tie to the spectacle. In fact, there is no substitute for getting off one's ass and becoming involved in genuinely interactive citizenship and democracy. Advocates of the superiority of cyberworlds denigrate the body as mere "meat" and "RL" as a boring intrusion into the pleasures of the media and computer worlds of cyberspace. We would avoid, however, demonizing cyberspace as a fallen realm of alienation and dehumanization, as do many of its technophobic philosophical critics (e.g., Virilio 1998a; Borgmann 1994, 1999), just as we would refrain from celebrating it as a new realm of emancipation, democracy, and creative activity.

We distinguish therefore between a more inventive and self-valorizing construction of cybersituations contrasted to the pseudointeraction of the corporate-produced interactive spectacle. Extending Debord's conception of the construction of situations into the spheres of new technologies, we suggest that producing cybersituations involves engaging individuals in activities that fulfill their own potential, further their interests, and promote oppositional activity aimed at progressive change and alternative cultural and social forms. This could consist of using cyberspace to advance struggles, such as to promote political demonstrations, actions, and organizations. It might include the construction of a website, computer-mediated space such as chat rooms, or discussion groups that provide alternative information and culture. Such cybersituations could engage individuals who are usually excluded from public discussions and could enlarge the sphere of democratic participation. In these self- or group-constructed environments, people can develop both form and content, using new technologies to advance their own projects, to express their own views and visions, and to interact in ways that they themselves decide.

Constructing cybersituations involves the appropriation, use, and reconstruction of technologies against the capitalist spectacle and other forms of domination, alienation, and oppression. The aesthetic strategies of the situationists included *détournement*, a means of deconstructing the images of bourgeois society by exposing their hidden manipulation or repressive logic (e.g., by changing the wording of a billboard); the *dérive*, an imaginative, hallucinatory "drift" through the urban environment (an urban variation on the surrealist stroll through the countryside); and the *constructed situation*, designed to unfetter, create, and experiment with desires (see the texts in Knabb 1981: 5–13, 43–47, 50–59).

There are conspicuous cyberequivalents of these categories. Hacking comprises a *détournement* within cyberspace, whereby computer activists break into government or corporate websites, using the tools of the interactive spectacle itself against institutions deemed to be pernicious. After the bombing of the Chinese embassy in Belgrade by NATO forces in May 1999, for instance, hackers broke into the NATO website to protest the action. There have been several examples of hackers invading Pentagon and Defense Department websites to deface them or to post critical messages. Hacker campaigns have also been organized against the governments of Mexico, Indonesia, and other countries.

In general, hackers protest against unpopular policies by defacing official websites or bombarding government servers with spam or logic bombs, attempting to shut them down.[29] One of the more spectacular hacker attacks against commercial e-business sites occurred in February 2000. Hackers temporarily blocked access to the popular Internet sites Yahoo (a web portal), Amazon.com (an Internet book company), CNN (a news site), and Buy.com (an e-business retail site). Attacks followed on the news site ZDNet and the online brokerage site E-Trade. This demonstration of the ease with which commercial Internet sites can be disabled sent jitters through the stock market, put the FBI and law enforcement agencies in motion, and set off a flurry of discussions of the need for better cybersecurity.[30]

Surfing the web can exemplify the Debordian *dérive*, in which one abstracts oneself from the cares of everyday life and seeks adventure, novelty, and the unexpected on the Internet. Such "cruising" is equivalent to the activity of the urban flaneur, celebrated by Walter Benjamin, in which one drifts though the hypertexts of the cyberworld, clicking from one destination and curiosity to another, sometimes merely observing and sometimes participating in more interactive endeavors. Such activities constitute novel forms of postmodern pleasure and help cultivate new subjectivities, interpersonal relationships, and communities—although, as we signal below, there are limitations and dangers to such activity.

Constructing cybersituations includes the creation of an anti-McDonald's website against the junk food corporation and then distributing the material through digital and print media. This site was developed by supporters of two British activists, Helen Steel and Dave Morris, who were sued by McDonald's for distributing leaflets denouncing the corporation's low wages, false advertising practices, involvement in deforestation, cruel treatment of animals, and promotion of an unhealthy diet. The activists counterattacked. With help from supporters, they organized a "McLibel" campaign, assembled a "McSpotlight" website with a tremendous amount of information criticizing the corporation, and mobilized experts to testify about and confirm their criticisms. A 3-year civil trial, Britain's longest ever, ended ambiguously on June 19, 1997, with the judge defending some of McDonald's claims against the activists, while substantiating some of the activists' criticisms (Vidal 1997: 299–315). The case created unprecedented bad publicity for McDonald's which was disseminated throughout the world via Internet websites, mailing lists, and discussion groups. The McLibel/McSpotlight group claims that their website was accessed over 15 million times and was visited over two million times in the month of the verdict alone (Vidal 1997: 326). The *Guardian* (February 22, 1996) reported that the site "claimed to be the most comprehensive source of information on a multinational corporation ever assembled" and characterized it as one of the more successful anticorporate campaigns.[31]

Of course, one can get sucked into the tentacles of the Internet spectacle, trapped in the interstices of the web, seduced by images, games, and consumption of goods and unable to connect with the outside world. The distinction between creative and empowering cybersituations versus (pseudo)interactive and disempowering spectacle is often difficult to make, but we believe that some such distinction is necessary in order to provide critical perspectives on and alternatives to the forms of interactive spectacle now evolving. While pseudointeraction provides escape into an ersatz (virtual) reality, activist use of technology enables individuals to create and interact more productively with others in their everyday lives and to strive to transform culture and society by generating new spaces of connection, freedom, and creativity. Constructing cybersituations thus provides potential articulations between cyberspace and the real world, while pseudointeraction merely entangles one ever deeper in the matrices of escapism and corporate entertainment.

Hence, "constructing a situation" in cyberspace involves producing an interactive realm that allows individuals to articulate their needs and interests, and to connect with people of similar outlooks and desires. It can also involve a refunctioning of technology, as when members of the French public recast the Minitel from a centralized source of official government information to an interactive space of connection and discourse from below (see Feenberg 1995). In the case of innovative MP3 and other music distribution technologies, both well-known and unknown artists can directly release their music to a listening audience without the mediation of the record industries that exploit artists, control artistic expression, and often enforce a bland homogeneity of music choices. MP3 and Napster, Gnutella, Netbrilliant, and various netcasting technologies also allow any person with a computer, the right software, and a little technical savvy to be their own DJ and radio station (even if sometimes distributing music illegally), thereby engendering more diversity of production, distribution, and consumption of music.[32]

Programs like *Freeware* and *Scour* make it possible to access and store programs ranging from music to text and video. Likewise, cheap digital-video cameras make possible the production of new types of low-cost film. *The Blair Witch Project*, a mockumentary about the supposed mysterious disappearance of a young documentary-film crew in the countryside of Maryland—was the film sensation of summer 1999.[33] Made on an extremely low budget, it exploited new video technologies and the Internet, which fostered tremendous subcultural interest in the phenomenon. Indeed, the Internet itself is becoming a venue for low-budget film, using digital film technologies to expand the possibilities for new voices and alternative cultures to contest the corporate hegemony and provide new forms of political and interactive culture.

To be sure, distinctions between empowering and creative activity versus disempowering and alienating activity are ideal types, since each individual is constructed in some way or another by the social environment in which he or she lives. But even the most controlled and structured interactive cyberspace allows more participation and involvement than the passive consumption of television or film images in the solitude of one's own subjectivity. One is never totally free of social influence. In cyberspace all technologically mediated communication is structured to some extent by computer protocols, codes, and programs. Moreover, we are not against the fun and pleasure offered by the interactive and media spectacles that we have been describing. Rather, we are criticizing the organization of an entire society structured around amusement, commodification, and consumption. Where commercial interests dominate the forms of culture, decisive issues are often not taken seriously, individuals are isolated in solipsistic activity and cut off from social practice, and, as Aldous Huxley put it, people exchange freedom for "fun."

In any case, the new forms of interactive spectacle are very ambiguous. On the one hand, they can provide more creative interaction with media and culture than viewing television or film and can promote social transformation rather than passivity. On the other hand, they ensnare individuals into technological systems that abstract them from their everyday life in favor of novel virtual worlds, the types and effects of which are difficult to conceptualize and evaluate. Yet while the form of technologically mediated interaction is always structured, limited, and coded, new technologies allow for the construction of alternative spaces that can attack and subvert the established culture. In this emergent site, one can express views and encourage alternatives hitherto excluded from mainstream media, and engage in innovative forms of democratic communication and political discussion. Consequently, the new cultural forums have many more voices and individuals participating than during the Era of Big Mainstream Media in which giant corporations controlled both the form and the content of what could be spoken and shown. Cyberdemocracy and technopolitics are too recent for us to adequately appraise their possibilities, limitations, and effects, but we believe they provide the promise of the sort of subversive politics against the capitalist spectacle that Debord encouraged.

TECHNOPOLITICS, NEW TECHNOLOGIES, AND THE NEW PUBLIC SPHERES

> We have merely used our new machines and energies to further processes which were begun under the auspices of capitalist and military enterprise.
> —LEWIS MUMFORD

> A community will evolve only when a people control their own communication.
> —FRANTZ FANON

Given the extent to which capital and its logic of commodification have colonized ever more areas of everyday life in recent years, it is somewhat astonishing that cyberspace is by and large decommodified for large numbers of people—at least in the overdeveloped countries like the United States.[34] In the United States, government and educational institutions, and some businesses, provide free Internet access and in some cases free computers, or at least workplace access. With flat-rate monthly phone bills (which we know do not exist in much of the world), one can thus have access to a cornucopia of information and entertainment on the Internet for free. The Internet is one of the few decommodified spaces in the ultracommodified world of technocapitalism. So far, the "information superhighway" is a freeway, although powerful interests would like to make it a tollroad. Indeed, powerful commercial interests are quickly transforming it into a giant mall, commercializing the Internet and transforming it into a megaconsumer spectacle (see Schiller 1999).

Obviously, much of the world does not even have telephone service, much less computers, and there are vast discrepancies in terms of who has access to computers and who participates in the technological revolution and cyberdemocracy today. Consequently, there have been passionate debates over the extent and nature of the "digital divide" between the information haves and have-nots. Critics of new technologies and cyberspace repeat incessantly that it is by and large young, white, middle- or upper-class males who are the dominant players in the cyberspaces of the present. While this is true, statistics and surveys indicate that many more women, people of color, seniors, and individuals from marginalized groups are becoming increasingly active.[35] In addition, it appears that computers are becoming part of the standard household consumer package in the overdeveloped world. They will perhaps be as common as TV sets in the years ahead and already they are much more important than television for work, social life, and education. Further, there are plans afoot to wire the entire world with satellites that would make the Internet and new communication technologies accessible to people who now do not even have telephones, TVs, or even electricity.[36]

However widespread and common computers and new technologies become, it is clear that they are of essential importance already for labor, politics, education, and social life. Hence, people who want to participate in the public and cultural life of the future will need to have computer access and computer literacy. Although there is a real threat that the computerization of society will intensify the current inequalities in relations of class, race, and gender power, there is also the possibility that a democratized and computerized public sphere might provide opportunities to overcome these injustices. Hence, cyberdemocracy and the Internet should be seen as a contested terrain. Radical democratic activists should look to its possibilities for resistance and the advancement of political education, action, and organization, while engaging in struggles over the digital divide. Dominant corporate and state powers, as well as conservative and rightist groups, have been making sustained use of new technologies to advance their agendas. If forces struggling for democratization and social justice want to become players in the cultural and political battles of the future, they must devise ways to use new technologies to advance a radical democratic and ecological agenda and the interests of the oppressed.

We could list copious examples of how the Internet and cyberdemocracy have been employed for oppositional political movements. A large number of insurgent intellectuals are already utilizing new technologies and public spheres in their political projects. The peasants and radical intellectuals who formed the Zapatista movement in Chiapas, Mexico, beginning in January 1994 used computer databases, guerrilla radio, and other forms of media to circulate their ideas and promote their causes. Every manifesto, text, and bulletin produced by the Zapatista Army of National Liberation who occupied land in the southern Mexican state of Chiapas was immediately circulated through the world via computer networks.[37]

In January 1995, when the Mexican government attacked the Zapatistas, they deployed computer networks to inform and mobilize individuals and groups throughout the world to support them in the struggle against repressive Mexican government action. There were many demonstrations in support of the rebels. Prominent journalists, human rights observers, and delegations traveled to Chiapas to demonstrate solidarity and to report on the uprising. The Mexican and U.S. governments were bombarded with messages calling for negotiations rather than repression. The Mexican government was forced to back down. As of this writing, the government is sporadically negotiating with the Zapatistas, who carried out a successful march to Mexico City in March 2001.

Seeing the progressive potential of advanced communication technologies, Frantz Fanon (1967) described the central role of the radio in the Algerian Revolution, and Lenin stressed the importance of film in spreading communist ideology after the Russian Revolution. Audiotapes were used to advance the insurrection in Iran and to disseminate alternative information by political movements throughout the world (see Downing 1984, 2000). The Tienanman Square democracy movement in China and various groups struggling against the remnants of Stalinism in the former communist bloc used computer bulletin boards and networks, to promote their movements. Anti-NAFTA groups made extensive use of the new communications technology (see Brenner 1994; Fredericks 1994). Such multinational networking and distribution of information failed to stop NAFTA, but did create alliances useful for the politics of the future. As Nick Dyer-Witheford (1999: 156) notes,

> The anti-NAFTA coalitions, while mobilizing a depth of opposition entirely unexpected by capital, failed in their immediate objectives. But the transcontinental dialogues which emerged checked—though by no means eliminated—the chauvinist element in North American opposition to free trade. The movement created a powerful pedagogical crucible for cross-sectoral and cross-border organizing. And it opened pathways for future connections, including electronic ones, which were later effectively mobilized by the Zapatista uprising and in continuing initiatives against *maquilladora* exploitation.

Thus, using new technologies to link information and practice to advance oppositional politics is neither extraneous to political battles nor merely utopian. Even if material gains are not won, often the information circulated or the alliances formed by such means can be of use. As we noted, two British activists were sued by McDonald's, counterattacked, and disseminated a tremendous amount of anticorporate information. Many labor organizations are also beginning to make use of the new technologies. Mike Cooley (1987) has written on how computer systems can reskill rather than deskill workers, while Shoshana Zuboff (1988) has discussed how high-tech can be appropriated to "informate" workplaces rather than automate them, expanding workers' knowledge and control over operations rather than reducing and eliminating it. The Clean Clothes Campaign, a movement started by Dutch women in 1990 in support of Filipino garment workers has supported strikes throughout the world, exposing exploitative working conditions.[38] In 1997, activists involved in Korean workers strikes and the Merseyside dock strike in England used websites to promote international solidarity.[39]

On the whole, labor organizations, such as the North South Dignity of Labor group, note that computer networks are useful for organizing and distributing information, but cannot replace print media, which are more accessible to many of its members; face-to-face meetings; and traditional forms of political action. Thus, the challenge is to articulate one's communications politics

with actual movements and struggles so that cyberpolitics is an arm of real battles rather than their replacement or substitute. The most efficacious Internet
projects have indeed intersected with activist movements encompassing campaigns to free political prisoners, boycotts of corporate projects, and various labor and even revolutionary struggles, as noted above.

One of the more instructive examples of the use of the Internet to foster
global struggles against the excesses of corporate capitalism occurred during
the protests in Seattle and throughout the world against the World Trade Organization (WTO) meeting in December 1999 and subsequent emergence of
a worldwide antiglobalization movement in 2000–2001. Behind these actions
was a global protest movement using the Internet to organize resistance to the
WTO and capitalist globalization, while championing democratization. Many
websites contained anti-WTO material and numerous mailing lists used the
Internet to distribute critical material and to organize the protest. The result
was the mobilization of caravans from throughout the United States to take
protestors to Seattle; many of these protestors had never met and were re-
cruited through the Internet. For the first time ever, labor, environmentalist,
feminist, socialist, animal rights, anarchist, and other groups organized to protest aspects of globalization and to form new alliances and solidarities for future struggles. In addition, protests occurred throughout the world, and a proliferation of anti-WTO material against the extremely secret group spread
throughout the Internet.[40]

Furthermore, the Internet provided critical coverage of the event, documentation of the various groups' protests, and debate over the WTO and globalization. Whereas the mainstream media presented the protests as "antitrade,"
featured the incidents of anarchist violence against property, and minimized
police violence against demonstrators, the Internet provided pictures, eyewit-
ness accounts, and reports of police brutality and the generally peaceful and
nonviolent nature of the protests. While the mainstream media framed the
protests negatively and privileged suspect spokespeople like Patrick Buchanan
as critics of globalization, the Internet provided multiple representations of the
demonstrations, advanced reflective discussion of the WTO and globalization,
and presented a diversity of critical perspectives.[41]

The Seattle demonstrations had some immediate consequences. The day
after the demonstrators made good on their promise to shut down the WTO
negotiations, Bill Clinton gave a speech endorsing the concept of labor rights
enforceable by trade sanctions, thus effectively making impossible any agreement during the Seattle meetings. In addition, at the World Economic Forum
in Davos a month later there was much discussion of how concessions were
necessary on labor and the environment if consensus over globalization and
free trade were to be possible. Importantly, the issue of overcoming divisions
between the information-rich and the information-poor, and improving the
lot of the disenfranchised and oppressed, bringing these groups the benefits of
globalization, were also seriously discussed at the meeting and in the media.

The Seattle demonstrations were followed by April 2000 demonstrations in Washington, DC, to protest the World Bank and the International Monetary Fund (IMF). The Internet again was used to organize the events and to disseminate information to the world concerning the policies of the institutions of capitalist globalization. The events made clear that the protestors were not against globalization per se, but were against neoliberal globalization. They opposed specific policies and institutions that produce intensified exploitation of labor, environmental devastation, growing divisions among the social classes, and the undermining of democracy. The emerging antiglobalization movements are contextualizing these problems in the context of a restructuring of capitalism on a worldwide basis for maximum profit with zero accountability and have made clear the need for regulation, rules, and globalization in the interests of people and not profit.

The new movements against globalization have thus placed the issues of global justice and environmental destruction squarely in the center of important political concerns of our time. Hence, whereas the mainstream media had failed to vigorously debate or even to report on globalization until the recent past, and rarely, if ever, critically discussed the activities of the WTO, World Bank, and IMF, there is now a widely circulating critical discourse regarding these institutions. Stung by criticisms, representatives of the World Bank, in particular, are pledging reform. Pressures are mounting concerning proper and improper roles for the major global institutions, highlighting their limitations and deficiencies, and the need for reforms like debt relief for overburdened developing countries to solve some of their fiscal and social problems.

Hence, to capital's globalization from above, cyberactivists have been attempting to carry out globalization from below, developing networks of solidarity and propagating oppositional ideas and movements throughout the planet. To the capitalist international of transnational corporate globalization, a Fifth International, to use Waterman's phrase (1992), of computer-mediated activism is emerging, one that is qualitatively different from the party-based socialist and communist internationals. Such networking links labor, feminist, ecological, peace, and other anticapitalist groups, providing the basis for a new politics of alliance and solidarity to overcome the limitations of postmodern identity politics.

In addition, a series of conflicts around gender, sex, and race are also being mediated by new communications technologies. After the 1991 Clarence Thomas hearings in the U.S. Senate on his fitness to be a Supreme Court justice, and the failure of the almost all-male U.S. Senate to disqualify the obviously unqualified Thomas, women turned to computer and other technologies to attack male privilege in the political system in the United States and to rally women to support women candidates. The result was the election of more women candidates in the 1992 election than in any previous election and continued increases in the election of women senators since then.

Many feminists have now established websites, mailing lists, and other forms of cybercommunication to advance their movements. Younger women, sometimes deploying the label "riot grrrls," have created electronically mediated 'zines, websites, and discussion groups to develop their ideas and to address their problems and struggles. African American women, Latinas, and other groups of women as well have been developing websites and discussion lists to advance their interests.

In addition, AIDS activists are employing new technologies to disseminate medical information and to activate their constituencies for courses of political action and organization. Moreover, African American activists have made use of broadcast and computer technologies to promote their cause. John Fiske (1994) has described some African American radio projects in the "technostruggles" of the present age and the important functions of the media in recent conflicts around race and gender. African American "knowledge warriors" are using radio, computer networks, and other media to circulate their ideas and "counterknowledge" on a variety of issues, contesting the mainstream, and offering alternative views and politics. Likewise, activists in communities of color—like Oakland, Harlem, and Los Angeles—are setting up computer and media centers to teach the skills necessary to survive the onslaught of the mediaization of culture and the computerization of society to people in their communities.

Indeed, a variety of local activists have been using the Internet to criticize government, to oppose corporate policies, and to organize people around specific issues. These efforts range from developing websites to oppose local policies, such as an attempt to transform a military airport into a civilian one in El Toro, California; to gadflies who expose corruption in local government; to citizen groups who use the Internet to inform, recruit, and organize individuals to become active in various political movements and struggles.[42] Thus, new communications technologies enable ordinary citizens and activists to themselves become intellectuals, to produce and disseminate information, and to participate in debates and struggles, thus helping to realize Gramsci's dictum that anyone could be an intellectual.

Obviously, rightwing and reactionary forces can and have used the Internet to promote their political agendas as well. In a short time, one can easily access an exotic witch's brew of websites maintained by the Ku Klux Klan; myriad neo-Nazi assemblages, the Aryan Nations; and various militia groups. Rightwing extremists are aggressively active on many computer forums, as well as radio programs and stations, public access television programs, fax campaigns, video and even rock music productions. These organizations are hardly harmless, having carried out terrorism of various sorts extending from church burnings to the bombings of public buildings. Adopting quasi-Leninist discourse and tactics for ultraright causes, these groups have been successful in recruiting working-class members devastated by the developments of global capitalism which has resulted in widespread unemployment for traditional forms of industrial, agricultural, and unskilled labor. Moreover, extremist websites have influenced alienated middle-class youth as well.

It is now de rigueur for mainstream politicians to run "e-campaigns" as a critical part of their overall strategy: as websites can provide information on the candidate, citizen feedback, and, of course, links for volunteer efforts and donations. It is widely held that without the Internet, former wrestler and independent candidate Jesse "The Body" Ventura would have lost his bid for governor of Minnesota, for his funding and influence grew primarily through a plain Internet site and a burgeoning e-mail list. Unlike one-way transmission TV ads, the sites of Bush and Gore in the 2000 presidential race featured interactive links for citizens to "get involved." Gore had special links for students, African Americans, Asians, Hispanics, and gays and lesbians. All such links were conspicuously absent on Bush's site, except for an "en espanol" link and a "Just For Kids!" page that likened a presidential campaign to a baseball game.

The Internet is thus a contested terrain, used by the Left, Right, and Center to advance their own agendas and interests. The political battles of the future may well be fought in the streets, factories, parliaments, and other sites of past conflicts, but all political struggle is now mediated by media, computer, and information technologies and increasingly will be so. Those interested in the politics and culture of the future should therefore be clear on the important role of the new public spheres and intervene accordingly.

Engaged citizens thus need to acquire new forms of technological literacy to intervene in the new public spheres of the media and information society. In addition to traditional literacy skills centered upon reading, writing, and speaking, engaged citizens and public intellectuals need to learn to use the new technologies to activate the public.[43] Computer and digital technologies thus expand the field and capacities of the intellectual as well as the possibilities for political intervention. During the Age of the Big Media, critical-oppositional intellectuals were by and large marginalized, unable to gain access to the major sources of information and communication. With the decentralization introduced by the Internet, however, new possibilities for "public intellectuals" exist to reach broad audiences. It is therefore the responsibility of the active citizen to creatively engage these new technologies, as well as to critically analyze the diverse developments of the cyberculture. This requires dialectical thinking that discriminates between the benefits and costs, the upsides and downsides, of new technologies and devising ways that the technological revolution can be used to promote positive values like education, democracy, enlightenment, and ecology. Active citizens thus face new challenges. The future of democracy depends in part on whether new technologies will be used for domination or democratization, and whether each individual will sit on the sidelines or participate in the development of new democratic public spheres.

NOTES

1. Attempts to chart the globalization of capital, decline of the nation-state, and rise of a new global culture include the essays in Featherstone (1990), Giddens (1990), Robertson (1991), King (1991), Bird et al. (1993), Gilroy (1993), Arrighi (1994), Lash and Urry (1994), Grewal and Kaplan (1994), Wark (1994), Featherstone et al. (1995), Axford (1995), Held (1995), Waters (1995), Hirst and Thompson (1996), Wilson and Dissayanake (1996), Albrow (1996), Cvetkovich and Kellner (1997), Kellner (1998), Dyer-Witheford (1999), Friedman (1999), Held et al. (1999), Schiller (1999), Robins and Webster (1999), and Lechner and Boli eds. (2000).

2. Negative critiques of globalization include Mander and Goldsmith (1996), Hirst and Thompson (1996), Schiller (1999), and Robins and Webster (1999). Positive takes on globalization include Friedman (1999).

3. Hence, although Manuel Castells (1996, 1997, 1998) has the most detailed theory of the new technologies and the rise of what he calls a "networked society," by refusing to link his analyses with the problematic of the postmodern, he does not adequately articulate the new—that is, what is different from the previous mode of social organization. Castells claims that Harvey (1989) and Lash (1990) say about as much about the postmodern as needs to be said (1996: 26ff.). With due respect to their excellent work, we believe that no two theorists or books exhaust the problematic of the postmodern, which involves transformations in theory, culture, society, politics, science, philosophy, and almost every other domain of experience, and is thus inexhaustible. Hence, although Castells has three weighty volumes that describes multiple dimensions of the network society, he does not engage the postmodern problematic, roots his analysis mostly in sociological literature, and does not have the theoretical and critical resources to analyze the full dimensions of the turbulent transformations that we are undergoing or to provide adequate critical perspectives on it.

4. Champions of technological revolution and the new economy like Toffler (1971) and Kelly (1994, 1999), as well as blatant apologists for capitalism such as Bill Gates (1995) and Thomas Friedman (1999), all ignore the continuing force of the logic of capital accumulation and the exploitation, conflict, and crises that it continues to generate. Instead, they sing praises to the wonders of the new technology and the new global economy and the wealth and benefits it will bring. Many critics of globalization, however, ignore the new technologies and interpret globalization in narrow economic terms as merely the imposition of the logic of capital upon ever more sectors of the world. For criticisms of technological determinism and "autonomous technology," see Winner (1977) and Feenberg (1991, 1995, 1999).

5. For an overview of these media mergers, see McChesney (1999). In an article on "Oligopoly," (New York Times, June 11, 2000: A1), Stephen Labaton writes: "During the 12 years of the Reagan and Bush administrations, an era widely remembered for frenized merger activity and devotion to a laissez-faire regulatory approach, there were 44,518 mergers and acquisitions in the United States, with a combined value of $2.12 trillion according to Thomson Financial Securities Data. By contrast, the seven-and-an-half years of the Clinton administration have witnessed 71,811 corporate deals valued at $6.6 trillion."

6. See New York Times, November 5, 1999: A1 and C19; Associated Press, February 7, 2000.

7. www.organic consumers.org, Vol. 1, No. 14, September 28, 1999.

8. The ideologues of the technological revolution and the information society are

forever arguing that education is the key to future prosperity, that it must be made available to all, and that it is thus the top social priority. Bill Clinton early on proclaimed that he wanted to be the "education president." In his 1997 State of the Union message, he stressed that he wanted to prioritize the expansion and strengthening of education during the rest of his term, in order to provide the "bridge to the 21st century" and to make the United States competitive in the information economy. Frank Webster quotes the new Labour Party prime minister Tony Blair maintaining that "education is the best economic policy there is for a modern economy." Gates (1995, 1999) and other promoters of new technologies also stress the importance of education for the new economy. It would be fine if education were to be expanded and made accessible to more individuals and if it were able to augment the realm of knowledge and literacies, rather than just to serve as a sophisticated enhancement of job training, focusing on transmitting the skills and knowledge that capital needs to expand and multiply. The danger, however, is that the knowledge revolution will expand commodification of education and its reconstruction to serve business imperatives.

9. Articles started appearing in the mid-1990s on the ubiquity of e-mail, chat rooms, listserves, MOOs, and MUDs; see Turkle (1995). One of the early advocates of virtual communities, Howard Rheingold (2000), had "second thoughts" that he disseminated through the Internet (see his website at www.rheingold.com). Books on "internet addiction" are starting to appear (see Young 1998); studies are also appearing on student gambling, stock market daytrading, and other addictive net activities; see *The Chronicle of Higher Education*, April 7, 2000.

10. Poster (1990) argues that the mode of production is now transcended in importance by the mode of information as a fundamental principle of organizing society. We would argue, however, that the modes of production and information are intertwined as a new stage of capitalism. In "Postmodern Virtualities" (1996), Poster highlights the importance of perceiving the connection of postmodernity with the new media and the new subjectivity, but does not link these phenomena with the restructuring of capital and globalization.

11. For an earlier and more extensive discussion of Cronenberg's films upon which we draw here, see Kellner (1989c). For Cronenberg's life and films, see Rodley (1992).

12. See Porton (1999), "The Film Director as Philosopher: An Interview with David Cronenberg," *Cineaste, 24*(4): 6.

13. On the history of the situationists, see Marcus (1989), Plant (1992), Wollen (1993), and the material in Substance 90 (1999). The key texts of the situationists and many interesting commentaries are found on various websites, such as www.nothingness.org/ SituationistInternational/journal.html; www.ccwf.cc.utexas/~panicbuy/HaTeMaiL/ situationist.html; and www.slip. net/~knabb. For our earlier reflections on the contributions and limitations of situationist thought, see Best and Kellner (1997, Ch. 3).

14. See Gromer, "It's a Wrap," *Popular Mechanics*, June 1998: 112-115.

15. Las Vegas is, of course, at the forefront of environmental art and advertising. Indeed, much of the city is a spectacle geared to lure consumers of the commodity spectacle to its pleasure palaces and gambling establishments:

> A 190-foot obelisk, from which lasers flash, is the equivalent of the traditional Las Vegas neon sign (Promoters claim that only two man-made objects can be seen from outer space: The Great Wall of China and Luxor's laser light). The entire Luxor setup is animated and computerized. A light show in front of the hotel focuses on a 60-foot screen of weather. As the sun goes down, the shimmering and luminescent face of King Tut appears in the air, projected against a screen of

raindrops from the fountains in front of the sphinx. Through the translucent face of the pharaoh, you can read a distant sign down the strip "Prime Rib Buffet."

Even the great beam and its reach skyward, consuming $1 million worth of electricity annually, suggest wider urban applications. Its designer, Zachary Taylor, foresees using this technology for forming "a new kind of skyline created by lasers." (Phil Patton, "Now Playing in the Virtual World," *Popular Science*, April 1994: 82)

16. Advertising has become a new way to raise funds to offset the dwindling resources of space travel. Seizing the initiative to bolster their cash-strapped program, Russia painted a 30-foot-high Pizza Hut logo on a rocket destined for the International Space Station in January 2000 in exchange for $2.5 million. Various groups are raising funds for privatized space exploration and colonies. Aerospace entrepreneur Peter Diamandis began a competition with a $10 million prize for the best designed spaceship that can make space travel an affordable journey in the megaspectacle for the near future (*CBS News*, November 5, 1999). Other entrepreneurs are already investing in space hotels; see "Space Tourism—Hot Ticket," *Los Angeles Times* (May 22, 2000).

17. Another source notes that "the average American household spent $1,813 in 1997 on entertainment—books, TV, movies, theater, toys—almost as much as the $1,841 spent on health care per family, according to a survey by the US Labor Department." Moreover, "the price we pay to amuse ourselves has, in some cases, risen at a rate triple that of inflation over the past five years" (*USA Today*, April 2, 1999: E1).

18. Environmental News Network, May 12, 1999.

19. feedmag.com/daily/dyo20499.html.

20. As reported in www.suck.com/fish/99/02/02.

21. "In Paris Couture, the Spectacle's the Thing," *New York Times*, July 21, 1998: C24.

22. *New York Times*, December 28, 1995: C1.

23. *New York Times*, August 26, 1998: C1 and C3.

24. *Los Angeles Times*, December 8, 1998: C3. For an examination of the incredible level of debt in the United States and its impact on people, see Schor (1997).

25. *Newsweek*, June 1, 1998: 64.

26. See the description in www.suck.com/fish/99/01/21.

27. See Brian Lowry " 'Big Brother's Watchers See Everything But Privacy,' " *Los Angeles Times*, February 12, 2000: A1 and A50 and "The Electronic Fishbowl," *New York Times*, May 21, 2000. The new reality shows exhibit the confluence of television and Internet entertainment. The Dutch show *Big Brother*, which featured a live website with four video streams that one could check out, attracted 52 million hits; the CBS series deployed roughly the same setup. It is interesting from the perspective of globalization that recent hit TV formulas have come from Europe to the United States. The 1999–2000 ABC sensation *Do You Want to Be a Millionaire?* was closely based on a hit British TV series, as was *Survivor.* Apparently, the crassest and most commercial aspects of globalization crosses borders the most easily.

28. www.nytimes.com/library/magazine/home/19990523mag-keegan.html.

29. The most spectacular stories of hackers are collected in Levy (1984), Hafner and Markoff (1991), and Sterling (1992). Note that "hackers" was initially a positive term for the creators of computer networks and systems, and later became a negative term describing illicit entry and vandalism in cyberspace. On the whole, while we are against posting computer viruses and bombs that infect entire servers and networks, and that constitute a form of cyberterrorism and wanton destructiveness, we believe that creative

hacking can constitute examples of Debordian *detournement* and the construction of cybersituations.

30. During the same period, the cyberhacker site RTMark claims that attacks against Internet toy giant eToys led the firm to withdraw a lawsuit against the popular art site etoy.com (see http://rtmark.com/autodesk.html). But the hacker whose program is believed to have enabled the recent e-commerce web assaults, a 20-year-old German computer whiz who goes by the name "Mixter," has denounced the attacks, calling the culprits "pretty clueless people who misuse powerful resources" (*Los Angeles Times*, February 12, 2000: A1). In fact, a 15-year-old Canadian boy using the netname "mafiaboy" was arrested for allegedly carrying out some of the February strikes against e-commerce sites, though there was speculation that his activity was exaggerated and that he was probably just a "script-kiddie" using existing hacker programs.

31. For the anti-McDonald's site, see www.mcspotlight.org.

32. MP3 allows computer users to compress music digitally into files that have near-CD quality. Napster has programs that search for MP3 files online and then download them to one's own computer—thus making possible the sharing of music libraries (see *New York Times*, "Powerful Music Software Has Industry Worried" [March 7, 2000] and *Salon*, "MP3 free-for-all" [February 3, 2000]). Yet well-publicized court rulings against Napster in May 2000 and February 2001 have rendered the future of net-music questionable, generating an impassioned debate about Internet distribution, ownership rights, and popular music. If Napster is suppressed, no doubt other technologies will emerge, assuring that new forms of production, distribution, and consumption of media culture continue to proliferate.

33. The film made the cover stories of both *Time* and *Newsweek*; for a discussion of the digital revolution in Hollywood filmmaking, see *Wired*, 1.06 (1993) and 8.05 (2000); on how "New Digital Cameras Poised to Jolt World of Filmmaking," see *New York Times*, November 19, 1999: A1 and C5. Other independent filmmakers have been making their product available on the web, gaining the attention of Hollywood producers and financers for their projects. The next logical move is to make an interactive film online on the web; a German filmmaker has begun such a project. In May 2000, Mike Figgis released *Time Code*, a film shot in digital video the previous fall with four-frame real-time simultaneous juxtapositions of overlapping stories.

34. In most parts of the world, individuals must pay telephone companies for each unit of time on the Internet, giving rise to movements for an affordable flat rate for monthly Interact access. For discussion of the access movement in England, promises from the telecommunications companies to provide a flat rate in the immediate future, and speculation that access still might not be affordable for many, see the dossier in the technology section of the *Times* of London, December 12, 1999.

35. In August 1999, a widely publicized U.S. Department of Commerce report contended that the "digital divide" between the information haves and have-nots was growing; by November, there were critiques that the survey data was severely out of date and that more reliable statistics indicated that the divide was lessening, that more women, people of color, and seniors were connected to the Internet, and that more than half of the United States was connected by late 1999. In 2000, several surveys indicated that the digital divide was mainly structured by class and education, and not by race. One should, however, be suspicious of statistics concerning Internet access and use, as powerful interests are involved who manipulate figures for their own purposes. Yet there is no doubt that a "digital divide" exists and various politicians, groups, and corporations are exploiting this problem for their own interests.

36. It was announced in April 1997 that Boeing Aircraft had joined Bill Gates in investing in a satellite communications company, Teledesic, which plans to send up 288 small low-orbit satellites to cover most of the Americas and then the world in 2002. This project could give up to 20 million people satellite Internet access at a given moment. See *USA Today*, April 30, 1997. In May 1998, Motorola joined the "Internet in the Sky" Project, scrapping its own $12.9 billion plan to build a satellite network capable of delivering high-speed data communications anywhere on the planet and instead joined the Teledesic project, pushing aside Boeing to become Teledesic's prime contractor (*New York Times*, May 22, 1998). An "Internet-in-the-Sky" would make possible access to new technologies for groups and regions that do not even have telephones, thus expanding the potential for democratic and progressive uses of new technologies. On the other hand, there are reports that the corporations proposing such projects are not pursuing them and thus, once again, state interventions may be necessary to develop progressive technologies that will serve all.

37. See Cleaver (1994), the documents collected in Zapatistas Collective (1994), and Castells (1997).

38. See www.cleanclothes.org/1/index.html.

39. For the Merseyside dock strike see www.gn.apc.org/labournet/docks. For an overview of the use of electronic communication technology by labor, see the studies by Moody (1988), Waterman (1990, 1992), Brecher and Costello (1994), and Drew (1998). Labor projects using the new technologies include the United States-based Labornet; the European Geonet; the Canadian LaborL; the South African WorkNet; the Asia Labour Monitor Resource Centre; Mujer a Mujer, representing Latina women's groups; and the Third World Network. PeaceNet in the United States is devoted to a variety of progressive peace and justice issues.

40. As a December 1 abcnews.com story titled "Networked Protests" put it:

> Disparate groups from the Direct Action Network to the AFL–CIO to various environmental and human rights groups have organized rallies and protests online, allowing for a global reach that would have been unthinkable just five years ago.
>
> As early as March, activists were hitting the news groups and list-serves—strings of e-mail messages people use as a kind of long-term chat—to organize protests and rallies.

In addition, while the organizers urged protesters not to engage in violent action, one website urged WTO protesters to help tie up the WTO's web servers, and another group produced an anti-WTO website that replicated the look of the official site (see RTMark's website, http://gatt.org/; the same group had produced a replica of George W. Bush's website with satirical and critical material, inciting the wrath of the Bush campaign). For compelling accounts of the anti-WTO demonstrations in Seattle and an acute analysis of the issues involved, see Paul Hawkens, "What Really Happened at the Battle of Seattle" (http://www.purefood.org/Corp/PaulHawken.cfm).

41. For current antiglobalization sites, see http://www.alternet.org/global.html.

42. See "Invasion of the Gadflies in Cyberspace," *Los Angeles Times*, May 18, 1998, and Castells (1997, Ch. 2–4).

43. For the new forms of multiliteracy needed to use the new technologies for education, communication, and politics, see Kellner (1998, 2000).

EPILOGUE
Challenges for the Third Millennium

Thought in contradiction must become more negative and more utopian in opposition to the status quo.
—HERBERT MARCUSE

The future is open territory; we're making it up as we go along.
—SARAH, IN *TERMINATOR 2: JUDGMENT DAY*

Human history becomes more and more a race between education and catastrophe.
—H. G. WELLS

The human adventure has passed through remarkable and surprising stages over the millennia. Some 6 to 8 million years ago, the hominid line of evolution developed as an offshoot of the great apes; over 100 thousand years ago, *Homo sapiens* emerged as a species endowed with unparalleled reasoning, linguistic, and technological abilities (see Stringer and McKie 1996). Breaking free of the chains of biological evolution to establish a far more dynamic social and technological evolution, human beings embarked on an incredible journey that reaches not only across the expanse of the globe, but also into the darkness of space.

While our species has displayed flashes of brilliance, altruism, and compassion, we have also evinced a violent and destructive side that is proving increasingly dangerous. Likewise, our long-developed sciences and technologies are both instruments of emancipation and utopian possibilities and potential forces of ruination and dystopian destruction. The economies that are natural extensions of the human need to produce and trade have grown out of their organic relation with culture and society to become empires and worlds in themselves, devouring the natural, social, and human resources that sustain them. Hence, as we enter the Third Millennium, standing at the crossroads of a most ambiguous and contradictory development, humanity faces fateful challenges and choices.

Although numerous human cultures have developed rich storehouses of ethical, philosophical, spiritual, and ecological wisdom, these are in danger of being buried and lost, inundated by increasingly globalized obsessions with scientific advancement, technical control, political hegemony, and economic growth. Both natural and social diversity are rapidly disappearing. Since the opening of the modern world, science, technology, and capitalism have co-evolved in an inseparable unity of interdependence, such that their advancement has become the overriding concern of the Western world for the last 4 centuries. In a nanosecond of historical time, modernity has developed so fast and spread so far that it has colonized the globe, depleted crucial resources, and decimated wilderness and wildlife. With over six billion people multiplying exponentially, humanity is now overshooting the Earth's carrying capacity; this problem is greatly exacerbated by the unsustainable consumerist lifestyles of the overdeveloped sectors of global capitalism.

Throughout this book we have documented how the coevolution of science, technology, and capitalism have produced powerful new information, multimedia, genetic, and space technologies that are propelling us into a new postmodern adventure as we enter the Third Millennium. In the present transition zone between the modern and the postmodern, the driving forces of change continue to alter the world at dizzying speeds. Science, technology, and capitalism are creating new mutations in nature, humanity, culture, everyday life, and identities. At the same time, the turbulent changes engender a process of critical reflection on the modern adventure and the norms that guided it, and spark new reconstructive visions and projects.

In some forms, then, the postmodern adventure merely perpetuates the dynamics of its modern predecessor—though often in even more destructive and dangerous modes, as with nuclear weapons and energy, chemical warfare, genetic engineering, and a predatory transnational capitalism. In other forms, ranging from multicultural science and feminist theories to social ecology and green democracy, new visions and new movements renounce the pathologies of the modern as they seek to recover and advance its great achievements in a new context. The inherent ambiguity of current transformations demands dialectical analysis of their positive and negative aspects and a keen political vision for promoting the life-enhancing and democratizing possibilities at hand.

One dramatic example of the ambiguity of modern technology is the rocket, an invention, Pynchon reminds us (see Chapter 1), that can either spread mass destruction on Earth or carry humankind from Earth to the stars. Ultimately, it is difficult to make a distinction between a "good" and a "bad" rocket, since the difference between civilian and military uses of technologies frequently implodes, and there are always unintended consequences of technological development. Just as radios and computers were originally used primarily by the military, so advancements in space travel and communications systems are unavoidably coopted for warfare and "defense." Nevertheless, many humanitarians, progressive scientists, and SF writers envision a time when human beings could end the violence that has marred their history, and use rocket technologies for peaceful missions, scientific advancement, and philosophical purposes that would constitute a fateful moment in the postmodern adventure. No one has stated this case more forcefully than astronomer and science-popularizer Carl Sagan.

MAKING CONTACT: CARL SAGAN AND THE POSTMODERN VOYAGE

> We began as wanderers, and we are wanderers still. We have lingered long enough on the shores of the cosmic ocean. We are ready at last to set sail for the stars.
> —CARL SAGAN

> There is no way back to the past. The choice is the Universe—or nothing.
> —H. G. WELLS

> Two possibilities exist: either we are alone in the universe or we are not. Both are equally terrifying.
> —ARTHUR C. CLARKE

Sagan does not use postmodern discourse, but he perceives the era of space travel as unique, as a qualitatively different stage in the modern project of journey and discovery, since "this is the epoch in which we began our journey to the stars" (1980: 284). Sagan excitedly reminds us that it is also the first period in which we have the technologies to enable contact with the alien life-forms he feels, according to Frank Drake's celebrated equation, exist as a matter of intriguing probability.[1] We ourselves see space travel as part of the postmodern, rather than part of the modern, adventure. For the first time, human beings fly not only within Earth's atmosphere, but also beyond it, having broken free of "gravity's rainbow" (see Chapter 1). Tomorrow they will venture toward other planets and radically new evolutionary possibilities.

Modernity was an era of immense discovery, of bold new mappings of the land, sea, and stars, of producing charts that dramatically altered scientific paradigms and human identities. Likewise, postmodernity is a continuation of this discovery process through new mappings of the brain, the human genome, the Earth (via global positioning systems and three-dimensional scannings taken from space), the Milky Way Galaxy and beyond, and actual travel to and landing on other planets. The term astronaut (Greek: astron, star; nautikos, ship) literally means one who sails the sea of stars. Yet this continuation of the modern voyage is so qualitatively different, and has such dramatically different implications, that it can legitimately be understood as a key part of the postmodern adventure.

Sagan (1977) was keenly aware of the crucial role technology has played in human evolution and the decisive importance technosciences play in the postmodern adventure that launches human beings into space and establishes new coevolutionary dynamics between the Earth and other planets in the galaxy. Sagan traces a direct line from Columbus and other early modern explorers of the land and sea to those in the space program who are the new explorers of the stars: "The Voyager spacecrafts [which, launched in 1977, collected and sent data on Jupiter, Saturn, Pluto, Uranus, and much of our Solar System] are the linear descendants of those sailing-ship voyages of [early modern] exploration" (1980: 121). As Sagan emphasizes, we already have become multiplanet travelers with Earth as our home base. Envisioning humans as standing on the shores of "the cosmic ocean," Sagan argues that we must take the plunge into the unknown. For Sagan, the next great human adventure will free us from the shackles of the Earth and its gravitational straightjacket to explore other planets, to live in space stations, to terraform and build space colonies, and to journey to the outer edges of the galaxy and perhaps beyond. The next stage in the human adventure would be to soar into a postgeocentric, multiplanet identity, such as dramatized by TV shows like *Star Trek* and *Deep Space Nine*, which feature a smorgasbord of advanced species and startling examples of the fifth discontinuity. Where Marx spoke of the "idiocy of rural life," Sagan alerts us to the limitations of an Earth-bound existence and the beckoning of the stars.[2]

For Sagan, what we are calling the postmodern adventure would have as profound an impact on human identity as did modern journeys centuries earlier. The exploration of the cosmos, Sagan points out, is a voyage of self-discovery, an attempt to map a cosmic genealogy since we are ultimately born from the stars, beings who are "starstuff gathering starlight." When life develops eyes and ears, the cosmos sees and hears; when it develops thought and intelligence, we become, as in a fantastic Hegelian evolution, the cosmos reflecting on itself—not mind knowing Mind, but mind knowing the matter of the universe from which consciousness was generated. Unlike people of ancient times, whose everyday life was intimately connected to the stars in the heavens, people living in our technoculture have grown so distant from the cosmos that, tragically, it seems remote and irrelevant to their lives. Focused on the project of the technological command of the earth, human beings have developed an overweening hubris whereby they attempt to place themselves at the helm of life. They have used and abused other species and fragile ecosystems to satisfy their burgeoning populations and, now, a world economic system rooted in insatiable growth imperatives. "Present global culture," Sagan states, "is a kind of arrogant newcomer. It arrives on the planetary stage following four and a half billion years of other acts, and after looking around for a few thousand years declares itself in possession of eternal truths" (1980: 276).

Opposed to the vision of the *Alien* films, where the fifth discontinuity is portrayed in horrifying and malevolent forms, Sagan sees an encounter with alien life as positive. Whereas the effect in *Alien* is for humans to close species rank against other life-forms, Sagan imagines a fifth discontinuity involving extraterrestrial beings that would widen our vision and experience. Contact with beings from space, Sagan believes, would lead to "a profound deprovincialization of the human condition" (1980: 259). It is very likely, Sagan believes, that the Watson we might speak to on the other end of the cosmic phone line would be far more intelligent and technologically and morally advanced than us, such that we could not but be humbled in our relatively primitive state of being. This could generate a radical deprovincialization effect—what we'll call the "D-effect," after Brecht's "A-effect"—which might indeed occur through contact, thereby forcing humanity to cross the fifth discontinuity. Yet it is clear from works like *Pale Blue Dot* (1994) that Sagan thinks scientific mappings of billions of galaxies alone are enough to promote awe and disarm cosmic arrogance.[3]

Unlike ecoprimitivists such as many members of Earth First!, Sagan argues that we need *more*, not *less*, science to extricate humanity from the mire of self-destruction: "The present epoch is a major crossroads for our civilization and perhaps for our species. Whatever road we take, our fate is indissociably bound up with science. It is essential as a matter of simple survival for us to understand science" (1980: xvii). Specifically, Sagan believes that further developments in science would advance the technologies needed for continued exploration of the stars. He hopes that space travel would facilitate even greater moral progress and could end human chauvinism toward one another and all forms of life. Sagan believes that by finding our true place in the multiverse, by understanding our cosmic roots, and by realizing that we live together on one fragile planet where national boundaries are utterly artificial, we might develop more peaceful and sustainable societies.

If nothing else, Sagan argues, contact with extraterrestrial life would teach us that an advanced technological civilization can endure; beyond that, such civilizations might offer important knowledge about how we might survive on our own decaying technocapitalist planet. A direct or satellite-mediated contact would mean "that someone has learned to live with high technology, that it is possible to survive technological adolescence. That alone, quite apart from the contents of the message, provides a powerful justification for the search for other civilizations" (Sagan 1980: 251). Thus, in Sagan's vision, contact could show that there is no inherent logic of technological destruction, no necessary path, as Adorno (1973) put it, from the slingshot to the atom bomb. Hence, we could hope that human beings can develop sciences and technologies that are advanced, sustainable, peaceful, and life-promoting, instruments of Eros rather than of Thanatos.

Sagan offers evocative visions of the fifth discontinuity as an opportunity for evolutionary growth; philosophizes suggestively about science, technology, and human evolution; and has contributed enormously to astronomy and public appreciation of science (see Poundstone 1999). Yet he advances surprisingly antiquated positivist conceptions of science as a universal vehicle for truth, and sharply opposes it to irrational, mythological, and "demonological" modes of thinking (see Sagan 1996). Sagan feels hopeful and optimistic about science and technology, and offers little consideration of their dark and potentially destructive side. While Sagan is no positivist, he is an uncritical realist, holding to a correspondence between the mathematical nature of the cosmos and the quantitative prowess of the human mind (see 1977: 243). In an acute critique, however, Richard C. Lewontin (1997) exposes the value- and theory-laden nature of all scientific observation and the often dogmatic, irrational, and mythological nature of science itself—as when it makes appeals to authority or extravagant claims to success.

Nor does Sagan adequately appreciate the fact that science and technology coevolve with capital, which puts enormous constraints on their emancipatory and democratic uses. He minimizes the dangers of military appropriations of space technologies and does not recognize that the causes of ecological catastrophe on Earth stem not simply from arrogant humanism or advanced technology, but also from a global capitalist economic system hellbent on devouring the planet. Confronting the crucial objection that space exploration is unjustifiable given the urgency of human needs on Planet Earth, however, Sagan claims that a single military plane costs more than a modest space exploration (1980: 263). If the U.S. budget could be demilitarized, in other words, there would not only be enough money for food, housing, and education, but also for funding the search for extraterrestrial intelligence (SETI) and the space program. The real problem lies less with NASA (although it certainly has its own failings and bureaucratic excesses) than with the Pentagon, the entire military–industrial complex, a "permanent war economy," and the politicians who fund it so extravagantly. Thus, many urge a dramatic restructuring of the military, a total ban on weapons of mass destruction, and allocation of the prodigious resources spent on war and destruction for peace and enhancing life (see Melman 1985; Shaw 1991).

In the long run, space exploration is unavoidable for, as Kaku (1997) argues, catastrophes such as a meteor strike could devastate our planet at any time. Moreover, even if we survive this catastrophic contingency, in 5 billion years the Sun will explode and vaporize the Earth. So, one way or the other, if the human adventure is to continue and be more than just a message in a bottle waiting for a future civilization to find, it must eventually leave the comfortable confines of the home planet and master space travel. This adventure would wed the human fate ever more closely to advanced science, technology, and a cyborg-like existence (see Savage 1994).

As interesting and paradigm shattering as contact with alien life would be, our world cannot wait for a cosmic Godot. Nor, indeed, is this necessary, since the wisdom and learning we need to harmonize advanced technology with ethics, compassion, social justice, and peaceful and ecological lifeways have been developed for millennia in both Eastern and Western traditions. The great challenge facing humanity, among other things, is to reduce its population, to restore what species and ecosystems it can, and to subvert consumerism in favor of sustainable lifestyles. We must also instill critical thinking skills as early as possible in our children and promote a "compassionate education" that teaches reverence for life. We need to revive the meaning and role of citizenship, and to develop a politics of alliance and solidarity that challenges the power of capital and the state, such as recently have emerged in the new antiglobalization coalitions on the streets of Seattle, Washington, DC, and elsewhere. It is imperative that citizens begin confronting—in public debates as opposed to isolated academic squabbles—topics such as sound conceptions and practices of science; socioethical modes of educating scientists, mathematicians, engineers, and medical doctors; new sensibilities toward nature; and new technologies, forms of political struggle and democracy, and identities.

THE APOCALYPTIC VISION OF PHILIP K. DICK

> Our present social continuum is disintegrating rapidly; if war doesn't burst it apart, it obviously will corrode away. . . . To avoid the topic of war and cultural regression . . is unrealistic and downright irresponsible.
> —Philip K. Dick

It is instructive to contrast Sagan's buoyant, technophilic, and optimistic vision of the future as an exciting evolutionary journey to the stars to the pessimistic, dystopian view of Philip K. Dick, who paints a bleak picture of the future of global capitalism and interplanetary space travel.[4] Astonishingly prolific, amazingly inventive, and always visionary, Dick in his best works attempts to measure the fallout of a proliferating technological society and to project foreboding visions of possible futures, as he extrapolates from contemporary economic, technological, political, and cultural developments. Like cyberpunk, which he anticipates and influenced, Dick sets his fantasies within a world drawn from contemporary configurations of global capitalism and the Cold War. His writings reveal deep fears of social breakdown, military technology and political tensions escalating out of control, and nuclear armageddon. He portrays a future in which demagogues use media culture to manipulate and dominate populations, and the development of cybernetic systems results in a society where humans are mastered by machines, technology, and in some cases superior species. Hence, implosion, posthumanism, the fifth discontinuity, and the fate of the human in technocapitalism are core themes of Dick's work.

Whereas for Sagan space travel is an object of poetic rapture, for Dick it is inherently ambiguous and potentially catastrophic. Although both see space travel as an inevitable outgrowth of science, technology, industry, and (for Dick at least) capitalism, Dick has grave worries about space technologies in the historical context of nuclear weapons, Cold War rivalries, global power politics, and predatory capitalism. Dick's epics of space colonialism, like *Martian Time-Slip* (1964), portray the class hierarchies and forms of political and technological domination developed on Earth replicated in the space colonies. His novel *The Three Stigmata of Palmer Eldritch* (1965) shows colonizers becoming addicted to drugs to overcome the bleak conditions of life on other planets. Moreover, his depictions of aliens in his voluminous short stories and novels were hardly benign. Sagan, of course, imagines alien intelligence in positive ways, in the manner of Steven Spielberg's *E. T.* (1982), and he seems to believe that worldly class, gender, race, and power issues can be transcended at escape velocity.

It is perhaps Dick's novel *Do Androids Dream of Electric Sheep?* (1987 [1968]) that provides his most compelling apocalyptic vision, while exhibiting quintessential Dickian themes of the implosion between the real and the artificial, humans and technology, and natural reality and simulation in a high-tech world—the same themes we have identified as major foci of the postmodern adventure. In the plot of the novel—which is significantly different from the film *Blade Runner* that is loosely based on it (see Kerman 1997)—Rick Deckard, a bounty hunter of renegades androids, is ordered to exterminate a group of highly advanced android Nexis-6 models who have escaped from the "off-colonies," where they were slaves, in order to prolong their short preprogrammed lives. Stronger, quicker, and smarter than humans, the androids pose a dangerous threat to humans and are menacing examples of a fifth discontinuity produced by technology. Deckard, however, increasingly empathizes with the androids, one of whom, Rachel, he becomes sexually involved with. Consequently, he is ever more troubled by the killing or "retiring" required by his job, as he gradually comes to recognize the android others as akin to human subjects.

Dick frames his story within the political economy of an interplanetary global capitalism, set in a bombscape of human ruination and massive species extinction. The androids were originally produced to help colonize Mars, when capitalism and corporations having devastated their home base, begin colonizing other planets. In a competitive race between two global giants, the Rosen Association and the Grozzi Corporation vie to market the most advanced androids. This war of technology has produced increasingly complex creatures who are seemingly identical with humans, sharing feelings such as love, empathy, desire, and fear of death. In the form of the Nexus-6 model produced by the Rosen Corporation, androids also have acquired a high level of self-reflexivity, which leads them to repudiate their slave status. Hence, as Marx saw in an earlier industrial context, capitalists created their own gravediggers by manufacturing increasingly complex workers who eventually acquire the will to rebel. Thus Dick provides a futuristic embodiment of Marx's vision of a rebellious proletariat.

A major theme of *Androids* is entropy, the incessant movement from birth to death, adolescence to senescence, order to disorder, heterogeneity to homo-geneity. As the second law of thermodynamics, "entropy" is a natural process; the cosmos, in Dick's terms, inexorably winds down to a state of "kipple." "No one can win against kipple . . . except temporarily and maybe in one spot. . . . It's a universal principle operating throughout the universe; the entire universe is moving toward a final state of total, absolute kippleization" (1987: 58). En-tropy is indeed the prototypical condition for Dick's futuristic world: cities are decaying; the natural environment is disappearing; the androids' short life spans are winding down; and the unfortunates stranded on earth are deteriorating in mind and body. Entropy is also evident in the "waning of affect," a symptom of postmodern subjectivity for theorists like J. G. Ballard and Fredric Jameson. In advanced stages of "civilization," individuals are so affectless that they have to rely on mechanical supplementation—via technologies such Dick's envisaged "mood organ" or "empathy box"—in order to feel. Dick ironically portrays an exhausted human species drained of all feeling, on the verge of being sup-planted by androids who are developing "human" feeling like empathy. He thereby signals an implosion between humans and machines, questions what is left of humanity in a high-tech world, and calls into doubt the long-term sur-vivability of a human species whose members lack positive emotional bonds with one another.

Dick makes it clear that just as individuals can hasten the entropy of their own bodies, social systems can quicken their own decay and that of the natural world. As an energy-devouring, resource-depleting, waste-producing, non-stop-guzzling megamachine of growth and accumulation, advanced capitalism rapidly accelerates entropic breakdown. While *Blade Runner* changed and ob-scured much in Dick's novel, it brilliantly captured the look and feel of a hyperintensive global system of production drowning in its own waste. The incessant downpour of radiation-saturated rain, the fire-belching smokestacks, the filthy refuse of the ultramodern metropolis, the densely overpopulated city streets and high-rise apartments, the glowing neon billboards and crisscrossing traffic of hovercraft vehicles, and the detritus of a multicultural society where even language breaks down into kippleized fragments underscore the presence of a dying, nihilistic, technocapitalism. Director Ridley Scott adds the ironic touch of metallic blimps moving ponderously across the nuclear-red skies, broadcasting advertisements for the good life in the out-colonies. The underclass denizens—mostly Asian and hybrid countercultural—live in crowded ghetto-like conditions on the ground level of the city, while the re-maining upper class dwells in luxurious high-rise apartments, reproducing the class structure portrayed in Fritz Lang's *Metropolis* (1927). This futuristic city—which became the prototype for the universe of cyberpunk—was recognizably Los Angeles, where the film was shot, but it could stand for any global and multicultural city of a postholocaust future, or the aftermath of a collapse of the global economy.

Typically, Dick's narratives do not have happy endings. Deeply disturbed with German fascism, he often sketches out totalitarian societies ruled by demagogues and authoritarians. More prescient than other writers of his day in regard to the dynamics of global capitalism, Dick portrays corporate forces using technology to exploit and control the population. Further, he was one of the first SF writers to explore a new virtual technoculture, in which the distinction between reality and illusion, the real and the virtual, implodes. The strong undercurrents of pessimism in Dick's work respond to Cold War conformity and stabilization in his 1950s and early 1960s writings, and then to the defeat of the counterculture, of which he was a precursor and participant, by the 1970s. While characters in his writings often manage to see through the socially manufactured illusions that stabilize the oppressive societies in which they live, they are unable to do anything to change them, and their revolt is depicted as futile. Nuclear apocalypse haunts his work. Cold War geopolitics are always in the background of his novels, which display ordinary people destroyed by political and technological forces beyond their understanding and control.

Hence, Dick's work embodies powerful visions of a world collapsing boundaries between technology and the human. He portrays tendencies in the present that will lead to future affliction, forecasts entropic decay of nature and society, and dissolves society and reality into grotesque configurations in which ordinary categories of space, time, and reality are ruptured. Dick drafts fantastic technological worlds with strange forms of media culture and art, simulacra, and a collapse of the boundaries of modernity that anticipate conceptions of hyperreality, implosion, and simulation in later French postmodern theory, especially Baudrillard and Virilio. In retrospect, Dick can be read as a dystopic visionary of the emerging postmodern adventure in which science and technology were creating new forms of the human, bringing about a highly ambiguous posthuman condition, and providing a dialectical foil to the optimistic and asocial visions of Sagan.

HUMAN IDENTITY POLITICS: *HOMO INDETERMINUS*

> It's all a question of story. We are in trouble just now because we do not have a good story. We are in between stories. The old story, the account of how the world came to be and how we fit into it, is no longer effective. Yet we have not learned the new story.
> —THOMAS BERRY

> The primary political and philosophical issue of the next century will be the definition of who we are.
> —RAY KURZWEIL

> Sometime in the next thirty years, very quietly one day we will cease to be the brightest things on earth.
> —JAMES McLEAR

As the contrast between Sagan and Dick indicates, the postmodern adventure brings with it dramatically different visions of science, technology, industry, the economy, and future developments in human evolution, such as space travel. Indeed, social life at large is fragmenting, as multiple forms of "identity politics" emerge around issues such as race, gender, religious outlook, national background, and sexual preference (see Best and Kellner 1997). There is yet another major form of identity under contestation at this moment, one that so far has been of little concern to postmodern social theorists. This involves the identity of the entire *human species*. As human beings continue to explore their evolutionary past and gain a more accurate knowledge of the intelligence of the great apes and other animals; further probe the depths of the cosmos in search of life far more advanced than themselves; develop increasingly sophisticated computers and forms of artificial intelligence and life; cross species boundaries and exchange genes with other animals; clone numerous species; and move toward bionic and genetically retooled bodies, the question inexorably arises: who is *Homo sapiens*? Are humans unique in any way? Because of the rapidly unfolding and far-reaching revolutions in science and technology, one is also forced to ask: What is left of humanism? Are we in a new posthuman condition that dethrones the sovereignty of Reason, upsets the reign of the Ego, and effects an implosion between human beings and technology? Have we mutated from *Homo sapiens* into *Homo silicon*, from fleshy beings into technobodies with cyberidentities? Will humans eventually have brain chips that will enable them to think millions of times faster than the limitations their tissue brain currently imposes? Will computers take on intellectual and emotional powers greater than those of the human and displace them from their self-appointed role as "the highest product of evolution"? With rapid advances in bionics and genetic engineering, are we ourselves moving into a fifth discontinuity of designer technobodies? Will uploading and downloading the mind to and from computers be an everyday act? Will humans have bodies at all? Will they achieve immortality?

Since Aristotle's celebrated notion of the "featherless biped," Western culture has struggled, and failed, to attain an adequate understanding of human beings. The specificity of human nature has been clouded in numerous ways, ranging from religious and anthropocentric attempts to define us as possessors of a soul made in the image of God, to sociobiological efforts to deny human beings any ontological uniqueness from insects and other DNA-bearing organisms. Traditionally, the riddle of human identity has been resolved through religion and philosophy. Today, however, we know the search for an answer depends on science, as it also requires a return to the broadest modes of cosmological and philosophical thinking and an engagement of the unique imaginative powers of literature and SF.

Human identity in Western culture has been formed in the crucible of the Judeo-Christian tradition, Greek and Roman classicism, medieval theology,

Renaissance humanism, and modern science and culture. All sources, whether religious or secular, concur in the belief that human beings are wholly unique beings, and therefore are radically separate from the Earth they inhabit and the "inferior beasts" surrounding them. No doubt, the most pervasive influence on Western human identity has been the biblical story of Genesis. According to the dominant interpretation, the myth commands human beings to take possession of a world made just for them, an Earth where their proper role is to "multiply and subdue" nature through technological prowess. In retrospect, this is a most unfortunate story upon which to found modern civilization, one that sets us apart from the living world around us. It demands a counternarrative that reweaves our bodies, psyches, and societies back into the folds of nature as many humans struggle to advance science, technology, and a moral learning process.

Since the 16th century, however, geocentric and anthropocentric identities have been dealt a series of powerful blows that earlier we discussed in terms of a series of discontinuities (see Chapters 3 and 4). Despite the heliocentric theories of Copernicus and Galileo and the development of a secular scientific culture, human beings nevertheless could feel comfortable in their alleged radical novelty and superiority in relation to "brute beasts." Comfortable, that is, until 1859, the year of publication for Darwin's *Origin of Species*, which posed a real challenge to anthropocentrism as the basis of human identity.

Only since Darwin's evolutionary studies in the mid-19th century have we truly begun to understand the forces of life and human identity. Moreover, it was not until 1960, when Jane Goodall made her historic journey to Gombe, Tanzania, that human beings acquired any real knowledge about the higher apes, specifically the chimpanzee, our closest evolutionary relative. Structurally, behaviorally, and genetically (a 98.6% match), human beings and chimpanzees are remarkably alike; in fact, chimpanzees are closer genetically to us than they are to orangutans (see Goodall 1971; Sagan and Druyan 1992; De Waal 1996).

Without an accurate comparative basis to our closest biological relatives, we could not have produced an adequate understanding of ourselves. We have been living, to borrow a phrase from Sagan and Druyan, in the "shadows of forgotten ancestors." Until Jane Goodall's work, the identity of *Homo sapiens* was still secure: only our species were *Homo faber* and *Homo loquens*—only we could make tools, use tools, and linguistically interact; only humans lived in behaviorally complex communities. Through Goodall's research, however, we have learned that chimpanzees also make and use tools. Moreover, Roger Fouts (1997) and others have demonstrated that chimpanzees and other higher apes can learn American Sign Language. Some chimps have developed a working vocabulary of hundreds of words, can communicate their thoughts and emotions to us, and can even, on their own accord, teach this language to their young. Alas, we have also learned that chimpanzees, like us, can be aggressive and violent, and that they have a highly complex social life which, while rule-governed and not merely instinctual, is hierarchical, patriarchal, and centered around power politics (see De Waal 1989, 1996)—suggesting still deeper connections between humans and the great apes.

Sagan and Druyan (1992) enumerate 36 characteristics that traditionally have been used to set human identity apart from that of other animals. They show that every criterion of alleged radical uniqueness is also found in chimpanzee cultures. Having refused the fallacious anthropocentric divide between the higher apes and us, one that typically underestimates their intelligence and overestimates our own, Sagan and Druyan seek to reconfigure our differences in a more scientifically accurate and ethically responsible way. For them, humans are biological beings with an evolutionary past that strongly conditions our behavior. But humans also are cultural beings with more information stored in their brains than in their genes, and thus that they can adapt to new conditions and learn new behaviors.

Specifically, Sagan and Druyan suggest, if aggression, territoriality, and xenophobia once served important purposes in our distant past, such as to identify a potentially hostile "other" and to protect the community, they are today dysfunctional. Now humanity needs to learn how to live peacefully and cooperatively in sustainable societies. "Many ancient voices speak within us. We are capable of muting some, once they no longer serve our best interests, and amplifying others as our need for them increases. This is cause for hope" (Sagan and Druyan 1992: 217). The project of amplifying the peaceful and cooperative voices of the past is of course a social project that requires new forms of education, communication, politics, and identity.

So, who is *Homo sapiens*? It is a very young and brash, but fragile, species of earthly life, one that asserted its presence on Earth, using its skills in language, cooperation, tool making, agriculture, and hunting to survive. A species that has coevolved with its tools and social organization, humanity, in an extraordinarily short period of time, has established its "dominion" on Earth, created and destroyed brilliant cultures, annihilated thousands of other species, and has now brought itself to the precipice of self-destruction. Yet humans have also produced science, technology, industry, and cultural forms that have improved their lives and provided the possibility to remake themselves at a higher level, which in turn allow the creation of better people, cultures, and social organization. If humans coevolve with their modes of science, technology, and economics, then clearly the worlds they create will in turn construct them for better or worse.

According to an influential anthropological narrative, we are all "out of Africa," having most likely evolved from the African continent a little over 100 thousand years ago, competing with other hominid species under difficult physical conditions (Stringer and McKie 1996). We know that *Homo sapiens* might well not have evolved, and that it could easily have joined the ranks of Neanderthal man, Cro-Magnon man, and millions of other life-forms that became extinct. But once again we are in danger of becoming extinct, if not through problems resulting from warfare and overpopulation, then through diseases and viruses or technology run amuck. These latter possibilities are graphically dramatized by Wil McCarthy's SF novel *Bloom* (1998), where nanocreatures escape their creators to decimate humanity (the remnants of which flee to an icy Jupiter moon) and spread throughout the entire solar system advancing their deadly "Mycosystem."

Human beings *are* unique in the degree to which they possess intelligence; no other species, to our knowledge, has written sonnets or sonatas, solved algebraic equations, or meditated on the contingency of life. But they are *not* unique in their possession of a neocortex; complex emotions like love, loneliness, empathy, and shame; sophisticated languages, behaviors, and communities; and perhaps even of an aesthetic sense (Masson and McCarthy 1995). Human beings are immensely complex, with a penchant for both violence and compassion, egoism and altruism. But they have overstated their uniqueness and separated themselves from the larger biocommunity, both conceptually and practically.[5]

Like any other group with an identity issue, "*Homo sapiens*" has created an *identity politics*. Clearly, human beings are a distinct group that differentiates itself from others in order to secure its own identity, in this case, from other *species*, rather than members of its own species, as in all other forms of identity politics. The creation of a human identity, particularly in the Western world, is inseparable from anthropocentrism, a human-centered worldview, and "speciesism." As analyzed by Peter Singer (1990), speciesism follows the exact same logic as racism or sexism: it establishes an absolute gulf between one group, human animals, and all other animals. Speciesism claims that one group is superior to another, and it concludes that the superior group has the right to exploit the inferior one. Interestingly, in every case of human-to-human domination, the inferior group is designated "non-" or "subhuman." Therefore a complex politics emerges around the discourse of "the human." The politics of human identity involve who counts as "human"; what privileges subsequently accrue to them; and whether or not the "human," however broadly or progressively defined, is an adequate marker for the boundaries of the moral community. Human identity is identity politics writ large. The consequences of human separatism and fragmentation from other animal groups are far more consequential than with any other form of identity politics.

Human*ism* is certainly not negative or predatory in all forms. Bookchin (1995a, 1995b), for one, has labored to recover and preserve the progressive aspects of modern humanism and to integrate it with ecological concerns. But although humanism promotes autonomy and critical reason, and is an immense gain over Christian theocentrism, in some forms it also promotes an arrogant, domineering mentality that seeks to colonize the Earth for human interests. Modern humanism also fails to understand the intricate ecological relations in which human life unfolds, and is unable to see that the harm human beings inflict on the planet and other species rebounds and redoubles to them.

Extreme positions invite extreme responses. The erroneous rejoinder to anthropocentrism has been radical biocentric positions that are misanthropic, mystical, and apolitical, and that go so far as to grant equal rights to all life-forms, including deadly viruses (see Ehrenfeld 1981). Baudrillard (1993) enjoins us to abandon our long-held, illusory subject positions and surrender to the object world. Taking this idea one step further, Paul and Cox (1996) and Moravec (1988) heap scorn on the flesh, proclaim the obsolescence of the body in a cybernetic world, and urge us to transfer our consciousness to machines in order to advance to the next stage in the evolution of intelligence. We don't just "jack in" to cyberspace, as in William Gibson's vision, rather we *are* cyberspace in our new brain state. In this vein, Kurzweil (1999) announces the coming of "the Age of Spiritual Machines" marked by neural implants, self-aware machines ("a new form of intelligence on earth"), and a growing importance of computers over human beings. Most extremely, the Voluntary Human Extinction Movement[6] invites the human species to initiate its own demise so that the natural world can regenerate.

We find no rationality in leaping from the false sovereignty of the Cartesian ego to the disembodied brain tape—vividly portrayed in Rucker's robot novels (see Chapter 4)— of Paul and Cox or Moravec. With Hayles (1999), we hold that the value of human existence is inseparably bound up with embodiment and sensuous existence, and that the radical posthumanist vision would lead to a life as meaningless and abstract as that of Byron the talking lightbulb in Pynchon's surreal fable (see Chapter 1). Moreover—and here's the worst part—we would never die and could not even scream in frustration. On the mechanistic assumption that the brain is a machine, Paul and Cox treat human identity as a simple matter and claim that it would be transferred whole and intact from flesh to machine (1996: 184, 190). In their cosmic cybertopia, no negative political or psychological dynamics transfer into cyberspace; there is a complete continuity of human identity and yet somehow there is a total break from the power politics of past human history, as if minds could avoid the struggle for recognition.

Thus, technological developments of the current era demand reflection on what constitutes the human, what is worth preserving, and how humans will relate to alien species and perhaps superior machines (if aliens make contact or if technoscience creates a superior machine race). These kind of questions frame the provocative SF of Octavia Butler, who has written a compelling posthuman narrative featuring intense implosions of the human and technology and stunning visions of the fifth discontinuity. In her celebrated "xenogenesis" trilogy (1987, 1988, 1989), Butler depicts a post-holocaust Earth whose survivors are taken away by an alien race to sleep until Earth's ecology can be regenerated and they are properly prepared for return. But the Oankali, an incredibly advanced and grotesquely (to humans) tentacled alien species, have an agenda of their own. They report that the human genetic structure is "fatally flawed": it is complex enough to create cultures of intriguing beauty and diversity, but nevertheless is programmed for territorialism, hierarchy, violence, and destruction. The Oankali, there-fore, propose to genetically blend features of human and Oankali genomes. While there are "resisters" who loathe the Oankali and struggle to maintain the purity of the human genome, they are sterile. Hence, the only way hu-manity can survive in the long run is by genetically merging with the Oankali. Both partners benefit in this gene trade: humans continue to live, albeit in an altered and improved form; Oankali become genetically richer as they advance along their path of dynamic evolution.

Depicting humans at an evolutionary dead end, Butler attacks xenophobia, novophobia (fear of the new), and technophobia, and suggests that substantive psychological and physiological changes are required if humans are to survive. Like Rucker's robots, Sagan's Vegans (aliens from Vega), and Dick's androids, But-ler's Oankali are potent symbols of otherness that raise complex issues about how humanity deals with issues of gender, sexuality, race, and species. More specifi-cally, Butler allegorizes the mixing of differences, at issue in current culture with racial hybridization, multiculturalism, androgyny and transgendering. Whereas the advanced Oankali embrace diverse cultures (indeed, they absorb and collect genetic information in their benevolent biocolonial ways) and take immense pleasure in the encounter with alterity, humans fear differences, which they reject and in some cases assault. Oankali, by contrast, survive only through endless change, embrace of complexity, and evolution, while humans are trapped in overspecialized roles and constricted behaviors like violence. For the Oankali, "Trade means change. Bodies change. Ways of living must change" (1988: 11). While the resisters cling to the human form, a new "construct" species—part Oankali, part human—emerges that is more peaceful, free of disease, ages more slowly, and is able to regenerate limbs, thereby evolving into a posthuman species quite obviously superior to its predecessor.

Unfortunately, Butler essentializes social conflicts under the rubric of the "Human Contradiction" (1988: 225), a fatal biological flaw that springs from the combination of ancient hierarchical drives and modern technological know-how. We agree with Butler that human beings have a dark side, with bi-ological and historical roots. But a key problem and contradiction in the con-temporary world is the disparity between the social production and the private appropriation of value, and the rich potentiality of advanced scientific, techno-logical, and economic systems, and the deprivations of global capitalism. Nev-ertheless, Butler dramatizes in a powerful way the limitations of the human species, the pressing need for conceptual and physical changes, the importance of diversity and intrahuman exchange, and the benefits of science and technol-ogy. Her trilogy is an evocative allegory of human and cultural transformation, and an affirmative vision of a genetically enriched future where the evolution of intelligence and complexity transcends the physical and moral limitations of the human species.

In one important sense, the "posthuman" means not the literal end of humanity, nor dramatic mutations in the human body brought on by various technologies. Rather, it signifies the end of certain misguided ways of conceiving of human identity and the nature of human relations to the social and natural environments, other species, and technology. A critical *postmodern humanism* would avoid the problems associated with both anthropocentrism and biocentrism, with the illusion of human sovereignty over nature and technology, and the fallacy of conflating species difference. It would eschew Moravec's (1988) absurd valorization of *Homo silicon*, and avoid all versions of atavism and "centrism" in favor of a rational and egalitarian use of science and technology that improves human life at the same time as it seeks to harmonize human society with the natural world.

Rather than subordinating nature to human beings or human beings to nature, a critical postmodern humanism would deconstruct these hierarchies in favor of complementary relationships. Like Kurzweil and numerous others, Sagan believes that the evolution of computers to intelligence is coming. He imagines a utopian cyborg merger where "the next major structural development in human intelligence is likely to be a partnership between intelligent humans and intelligent machines" (1977: 236). Similarly, Haraway's cyborg politics envisions a world where "people are not afraid of their joint kinship with animals and machines, not afraid of permanently partial identities and contradictory standpoints" (1991: 154). What is remarkable about the positions of Sagan, Haraway, Dick, and Butler is their lack of both speciesism and technophobia, their openness toward creating new human identities, their equilibrium, sanity, and compassion in the midst of radical change and historical transitions.

Thus, a critical postmodern humanism would strive for the "new sensibility" toward nature championed by Marcuse (1964), and for the ethics of "reverence for life" Albert Schweitzer (1987) upheld as the highest expression of our humanity. It would also be open to all kinds of creative interactions with computers, robots, and machines that would enhance our lives. A postmodern humanism would affirm the need to create new human identities that neither loathe past origins in animality, nor fear future interaction with technology. Computers and human intelligence need not be antagonistic; they can instead be complementary. Here, we agree with Kelly's modified humanist idea that we should let technology go "out of control" in conditions where left to its own operations it can produce better results than when rigidly programmed or controlled by engineers. Also, while being extremely cautious and sensitive to potential dangers, we believe that one should be open to genetic-based cures for disease and enhancing human brains and bodies through all available technological means.

The relations human beings form with the Earth, animals, and machines, however, depend on the alliances they create with themselves in political movements that challenge the ecocidal and nihilistic foundations of techno-science and technocapitalism, which reduce all life to objects of power and profit. This reconstructive project demands new social movements and identi-ties shaped around radical democracy and ecology. More broadly, there is a des-perate need for a new consciousness, for new *cosmopolitan identities*, for human beings to begin seeing themselves not as citizens of one nation or another, but as citizens of the Earth—indeed, of the cosmos itself. The human species could benefit greatly by seeing that it is a small part of an evolutionary process in which it coevolves with other species, its natural environment, science and technology, and the cosmos itself. A coevolutionary narrative would situate the human adventure in the protean drama of evolution and would make human beings aware of their dependence on other people, other species, and the natu-ral world. In view of postmodern fragmentation and increasing global conflict, a more cosmopolitan identity can militate against parochial nationalisms, war-ring identity politics, arrogant humanism, and rampant egoism and narcissism. Homocentric dramas need to be superseded by cosmological narratives that contextualize human life in the larger evolution of the universe, seeing human beings and the Earth as part of a coevolutionary odyssey that may have pro-duced conscious life many times over.

We can agree with Thomas Berry (1988) on the importance of narratives for determining human meaning, values, and practices, but we do not concur, as he insists, that it is "all a question of story." It is also a question of insight and theory, of how we conceptualize the world and our values, and of politics, of how people struggle against hierarchies and domination, and what alternative institutions they seek to put in their place. Yet it is a promising sign that sci-ence, which has done so much to eradicate our ties to life, is beginning to help rebuild these connections through new holistic and ecological theories. *Homo sapiens* truly is "in between stories." A key task for the future is to write and disseminate a new story that emphasizes our responsibilities in the larger com-munity that engulfs us, the biocommunity in which human beings are only one of millions of interdependent, coevolving species. While human beings are free to write their own social and ethical laws, and to use nature to advance human well-being, most have yet to learn that they must also conform to the limits and dynamics of nature. Ecological balance and human sustainability is inconsistent with the burgeoning population, insatiable consumption levels, and ideology of limitless growth marring cultures in both the West and the East. The new story will inform us that humanity survives and flourishes not by opposing itself to nature, as the old Adam and Eve story teaches, but rather by harmonizing with all that has come before it in the multibillion year odys-sey of evolution. This would entail that the natural and social worlds diversify together, a coevolutionary process that is now terminating with human over-population, the environmental ravages of global technocapitalism, and species extinction.

The discourse of limits, however, so essential to the new story, is ambiguous and problematic. On one extreme, technophobic views err in positing essentialist concepts of the natural as a pregiven boundary not to be transgressed by science and technology, and they set up a crude dualism between authentic "reality" and inauthentic "artificiality." Against this, we would argue that there is no viable definition of "nature" that excludes human beings, and point out that "limits" can be prisons. Moreover, proscriptions against technological manipulation of nature should proceed from extrinsic not from intrinsic grounds, assessing actual or potential negative consequences of change and development. However, since the natural world is not a cornucopia of infinite resources, fragile holistic interrelationships of ecosystems suffer degradation and disrepair, and human beings cannot thrive independent of a flourishing Earth. Technophilic views therefore err in seeing nature as infinitely malleable and open to any and all technological manipulations. Thus, while a discourse of limits must recognize that the enhancement of human life and the furthering of social evolution is tied to the development of science and technology and the opening of new vistas, it must also establish boundaries and harmonious modes of coevolution between human beings and their natural surroundings and life context.

RECONSTRUCTING THEORY AND POLITICS IN THE NEW MILLENNIUM

> We exist in a sea of powerful stories: They are the conditions of finite rationality and personal and collective life histories. There is no way out of stories, but no matter what the One-Eyed Father says, there are many possible structures, not to mention contents, of narration. Changing the stories, in both material and semiotic senses, is a modest intervention worth making.
>
> —DONNA HARAWAY

> Our tragedy lies in the richness of the available alternatives, and in the fact that so few of them are ever seriously explored.
>
> —TOM ATHANASIOU

> Pessimism of the intellect, optimism of the will.
>
> —ANTONIO GRAMSCI

With the human species entering the Third Millennium, it encounters perhaps the most dramatic scientific and technological revolutions in history and the massive global restructuring of capitalism. This postmodern adventure forces us to rethink the basic categories and methods of theory, to invent useful practical and political responses to the great transformation that we are undergoing, and thus to reshape theory and politics for the future. Such a transformative project is not an idealist reflex of theory, but one demanded by the striking developments of the present age. The turbulent metamorphoses of the contemporary era provide opportunities for progressive interventions in arenas ranging from education and the workplace to struggles over world trade and global democracy.

As we noted in Chapter 3, scientists and philosophers alike are engaging in the reshaping of science. Many are now rejecting mechanistic, deterministic, and positivist models, and producing new understandings and more ecologically and ethically oriented work. Likewise, as we showed in Chapters 4 and 5, individuals are reconfiguring technology to make it a more creative force for culture and communication and a key weapon for radical democratic politics. Current struggles against globalization from below indeed provide the potential for new movements to overcome social fragmentation and to create a more ecological, egalitarian, and just social order.

Embracing these projects, we note that many serious efforts for transformations of theory, politics, society, and identities are underway; they range from new theoretical mappings and critiques to political battles over biotechnology and capitalist globalization, to efforts to remake institutions like the schools and family. But the forces of capitalism also have their own reconstructive project, of course. Thus it is necessary to keep up with and counter capitalism's ever-changing tactics of conquest and domination with alternative projects of radical democracy. The postmodern adventure is thus a contested field with competing groups struggling to transform all domains of everyday life.

While the planet spirals ever deeper into social and natural disaster, with all things becoming ever more tightly knit into the tentacles of global capitalism, there is a burning need for new maps and compasses to help steer us into a viable mode of existence. Karl Marx's 1843 call for a "ruthless criticism of everything existing" has never been more urgent and appropriate, but all too often today critique is merely academic and stratospheres away from concrete action. Yet social critique and change in the slaughterhouse of capitalism needs to be guided and informed by powerful descriptions of what *is*: the degraded forfeiture of human potential in a world where over a billion people struggle for mere existence and live on less than one dollar a day. In addition, transformative projects require bold new visions of what *can be*, developing imaginative projections of how human beings might harmoniously relate to one another and the living/dying Earth.

Where some people fatalistically concede defeat, others declare this to be the best of all possible worlds (we'd hate to see the worst) and announce the end of history (Fukuyama and Baudrillard). However, one of the first preconditions for change is the realization that things could be otherwise, that humanity has choices, and, indeed, that we are currently at a crucial crossroads where "the fate of the Earth" hangs in balance. What choices we make, how we act or fail to act in the next few decades, might decide the ultimate outcome for all advanced life.

A sobering diagnosis of current crises must be counterbalanced by hope for regeneration of the planet and humanity, accompanied by positive, alternative visions of social organization, politics, and ethics. To be sure, the way forward is shadowed by doubt and uncertainty. The maps of the modern era, though partly in shreds, can guide us in some ways, but in other ways they can only lead us further down the paths of catastrophe since they have steered advanced Western societies (and increasingly the entire world) into their present cultural and historical impasse. A regenerative future demands new maps, a different compass, and a transformative orientation. This new orientation requires an appraisal of the present situation and new theories, new ethics, and new politics to reconfigure existing frameworks. In these tasks, postmodern critiques and concepts have much to offer, while suffering important limitations of their own.

The old determinist maps of reality are obsolete and increasingly hazardous to employ. They were based on erroneous notions of linear causality, simple cause-and-effect models, dualistic thinking, and a "quest for certainty" that divorces theory from practice and attempts to eliminate ambiguity and contingency from knowledge and life (see Dewey 1979). At their best, the new maps, which have come to be called "postmodern," and which have been assembled from elements in the fields of art, philosophy, social theory, and science, often allow for more complex and adequate modes of thinking. The most advanced new postmodern mappings abandon naive attempts to impose crude ordering schemes on reality, renouncing the dangerous obsession with repressive and reductive control of the social and natural worlds. They substitute multi-perspectivist thinking for reductionist, realist, and essentialist positions, and enable individuals better to theorize and deal with contingency, paradox, ambiguity, particularity, multiplicity, and relationships. They challenge anthropocentrism and its dualistic vision of the human place in nature, and disassemble hierarchies of all kinds in favor of relations of complementarity. The new perspectives of chaos and complexity theory stress self-organization and the creation of fresh cultural and social forms that can be born out of current turbulence and disequilibrium, as we approach threshold points of change. Such alternative postmodern theoretical guidelines, while not always articulated adequately, are important, for they can inform a reconstructed ethics, politics, and set of social practices that can enhance democracy and individuality, and create less domineering and more life-enhancing relationships with nature. Humans can learn to see their natural and social environments as potentials for gratification and cooperation rather than as objects to be dominated and manipulated.

Of course, as we have argued elsewhere (Best and Kellner 1991, 1997), many versions of postmodern theories are excessively irrational, relativistic, individualistic, nihilistic, and antimodern. We reject such positions in favor of a more positive and transformative critical postmodern theory. The restructuring of theory and politics called for by Dewey in the Progressive Era, and by critical theorists like Marcuse, feminists, multiculturalists, poststructuralists, and postmodernists in recent decades, is driven now by bold developments in technoscience and the global economy. The coevolution of science, technology, and capitalism is creating mutations within the human adventure itself, confronting us with fantastic new forms of communication and information technology, multimedia, biotechnology, nanotechnologies, and rapidly evolving forms of culture, society, and economy. These turbulent and frightening developments pose great dangers for the human species, but also offer opportunities for more democratizing, egalitarian, and ecological social relations, values, and practices.

As humans coevolve with their economies, tools, cultures, and theories, they produce new mappings to make sense of their world and create new practices to achieve their desired values. Hence, the reconstruction of theory and practice is rooted in the coevolutionary adventure itself and involves imaginative co-constructions of those forces that are propelling us into an ever more quickly arriving and unpredictable future. However things are presently constructed, they can be deconstructed and reconstructed by human beings in different ways. Whatever futures might be likely or probable, such as one of global social and environmental collapse, they can be anticipated and prevented in favor of quite different results.

Unless we first imagine various futures, both good and bad, and utilize socially progressive and ecological visions as ethical and institutional maps, we will have nothing to guide us in the constitution of a viable world, and we will travel through time like lost seafarers. Such an imaginative project is undertaken, for example, in Allen Hammond's *Which World? Scenarios for the 21st Century: Global Destinies, Regional Choices* (1998). Hammond examines longterm trends in various regions and the globe as a whole. He envisages three main possibilities for humanity: we can journey into the Market World of untrammeled capitalism, the Fortress World of social collapse and authoritarian control, or the Transformed World of benign capitalism that prioritizes social justice and seeks a rapprochement with nature. In line with a systems and chaos theory approach, Hammond insists that while current trends may predispose societies to certain outcomes, these futures are too complex and too contingent on uncertain variables for exact prediction.

Hammond begins by stressing the importance of creating stories or "scenarios" as critical maps of the present and guideposts for the future. He then broadly describes the nature of the three worlds/roads he believes face us in the current crossroads of social evolution. Finally, he applies each scenario to various regions of the world, always with a careful eye on how each region interacts with the global economy as a whole and how social development is inextricably bound to the ecological systems of the Earth.

But if Hammond's menu of options seems limited, something like what a steakhouse offers a vegetarian, indeed it is. For the neoliberal author fails to consider a wide range of alternatives such as a revitalized socialist economics, left-green ecopolitics, anarchist or radical democratic movements, or the coalitions currently being formed by opponents of globalization. Still, although it leaves out a vision of a Postcapitalist Green World that rebuilds political and economic institutions for participatory democracy, the value of Hammond's book is its concrete projection of some different futures that may await us, and which depend upon our individual and collective choices. Indeed, one of the major crises today is a crisis of the imagination. In the tradition of neo-Marxism, and the work of thinkers like Herbert Marcuse and Murray Bookchin, it has been recognized that so-called utopian visions are not, when authentic, starry-eyed dreams of abstract ideals. They are at their best empirically grounded in actual social tendencies and the real potential for a rational, egalitarian, ecological, and compassionate mode of life. For such utopians, the "ought" can become an "is."

As an example of our reconstructive project, we find value in combining modern Enlightenment notions of community, rights, and solidarity with a postmodern ethics of difference, contingency, and nonfoundationalism. This could lead to creation of a new ethics that balances principles of individuality and community, difference and unity, particularity and universality. The Kantian notion of a Kingdom of Ends still contributes to ethical vision, especially now, when politics is being reduced to amoral assertions of self-interest via competing groups that refuse to search for commonality or reach consensus. Kant's conception of perpetual peace might also be reconfigured for the present in the light of the proliferation of violence and war, as should the nonviolent perspectives of Gandhi and Martin Luther King. One might also learn from the classical Greek synthesis of ethics and politics about the need to combine these domains, as well as to preserve the substance of both individual and communal life, in the quest for more social harmony and well-being. Further, one should overcome the limitations of all anthropocentric and humanistic ethics, however progressive, democratic, and enlightened, which assign moral status and value only to humans, positioning the animal kingdom and the natural world as mere "resources" for human use.

New relationships to nature and other species need to be developed that could enable people to appreciate the intrinsic value of the natural world, to seek creative forms of interaction and enjoyment with nature, and to fight the pollution, depletion, and destruction of nature and life. In addition, it is important to mediate the fact/value distinction in science, to reshape science so that ethical concerns and values are central to its conceptual apparatus. This was a quest of Herbert Marcuse (1964) and has been taken up by some versions of environmental thought, feminism, and postmodern science (Haraway 1997). The dominant positivist and neopositivist stances within mainstream science continue to fetishize detachment and seek solace in myths of objectivity. Moreover, the conventional approach is to limit discussion to procedures of research by individual scientists rather than infusing science as a whole with more embracing social values of accountability, human and animal welfare, social justice, ecology, and the like (conversation with Sandra Harding, June 2000).

The reconfiguration of science, ethics, and society requires the reconstruction of education. As H. G. Wells notes in an epigraph that opens this Epilogue, education can save us from catastrophe. As John Dewey consistently argued, the transformation of education is crucial to the democratization of society. We would argue that technological revolution and globalization are dramatically reshaping education and that a major challenge of the present age is to reshape education to make it serve the interests of democratization rather than intensified corporate hegemony. This will require teaching multiple literacies to critically engage new technologies and to attempt to overcome the "digital divide." A democratizing reconstruction of education should thus provide the skills necessary to actively participate in the new technoculture and society to all groups and individuals (for an elaboration of this argument, see Kellner 1998, 2000).

The democratic reconfiguration of education, science, and society still requires philosophy and philosophical visions of the good life. Science and social theory can tell us what the world is, but by themselves not how to live in it. Hence, it is crucial to activate the philosophical imagination and generate visions of the good society. But possibilities for the good life and the good society mutate as new sciences, technologies, and sociopolitical tendencies emerge. One must therefore constantly rethink the possibilities of liberation, democracy, Enlightenment, and freedom from these changing perspectives.

While cultural politics can help us to understand groups and individuals different from ourselves, spark thought and action, promote new sensibilities, and enhance our lives in a variety of ways (see Best and Kellner 1997; Giroux 2000), it is still important to develop new forms of political organization and struggle. For instance, to overcome the environmental crisis will require massive global efforts of political organization and new forms of struggle, alliance, and enlightenment. This requires collective acts of will and imagination, rather than the prevailing fragmentation of identity politics, whose one-sidedness and limitations we must overcome. For substantive change to occur, expansive, democratizing visions must supplant the "modest" visions of postmodern politics that limit action to mere local changes or local reform.

There are conflicting potentials in the present social situation. On the one hand, postmodern fragmentation and pluralization has taken the differentiating features of modernity into a spiral of otherness and difference, expanding social dissolution and conflict. This form of postmodern fragmentation involves a breaking up of unities (communities, traditions, even national cultures) that once provided resources for identity, were empowering, and enabled individuals to create better lives for themselves. Their disintegration is a loss, yet these very unities also contained oppressive features in the form of cultural hierarchies, relations of subordination and domination, backwardness, and chauvinisms of various sorts. Their erosion creates openings for cosmopolitan identities and a more pluralized social condition that gives groups and individuals excluded from political and cultural participation expanded opportunities for cultural creation and political involvement.

Thus, crises contain opportunities for progressive change, and fragmentation creates exciting openings and empowering possibilities as well as dispiriting and destructive tendencies. What does the near future hold for humankind? Will we continue to overpopulate the planet, move toward technocracy, develop violent cultures, overproduce nuclear weapons, exacerbate the already obscene disparities between the rich and the poor, advance trends toward global warming, destroy other species, deplete the Earth's natural resources, and utterly self-destruct? Will life end apocalyptically by epidemic disease or by a nuclear bang, or will there be enough fragments of humanity left to survive for a short time, as in contrasting conditions of drought and flood depicted by *Mad Max* (1979) and *Waterworld* (1995), before it ends in a pathetic whimper? Will we mutate into cyborgs or bionic beings and live out our lives in spaceships and space stations? Will we make "contact" and be saved by the superior wisdom and technologies of space aliens, or will they devour us as resources for their megamachines? Or will we learn to harmonize our advanced technological society with the natural world and take on responsible roles as stewards of the Earth?

The greatest adventure ever faced by the human species is staring us right in the face: Can we use our advanced intelligence and technologies toward constructive rather than destructive ends? Can we learn to live together on this planet? Can we diversify and live together peacefully? Can we regain respect and reverence for life? The next few generations hold the fate of the evolution of all life on Earth in their hands. The window of opportunity is closing.

The postmodern adventure holds more promise, more danger, and more surreality than any previous adventure known to humanity. We must seek possibilities in the present to move toward a better future. The postmodern adventure is just beginning and alternative futures unfold all around us. Western societies inhabit a historically unique terrain between the modern and the postmodern, and we need a variety of theoretical and political perspectives to make sense of the momentous changes that are now occurring. In the Third Millennium, the choices agents make will determine whether the adventure of evolution itself will continue in creative ways on this planet, producing ever more biodiversity, or collapses into the sixth and perhaps final extinction crisis in the history of the Earth (see Leakey and Lewin 1995).

As science, technology, and capitalism continue to coevolve into an ever denser global network, the ultimate question is whether we can reshape the driving forces of change to harmonize social with natural evolution, such that diversity and complexity grow in both spheres. Or will current developments produce the death of the human, the despoliation of the Earth, and even the demise of all complex life? Neither option is preordained, both are possible futures, and this tension and ambiguity itself is a core feature of the postmodern adventure.

NOTES

1. Drake's equation concludes that there are 50,000 planets in our solar system that have intelligent life. Numerous scientists have objected that his variables and reasoning are arbitrary, and that his result is far too optimistic. In their book *Rare Earth*, for example, Donald Brownlee and Peter Ward (2000) draw on new findings in astronomy, geology, and paleontology to argue that the odds of another Earth-like planet existing in the entire cosmos are exceedingly rare. Recent findings in exobiology, however, which prove that life is able to thrive in very hostile conditions, might support Drake's thesis. Drake finds Brownlee and Ward's work too pessimistic, stating that "the basic flaw in all [such] arguments is that they don't allow for the opportunistic nature of life, its ability to accommodate or alter itself to cope with environmental change" ("Maybe We Are Alone in the Universe, After All," www.nytimes.com/library/national/science/020800sci-space-life.html). The controversy rages on.

2. On the history and politics of the space program, see McDougall (1985) and Burrows (1990). For recent books on space technology and travel colonization, see Burrows (1998).

3. It is important to emphasize that for Sagan, space research and space travel have not only philosophical implications, but also crucial pragmatic value, since the study of the atmospheres and matter of other planets like Venus can tell us much about the ecological dynamics and fate of our own Earth. Throughout *Pale Blue Dot* (1994), Sagan makes convincing arguments about the importance of space research for ecology, noting that key insights into the dangers with chlorofluorocarbons (CFCs) (which destroy the ozone layer) and problems with global warming were gleaned by scientists studying other planets. See especially chapter 14, "Exploring Other Worlds and Protecting This One" (216–229). Sagan's dual optic—philosophical and pragmatic—for arguing the importance of the space programs is well articulated in this passage: "When I look at the evidence, it seems to me that planetary exploration is of the most practical and urgent utility for us here on Earth. Even if we were not roused by the prospect of exploring other worlds, even if we didn't have a nanogram of adventuresome spirit in us, even if we were only concerned for ourselves and in the narrowest sense, planetary exploration would still constitute a superb investment" (1995: 229). Importantly, Sagan insists on the need to bring science down to earth, to advance an interdisciplinary research program, and to articulate a coevolutionary cosmology that intimately links the Earth to other planets in its solar system, such as in the possibility that Mars may have seeded life on Earth, or the other way around.

4. Dick published 80 stories and 13 novels from 1951 to 1958 (Sutin 1989: 85), an intensity and productivity that continued through the 1960s, in which he published as many as 11 novels in 1 year. Five volumes of his collected short stories are in print and a large number of his novels have been reprinted. Dick has indeed become a cult figure, with a loyal following, a major SF prize named after him, and movies and TV shows of his work regularly appearing. He was generally ignored during his life, often living in extreme poverty and turmoil. On Dick, see Sutin (1989) and Hayles (1999).

5. Yet another scientific blow to anthropocentrism came in February 2001, when the rival teams mapping the human genome discovered that human beings have only about 30,000–40,000 genes, far less than the commonly projected number of 100,000. This means that at the genetic level, humans are not significantly more complicated than simple invertebrate animals. If these findings are correct, the pufferfish, which has 50,000 genes, is more genetically complex than human beings. Also, Dr. Craig Venter claims he found only 300 human genes that lacked a recognizable counterpart in the mouse; see Wade (2001). But others challenge this. On the latest research, and the controversy raging on about the number of human genes and the meaning of the data, see Nicholas Wade, "Genome Analysis Shows Humans Survive on Low Number of Genes," www.nytimes.com/2001/02/11/health/11GENO.html and Kristen Philipkowski, "Gene Map: Help or Hype?" www.wirednews.com/news/print/0,1294,41718,00.htm.

6. www.vhemt.org.

BIBLIOGRAPHY

The reference list assembled here contains the books and key scholarly articles which we have drawn on and cited in our studies. Newspaper and magazine articles and Internet sources generally are referenced either in the text itself or in the notes at the end of each chapter.

Adams, James. (1998). *The Next World War.* New York: Simon and Schuster.

Adorno, Theodor W (1973). *Negative Dialectics.* New York: Continuum.

Albrow, Martin. (1996). *The Global Age.* Cambridge, UK: Polity Press.

Al-Hadithy, Nabil. (1992). "The Education of American Consciousness" in *War after War,* ed. Nancy J. Peters. San Francisco: City Lights Books.

Andrews, Lori B. (1999). *The Clone Age: Adventures in the New World of Reproductive Technology.* New York: Henry Holt and Company.

Arditti, Rita, Pat Brennan, and Steve Cavrak, eds. (1980). *Science and Liberation.* Boston: South End Press.

Argyros, Alexander. (1992). *A Blessed Rage for Order: Deconstruction, Evolution, and Chaos.* Ann Arbor: University of Michigan Press.

Arnett, Peter. (1994). *Live From the Battlefield.* New York: Simon and Schuster.

Aronowitz, Stanley, and William de Fazio. (1994). *The Jobless Future.* Minneapolis: University of Minnesota Press.

Aronson, Ronald. (1983). *Dialectics of Disaster.* London: Verso.

Arquilla, John, and David Ronfeldt. (1996). *Advent of Netwar.* Santa Monica, CA: Rand.

Arrighi, Giovanni. (1994). *The Long Twentieth Century.* London and New York: Verso Books.

Asimov, Isaac. (1979). "The Science-Fiction Breakthrough," in H. G. Wells, *Three Novels of the Future.* Garden City, NY: Doubleday.

_____. (1990). "Little Lost Robot," in *Robot Dreams.* New York: Ace Books.

Athanasiou, Tom. (1996). *Divided Planet: The Ecology of Rich and Poor.* Boston: Little, Brown.

Axford, Barrie. (1995). *The Global System.* Cambridge, UK: Polity Press.

Bacon, Francis. (1960). *The New Organon*, ed. Fulton H. Anderson. New York: Macmillan.

Bailey, Ronald. (1993). *Ecoscam: The False Prophets of Ecological Collapse.* New York: St. Martin's Press.

Barber, Benjamin. (1996). *Jihad vs. McWorld: How Globalism and Tribalism Are Reshaping the World.* New York: Ballantine Books.

Barbrook, R., and A. Cameron. (1995). "The California Ideology," *Mute*(3). Available: http://www.wmin.ac.uk/media/hrc/ci/califl.html

Barrow, John D. (1991). *Theories of Everything: The Quest for Ultimate Explanation.* New York: Fawcett Columbine.

Barsook, Paulina. (2000). *Cyberselfish: A Critical Romp through the Terribly Libertarian Culture of High Tech.* New York: Public Affairs.

Barthes, Roland. (1975). *The Pleasures of the Text.* New York: Hill & Wang.

Bateson, Gregory. (1972). *Steps to an Ecology of Mind.* New York: Ballantine Books.

_____. (1979). *Mind and Nature: A Necessary Unity.* New York: Bantam Books.

Baudrillard, Jean. (1975). *The Mirror of Production.* St. Louis: Telos Press.

_____. (1981 [1973]). *For a Critique of the Political Economy of the Sign.* St. Louis: Telos Press.

_____. (1983a). *Simulations.* New York: Semiotext(e).

_____. (1983b). *In the Shadow of the Silent Majorities.* New York: Semiotext(e).

_____. (1983c). "The Ecstasy of Communication," in *The Anti-Aesthetic* (pp. 126–134), ed. Hal Foster. Port Townsend, WA: Bay Press.

_____. (1988a). *America.* London: Verso Books.

_____. (1988b). "The Year 2000 Has Already Happened," in *Body Invaders: Panic Sex in America* (pp. 35–44), ed. Arthur Kroker and Marilouise Kroker. Montreal: New World Perspectives.

_____. (1989). "The Anorexic Ruins," in *Looking Back at the End of the World* (pp. 29–45), ed. Dietmar Kamper and Christoph Wulf. New York: Semiotext(e).

_____. (1990). *Fatal Strategies.* New York: Semiotext(e).

_____. (1993). *Symbolic Exchange and Death.* London: Sage.

_____. (1995). *The Gulf War Never Happened.* Cambridge, UK: Polity Press.

_____. (1996c [1968]). *The System of Objects.* London: Verso Books.

_____. (1998 [1970]). *The Consumer Society.* London: Sage.

Bauman, Zygmuny. (1989). *Modernity and the Holocaust.* Cambridge, UK: Polity Press.

Becker, Carl L. (1964). *The Heavenly City of the Eighteenth-Century Philosophers.* New Haven, CT: Yale University Press.

Bell, Daniel. (1962). *The End of Ideology.* New York: Free Press.

_____. (1976). *The Coming of Post-Industrial Society.* New York: Basic Books.

Benedikt, Michael, ed. (1991). *Cyberspace: First Steps.* Cambridge, MA: MIT Press.

Benjamin, Walter. (1969). *Illuminations.* New York: Schocken Books.

Benyus, Janine M. (1997). *Biomimicry: Innovation Inspired from Nature.* New York: Morrow.

Berlet, Chip, and Matthew N. Lyons. (2000). *Right-Wing Populism in America: Too Close for Comfort.* New York: Guilford Press.

Berman, Marshall. (1982). *All That Is Solid Melts in the Air.* New York: Simon and Schuster.

Berman, Morris. (1981). *The Reenchantment of the World.* New York: Bantam Books.

Bernal, Martin. (1989). *Black Athena: The Afroasiatic Roots of Classical Civilization: Vol 1.* New Brunswick, NJ: Rutgers University Press.

Berry, Thomas. (1988). *The Dream of the Earth.* San Francisco: Sierra Club Books.

Berry, Thomas, and Brian Swimme. (1992). *The Universe Story: From the Primordial Flaring Forth to the Ecozoic Era.* New York: HarperCollins.

Bertman, Stephen. (1998). *Hyperculture.* New York: Praeger.

Best, Steven. (1992). "Creative Paranoia: A Postmodern Aesthetic of Cognitive Mapping in *Gravity's Rainbow,*" *Centennial Review, 36*(1): 59–88.

_____. (1995). *The Politics of Historical Vision.* New York: Guilford Press.

Best, Steven, and Douglas Kellner. (1987). "(Re)Watching Television: Notes Toward a Political Criticism," *diacritics* 97–113.

_____. (1991). *Postmodern Theory: Critical Interrogations.* New York: Guilford Press.

_____. (1997). *The Postmodern Turn.* New York: Guilford Press.

_____. (1999). "Kevin Kelly's Complexity Theory: The Politics and Ideology of Self-Organizing Systems," *Organization and Environment, 12*(2): 141–162.

_____. (2000). "Afloat in Cloud Cuckoo Land? Some Critical Comments on the Symposium 'Manufacturing Nature, Naturalizing Machines,' " *Organization and Environment, 13*(1): 102–104.

Bibby, Michael, ed. (2000). *The Vietnam War and Postmodernity.* Amherst: University of Massachusetts Press.

Biehl, Janet. (1991). *Rethinking Ecofeminist Politics.* Boston: South End Press.

Birch, Charles. (1988). "A Postmodern Challenge to Biology," in *The Reenchantment of Science: Postmodern Proposals* (pp. 69–78), ed. David Ray Griffin. Albany: State University of New York Press.

Bird, Jon, Barry Curtis, Tim Putnam, and George Robertson, eds. (1993). *Mapping the Futures: Local Cultures, Global Change.* London and New York: Routledge.

Birke, Linda, and Ruth Hubbard. (1995). *Reinventing Biology: Respect for Life and the Creation of Knowledge.* Bloomington: Indiana University Press.

Birkerts, Sven. (1995). *The Gutenberg Elegies: The Fate of Reading in an Electronic Age.* New York: Fawcett.

Blackwell, James. (1991). *Thunder in the Desert.* New York: Bantam Books.

Bloch, Ernst. (1986). *The Principle of Hope.* Cambridge, MA: MIT Press.

Bloch, Ernst, et al. (1977). *Aesthetics and Politics.* London: New Left Books.

Blum, William. (1995). *Killing Hope: U.S. Military and CIA Interventions Since World War II.* New York: Dimensions.

Boggs, Carl. (2000). *The End of Politics.* New York: Guilford Press.

Bohm, David. (1957). *Causality and Chance in Modern Physics.* Philadelphia: University of Pennsylvania Press.

_____. (1988). "Postmodern Science and a Postmodern World," in *The Reenchantment of Science: Postmodern Proposals* (pp. 57–68), ed. David Ray Griffin. Albany: State University of New York Press.

Bohr, Niels. (1958). *Atomic Theory and Human Knowledge.* New York: Wiley.

Boje, David M., and Robert F. Dennehy. (1994). *Managing in the Postmodern World.* Dubuque, IA: Kendall/Hunt.

Boje, David M., Robert P. Gephart, and Joseph Thatchenkery. (1996). *Postmodern Management and Organization Theory*. Thousand Oaks, CA, and London: Sage.

Bookchin, Murray. (1974). *The Limits of the City*. New York: Harper Colophon.

———. (1992). *Urbanization without Cities: The Rise and Decline of Citizenship*. Montreal: Black Rose Books.

———. (1994). *Which Way for the Ecology Movement?* Edinburgh and San Francisco: AK Press.

———. (1995a). *Re-Enchanting Humanity*. London: Cassell Press.

———. (1995b). *The Philosophy of Social Ecology: Essays on Dialectical Naturalism* (rev. ed.). Montreal: Black Rose Books.

Boorstin, Daniel. (1961). *The Image*. New York: Random House.

———. (1985). *The Discoverers: A History of Man's Search to Know His World and Himself*. New York: Random House.

Bordo, Susan R. (1987). *The Flight to Objectivity: Essays on Cartesianism and Culture*. Albany: State University of New York Press.

Borgmann, Albert. (1994). *Across the Postmodern Divide*. Chicago: University of Chicago Press.

———. (1999). *Holding onto Reality*. Chicago: University of Chicago Press.

Boyer, Paul. (1985). *By the Bomb's Early Light*. New York: Pantheon Books.

Brand, Stewart. (1968). *Whole Earth Catalog*. San Francisco: Whole Earth Press.

Brecher, Jeremy, and Tim Costello. (1994). *Global Village or Global Pillage? Economic Reconstruction from the Bottom Up*. Boston: South End Press.

Brenner, Joseph. (1994). *Internationalist Labor Communication by Computer Network: The United States, Mexico, and Nafta,* unpublished paper,

Brians, Paul. (1987). *Nuclear Holocausts: Atomic War in Fiction, 1895–1984*. Kent, OH: Popular Press.

Bright, Chris. (1998). *Life Out of Bounds: Bioinvasion in a Borderless World*. New York: Norton.

Brockman, John, ed. (1995). *The Third Culture*. New York: Simon and Schuster.

Brown, Julian. (2000). *Minds, Machines, and the Multiverse: The Quest for the Quantum Computer*. New York: Simon and Schuster.

Brown, Norman O. (1955). *Life Against Death*. New York: Random House.

Brown, Stephen Walter. (1998). *Postmodern Marketing*. New York: Routledge.

Brownlee, Donald, and Peter Douglas Ward. (2000). *Rare Earth: Why Life Is Uncommon in the Universe*. New York: Copernicus Books.

Bruno, Giuliana. (1990). "Ramble City: Postmodernism and *Blade Runner*," in *Alien Zone: Cultural Theory and Contemporary Science Fiction* (pp. 183–195), ed. Annette Kuhn. London and New York: Verso Books.

Buchanan, R. A. (1992). *The Power of the Machine: The Impact of Technology from 1700 to the Present*. New York: Penguin Books.

Buckley, Walter. (1968). *Modern Systems Research for the Behavioral Scientist: A Sourcebook*. Chicago: Aldine.

Buktaman, Scott. (1993). *Terminal Identity: The Virtual Subject in Post-Modern Science Fiction*. Durham, NC, and London: Duke University Press.

Burrows, William E. (1990). *Exploring Space: Voyages in the Solar System and Beyond*. New York: Random House.

———. (1998). *This New Ocean: The Story of the First Space Age*. New York: Random House.

Butler, Octavia. (1987). *Dawn*. New York: Warner Books.

————. (1988). *Adulthood Rites*. New York: Warner Books.

————. (1989). *Imago*. New York: Warner Books.

Butler, Samuel. (1998). *Erewhon*. New York: Prometheus Books. (originally published 1872)

Caldicott, Helen. (1997). *Metal of Dishonor: How Depleted Uranium Penetrates Steel, Radiates People and Contaminates the Environment*. New York: International Action Center.

Capra, Fritjof. (1982). *The Turning Point: Science, Society, and the Rising Culture*. New York: Bantam Books.

————. (1996). *The Web of Life: A New Scientific Understanding of Living Systems*. New York: Anchor Books.

Carter, Dale. (1988). *The Final Frontier*. London and New York: Verso Books.

Castells, Manuel. (1989). *The Informational City: The Space of Flows*. Oxford, UK: Blackwell.

————. (1996). *The Rise of the Network Society*. Oxford, UK: Blackwell.

————. (1997). *The Power of Identity*. Oxford, UK: Blackwell.

————. (1998). *End of Millenium*. Oxford, UK: Blackwell.

Casti, John L. (1995). *Complification: Explaining a Paradoxical World through the Science of Surprise*. New York: HarperPerennial.

Cavalieri, Paola, and Peter Singer. (1995). *The Great Ape Project: Equality beyond Humanity*. New York: St. Martin's Press.

Clark, Ramsey. (1992). *The Fire This Time: U.S. War Crimes in the Gulf*. New York. Thunder's Mouth Press.

Clark, Ramsey, et al. (1991). *War Crimes: A Report on United States War Crimes against Iraq*. Washington, DC: Maisonneuve Press.

Clarke, Arthur C. (1968). *2001: A Space Odyssey*. New York: Signet.

Clarke, Simon, et al. (1980). *One-Dimensional Marxism*. London: Allison & Busby.

Cleaver, Harry. (1994). "The Chiapas Uprising," *Studies in Political Economy, 44*: 141–157.

Colborn, Theo, Dianne Dumanoski, and John Peterson Myers. (1996). *Our Stolen Future*. New York: Penguin Books.

Commoner, Barry. (1972). *The Closing Circle*. New York: Bantam Books.

Cooke, Miriam. (1991). "Postmodern Wars." *Journal of Urban and Cultural Studies, 2*(1): 27–40.

Cooley, Mike. (1987). *Architect or Bee? The Human Price of Technology*. London: Hogarth.

Coveney, Peter, and Roger Highfield. (1995). *Frontiers of Complexity: The Search for Order in a Chaotic World*. New York: Ballantine Books.

Craige, Betty Jean. (1996). *American Patriotism in a Global Society*. Albany: State University of New York Press.

Crandall, B. C. (1996). *Nanotechnology: Molecular Speculations on Global Abundance*. Cambridge, MA: MIT Press.

Crichton, Michael. (1990). *Jurassic Park*. New York: Ballantine Books.

Crosby, Alfred W. (1997). *The Measure of Reality: Quantification and Western Society, 1250–1600*. Cambridge, UK: Cambridge University Press.

Cumings, Bruce. (1992). *War and Television*. London: Verso Books.

Cvetkovich, Ann, and Douglas Kellner, eds. (1997). *Articulating the Global and the Local. Globalization and Cultural Studies.* Boulder, CO: Westview Press.

Czitrom, Daniel. (1982). *Media and the American Mind.* Chapel Hill: University of North Carolina Press.

Daly, Herman E., and Kenneth N. Townsend, eds. (1993). *Valuing the Earth: Economics, Ecology, Ethics.* Cambridge, MA: MIT Press.

Darnton, Robert, and Daniel Roche, eds. (1989). *Revolution in Print.* Berkeley and Los Angeles: University of California Press.

Davies, Paul. (1978). *The Runaway Universe.* New York: Harper & Row.

Davies, Paul, and J. Brown, eds. (1988). *Superstrings: A Theory of Everything?* Cambridge, UK: Cambridge University Press.

Dawkins, Richard. (1989). *The Selfish Gene.* Oxford and New York: Oxford University Press.

Debord, Guy. (1967). *Society of the Spectacle.* Detroit, MI: Black and Red.

De Landa, Manuel. (1991). *War in the Age of Intelligent Machines.* New York: Zone Books.

Deleuze, Gilles, and Felix Guattari. (1977). *Anti-Oedipus.* New York: Viking Press.

_____. (1987). *A Thousand Plateaus.* Minneapolis: University of Minnesota Press.

Derrida, Jacques. (1976). *Of Grammatology.* Baltimore: Johns Hopkins University Press.

_____. (1981a). *Positions.* Chicago: University of Chicago Press.

_____. (1981b). *Dissemination.* Chicago: University of Chicago Press.

_____. (1982). *Margins of Philosophy.* Chicago: University of Chicago Press.

Dery, Mark. (1996). *Escape Velocity: Cyberculture at the End of the Century.* New York: Grove Press.

DeSalle, Rob, and David Lindley. (1997). *The Science of "Jurassic Park" and "The Lost World".* New York: Basic Books.

Descartes, René. (1998). *A Discourse on Method.* New York: Penguin Books.

Devlin, Keith. (1997). *Goodbye Descartes: The End of Logic and the Search for a New Cosmology of the Mind.* New York: Wiley.

De Waal, Frans. (1989). *Chimpanzee Politics: Power and Sex among Apes.* Baltimore: Johns Hopkins University Press.

_____. (1996). *Good Natured: The Origins of Right and Wrong in Humans and Other Animals.* Cambridge, MA: Harvard University Press.

Dewey, John. (1979). *Theory and Practice.* New York: Paragon Books.

_____. (1995). *Democracy and Education.* New York: Free Press.

Diamond, Jared. (1997). *Guns, Germs, and Steel: The Fates of Human Societies.* New York: W.W. Norton & Co.

Diamond, Sara. (1995). *Roads to Dominion: Right-Wing Movements and Political Power in the United States.* New York: Guilford Press.

Dick, Philip K. (1957). *Eye in the Sky.* New York: Collier.

_____. (1964). *Martian Time-Slip.* New York: Ace.

_____. (1965). *The Three Stigmata of Palmer Eldritch.* New York: Vintage.

_____. (1987). *Do Androids Dream of Electric Sheep?* New York: Ballantine Books.

Dossey, Larry. (1982). *Space, Time, and Medicine.* Boulder, CO: Shambala Books.

Dowie, Mark. (1995). *Losing Ground: American Environmentalism at the Close of the Twentieth Century.* Cambridge, MA: MIT Press.

Downing, John. (1984). *Radical Media.* Boston: South End Press.

_____. (2000). *Radical Media* (2nd, rev. ed.). London: Sage.

Drew, Jesse. (1998). *Global Communications in the Post-Industrial Age: A Study of the Communications Strategies of U.S. Labor Organizations*, Ph.D. Dissertation, University of Texas.

Drexler, K. Eric. (1987). *Engines of Creation: The Coming Era of Nanotechnology*. New York: Anchor Books.

Drucker, Peter. (1993). *Post-Capitalist Society*. New York: HarperBusiness.

Dunnigan, James F., and Austin Bay. (1992). *From Shield to Storm: High-Tech Weapons, Military Strategy, and Coalition Warfare in the Persian Gulf*. New York: Morrow.

Dyer-Witheford, Nick. (1999). *Cyber-Marx: Cycles and Circuits of Struggle in High-Technology Capitalism*. Urbana and Chicago: University of Illinois Press.

_____. (2000). *The Contest for General Intellect*. Chicago: University of Illinois Press.

Dyson, George B. (1996). *Good Natured: The Origins of Right and Wrong in Humans and Other Animals*. Cambridge, MA: Harvard University Press.

_____. (1997). *Darwin among the Machines: The Evolution of Global Intelligence*. Reading, MA: Perseus Books.

Ebert, Teresa L. (1996). *Ludic Feminism and After: Postmodernism, Desire, and Labor in Late Capitalism*. Ann Arbor: University of Michigan Press.

Edwards, Paul. (1996). *The Closed World: Computers and the Politics of Discourse in Cold War America*. Cambridge, MA: MIT Press.

Ehrenfeld, David. (1981). *The Arrogance of Humanism*. Oxford, UK: Oxford University Press.

Eigen, Manfred. (1971). "Molecular Self-Organization and the Early Stages of Evolution," *Quarterly Review of Biophysics, 4*:

Eisenstein, Elizabeth L. (1983). *The Printing Revolution in Early Modern Europe*. Cambridge, UK: Cambridge University Press.

Ellul, Jacques. (1964). *The Technological Society*. New York: Knopf.

Erlich, Paul R. (1968). *The Population Bomb*. New York: Ballantine Books.

Erlich, Paul R., Anne H. Erlich, and John P. Holdren. (1993). "Availability, Entropy, and the Laws of Thermodynamics" in *Valuing the Earth: Economics, Ecology, Ethics* (pp. 69–73), ed. Herman E. Daly and Kenneth N. Townsend. Cambridge, MA: MIT Press.

Esterbrook, Gregg. (1995). *A Moment on Earth: The Coming Age of Environmental Optimism*. New York: Viking Press.

Fanon, Frantz. (1967). *For a Dying Colonialism*. New York: Grove Press.

Featherstone, Mike, ed. (1990). *Global Culture: Nationalism, Globalization, and Modernity*. London: Sage.

Featherstone, Mike, Scott Lash, and Roland Robertson, eds. (1995). *Global Modernities*. London: Sage.

Feenberg, Andrew. (1991). *Critical Theory of Technology*. New York: Oxford University Press.

_____. (1995). *Alternative Modernity*. Berkeley and Los Angeles: University of California Press.

_____. (1999). *Questioning Technology*. New York and London: Routledge.

Ferris, Timothy. (1997). *The Whole Shebang: A State-of-the-Universe(s) Report*. New York: Simon and Schuster.

Feyerabend, Paul. (1978a). *Against Method: Outline of an Anarchistic Theory of Knowledge*. London: Verso Books.

_____. (1978b). *Science in a Free Society*. London: Verso Books.

Fiske, John. (1994). *Media Matters*. Minneapolis, MN: University of Minnesota Press.

FitzGerald, Francis. (2000). *Way Out There in the Blue*. New York: Simon and Schuster.

Foster, Hal. (1983). "Introduction," in *The Anti-Aesthetic* (pp. ix–xvi), ed. Hal Foster. Port Townsend, WA: Bay Press.

Foucault, Michel. (1972a). *The Archaeology of Knowledge*. New York: Pantheon Books.

_____. (1972b). *Power/Knowledge*. New York: Pantheon Books.

_____. (1973). *The Order of Things*. New York: Vintage Books.

_____. (1975). *Discipline and Punish*. New York: Pantheon Books.

_____. (1977). *Language, Counter-Memory, Practice*. Ithaca, NY: Cornell University Press.

_____. (1980). *The History of Sexuality: Vol. 1*. New York: Vintage Books.

Fouts, Roger. (1997). *Next of Kin: What Chimpanzees Have Taught Me about Who We Are*. New York: Morrow.

Fox, Michael W. (1999). *Beyond Evolution: The Genetically Altered Future of Plants, Animals, the Earth . . . and Humans*. New York: Lyons Press.

Frankel, Boris. (1987). *The Post-Industrial Utopians*. Cambridge, UK: Polity Press.

Franklin, H. Bruce. (1995). *Future Perfect*. New Brunswick, NJ: Rutgers University Press.

Fredericks, Howard. (1994). *North American NGO Networking against NAFTA: The Use of Computer Communications in Cross-Border Coalition Building*, paper presented at the XVII International Congress of the Latin American Studies Association.

Friedman, Norman. (1991). *Desert Victory*. Annapolis, MD: Naval Institute Press.

Friedman, Thomas. (1999). *The Lexus and the Olive Tree*. New York: Farrar Straus Giroux.

Frye, Northrop. (1976). *The Sacred Scripture*. Cambridge, MA: Harvard University Press.

Fukuyama, Francis. (1992). *The End of History and the Last Man*. New York: Free Press.

Fuller, Steve. (1991). *Social Epistemology*. Bloomington: Indiana University Press.

_____. (1995). *Philosophy of Science and Its Discontents*. New York: Guilford Press.

Frye, Marilyn. (1983). "In and out of Harm's Way: Arrogance and Love," in *The Politics of Reality* (pp. 66–72). Trumansburg, NY: Crossing Press.

Gane, Mike. (1991). *Baudrillard: Critical and Fatal Theory*. London: Routledge.

_____, ed. (1993). *Baudrillard Live: Selected Interviews*. London: Routledge.

Garrett, Laurie. (1994). *The Coming Plague: Newly Emerging Diseases in a World out of Balance*. New York: Penguin Books.

Gates, Bill. (1995). *The Road Ahead*. New York: Viking Press.

_____. (1999). *Business at the Speed of Thought*. New York: Viking Press.

Gelernter, David. (1992). *Mirror Worlds*. New York: Oxford University Press.

_____. (1997). *Machine: Beauty, Elegance, and the Heart of Computing*. New York: Basic Books.

Gell-Mann, Murray. (1994). *The Quark and the Jaguar: Adventures in the Simple and the Complex*. New York: Freeman.

Gerbner, George. (1992). "Persian Gulf War: The Movie," in *Triumph of the Image* (pp. 243–262), ed. Hadmid Mowlana, George Gerbner, and Herbert I. Schiller. Boulder, CO: Westview Press.

Gershenfeld, Neil. (1999). *When Things Start to Think*. New York: Holt.

Gibson, J. William. (1987). *The Perfect War*. New York: Morrow.

_____. (1994). *Warrior Dreams: Violence and Manhood in Post-Vietnam America*. New York: Hill & Wang.

_____. (2000). "Crises in American War Culture at the Millennium," *Veterans for Peace*. Vol. 1, No. 1. (Spring): 1-8, 17-18.

Gibson, William. (1984). *Neuromancer*. New York: Dell.

_____. (1999). *All Tomorrow's Parties*. New York: Putnam.

Giddens, Anthony. (1990). *Consequences of Modernity*. Cambridge, UK, and Palo Alto, CA: Polity Press and Stanford University Press.

Gilder, George. (1989). *Microcosm*. New York: Simon and Schuster.

Gilroy, Paul. (1993). *The Black Atlantic: Modernity and Double Consciousness*. Cambridge, MA: Harvard University Press.

Giroux, Henry. (2000). *Impure Acts: The Practical Politics of Cultural Studies*. London and New York: Routledge.

Gitlin, Todd, ed. (1986). *Watching Television*. New York: Pantheon Books.

Glanz, James. (2001). "Tiniest of Particles Pokes Big Hole in Physics Theory," *www.nytimes.com/2001/02/09/science/09PHYS.html*.

Gleick, James. (1987). *Chaos*. New York: Viking Penguin.

Goodall, Jane. (1971). *In the Shadow of Man*. Boston: Houghton Mifflin.

Goodwin, Brian. (1994). *How the Leopard Changed Its Spots: The Evolution of Complexity*. New York: Scribner's.

Gottdiener, Mark. (1995). *Postmodern Semiotics*. Oxford, UK: Blackwell.

_____. (1997). *The Theming of America: Dreams, Visions, and Commercial Spaces*. Boulder, CO: Westview Press.

Gottdiener, Mark, et al. (1999). *Las Vegas: The Social Production of an All-American City*. Oxford: Blackwell.

Gould, Stephen Jay. (1980). *The Panda's Thumb: More Reflections in Natural History*. New York: Norton.

_____. (1993). "Dinomania," *New York Review of Books*, August 12: 51–55.

_____. (1997). *Questioning the Millennium: A Rationalist's Guide to a Precisely Arbitrary Countdown*. New York: Harmony Books.

Grabbe, Jo. Orlin. (1994). "In Praise of Chaos," *Liberty*, March: 17–20.

Gramsci, Antonio. (1971). *Prison Notebooks*. New York: International Publishers.

Gray, Chris Hables. (1989). "The Cyborg Soldiers: The U.S. Military and the Postmodern Warrior," in *Cyborg Worlds: The Military Information Society* (pp. 159–178), ed. Les Levidow and Kevin Robins. London: Free Association Books.

_____. (1997). *Postmodern War*. New York: Guilford Press.

Gray, Chris Hables, Heidi J. Figueroa-Sarriera, and Steven Mentor, eds. (1995). *The Cyborg Handbook*. London and New York: Routledge.

Greider, William. (1998). *Fortress America: The American Military and the Conse-quences of Peace.* New York: Public Affairs.

Grewal, Inderpal, and Caren Kaplan, eds. (1994). *Scattered Hegemonies: Postmodernity and Transnational Feminist Practices.* Minneapolis: University of Minnesota Press.

Gribbin, John. (1993). *In the Beginning: The Birth of the Living Universe.* Boston: Back Bay Books.

Griffin, David Ray, ed. (1988a). *The Reenchantment of Science: Postmodern Proposals.* Albany: State University of New York Press.

_____, ed. (1988b). *Spirituality and Science: Postmodern Visions.* Albany: State University of New York Press.

Gross, Paul R., and Norman Levitt. (1994). *Higher Superstition: The Academic Left and Its Quarrels with Science.* Baltimore: Johns Hopkins University Press.

Grossberg, Lawrence. (1987). "The In-Difference of Television," *Screen, 28*(2): 28–46.

Gunther, Judith, Suzanne Kantra, and Robert Langreth. (1994). "Digital Warrior," *Popular Science,* September: 60–65.

Guth, Alan H. (1997). *The Inflationary Universe: The Quest for a New Theory of Cosmic Origins.* Reading, MA: Addison Wesley.

Habermas, Jürgen. (1979). *Communication and the Evolution of Society.* Boston: Beacon Press.

_____. (1984). *Theory of Communicative Action: Vol. 1.* Boston: Beacon Press.

_____. (1987). *Theory of Communicative Action: Vol. 2.* Boston: Beacon Press.

_____. (1989). *The Public Sphere.* Cambridge, MA: MIT Press.

Hafner, Katie, and John Markoff. (1991). *Cyberpunk: Outlaws and Hackers on the Computer Frontier.* New York: Simon and Schuster.

Haining, Peter, ed. (1994). *The Frankenstein Omnibus.* Edison, NJ: Chartwell Books.

Hall, Stephen S. (1993). *Mapping the Next Millennium.* New York: Vintage.

Hammond, Allen. (1998). *Which World? Scenarios for the 21st Century: Global Destinies, Regional Chorus.* Washington, DC: Island Press.

Haraway, Donna. (1989). *Primate Visions: Gender, Race, and Nature in the World of Modern Science.* New York: Routledge.

_____. (1991). *Simians, Cyborgs, and Women: The Reinvention of Nature.* New York: Routledge.

_____. (1997). *Modest_Witness@Second_Millennium: FemaleMan Meets OncoMouse: Feminism and Technoscience.* New York: Routledge.

Harding, Sandra. (1986). *The Science Question in Feminism.* Ithaca, NY: Cornell University Press.

_____. (1991). *Whose Science? Whose Knowledge? Thinking from Women's Lives.* Ithaca, NY: Cornell University Press.

_____, ed. (1993). *The "Racial" Economy of Science.* Bloomington: Indiana University Press.

_____. (1994). "Is Science Multicultural? Challenges, Resources, Opportunities, Uncertainties," *Configurations,* 2:301–330.

_____. (1998). *Is Science Multicultural? Postcolonialism, Feminism, and Epistemologies.* Bloomington: Indiana University Press.

Harrison, Brady. (2000). "'This movie is a thing of mine': Simulations, Subjectivity, and History in *Dispatches,*" in *The Vietnam War and Postmodernity* (pp. 101–116), ed. Michael Bibby. Amherst: University of Massachusetts Press.

Harvey, David. (1989). *The Condition of Postmodernity.* Oxford, UK: Blackwell.

Hawking, Stephen W. (1988). *A Brief History of Time: From the Big Bang to Black Holes.* New York: Bantam Books.

Hawkins, Michael. (1997). *Hunting Down the Universe: The Missing Mass, Primordial Black Holes, and Other Dark Matters.* Reading, MA: Helix Books.

Hawley, T. M. (1992). *Against the Fires of Hell: The Environmental Disaster of the Gulf War.* New York: Harcourt Brace Jovanovich.

Hayles, N. Katherine. (1984). *The Cosmic Web: Scientific Field Models and Literacy Strategies in the Twentieth Century.* Ithaca, NY: Cornell University Press.

_____. (1990). *Chaos Bound: Orderly Disorder in Contemporary Literature and Science.* Ithaca, NY: Cornell University Press.

_____, ed. (1991). *Chaos and Order: Complex Dynamics in Literature and Science.* Chicago: University of Chicago Press.

_____. (1999). *How We Became Posthuman: Virtual Bodies in Cybernetics, Literature, and Informatics.* Chicago: University of Chicago Press.

Heidegger, Martin. (1962). *Being and Time.* New York: Harper & Row.

_____. (1977). *The Question Concerning Technology.* New York: Harper & Row.

Heikal, Mohammed. (1992). *Illusions of Triumph: An Arab View of the Gulf War.* New York: HarperCollins.

Heisenberg, Werner. (1958). *Physics and Philosophy.* New York: Harper & Row.

_____. (1971). *Physics and Beyond.* New York: Harper & Row.

Held, David. (1995). *Democracy and the Global Order.* Cambridge, UK, and Palo Alto, CA: Polity Press and Stanford University Press.

Held, David, Anthony McGrew, David Goldblatt, and Jonathan Perraton. (1999). *Global Transformations.* Palo Alto, CA, and Cambridge, UK: Stanford University Press and Polity Press.

Hendin, Josephine. (1978). *Vulnerable People: A View of American Fiction since 1945.* New York: Oxford Univerity Press.

Henriksen, Margot. (1997). *Dr. Strangelove's America.* Berkeley and Los Angeles: University of California Press.

Herbert, Nick. (1985). *Quantum Realities: Beyond the New Physics.* New York: Anchor Books.

Herr, Michael. (1978). *Dispatches.* New York: Avon.

Hersh, Seymour. (1998). *Against All Enemies. Gulf War Syndrome: The War between America's Ailing Veterans and Their Government.* New York: Simon and Schuster.

Hesse, Mary. (1980). *Revolutions and Reconstructions in the Philosophy of Science.* Bloomington: Indiana University Press.

Hey, Tony, and Patrick Walters. (1997). *Einstein's Mirror.* Cambridge, UK: Cambridge University Press.

Hirst, Paul, and Grahame Thompson. (1996). *Globalization in Question.* Cambridge, UK: Polity Press.

Ho, Mae-Wan. (1998). *Genetic Engineering: Dream or Nightmare? The Brave New World of Bad Science and Big Business.* Bath, UK: Gateway Books.

Horgan, John. (1996). *The End of Science: Facing the Limits of Knowledge in the Twilight of the Scientific Age.* Reading, MA: Helix Books.

Horkheimer, Max, and Theodor W. Adorno. (1972). *Dialectic of Enlightenment.* New York: Continuum.

Hutchison, Micheal. (1991). *Mega-Brain: New Tools and Techniques for Brain Growth and Mind Expansion.* New York: Ballantine Books.

Huxley, Aldous. (1958). *Brave New World Revisited.* New York: Harper and Row.

Huxley, Aldous. (1989 [1931]). *Brave New World.* New York: HarperPerennial.

Ignatieff, Michael. (2000). *Virtual War: Kosovo and Beyond.* New York: Henry Holt.

Jakitis, John M. (1986). "Two Versions of an Unfinished War," *Cultural Critique, 3*: 191–210.

James, George. (1992). *Stolen Legacy: Greek Philosophy Is Stolen Egyptian Philosophy.* Lawrenceville, NJ: Africa World Press.

Jameson, Fredric. (1981). *The Political Unconscious.* Ithaca, NY: Cornell University Press.

_____. (1984). "Postmodernism, or The Cultural Logic of Late Capitalism," *New Left Review, 146*: 53–92.

_____. (1988). "Cognitive Mapping," in *Marxism and the Interpretation of Culture* (pp. 347–358), ed. Cary Nelson and Lawrence Grossberg. Urbana: University of Illinois Press.

_____. (1991). *Postmodernism, or, The Cultural Logic of Late Capitalism.* Durham, NC, and London: Duke University Press.

Jaspers, Karl. (1961). *The Atom Bomb and the Future of Man.* Chicago: University of Chicago Press.

Jeffords, Susan. (1989). *The Remasculinization of America.* Bloomington: Indiana University Press.

Jeffords, Susan, and Lauren Rabinovitz, eds. (1994). *Seeing through the Media: The Persian Gulf War.* New Brunswick, NJ: Rutgers University Press.

Johnson, George. (1995). *Fire in the Mind: Science, Faith, and the Search for Order.* New York: Vintage Books.

Johnson, Steven. (1997). *Interface Culture: How New Technology Transforms the Way We Create and Communicate.* New York: Dimensions.

Joy, Bill. (2000). "Why the Future Doesn't Need Us," *Wired,* July: 238–246.

Kaku, Michio. (1994). *Hyperspace: A Scientific Odyssey through Parallel Universes, Time Warps, and the 10th Dimension.* New York: Anchor Books.

_____. (1997). *Visions: How Science Will Revolutionize the 21st Century.* New York: Anchor Books.

Kauffman, Stuart A. (1991). "Antichaos and Adaptation," *Scientific American,* August: 78–84.

_____. (1995). *At Home in the Universe: The Search for the Laws of Self-Organization and Complexity.* New York: Oxford University Press.

Kaufman, Wallace. (1994). *No Turning Back: Dismantling the Fantasies of Environmental Thinking.* New York: Basic Books.

Keeble, Richard. (1999). *Secret State, Silent Press: New Militarism, the Gulf and the Modern Image of Warfare.* Luton, UK: University of Luton Press.

Keen, Sam. (1986). *Faces of the Enemy.* New York: Harper & Row.

Keller, Evelyn Fox. (1983). *A Feeling for the Organism: The Life and Work of Barbara McClintock.* New York: Freeman.

Kellner, Douglas. (1989a). *Critical Theory, Marxism, and Modernity.* Cambridge, UK, and Baltimore: Polity Press and Johns Hopkins University Press.

_____. (1989b). *Jean Baudrillard: From Marxism to Post-Modernism and Beyond.*

Cambridge, UK, and Palo Alto, CA: Polity Press and Stanford University Press.

_____. (1989c). "Body Invaders/Cronenberg/Panic Film"; *Canadian Journal of Social and Political Theory*, Vol. 13, No. 3: 89–101.

_____. (1990). *Television and the Crisis of Democracy.* Boulder, CO: Westview Press.

_____. (1992). *The Persian Gulf TV War.* Boulder, CO: Westview Press.

_____, ed. (1994). *Baudrillard. A Critical Reader.* Oxford: Blackwell.

_____. (1995a). *Media Culture.* London and New York: Routledge.

_____. (1995b). "Intellectuals and New Technologies," *Media, Culture, and Society,* 17: 201–217.

_____. (1996). "Advertising, Fashion, and Consumer Culture," in *Questioning the Media: A Critical Introduction* (2nd, rev. ed., pp. 242–254), ed. John Downing, Ali Mohammadi, and Annabelle Sreberny-Mohammadi. London: Sage.

_____. (1997). "Intellectuals, the New Public Spheres, and Technopolitics," *New Political Science,* 41–42: 169–188.

_____. (1998). "Multiple Literacies and Critical Pedagogy in a Multicultural Society," *Educational Theory,* 48(1): 103–122.

_____. (1999). "Virilio, War, and Technology: Some Critical Reflections," *Theory, Culture and Society, 16*(5–6): 103–125. Reprinted in Armitage, John, ed. (2000). *Paul Virilio: From Modernism to Hypermodernism and Beyond* (pp. 103–125). London: Sage.

_____. (2000). "New Technologies/New Literacies: Reconstructing Education for the New Millennium," *Teaching Education, 11*(3): 245–265.

_____. (forthcoming). *36 Days: Media Spectacle and the Theft of Election 2000.* Lanham, MD: Rowman and Littlefield.

Kellner, Douglas, and Michael Ryan. (1988). *Camera Politica: The Politics and Ideologies of Contemporary Hollywood Film.* Bloomington: Indiana University Press.

Kellner, Douglas, and Dan Streible, eds. (2000). *Film, Art and Politics: An Emile de Antonio Reader.* Minneapolis: University of Minnesota Press.

Kelly, Kevin. (1995). *Out of Control: The New Biology of Machines, Social Systems, and the Economic World.* New York: Addison Wesley.

_____. (1998). *New Rules for the New Economy.* New York: Viking Press.

_____. (2000). "Pro-Choice: The Promise of Technology," *Organization and Environment,* 12(4), 428–429.

Kendrick, Michelle. (1994). "Kicking the Vietnam Syndrome," in *Seeing through the Media: The Persian Gulf War,* ed. Susan Jeffords and Lauren Rabinovitz. New Brunswick, NJ: Rutgers University Press.

Kerman, Judith B., ed. (1997). *Retrofitting "Blade Runner."* Bowling Green, OH: Popular Press.

Khury, Muin J., and Ruth S. Thornburg. (2001). "Will Genetics Revolutionize Medicine?," www.geneletter.com/01-02-01/features/prn_medicine.html.

King, Anthony D., ed. (1991). *Culture, Globalization and the World-System: Contemporary Conditions for the Representation of Identity.* Binghamton: Art Department, State University of New York.

Klemm, Friedrich. (1964). *A History of Western Technology.* Cambridge, MA: MIT Press.

Knabb, Ken, ed. (1981). *Situationist International Anthology.* Berkeley, CA: Bureau of Public Secrets.

Knightly, Philip. (1975). *The First Casualty.* New York: Harcourt Brace Jovanovich.

Kolata, Gina. (1998). *Clone: The Road to Dolly and the Path Ahead.* New York: Morrow.

Kosko, Bart. (1993). *Fuzzy Thinking: The New Science of Fuzzy Logic.* New York: Hyperion.

Krader, Lawrence. (1982). "Theories of Evolution, Revolution and the State," in Eric J. Hobsbawn, editer, *The History of Marxism.* Bloomington, Ind.: Indiana University Press: 192-226.

Kroker, Arthur. (1992). *The Possessed Individual.* New York: St. Martin's Press.

Kroker, Arthur, and Michael Weinstein. (1994). *Data Crash.* New York: St. Martin's Press.

Kuberski, Philip Francis. (1986). "Genres of Vietnam," *Cultural Correspondence,* 3: 168–188.

Kuhn, Thomas S. (1970). *The Structure of Scientific Revolutions* (2d ed.). Chicago: University of Chicago Press.

Kurzweil, Ray. (1990). *The Age of Intelligent Machines.* Cambridge, Mass: MIT Press.

_____. (1999). *The Age of Spiritual Machines: When Computers Exceed Human Intelligence.* Cambridge, MA: MIT Press.

Landow, George. (1995). *Hypertext 2.0.* Baltimore: Johns Hopkins University Press.

Lanham, Richard. (1993). *The Electronic Word: Democracy, Technology, and the Arts.* Chicago: University of Chicago Press.

Lash, Scott. (1990). *A Sociology of Postmodernism.* London and New York: Routledge.

Lash, Scott, and John Urry. (1987). *The End of Organized Capitalism.* Cambridge: Polity Press.

_____. (1994). *Economies of Signs and Space.* London: Sage.

Latour, Bruno. (1987). *Science in Action: How to Follow Scientists and Engineers through Society.* Cambridge, MA: Harvard University Press.

Leakey, Richard, and Roger Lewin. (1995). *The Sixth Great Extinction: Patterns of Life and the Future of Humankind.* New York: Doubleday.

Lechner, Frank J., and John Boli, eds. (2000). *The Globalization Reader.* Malden, MA and Oxford, UK: Blackwell.

Lederman, Muriel, and Ingrid Bartsch, eds. (2001). *The Science and Gender Reader.* New York: Routledge.

Lefebvre, Henri. (1984). *Everyday Life in the Modern World.* New Brunswick, NJ: Transaction Books.

_____. (1991 [1947; 1958]). *Critique of Everyday Life.* London: Verso Books.

Lefkowitz, Mary. (1997). *Not Out of Africa: How Afrocentrism Became an Excuse to Teach Myth as History.* New York: Basic Books.

Lefkowitz, Mary, and Guy MacLean Rogers. (1996). *Black Athena Revisited.* Chapel Hill: University of North Carolina Press.

Leiss, William. (1974). *The Domination of Nature.* Boston: Beacon Press.

Leopold, Aldo. (1989). *A Sand County Almanac.* New York: Oxford University Press.

Lessard, Bill, and Steve Baldwin. (2000). *Net Slaves: True Tales of Working the Web.* New York: McGraw Hill.

Leverenz, David. (1976). "On Trying to Read *Gravity's Rainbow*," in *Mindful Pleasures: Essays in Thomas Pynchon* (pp. 229–250), ed. George Levine and David Leverenz. Boston and Toronto: Little, Brown.

Levidow, Les, and Kevin Robins, eds. (1989). *Cyborg Worlds: The Military Information Society*. London: Free Association Books.

Levin, Harry. (1966). "What Was Modernism?," in *Refractions* (pp. 28–52). New York: Oxford University Press.

Levins, Richard, and Richard Lewontin. (1985). *The Dialectical Biologist*. Cambridge, MA: Harvard University Press.

Levy, Stephen. (1985). *Hackers*. New York: Dell Books.

_____. (1992). *Artificial Life: A Report from the Frontier Where Computers Meet Biology*. New York: Random House.

Lewis, Justin, Sut Jhally, and Michael Morgan. (1991). *The Gulf War: A Study of the Media, Public Opinion, and Public Knowledge*. Amherst, MA: Center for the Study of Communication.

Lewis, Lisa. (1990). *Gender Politics and MTV*. Philadelphia: Temple University Press.

Lewontin, Richard C. (1992). *Biology as Ideology: The Doctrine of DNA*. New York: HarperCollins.

_____. (1997). "Billions and Billions of Demons" (www.nybooks.com/nyrev/WWWarchdisplay.cgi?19970109028R).

Lewontin, Richard C., Steven Rose, and Leon J. Kamin. (1984). *Not in Our Genes: Biology, Ideology, and Human Nature*. New York: Pantheon Books.

Lovelock, James F. (1979). *Gaia: A New Look at Life on Earth*. Oxford, UK: Oxford University Press.

_____. (1988). *The Ages of Gaia: A Biography of Our Living Earth*. New York: Norton.

Lowenthal, Leo. (1961). *Literature, Popular Culture, and Society*. Englewood Cliffs, NJ: Prentice-Hall.

Lukács, Georg. (1964a). *Studies in European Realism*. New York: Grosset & Dunlap.

Lukács, Georg. (1964b). *Realism in Our Time*. New York: Harper.

Lyotard, Jean François. (1984). *The Postmodern Condition*. Minneapolis: University of Minnesota Press.

_____. (1986–1987). "Rules and Paradoxes and Svelte Appendix," *Cultural Critique*, 5: 209–219.

MacArthur, John R. (1992). *Second Front: Censorship and Propaganda in the Gulf War*. New York: Hill & Wang.

Maddox, John. (1998). *What Remains to Be Discovered: Mapping the Secrets of the Universe, the Origins of Life, and the Future of the Human Race*. New York: Free Press.

Mandel, Ernest. (1975). *Late Capitalism*. London: New Left Books.

Mander, Jerry. (1978). *Four Arguments for the Elimination of Television*. New York: Morrow.

_____. (1991). *In the Absence of the Sacred*. San Francisco: Sierra Club Books.

Mander, Jerry, and Edward Goldsmith. (1996). *The Case against the Global Economy*. San Francisco: Sierra Club Books.

Marcus, Greil. (1989). *Lipstick Traces*. Cambridge, MA: Harvard University Press.

Marcuse, Herbert. (1955). *Eros and Civilization*. Boston: Beacon Press.

_____. (1964). *One-Dimensional Man*. Boston: Beacon Press.

_____. (1968). *Negations.* Boston: Beacon Press.

_____. (1969). *An Essay on Liberation.* Boston: Beacon Press.

_____. (1972). *Counterrevolution and Revolt.* Boston: Beacon Press.

_____. (1978). *The Aesthetic Dimension.* Boston: Beacon Press.

_____. (1998 [1941]). "Some Social Implications of Modern Technology," in *Technology, War and Fascism: Collected Papers of Herbert Marcuse, Vol. 1* (pp. 39–66), ed. Douglas Kellner. London and New York: Routledge.

Margulis, Lynn, and Dorion Sagan. (1986). *Microcosmos: Four Billion Years of Microbial Evolution.* Berkeley and Los Angeles: University of California Press.

Marx, Karl. (1973). *Grundrisse.* Baltimore: Penquin Books.

_____. (1975). *Collected Works.* Vol 1. New York: International Publishers.

_____. (1976). *Collected Works.* Vol 6.. New York: International Publishers.

Marx, Karl, and Friedrich Engels. (1978). *The Marx–Engels Reader* (2nd ed.), ed. Robert C. Tucker. New York: Norton.

Mason, Jim. (1993). *An Unnatural Order. Uncovering the Roots of Our Domination of Nature and Each Other.* New York: Simon and Schuster.

Masson, Jeffrey Moussaieff, and Susan McCarthy. (1995). *When Elephants Weep: The Emotional Lives of Animals.* New York: Delacorte Press.

Matson, Floyd D. (1966). *The Broken Image: Man, Science and Society.* New York: Anchor Books.

Mayr, Ernst. (1988). *Toward a New Philosophy of Biology: Observations of an Evolutionist.* Cambridge, MA: Harvard University Press.

Mazlish, Bruce. (1993). *The Fourth Discontinuity.* New Haven, CT, and London: Yale University Press.

Mazurek, Jan, and Nicholas Ashford. (2000). *Making Microchips: Policy, Globalization, and Economic Restructuring in the Semiconductor Industry.* Cambridge, MA: MIT Press.

McCaffery, Larry. (1986). *Introduction to Postmodern Fiction: A Bio-Bibliographical Guide.* New York: Greenwood Press.

_____. (1991). *Storming the Reality Studio.* Durham, NC, and London: Duke University Press.

McCarthy, Wil. (1998). *Bloom.* New York: Random House.

McDougall, Walter A. (1985). . . . *The Heavens and the Earth: A Political History of the Space Age.* New York: Basic Books.

McHale, Brian. (1987). *Postmodernist Fiction.* New York and London: Methuen.

_____. (1992). *Constructing Postmodernism.* New York and London: Routledge.

McLuhan, Marshall. (1962). *The Gutenberg Galaxy.* New York: Signet Books.

_____. (1964). *Understanding Media: The Extensions of Man.* New York: Signet Books.

Melman, Seymour. (1975). *Pentagon Capitalism: The Management of the New Imperialism.* New York: Simon and Schuster.

_____. (1985). *The Permanent War Economy: American Capitalism in Decline.* New York: Simon and Schuster.

Mendelson, Edward. (1976). "Gravity's Encyclopedia," in *Thomas Pynchon's "Gravity's Rainbow"* (pp. 161–196), ed. Harold Bloom. New York: Chelsea House.

Merchant, Carolyn. (1983). *The Death of Nature: Women, Ecology, and the Scientific Revolution.* New York: Harper & Row.

Mills, C. Wright. (1956). *The Power Elite.* Boston: Beacon Press.

Mitchell, W. J. T. (1998). *The Last Dinosaur Book: The Life and Times of a Cultural Icon.* Chicago: University of Chicago Press.

Monbiot, George. (1999). "Labs Are Full of Researchers Who Can't See Beyond the Microscope," www.iatp.org/iatp/News/news.cfm?News_ID=187.

Monod, Jacques. (1971). *Chance and Necessity.* New York: Knopf.

Moody, Kim. (1988). *An Injury to One.* London: Verso Books.

Moore, Thomas. (1987). *The Style of Connectedness: "Gravity's Rainbow" and Thomas Pynchon.* Columbia: University of Missouri Press.

Moravec, Hans. (1988). *Mind Children: The Future of Robot and Human Intelligence.* Cambridge, MA: Harvard University Press.

Mowlana, Hadmid, George Gerbner, and Herbert I. Schiller, eds. (1992). *Triumph of the Image.* Boulder, CO: Westview Press.

Muddiman, Dave. (1998). "The Universal Library as Modern Utopia: The Information Society of H. G. Wells," *Library History,* 14: 85"101.

Mumford, Lewis. (1963 [1934]). *Technics and Civilization.* New York: Harcourt, Brace, and World.

———. (1964). *The Myth of the Machine: The Pentagon of Power.* New York: Harcourt, Brace, and Jovanovitch.

Nash, Roderick. (1989). *The Rights of Nature: A History of Environmental Ethics.* Madison: University of Wisconsin Press.

Negri, Antonio. (1984). *Marx beyond Marx: Lessons on the Grundrisse.* New York: Autonomedia.

Negroponte, Nicholas. (1995). *Being Digital.* New York: Knopf.

Nerlich, Michael. (1987). *The Ideology of Adventure: Studies in Modern Consciousness, 1100–1750* (2 vols.). Minneapolis: University of Minnesota Press.

Noble, David. (1998). *The Religion of Technology.* New York: Knopf.

Norris, Christopher. (1990). *What's Wrong with Postmodernism?* Baltimore: Johns Hopkins University Press.

Nuttall, Jeff. (1968). *Bomb Culture.* New York: Delta.

Oelschlaeger, Max. (1991). *The Idea of Wilderness: From Prehistory to the Age of Ecology.* New Haven, CT: Yale University Press.

Offe, Claus. (1985). *Disorganized Capitalism.* Cambridge, UK: Polity Press.

O'Neill, John. (1996). "Dinosaurs-R-Us: The (Un)Natural History of *Jurassic Park,*" in *Monster Theory: Reading Culture,* ed. Jeffrey Jerome Cohen. Minneapolis: University of Minnesota Press.

Ordway, Frederick I., and Mitchell R. Sharpe. (1979). *The Rocket Team.* New York: Random House.

Paul, Gregory S., and Earl D. Cox. (1996). *Beyond Humanism: CyberEvolution and Future Minds.* Rockland, MA: Charles River Media.

Peat, David E. (1988). *Superstrings and the Search for the Theory of Everything.* Lincolnwood, IL: Contemporary Books.

Pence, Gregory E. (1998). *Who's Afraid of Human Cloning?* Lanham, MD: Rowman and Littlefield.

Plant, Sadie. (1992). *The Most Radical Gesture.* London and New York: Routledge.

Polanyi, Karl. (1957). *The Great Transformation: The Political and Economic Origins of Our Time.* Boston: Beacon Press.

Popper, Karl R. (1963). *Conjectures and Refutations: The Growth of Scientific Knowledge.* Routledge and Kegan Paul.

Poster, Mark. (1990). *The Mode of Information.* Cambridge, UK, and Chicago: Polity Press and University of Chicago Press.

_____. (1996). "Postmodern Virtualities," in *Cyberspace/Cyberbodies/Cyberpunk,* ed. Mike Featherstone and Roger Burrows. London and Thousand Oaks, CA: Sage.

Postman, Neil. (1985). *Amusing Ourselves to Death: Public Discourse in the Age of Show Business.* New York: Viking Press.

_____. (1992). *Technopoly: The Surrender of Culture to Technology.* New York: Vintage Books.

Poundstone, William. (1999). *Carl Sagan: A Life in the Cosmos.* New York: Holt.

Powell, Colin. (1996). *My American Journey.* New York: Ballantine.

Prigogine, Ilya. (1996). *The End of Certainty: Time, Chaos, and the New Laws of Nature.* New York: Free Press.

Prigogine, Ilya, and Isabelle Stengers. (1984). *Order Out of Chaos.* New York: Bantam Books.

Pynchon, Thomas. (1963). *V.* New York: Lippincott.

_____. (1973). *Gravity's Rainbow.* New York: Viking Compass.

_____. (1984). *Slow Learner: Early Stories.* Boston: Little, Brown.

_____. (1990). *Vineland.* Boston: Little, Brown.

Regis, Ed. (1995). *Nano: The Emerging Science of Nanotechnology.* Boston: Little, Brown.

Reich, Charles A. (1970). *The Greening of America.* New York: Random House.

Rheingold, Howard. (2000). *The Virtual Community* (2nd ed.). Cambridge, MA: MIT Press.

Rhodes, Richard. (1995). *The Making of the Atomic Bomb.* New York: Touchstone.

_____. (1999). *Visions of Technology.* New York: Simon and Schuster.

Ricoeur, Paul. (1984). *Time and Narrative: Vol. 1.* Chicago: University of Chicago Press.

Ridley, Matt. (1999). *Genome: The Autobiography of a Species in 23 Chapters.* New York: HarperCollins.

Rifkin, Jeremy. (1989). *Entropy: Into the Greenhouse World.* New York: Bantam Books.

_____. (1992). *Beyond Beef: The Rise and Fall of the Cattle Culture.* New York: Dutton.

_____. (1995). *The End of Work: The Decline of the Global Labor Force and the Dawn of the Post-Market Era.* New York: Tarcher/Putnam.

_____. (1998). *The Biotech Century: Harnessing the Gene and Remaking the World.* New York: Tarcher/Putnam.

Ritzer, George. (1998). *Enchanting a Disenchanted World: Revolutionizing the Means of Consumption.* Thousand Oaks, CA: Pine Forge Press.

Robertson, Roland, ed. (1991). *Globalization.* London: Sage.

Robins, Kevin, and Frank Webster. (1999). *Times of the Technoculture.* New York: Routledge.

Rochlin, Eugene. (1997). *Trapped in the Net.* Princeton, NJ: Princeton University Press.

Rodley, Chris. (1992). *Cronenberg on Cronenberg.* Boston and London: Faber & Faber.

Roegen, Nicholas Georgescu. (1993a). "The Entropy Law and the Economic

Problem," in *Valuing the Earth: Economics, Ecology, Ethics* (pp. 75–88), ed. Herman E. Daly and Kenneth N. Townsend. Cambridge, MA: MIT Press.

———. (1993b). "Selections from 'Energy and Economic Myths,' " in *Valuing the Earth: Economics, Ecology, Ethics* (pp. 89–112), ed. Herman E. Daly and Kenneth N. Townsend. Cambridge, MA: MIT Press.

Rollin, Bernard. (1995). *The Frankenstein Syndrome: Ethical and Social Issues in the Genetic Engineering of Animals.* Cambridge, UK: Cambridge University Press.

Rorty, Richard, ed. (1967). *The Linguistic Turn.* Chicago: University of Chicago Press.

———. (1979). *Philosophy and the Mirror of Nature.* Princeton, NJ: Princeton University Press.

———. (1989). *Irony, Contingency, and Solidarity.* New York: Cambridge University Press.

———. (1991). *Objectivity, Relativism, and Truth.* New York: Cambridge University Press.

Ross, Andrew, (1991), *Strange Weather: Culture, Science, and Technology in the Age of Limits.* New York: Verso Books.

———. (1994). *The Chicago Gangster Theory of Life: Nature's Debt to Society.* London: Verso Books.

———. (1996). *Science Wars.* Durham, NC: Duke University Press.

———. (1998). *Real Love: In Pursuit of Cultural Justice.* New York: New York University Press.

Roszak, Theodore. (1968). *The Making of a Counter Culture.* New York: Doubleday.

———. (1973) *Where the Wasteland Ends.* New York: Doubleday.

———. (1986). *The Cult of Information.* New York: Pantheon Books.

———. (1992). *The Voice of the Earth.* New York: Simon and Schuster.

Rothfeder, Jeffrey. (1985). *Minds over Matter: A New Look at Artificial Intelligence.* New York: Simon and Schuster.

Rucker, Rudy. (1991). *Transreal!* Englewood, CO: WCS Books.

———. (1994). *Live Robots: Two in One Volume of Software/Wetware.* New York: Avon Books.

———. (1999), *Freeware.* New York: Avon Books.

———. (2000). *Realware.* New York: HarperCollins.

Sagan, Carl. (1977). *The Dragons of Eden: Speculations on the Evolution of Human Intelligence.* New York: Ballantine Books.

———. (1980). *Cosmos.* New York: Ballantine Books.

———. (1994). *Pale Blue Dot: A Vision of the Human Future in Space.* New York: Random House.

———. (1996). *The Demon-Haunted World: Science as a Candle in the Dark.* New York: Ballantine Books.

Sagan, Carl, and Ann Druyan. (1992). *Shadows of Forgotten Ancestors: A Search for Who We Are.* New York: Ballantine Books.

Sale, Kirkpatrick. (1990). *The Conquest of Paradise.* New York: Knopf.

———. (1995). "Is There Method in His Madness?," *Nation,* September 25: 305–311.

Sanders, Scott. (1976). "Pynchon's Paranoid History," in *Mindful Pleasures: Essays on Thomas Pynchon,* ed. George Levine and David Leverenz. Boston: Little, Brown.

Sartell, Joe. (1993). "*Jurassic Park:* or, Sympathy for the Dinosaur," *Bad Subjects*, May.

Savage, Marshall T. (1994). *The Millennial Project: Colonizing the Galaxy in Eight Easy Steps.* Boston: Little, Brown.

Schaller, Michael, Virginia Scharff, and Robert D. Schulzinger. (1998). *Coming of Age: America in the Twentieth Century.* Boston: Houghton Mifflin.

Schiller, Dan. (1999). *Digital Capitalism.* Cambridge, MA: MIT Press.

Schneider, Stephen H. (1989). *Global Warming: Are We Entering the Greenhouse Century?* New York: Vintage Books.

Schor, Juliet. (1997). *The Overspent American.* New York: HarperCollins.

Schumpeter, Joseph. (1962). *Capitalism, Socialism, and Democracy.* New York: Harper & Row.

Schwartau, Winn. (1996). *Information Warfare.* New York: Thunder's Mouth Press.

Schwarzkopf, Norman. (1992). *It Doesn't Take a Hero.* New York: Bantam Books.

Schweitzer, Albert. (1987). *The Philosophy of Civilization: Part 1, The Decay and Restoration of Civilization; Part 2, Civilization and Ethics.* Ithaca, NY: Prometheus Books.

Session, George. (1992). "Radical Environmentalism in the '90s," *Wild Earth* Fall: 64–67.

Shapiro, Michael J. (1997). *Violent Cartographies: Mapping Cultures of War.* Minneapolis: University of Minnesota Press.

Shaw, Martin. (1991). *Post-Military Society.* Philadelphia: Temple University Press.

Sheldrake, Rupert. (1988). "The Laws of Nature as Habits: A Postmodern Basis for Science," in *The Reenchantment of Science: Postmodern Proposals* (pp. 79–86), ed. David Ray Griffin. Albany: State University of New York Press.

————. (1990). *The Rebirth of Nature: The Greening of Science and God.* London: Random Century Group.

Shelley, Mary. (1993 [1818]). *Frankenstein.* Oxford, UK, and New York: Oxford University Press.

Shenk, David. (1997). *Data Smog: Surving the Information Glut.* New York: HarperCollins.

Shiva, Vandana. (1993). *Monocultures of the Mind: Perspectives on Biodiversity and Biotechnology.* London: Zed Books.

————. (1997). *Biopiracy: The Plunder of Nature and Knowledge.* Boston: South End Press.

Shlain, Leonard. (1991). *Art and Physics: Parallel Visions in Space, Time, and Light.* New York: Morrow.

Siegel, Mark Richard. (1978). *Pynchon: Creative Paranoia in "Gravity's Rainbow".* New York: Kennikat Press.

Simpson, Lorenzo C. (1995). *Technology, Time, and the Conversations of Modernity.* New York and London: Routledge.

Singer, Peter. (1990). *Animal Liberation.* New York: Avon Books.

Slouka, Mark. (1995). *War of the Worlds.* New York: Harper & Row.

Smart, Barry. (1992). *Modern Conditions, Postmodern Controversies.* London: Routledge.

————. (1993). *Postmodernity.* London: Routledge.

Smith, Adam. (1965). *An Inquiry into the Nature and Causes of the Wealth of Nations.* New York: Modern Library.

Smith, Bradley. (1983). *The Shadow Warriors.* New York: Basic Books.

Smith, Huston. (1982). *Beyond the Post-Modern Mind*. New York: Crossroad.
Smith, Perry. (1991). *How CNN Fought the War.* New York: Birch Lane Press.
Smolin, Lee. (1997). *The Life of the Cosmos*. New York and Oxford, UK: Oxford University Press.
Snow, C. P. (1964). *The Two Cultures: And a Second Look*. Cambridge, UK: Cambridge University Press.
Soja, Edward. (1989). *Postmodern Geographies*. London: Verso Books.
_____. (1996). *ThirdSpace*. Cambridge, MA, and Oxford, UK: Blackwell.
Soule, Michael, and Gary Lease, eds. (1995). *Reinventing Nature? Responses to Postmodern Deconstruction*. Washington, DC: Island Press.
Spark, Muriel. (1987 [1951]). *Mary Shelley. A Biography.* New York: Dutton.
Spence, Gerry. (1995). *From Freedom to Slavery.* New York: St. Martin's Press.
Spretnak, Charlene. (1990). "Ecofeminism: Our Roots and Flowering," in *Reweaving the World: The Emergence of Ecofeminism* (pp. 3–14), ed. Irene Diamond and Gloria Orenstein. San Francisco: Sierra Club Books.
_____. (1991). *States of Grace: The Recovery of Meaning in the Postmodern Age*. New York: HarperCollins
Stephenson, Neal. (1992). *Snow Crash*. New York: Bantam Books.
_____. (1995). *The Diamond Age*. New York: Bantam Books.
Sterling, Bruce, ed. (1986). *Mirrorshades: The Cyberpunk Anthology.* New York: Ace Books.
_____. (1988). *Islands in the Stream*. New York: Ace Books.
_____. (1989). *Crystal Express.* New York: Ace Books.
_____. (1992). *The Hacker Breakdown: Law and Disorder on the Electronic Frontier.* New York: Bantam Books.
_____. (1994). *Heavy Weather.* New York: Bantam Books.
_____. (1996). *Holy Fire.* New York: Bantam Books.
Stock, Gregory. (1993). *Metaman: The Merging of Humans and Machines into a Global Superorganism*. New York: Simon and Schuster.
Stockwell, John. (1978). *In Search of Enemies: A CIA Story.* New York: Norton.
Stoll, Clifford. (1995). *Silicon Snake Oil: Second Thoughts on the Information Highway.* New York: Doubleday.
Strauss, David Levi. (1992). "(Re)Thinking Resistance," in *War After War*, ed. Nancy J. Peters. San Francisco: City Lights Press.
Stringer, Christopher, and Robin McKie. (1996). *African Exodus: The Origins of Modern Humanity.* New York: Holt.
Sutin, Lawrence. (1989). *Divine Invasions: A Life of Philip K. Dick*. New York: Harmony Books.
_____, ed. (1995). *The Shifting Realities of Philip K. Dick: Selected Literary and Philosophical Writings.* New York: Vintage.
Swimme, Brian. (1988). "The Cosmic Creation Story," in *The Reenchantment of Science: Postmodern Proposals* (pp. 47–56), ed. David Ray Griffin. Albany: State University of New York Press.
Swimme, Brian, and Thomas Berry. (1992). *The Universe Story: From the Promordial Flaring Forth to the Ecozoic Era—A Celebration of the Unfolding of the Cosmos.* New York: HarperCollins
Tabbi, Joseph. (1995). *Postmodern Sublime*. Ithaca, NY, and London: Cornell University Press.

Tanner, Tony. (1982). *Thomas Pynchon*. London and New York: Metheun.

Taylor, Peter J. (1997). "Afterword: Shifting Positions for Knowing and Intervening in the Cultural Politics of the Life Sciences," in *Changing Life: Genomes, Ecologies, Bodies, Commodities* (pp. 203–224), ed. Peter J. Taylor, Saul Halfon, and Paul N. Edwards. Minneapolis: University of Minnesota Press.

Taylor, Peter J., Saul Halfon, and Paul N. Edwards, eds. (1997). "Afterword: Shifting Positions for Knowing and Intervening in the Cultural Politics of the Life Sciences," in *Changing Life: Genomes, Ecologies, Bodies, Commodities.* Minneapolis: University of Minnesota Press.

Tobias, Michael. (1994). *World War Three: Population and the Biosphere at the End of the Millenium*. Santa Fe, NM: Bear and Co.

Toffler, Alvin. (1991). *Third Wave.* New York: Bantam Books.

Toulmin, Stephen. (1982a). "The Construal of Reality: Criticism in Modern and Postmodern Science," in *The Politics of Interpretation*, ed. W. J. T. Mitchell. Chicago: University of Chicago Press.

———. (1982b). *The Return to Cosmology: Postmodern Science and the Theology of Nature.* Berkeley and Los Angeles: University of California Press.

Turkle, Sherry. (1984). *The Second Self: Computers and the Human Spirit.* New York: Simon and Schuster.

———. (1995). *Life on the Screen: Identity in the Age of the Internet.* New York: Simon and Schuster.

Varela, Francisco J. (1979). *Principles of Biological Autonomy.* New York and Oxford, UK: Elsevier North Holland.

Vattimo, Gianni. (1988). *The End of Modernity.* London: Polity Press.

Vidal, John. (1997). *McLibel: Burger Culture on Trial.* New York: New Press.

Virilio, Paul. (1986 [1977]). *Speed and Politics.* New York: Semiotext(e), Foreign Agents Series, Autonomedia.

———. (1989 [1984]). *War and Cinema: The Logistics of Perception.* London: Verso Books.

———. (1990 [1978]). *Popular Defense and Ecological Struggles.* New York: Semiotext(e), Foreign Agents Series, Autonomedia.

———. (1991a [1980]). *The Aesthetics of Disappearance.* New York: Semiotext(e), Foreign Agents Series, Autonomedia.

———. (1991b [1984]). *The Lost Dimension.* New York: Semiotext(e), Foreign Agents Series, Autonomedia.

———. (1994 [1988]). *The Vision Machine.* Bloomington: University of Indiana Press.

———. (1995a). "Global Algorithm 1.7: The Silence of the Lambs: Paul Virilio in Conversation," in *C-Theory*, www.freedonia.com/ctheory.

———. (1995b). "Speed and Information: Cyberspace Alarm!" in *C-Theory*, www.freedonia.com/ctheory.

———. (1995c). "The Information Bomb: A Conversation between Paul Virilio and Friedrich Kittler, translated and forthcoming in *New Cultural Theory and Techno-Politics*, ed. John Armitrage.

———. (1995d [1993]). *The Art of the Motor.* Minneapolis: University of Minnesota Press.

———. (1996). *Cybermonde: La politique de pire.* Paris: Textuel.

———. (1997a). "Cyberwar, God and Television: An Interview with Paul Virilio,"

in *Digital Delirium* (pp. 41–48), ed. Arthur Kroker and Marilouise Kroker. New York: St. Martin's Press.
_____. (1997b [1995]). *Open Sky.* London: Verso Books.
_____. (1998a). *The Virilio Reader,* ed. James Der Derian. Malden, MA, and Oxford, UK: Blackwell.
_____. (1998b [1990]). *Polar Inertia.* London: Sage.
Virilio, Paul, and Sylvere Lotringer. (1983). *Pure War.* New York: Semiotext(e), Foreign Agents Series, Autonomedia.
Vonnegut, Kurt. (1980). *Player Piano.* New York: Laurel.
Waldrop, M. Mitchell. (1992). *Complexity: The Emerging Science at the Edge of Order and Chaos.* New York: Simon and Schuster.
Wark, McKenzie. (1994). *Virtual Geography: Living with Global Media Events.* Bloomington: University of Indiana Press.
Warren, Karen J. (1993). "The Power and Promise of Ecological Feminism," in *Environmental Philosophy* (pp. 320–341), ed. Michael Zimmerman, J. Baird Callicott, George Sessions, Karen J. Warren, and John Clark. Upper Saddle River, NJ: Prentice Hall.
Waterman, Peter. (1990). "Communicating Labor Internationalism: A Review of Relevant Literature and Resources," *Communications: European Journal of Communications,* 15(1–2): 85–103.
_____. (1992). "International Labour Communication by Computer: The Fifth International?," in *Working Paper Series 129* (pp. 1–32). The Hague, The Netherlands: Institute of Social Studies.
Waters, Malcolm. (1995). *Globalization.* London: Routledge.
Webster, Frank. (1995). *Theories of the Information Society.* London and New York: Routledge.
Weinberg, Steven. (1994). *Dreams of a Final Theory: The Scientist's Search for the Ultimate Laws of Nature.* New York: Vintage Books.
Weisenburger, Steven. (1981). "The End of History? Thomas Pynchon and the Uses of the Past," in *Critical Essays on Thomas Pynchon* (pp. 140–156), ed. Richard Pearce. Boston: M. K. Hall.
_____. (1988). *A "Gravity's Rainbow" Companion.* Athens: University of Georgia Press.
Wells, H. G. (1902). *Anticipations of the Reaction of Mechanical and Scientific Progress.* London: T. Fisher Unwin.
_____. (1938). *World Brain.* London: Metheun.
_____. (1965). *The Food of the Gods.* New York: Airmont.
_____. (1979). *Three Novels of the Future.* Garden City, NY: Doubleday.
_____. (1996a). *The Invisible Man.* New York: Oxford University Press.
_____. (1996b). *"The Time Machine" and "The Island of Dr. Moreau".* New York: Oxford University Press.
_____. (1996c). *The Country of the Blind and Other Stories.* New York: Oxford University Press.
White, Hayden. (1990). *The Content of the Form: Narrative Discourse and Historical Representation.* Baltimore: Johns Hopkins University Press.
White, Lynn, Jr. (1968). *Machina ex Deo: Essays in the Dynamism of Western Culture.* Cambridge, MA: MIT Press.
Whitehead, Alfred North. (1967). *The Adventure of Ideas.* New York: Mentor.

Wilford, John Noble. (2001). "Found: 2 Planetary Systems. Result: Astronomers Stunned," *www.nytimes.com/2001/01/10/science/10PLAN.html.*

Wilmut, Ian, Keith Campbell, and Colin Tudge. (2000). *The Second Creation: Dolly and the Age of Biological Control.* New York: Farrar Straus Giroux.

Wilson, E. O. (1998a). *Consilience.* New York: Knopf.

———. (1998b). "Back from Chaos," *Atlantic Monthly,* March: 54–62.

———. (1998c). "The Ionian Instauration: An Interview with E. O. Wilson on His Latest Controversial Book: *Consilience: The Unity of Knowledge,*" *Skeptic,* 6(1): 76–85.

Wilson, Rob. (1992). " 'Sublime Patriot,' " *Polygraph, 5*: 67–77.

Wilson, Rob, and Wilmal Dissayanake, eds. (1996). *Global/Local: Cultural Production and the Transnational Imaginary* (Asia–Pacific Series). Durham, NC: Duke University Press.

Winner, Langdon. (1977). *Autonomous Technology: Technology Out-of-Control as a Political Theme.* Cambridge, MA: MIT Press.

Winter, Deborah DuNann. (1996). *Ecological Psychology: Healing the Split between Planet and Self.* New York: HarperCollins.

Wolf, Michael J. (1999). *Entertainment Economy: How Mega-Media Forces Are Transforming Our Lives.* New York: Times Books.

Wollen, Peter. (1993). *Raiding the Icebox: Reflections on Twentieth Century Culture.* Bloomington: Indiana University Press.

Wood, Denis. (1992). *The Power of Maps.* New York: Guilford Press.

Worster, Donald. (1979). *Nature's Economy: The Roots of Ecology.* New York: Anchor Books.

———. (1985). *Nature's Economy: A History of Ecological Ideas.* Cambridge, UK: Cambridge University Press.

Wright, Will. (1992). *Wild Knowledge: Science, Language, and Social Life in a Fragile Environment.* Minneapolis: University of Minnesota Press.

Young, Kimberly S. (1998). *Caught in the Net: How to Recognize the Signs of Internet Addiction—And a Winning Strategy for Recovery.* New York: Wiley.

Zapatistas Collective. (1994). *Zapatistas: Document of the New Mexican Revolution.* New York: Autonomedia.

Zuboff, Shoshana. (1988). *In the Age of the Smart Machine: The Future of Work and Power.* New York: Basic Books.

INDEX

ABOUT THE AUTHORS

Steven Best is Associate Professor and Chair of Philosophy at the University of Texas, El Paso. The author of *The Politics of Historical Vision*, he is coauthor (with Douglas Kellner) of *Postmodern Theory* and *The Postmodern Turn*.

Douglas Kellner is George Kneller Chair in the Philosophy of Education at the University of California, Los Angeles. He is coauthor of *Postmodern Theory* and *The Postmodern Turn*, and author of several other books on social theory, politics, history, and culture.